PRINCIPLES OF ENVIRONMENTAL ECONOMICS

This text offers a systematic exposition of environmental and natural resource economics. It presents the economic and ecological principles essential for a clear understanding of contemporary environmental and natural resource issues and policy considerations. Environmental and natural resource issues are considered in a broad, interdisciplinary context that does not treat them as just another subset of applied economics. The main subject areas include:

- basic economic concepts specifically relevant to environmental economics
- the economics of natural resource scarcity
- ecology, economics and the biophysical constraints to economic growth
- ecological economics
- the economics of sustainable development
- the economics of pollution
- valuing the environment
- the economics of natural resources
- population, development and the environment

The author develops specific tools to illuminate the central problems of environmental economics. Fundamental economic concepts specifically relevant to environmental and resource economics are introduced and then integrated with ecological principles and approaches. This text presents an integrated understanding of environmental and resource economics that acknowledges the disciplinary tie between economics and ecology.

This student-friendly textbook contains a variety of study tools including learning points, boxed features, case studies, revision questions and discussion questions. Written in a clear and accessible style, *Principles of Environmental Economics* considers a variety of real-world examples to illustrate the policy relevance and implications of key economic and ecological concepts.

Ahmed M. Hussen is a Professor and Chair of the Department of Economics, Kalamazoo College, Michigan, USA.

Principles of Environmental Economics

Economics, ecology and public policy

Ahmed M. Hussen

LONDON & NEW YORK

First published 2000 by Routledge
11 New Fetter Lane, London EC4P 4EE

Simultaneously published in the USA and Canada
by Routledge
29 West 35th Street, New York, NY 10001

Typeset in Plantin and Rockwell by
Keystroke, Jacaranda Lodge, Wolverhampton
Printed and bound in Great Britain by
TJ International Ltd, Padstow, Cornwall

British Library Cataloguing in Publication Data
A catalogue record for this book is available from the British Library

Library of Congress Cataloging in Publication Data
Hussen, Ahmed M.
     Principles of environmental economics : economics, ecology and
public policy / Ahmed M. Hussen.
          p.   cm.
     Includes bibliographical references and index.
     1. Environmental economics. 2. Ecology. 3. Environmental policy.
I. Title.
HC79.E5H875   1999
333. 7–dc21   99–17809
                                                                   CIP

ISBN 0–415–19570–5 (hbk)
ISBN 0–415–19571–3 (pbk)

Contents

Figures

Tables

Case studies

Exhibits

Preface

The primary objective of this book is to present the economic and ecological principles essential for a clear understanding of the complex contemporary environmental and natural resource issues and policy considerations. Several textbooks have been written on this subject in recent years. One may ask, then, what exactly differentiates this one from the others?

LEVEL

This book is written for an introductory-level course in environmental and resource economics. It is primarily designed for college sophomores and juniors who want to study environmental and resource concerns with an interdisciplinary focus. The academic majors of these students could be in any field of study, but the book would be especially appropriate for students with majors in economics, political science, environmental studies or biological sciences.

Several other textbooks may claim to have the above-stated features. However, very few, if any, offer two chapters that are exclusively designed to provide students with fundamental economic concepts specifically relevant to environmental and resource economics. In these chapters, economic concepts such as demand and supply analysis, willingness to pay, consumers' and producers' surplus, rent, marginal analysis, Pareto optimality, factor substitution and alternative economic measures of scarcity are thoroughly and systematically explained. The material in these two chapters (Chapters 2 and 3) is *optional*. They are intended to serve as a good review for economics students and a very valuable foundation for students with a major in a field other than economics. This book requires no more than a semester course in microeconomics. Thus, unlike many other textbooks in this field, it does not demand a knowledge of intermediate microeconomics, either implicitly or explicitly.

The claim that environmental and resource economics should be studied within an interdisciplinary context is taken *very* seriously. Such a context requires students to have, in addition to microeconomics, a good understanding of the basic principles of the natural and physical sciences that govern the natural world. This book addresses this concern by devoting a chapter to ecology. This is done not only to make certain relevant ecological principles understandable to non-science students, but also to clearly present the disciplinary tie between economics and ecology. This chapter assumes no prior knowledge in ecology. Instead, it discusses thoroughly and systematically ecological concepts such as ecosystem, ecosystem structure, material recycling, the law of matter and energy, entropy, and the interrelationships of succession, stability, resilience and complexity of ecological systems. These are concepts especially pertinent to the understanding of biophysical limits and to recent concerns with global issues such as loss of biodiversity and climate change.

This book is primarily a theoretical exposé of environmental and resource economics. The emphasis is on a systematic development of theoretical principles and conceptual frameworks essential for a clear understanding and analysis of environmental and resource issues. To catch students' imagination and attention, as well as to reinforce understandings of basic theoretical principles, case studies and "exhibits" are incorporated into most of the chapters. These are taken from newspaper clippings, brief magazine articles, articles and summaries of empirical studies from professional journals, and excerpts of publications from government and private research institutions.

ORIENTATION

Unlike other textbooks in this area, this book is written in the belief that a course in environmental and resource economics cannot be treated as just another applied course in economics. It must include both economic and ecological perspectives and, in so doing, must seek a broader context within which environmental and natural resource issues can be understood and evaluated. In this regard, the book does *not* approach environmental and natural resource problems from only or even predominantly a standard economic perspective.

From my experience of nearly two decades of teaching a course in environmental and resource economics, I have come to realize that it is extremely difficult for students to understand and appreciate the subtle differences between the economic and ecological perspectives until they are made aware of the "axiomatic" foundations (the conceptual starting point of analysis) of each of these perspectives. With this in mind, this book starts with a careful examination of the preanalytic or axiomatic assumptions of standard economic perspectives concerning resources, resource scarcity and the role that natural resources play in the economic process. Similarly, the axiomatic assumptions pertaining to the ecological perspective are discussed in another chapter. Thus, the clear delineation of the *anthropocentric* and *biocentric* views of natural resources and their scarcity is a unique feature of this textbook.

Most texts on environmental and resource economics are neoclassical in their orientation. For this reason the emphasis is mainly on intertemporal *optimal allocation* among alternative uses of the total resource flow, including the services of the natural environment. In this regard the over-riding concern is *efficiency*. This book does not disregard the importance of this approach, but it adds to it another important dimension: the concern for achieving the *optimal scale* of total resource flow relative to the environment. The key issue here is to keep the economic scale within the ecological carrying capacity and this requires the recognition of *biophysical limits*. Several chapters are assigned to discuss alternative views on biophysical limits to economic growth and the economics of sustainable development. This, as will be evident shortly, is one of the most distinguishing features of this book.

ORGANIZATION

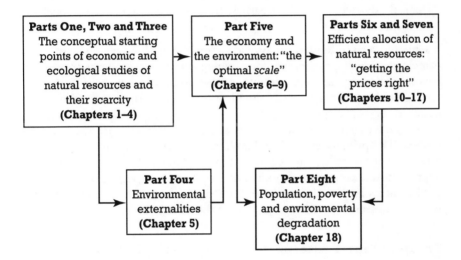

The book consists of eighteen chapters which are grouped into eight parts, as shown in the diagram. The five boxes represent the major organizational themes of the book. As indicated by the direction of the arrows, these five themes or major groupings are related in both specific and general terms. The exact nature of these relationships will become evident from the discussions that follow.

Fundamental economic and ecological concepts and perspectives

The four chapters of Parts One, Two and Three constitute what I consider to be the conceptual starting point of economic and ecological analyses of natural resources and their scarcity. Chapter 1 deals with the "axiomatic" assumptions that are fundamental to the understanding of the standard economic perception of natural resources and their role in the economic process. An early explanation of these assumptions, even if it does not serve to correct logical errors, helps clarify the position neoclassical economists tend to have on natural resource issues in general.

Chapters 2 and 3 offer comprehensive treatment of all the basic concepts essential for understanding the economic approach to natural resource and environmental policy. Furthermore, for the most part this is done using no more than the traditional demand and supply analysis. The two chapters are written with three specific objectives in mind:

1 To show how, in general, resources are allocated in a competitive market economy.
2 To identify and carefully assess the relative merits of several alternative indicators of emerging natural resource scarcity.
3 To explain the economic arguments on how scarcity of natural resources can be alleviated through factor substitution possibilities and/or techno- logical advances. As stated earlier, these two chapters are optional for students with a strong economic background.

Chapter 4 is intended to provide students with basic concepts and principles of ecology, thereby encouraging economics students to venture beyond the realm of their discipline. The position taken here is that no serious student of environmental and resource economics can afford to be ignorant of the important lessons of ecology. However, it should be understood that the inquiry on this subject matter is quite focused and limited. The primary intent is to familiarize students with carefully selected ecological concepts and principles so that they will acquire at the end, if not appreciation, a clear understanding of ecologists' perspective of the natural world and its relationship with the human economy. This is also a chapter of vital importance to the recognition of the existence of *biophysical limits*.

Environmental externalities and market failure

Part Four, which consists of a single chapter, Chapter 5, represents the second organizational theme of the text. This part covers fundamental concepts in environmental economics. It demonstrates how the basic concepts in ecology and economics studied in Parts One, Two and Three can be used to help us understand and resolve the problem of environ- mental pollution. Concepts such as the waste absorptive capacity of the environment, externalities, market failures and environmental regulations and their macroeconomic effects are discussed in this chapter. These are also concepts which are important to understand for the discussion in Part Five.

Biophysical limits to economic growth

The four chapters in Part Five are unique in their organization and contain some topics that are rarely discussed in standard textbooks on environ- mental and resource economics. The major concern here is the *scale* of the economy relative to the natural environment.

Chapters 6, 7 and 8 discuss the limit to economic growth from three distinctive perspectives: Malthusian, neoclassical and ecological economics, respectively. Chapter 9 deals with the economics of sustainable development. The key questions that these four chapters address are:

1 Can we expect unlimited economic growth in a world endowed with finite resources?
2 If ecological limits are important factors in determining future trends of economic growth, what steps or precautions should be taken in order to avoid transgressing these natural limits?

The economics of environmental and natural resources management

The unifying feature of Parts Six and Seven (which consist of Chapters 10–17) is the fact that they deal with environmental and resource economic issues from a predominantly neoclassical perspective. The emphasis in these chapters is on "getting the prices right." That is, environmental resources are optimally allocated provided market prices reflect their "true" scarcity values.

Chapters 10–15, the economics of environmental resources, deal with the standard economic approaches to environmental policies and valuations. Chapter 10 develops theoretical models that can be used as a policy guide to control environmental pollution. In Chapters 11 and 12, a number of pollution control policy instruments are thoroughly discussed and analyzed. The scientific, economic and public policy issues of environmental pollution that have a global dimension are discussed in Chapter 13. Chapter 14 examines alternative economic approaches to measuring environmental benefits (damage). Chapter 15 deals with economic valuation of environmental projects using a cost–benefit analysis framework.

Chapters 16 and 17 explore the fundamental principles of the economics of renewable and nonrenewable resources. Individually, Chapter 16 covers the basic economic theory of renewable resources as it is applied to biological resources and to fishery in particular. Chapter 17 deals with the basic elements of the economic theory of nonrenewable resources.

An important point to emphasize here is that even though the seven chapters in Parts Six and Seven are predominantly neoclassical in their orientation, *this should not suggest the total abandonment of the ecological theme that is central to this text.* As much as possible, the major conclusions drawn from each chapter are subjected to critical appraisal on the basis of their conformity or lack thereof to relevant ecological principles.

Population, economic development and environmental degradation

Part Eight, which is composed of a single chapter, Chapter 18, analyzes the contemporary population, resources and environmental problems of the developing nations. The main concerns are poverty and rapid environmental degradation on a global scale. In addressing these issues, the concern is not only efficiency but also the *scale* of the global economy relative to the environment. In this respect, the issues discussed in this chapter have the added feature of integrating the concepts learned in both Part Five (where scale is the emphasis) and Parts Six and Seven (where efficiency is the emphasis).

Acknowledgments

The experience of being the sole author of a textbook on a subject which requires an interdisciplinary focus has indeed been daunting. Undoubtedly, the completion of this project would not have been possible without the help and encouragement of many professional associates, students and family members. In this sense, I cannot truly claim to be the sole author of this text.

I am deeply indebted to Fumie, my wife, and Christine R. Fahndrich, my student, who read and edited the first draft. Nothing written in this text passed to other readers without first being read by my wife.

I would like to thank several individuals for their specific and significant contributions to this text. These people include the following: Marvin Soroos for authoring Chapter 13 (the chapter on global environmental pollution); Paul Olexia for his close reading and for his concrete and insightful suggestions on how to improve the material covered in Chapter 4 (the chapter on ecology); Mike Travis for his very careful reading of Chapter 16 (the chapter on renewable resources); Glen Britton for his contribution to Case Study 9.1 and for suggesting alternative approaches and valuable literature bearing on the subject; and Mike Bernasek for reading and commenting on Part Five (Chapters 6–9), and, most importantly, for his encouragement.

I would like also to express my deeply felt gratitude to my colleagues from the Economics Department, Kenneth Reinert, Charles Stull, James Stansell and Phil Thomas, for reading parts of the text and for their helpful comments and suggestions.

This book uses numerous quoted remarks, exhibits and case studies. These works are not included for mere appearance or style; they significantly contribute to the effectiveness of the book in conveying certain important ideas. Obviously, my debt to those whose work I have quoted and summarized is immeasurable. However, I have the sole responsibility for the interpretation placed on these works.

I actually started writing this book three years ago. However, the idea of writing a textbook on environmental and resource economics had been on my mind for much of the eighteen years that I have been actively engaged in teaching courses in this subject. This enduring desire to write a text would not have been possible without the positive stimulus and, in some instances, tangible support that I have been fortunate to receive from my students. In this regard, I am deeply indebted to all those who have taken courses from me dealing with topics on environmental and resource issues.

A special word of thanks to my editor, Alison Kirk, for her thoughtful, professional and supportive role in the early development of this textbook. Special thanks too to Andreja Zivkovic for his effective editorial guidance and assistance during the time Alison Kirk was on leave. Many thanks also to Goober Fox for his cooperative spirit and for his many helpful contributions as desk editor. I would also like to express my sincere appreciation of the valuable comments I received from several anonymous reviewers during the various stages of the text development. I am especially indebted to the last group of four anonymous reviewers for their close reading of the entire manuscript and for providing me with concrete ideas and suggestions as to how the book could be improved.

Finally, I would like to express my sincere gratitude to my two daughters, Sophia and Aida, for their contributions to proofreading and editing. Most of all, it would have been extremely difficult to complete this project without their constant cheering and encouragement. I am also forever indebted to Fumie, my wife, for the continued support, love and unconditional commitment she has shown to me and to our two daughters. I dedicate this book to her and to the mother of all mothers, the planet EARTH.

Introduction: Overview of Environmental and Resource Economics as a Subdiscipline in Economics

Labor is the father and nature is the mother of wealth.
(Petty 1899: 2: 377)

THE CONCEPT OF NATURAL RESOURCES

The study of natural resources, the subject matter of this book, involves theories and concepts that seem to be continually evolving with the passage of time and with our improved understanding of the natural circumstances that govern these resources. For example, the preclassical or Physiocratic school (1756–78) and classical economists (1776–1890) typically used *land* as a generic term to describe natural resources. To these economists, land or natural resources represented one of the three major categories of basic resources essential to the production of goods and services – the other two being labor and capital.

This three-way classification of basic resources or factors of production seems to persist, although our understanding of natural resources and their roles in the economic process has changed markedly. Advances in the natural and physical sciences have increased our knowledge of the laws that govern the natural world. Furthermore, as the human economy continues to expand, its impacts on the natural world have become sizable and potentially detrimental. Inevitably our conception of natural resources tends to be influenced by our current understanding of the human economy and its interrelationship with the natural world.

Broadly defined, natural resources include all the "original" elements that comprise the Earth's natural endowments or the life-support systems: air, water, the Earth's crust and radiation from the sun. Some representative examples of natural resources are arable land, wilderness areas, mineral fuels and nonfuel minerals, watersheds, and the ability of the natural environment to degrade waste and absorb ultraviolet light from the sun.

Natural resources are generally grouped into two major categories: renewable and nonrenewable natural resources. Renewable resources are those resources that are capable of regenerating themselves within a relatively short period, provided the environment in which they are nurtured is not unduly disturbed. Examples include plants, fish, forests, soil, solar radiation, wind, tides and so on. These renewable resources can be further classified into two distinct groups: biological resources and flow resources.

Biological resources consist of the various species of plants and animals. They have one distinctive feature that is important for consideration here. While these resources are capable of self-regeneration, they can be irreparably damaged if they are exploited beyond a certain critical threshold. Hence, their use should be limited to a certain critical zone. As will be explained later, both the regenerative capacity of these resources and the critical zone are governed by natural biological processes. Examples of this type of resource are fisheries, forests, livestock, and all forms of plants.

Flow resources include solar radiation, wind, tides and water streams. Continuous renewal of these resources is largely dictated by atmospheric and hydraulic circulation, along with the flow of solar radiation. Although these resources can be harnessed for specific use (such as energy from solar radiation or waterfalls), the rate at which the flows of these potential resources are regulated is largely governed by nature. This does not, however, mean that humans are totally incapable of either augmenting or decreasing the amount of flow of these resources. A good illustration of this would be the effect greenhouse gas emissions (in particular carbon dioxide emissions) have on global warming.

Nonrenewable resources are resources that either exist in fixed supply or are renewable only on a geological timescale, whose regenerative capacity can be assumed to be zero for all practical purposes. Examples of these resources include metallic minerals like iron, aluminum, copper and uranium; and nonmetallic minerals like fossil fuels, clay, sand, salt and phosphates.

Nonrenewable resources can be classified into two broad categories. The first group includes those resources which are recyclable, such as metallic minerals. The second group consists of nonrecyclable resources, such as fossil fuels.

As indicated by the title of this introductory section, mainly for pedagogical purposes the study of natural resources is subdivided into two major subfields: *environmental economics* and *resource economics*. The difference between these two subfields is primarily a matter of focus. In environmental economics the primary focus is on how to use or manage the natural environment (air, water, landmass) as a valuable resource for the disposal of waste. The material in Chapter 5 and Chapters 10–15 covers concepts and issues specifically related to environmental economics. In natural resource economics the emphasis is on the intertemporal allocation of extractive nonrenewable resources (such as petroleum, iron ore, potash, etc.) and the harvest of renewable resources (such as fish, forest products, and other plant and animal varieties). These are the subject matter of Chapters 16 and 17.

THE ECONOMY AND THE NATURAL ENVIRONMENT: AN EMERGING PARADIGM

The new understanding in environmental and resource economics is that the natural environment and the human economy are two interrelated systems. They are interrelated in the sense that a change in one could have significant effect(s) on the function of the other. This is because the human economy has grown to a size that can no longer be considered negligible relative to the natural world. Hence, consideration of *scale* (the size of the economy relative to the natural world) is, although still neglected, a significant issue that needs to be addressed in environmental and resource economics.

As shown in the diagram, in specific terms the economy is assumed to depend on the natural environment for three distinctive purposes: (a) the extraction of nonrenewable resources and the harvest of renewable resources to be used in the production process; (b) the disposal and assimilation of wastes; and (c) the consumption of environmental amenities. What this suggests is that the economy cannot be viewed as an *open system*. Its continued functioning depends on resources that trace their origin and existence to the natural phenomena or the processes that occur in nature, as will become evident from Chapter 4.

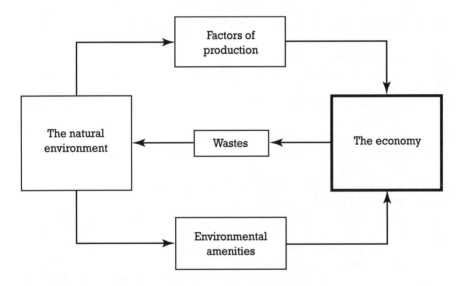

Schematic view of the interrelationship between the natural environment and the economy

Thus, broadly viewed, the economy is assumed to be completely dependent on the natural environment for raw materials, amenities and the disposal of waste materials. Furthermore, the capacity of the environment to carry out the above economic functions cannot be considered limitless. As with any other branch of economics, fundamental to the study of environmental and resource economics is the problem of scarcity – or, more specifically, biophysical scarcity. The implication of this for economic growth is a subject matter thoroughly discussed in Chapters 6–9.

ENVIRONMENTAL AND RESOURCE ECONOMICS: SCOPE AND NATURE

As a subdiscipline of economics, environmental and resource economics started in the 1960s – the early years of the so-called environmental movement. However, despite its brief history, over the past three decades it has become one of the fastest-growing fields of study in economics. The growing popularity of this field of inquiry parallels the increasing awareness of the interconnectedness between the economy and the environment – more specifically, the increasing recognition of the significant roles that nature plays in the economic process as well as in the formation of economic value.

The nature and scope of the issues addressed in environmental and resource economics are quite varied and all-encompassing. Below is a list of some of the major general topics addressed in this field of study. The list is also representative of the issues addressed in this book.

- the call for a renewed perception and understanding of resource scarcity;
- the need to reestablish the disciplinary ties between ecology and economics;
- the causes of environmental degradation;
- the difficulties associated with assigning ownership rights to environmental resources;
- the trade-off between environmental degradation and economic goods and services;
- assessing the monetary value of environmental damage;
- the ineffectiveness of the market, if left alone, in allocating environmental resources;
- the difficulties associated with measuring the size of resource stocks of biological and geological origin;
- economic indicators of natural resource scarcity and their limitations;
- public policy instruments that can be used to slow, halt and reverse the deterioration of environmental resources and/or the overexploitation of renewable and nonrenewable resources;
- the macroeconomic effects of environmental regulations and other resource conservation policies;
- the extent to which technology can be used as a means of ameliorating resource scarcity – that is, limits to technology;
- the extent to which past experience can be used to predict future events that are characterized by considerable economic, technological and ecological uncertainties;
- population problems: past, present and future;

- the interrelationships among population, poverty and environmental degradation in the developing countries of the world;
- resource problems that transcend national boundaries, and thus require international cooperation for their resolution;
- the limits to economic growth;
- ethical and moral imperatives for resource conservation – concerns for the welfare of future generations;
- the necessity and viability of sustainable development.

This list by no means exhausts the issues that can be addressed in environmental and resource economics. However, the issues contained in this list do provide important clues concerning some of the fundamental ways in which the study of environmental and resource economics is different from other subdisciplines in economics.

First, the ultimate limits to resource availability are imposed by nature. That is, their origin, interactions and reproductive capacity are largely governed by nature.

Second, most of these resources have no readily available markets: for example, clean air, ozone, the genetic pool of a species, the price of petroleum fifty years from now, etc.

Third, *time* plays a very important role in the allocation and distribution of these resources. The major problem is generally recognized as "How long and under what conditions can human life continue on earth with finite stocks of *in situ* resources, renewable but destructible resource populations, and limited environmental systems?" (Howe 1979: 3). No serious study in environmental and resource economics can be entirely static.

Fourth, no serious environmental and resource economic study can be entirely descriptive. *Normative* issues such as intergenerational fairness and distribution of resources between the poor and rich nations are very important.

Fifth, uncertainties are unavoidable considerations in any serious study of environmental and natural resource issues. These uncertainties may take several forms, such as prices, resource stock size, irreversible environmental damage, or unexpected and sudden resource depletion.

Such is the nature of the subject matter that we are about to begin exploring in this book.

REFERENCES

Howe, C. W. (1979) *Natural Resource Economics*, New York: John Wiley.
Petty, W. (1899) *The Economic Writings of Sir William Petty*, ed. C. H. Hull, Cambridge.

part one

THE "PREANALYTIC" VISION OF NATURAL RESOURCES: THE STANDARD ECONOMIC PERSPECTIVE

The perennial problem in natural resource economics is how to deal with emerging natural resource scarcity viewed from the long run and from societal perspectives. How this long-term economic concern of society is understood and addressed depends to a large extent on people's perception of the relationships between the economic and the natural world.

Standard economic visions of natural resources, and the roles they play in the attainment of human material needs, are generally at odds with those of most physical scientists, and most notably with those of ecologists. Part One, which comprises a single chapter, Chapter 1, examines the basic physical and institutional elements that are fundamental to the understanding of the standard economic perception of natural resources and their role in the economic process. This chapter reveals what could be considered the mainstream economists' "preanalytic" vision of the economy and its relationship with the natural world. What can be observed from the discussion in this chapter is the treatment of the natural environment as one of the many "fungible" assets that can be used to satisfy human needs. In this regard, the emphasis is on the general problems of resource scarcity. This being the case, the roles of consumers' preferences, efficiency, markets and technology are stressed.

This view is contrasted in Part Three with the ecological perspective on the natural environment as it relates to human economy.

chapter
one

THE CONCEPT OF RESOURCES AND RESOURCE SCARCITY:
An Economic Perspective

---

learning objectives

After reading this chapter you will be familiar with the following:

- the traditional economic classification of basic resources;
- the "anthropocentric" tendencies of the standard economic notions of natural resources;
- fungibility of resources;
- resource scarcity, opportunity cost and efficiency;
- the rudiments of a market economy and its basic constituents;
- the production possibility frontier;
- the difference between efficiency and optimality;
- flow versus stock concepts of resources;
- the neoclassical economic perspective of the human economy and the extent to which it depends on the natural world.

Before any element can be classified as a resource, two basic pre-conditions must be satisfied: first, the knowledge and technical skills must exist to allow its extraction and utilization; and second, there must be a demand for the materials or services produced. If either of these conditions is not satisfied then the physical substances remain *neutral stuff*. It is, therefore, human ability and need which create resource value, not merely physical presence.

(Rees 1985: 11)

1.1 INTRODUCTION

The primary objective of this chapter is to establish a clear understanding of the axiomatic, or preanalytic, conceptions of mainstream economics concerning natural resources and their role in the economic process. This is a crucial first step in identifying the ideological basis of neoclassical environmental and resource economics. In general, the phrase "neoclassical economics" refers to what has been regarded as the dominant (or the "normal," in the Kuhnian sense) approach to economic analyses since about the 1870s.

Sections 1.2–1.4 provide overviews of the concept of resources in general and the role of social institutions in coordinating economic activities. These issues are addressed from a purely neoclassical economic perspective. In Sections 1.5 and 1.6 the focus shifts to exploring the broader implications of this particular worldview of resources, using Costa Rica as a case study.

1.2 THE CONCEPT OF RESOURCES

In broad terms, a resource can be defined as anything that is directly or indirectly capable of satisfying human wants. Traditionally, economists classify resources into three broad categories: labor, capital and natural resources. *Labor* encompasses the productive capacity of human physical and/or mental efforts measured in terms of ability to do work or produce goods and services. Examples are a worker on an auto assembly line, a high-school teacher and a commercial truck driver. *Capital* refers to a class of resources that is produced for the purpose of creating a more efficient production process. In other words, it is the stock of produced items available not for direct consumption, but for further production purposes. Examples include machines, buildings, computers and education (acquired skill). *Natural resources* are the stock of living and nonliving materials found in the physical environment, and which have an identifiable potential use to human beings (Randall 1987). Agricultural land, deposits of ferrous and nonferrous minerals, water, fisheries, and wilderness and its multiple products are examples of natural resources.

At this point, *four* key issues need to be clarified regarding this economic notion of resources. First, it is rare that basic resources (labor, capital and natural resources) are used for direct consumption without some modification. Resources are often used as *factors of production* or as means to produce final goods and services that are capable of directly satisfying human needs. In other words, basic resources are often viewed as a means to an end, rather than ends in themselves. The second and somewhat related issue is that, as the quotation at the beginning of the chapter clearly indicates, the economic notion of resources is strictly *anthropocentric*. That is, the economic value of any resource is defined by human needs and nothing else – which implies that resources have no *intrinsic* value (value which depends solely on the nature of the thing in question) (Attfield 1998). Case Study 1.1 illustrates the anthropocentric view of resources. The worthiness of a watershed service (water purification process by root systems and soil microorganisms) is identified solely by its commercial value. The fact that the watershed under consideration may have other, noneconomic value is not considered.

The third issue that needs to be understood is that each of the above resource categories is of *economic concern* to the extent that they are *scarce* – found in limited quantities and/or qualities. The fourth issue deals with the fact that as factors of production, resources are used in combinations. Furthermore, resources are generally considered to be *fungible* (Solow 1993). That is, one kind of resource (such as a machine) can be freely replaced by another (such as labor) in the production process; or one type of energy resource (such as petroleum) can be replaced by another form of energy (such as natural gas). This is also evident in Case Study 1.1 where it is suggested that water purification for the city of New York can be undertaken either by investing in the preservation of "natural capital" (a forest watershed) or by building a filtration plant – physical capital. Fungibility implies that no particular resource is considered to be absolutely essential for production of goods and services (more on this in Chapters 3 and 7). However, as will be evident from the discussion in the next section, fungibility does not in any way suggest an escape from the general problem of resource scarcity.

CASE STUDY 1.1 ECONOMIC RETURNS FROM THE BIOSPHERE

Garciela Chichilnisky and Geoffrey Heal

. . . The environment's services are, without a doubt, valuable. The air we breathe, the water we drink and the food we eat are all available only because of services provided by the environment. How can we transform these values into income while conserving resources?

We have to "securitize" (sell shares in the return from) "natural capital" and environmental goods and services, and enroll market forces in their conservation. This means assigning to corporations – possibly by public–private corporate partnerships – the obligation to manage and conserve natural capital in exchange for the right to the benefits from selling the services provided.

In 1996, New York City invested between $1 billion and $1.5 billion in natural capital, in the expectation of producing cost savings of $6 billion–$8 billion over ten years, giving an internal rate of return of 90–170 percent in a payback period of four to seven years. This return is an order of magnitude higher than is usually available, particularly on relative risk-free investments. How did this come about?

New York's water comes from a watershed in the Catskill Mountains. Until recently, water purification processes by root systems and soil microorganisms, together with filtration and sedimentation during its flow through the soil, were sufficient to cleanse the water to the standards required by the US Environmental Protection Agency (EPA). But sewage fertilizer and pesticides in the soil reduced the efficacy of this process to the point where New York's water no longer met EPA standards. The city was faced with the choice of restoring the integrity of the Catskill ecosystems or of building a filtration plant at a capital cost of $6 billion–$8 billion, plus running costs of the order of $300 million annually. In other words, New York had to invest in natural capital or in physical capital. Which was more attractive?

Investing in natural capital in this case meant buying land in and around the watershed so that its use could be restricted, and subsidizing the construction of better sewage treatment plants. The total cost of restoring the watershed is expected to be $1 billion–$1.5 billion . . .

To address its water problem New York City has floated an "environmental bond issue," and will use the proceeds to restore the functioning of the watershed ecosystems responsible for water purification. The cost of the bond issue will be met by the savings produced: avoidance of a capital investment of $6 billion–$8 billion, plus the $300 million annual running costs of the plant. The money that would otherwise have paid for these costs will pay the interest on the bonds. New York City could have "securitized" these savings by opening a "watershed saving account" into which it paid a fraction of the costs avoided by not having to build and run a filtration plant. This account would then pay investors for the use of their capital.

Source: Nature Vol. 391, February 12, 1998, pp. 629–630. Reprinted by permission.

1.3 SCARCITY AND ITS ECONOMIC IMPLICATIONS

At the root of any economic study is the issue of resource scarcity. In fact, as a discipline, economics is defined as the branch of social science that deals with the allocation of scarce resources among competing ends. What exactly do economists mean by resource scarcity? What are the broader implications of scarcity?

For economists, scarcity is the universal economic problem. Every human society, whether a tribal society such as the Aborigines in Australia or an economically and technologically advanced society such as Japan, is confronted with the basic problem of scarcity. That is, at any point in time, given societal resource endowments and technological know-how, the total sum of what people want to have (in terms of goods and services) is far greater than what they can have (Kohler 1986).

Considering that human wants for goods and services are immense and, worse yet, insatiable in a world of scarcity, what can be done to *maximize* the set of goods and services that people of a given society can have at a point in time? This question clearly suggests that the significant economic problem involves *rationing* limited resources to satisfy human wants and, accordingly, has the following four general implications:

1 *Choice* The most obvious implication of scarcity is the need to choose. That is, in a world of scarcity, we cannot attain the satisfaction of all our material needs completely. Hence, we need to make choices and set priorities.

2 *Opportunity cost* Every choice we make has a cost associated with it; one cannot get more of something without giving up something else. In other words, an economic choice always entails sacrifice or opportunity cost – the highest-valued alternative that must be sacrificed to attain something or satisfy a want. In a world of scarcity, "there is no such thing as a free lunch."

3 *Efficiency* In the presence of scarcity, no individual or society can afford to be wasteful or inefficient. The objective is, therefore, to maximize the desired goods and services that can be obtained from a given set of resources. *This state of affairs is attained when resources are fully utilized (full employment) and used for what they are best suited in terms of production (i.e., there is no misallocation of resources).* Furthermore, efficiency implies that the best available technology is being used (McConnell and Bruce 1996).

4 *Social institutions* As noted earlier, the essence of scarcity lies in the fact that people's desire for goods and services exceeds society's ability to produce them at a point in time. In the presence of scarcity, therefore, the allocation and distribution of resources always cause *conflicts*. To resolve these conflicts in a systematic fashion, some kind of institutional mechanism(s) needs to be established. For example, in many parts of the contemporary world, the *market system* is used as the primary means of rationing scarce resources. How this system operates conceptually is briefly discussed in the next section.

1.4 A SCHEMATIC VIEW OF THE ECONOMIC PROCESS

In this section, using a circular flow diagram (an approach familiar to anyone who has taken a course in introductory economics) an attempt will be made to specify the institutional components that are basic to a market economy. As a working definition, an *economy* can be viewed as a rather complex institutional mechanism designed to facilitate the production, consumption and exchange of goods and services, given resource scarcity and technology, the preferences of households, and the legal system for resource ownership rights (Randall 1987). All economies are alike in the sense that they are devised to help facilitate the production, consumption and exchange of goods and services, and they are constrained by resource scarcity and technology. On the other hand, economies differ in the degree of empowerment given to households and firms in their ability to make economic choices, and the legal view of property ownership rights. For example, in a capitalistic and market-oriented economy, freedom of choice and private ownership of property are strongly held institutional principles. In contrast, in a centrally planned economy, the production and distribution of goods are dictated by bureaucratic choices, with resource ownership retained by the state.

The circular flow diagram in Figure 1.1 is designed to show that the operation of a market-oriented economy is composed of the following elements:

1 *Economic entities* (households and firms) Households are the final users of goods and services and the owners of resources. In a market economy, given resource scarcity the primary goal is to find effective ways to address the material needs of consumers (households). At least in principle, consumers' well-being is the primary goal of a market-oriented economy. Although households are final users of goods and services, firms enter the economic process as transformers of basic resources (labor, capital and natural resources) into goods and services, and *this is done on the basis of consumers' preferences (demand)*.

2 *Markets* Markets represent an institutional arena in which exchanges (buying and selling) of final goods and services and factors of production (labor, capital and natural resources) take place. Traditionally, economists group markets into two broad categories, namely product and factor markets. The *product market* is where the exchange of *final* goods and services occurs. In this market, demand and supply provide information about households and firms, respectively. The *factor market* refers exclusively to the buying and selling of basic resources, such as labor, capital and natural resources. In this submarket, demand imparts market information about firms and supply provides information about households. That is, households are the suppliers of labor, capital and natural resources, while firms are the buyers, and in turn use these items to produce final goods and services for the product market. Clearly, then, the roles played in the factor market by households and firms respectively are the reverse of their roles in the product market.

   In both the product and the factor markets, information about resource scarcity is transmitted through prices. These prices are formed through the interactions of market demand and supply; and, under certain conditions, market prices can be used as reliable indicators of both present and future resource scarcities (a subject to be discussed in Chapters 2 and 3). Furthermore, using prices from the product market, economists customarily measure aggregate economic performance of a given economy or a country by the *total* market value of all the goods and services produced for *final use* within a given period, usually a year. This is called gross domestic product (GDP) when the total market value of the final goods and services produced is attributable to factors of production (labor, capital and natural resources) originating exclusively from a given country (more on this in the next section).

3 *Nonmarket public and private institutions* A market does not function in a vacuum; that is, for a market to operate efficiently, ownership rights need to be clearly defined and enforced. This requires the establishment of public agencies designed to articulate and enforce the rules and regulations by which ownership rights are attained, relinquished (transferred) and enforced (more on this in Chapters 2 and 5). In addition, competition in the marketplace is fostered through public intervention in some instances. The public and private entities (social institutions) that legislate the rules for assigning resource ownership rights and regulate the degree of competition in the marketplace are represented by the box at

the center of Figure 1.1. On one view, what flows from this box to households, firms and markets is not physical goods but information services. In general, the main function of these flows of information is to ensure that economic agents (households and firms) are playing by some socially predetermined rules of the game. In this regard, *ideally*, social institutions are perceived as being rather like a conductor of a symphony orchestra or a traffic director at a busy intersection.

Viewed this way, social institutions have important economic functions. However, they should not be assumed to be either perfect or costless (North 1995). When they are not functioning well, the information communicated through them can distort market signals (prices) and in so doing, significantly affect the allocation of scarce resources. This will become evident in Chapters 2 and 5.

The discussions so far have dealt with (a) the general concept of resources and their broad classification; (b) resource scarcity and its socioeconomic implications (choice, opportunity cost, efficiency and social institutions); and (c) a schematic view of the basic institutional components of a market economy. It is important to note that these are from a purely neoclassical economic perspective. The next section attempts to explore the implications of this type of "worldview" for resource concerns and focuses on natural resources – the subject matter of this book. Costa Rica is used as a case study, a nation whose recent efforts to "preserve" its vital natural resources have been considerable (see Exhibit 1.1). This exhibit, along with the discussions in the next section, further illustrates the anthropocentric tendencies of the standard economic notions of natural resources, and resources in general.

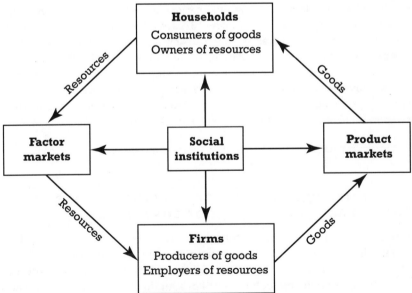

Figure 1.1 Circular flow diagram of the economic process

EXHIBIT 1.1 ECOTOURISM, FORESTLAND PRESERVATION AND THE ECONOMY OF COSTA RICA

Costa Rica, a small nation with a primarily agrarian economy, is well known for its wilderness preserves. About 35 percent of the country's total land area is covered with vast tracts of virgin tropical forests. Much of this forestland supports a variety of trees, including rich stands of ebony, balsa, mahogany, and cedar – which all have significant commercial value. The animal population includes puma, jaguar, deer and monkeys. Furthermore, Costa Rica's forest is an important repository of many plants and biological species with significant ecological, if not economic, values. It is reported that Costa Rica's forest ecosystem houses literally thousands of species of plants and animals. It is also important to note that the forestland contains the watersheds that constantly replenish the many river tributaries essential for providing one of the most critical energy resources of Costa Rica: waterpower.

The forest with its multiple products is important to the Costa Rican economy for more than its obvious commercial values, and in recent years has been increasingly used for a specific type of service: *ecotourism*. This entails preservation of a forest ecosystem to attract tourists interested in having direct experience of or contact with nature. This development, among others, requires a significantly different use of Costa Rica's natural resources – preserving forestland for its *service* value rather than the expansion of agricultural and cattle-ranching activities. In recent years, Costa Rica has been regarded as the Mecca of ecotourism; and it is a major contributor to Costa Rica's fast-growing service sector. Currently, the service sector accounts for 58 percent of Costa Rica's GDP (World Resources Institute 1998), and between 1985 and 1995, Costa Rica's economy has grown at a healthy average annual rate of 4.5 percent.

Ecotourism is a relatively recent industry in Costa Rica. The recent push to ecotourism emerged in large part from Costa Rica's unsettling experience with deforestation in the previous two decades. More specifically, during the 1970s and the early 1980s, Costa Rica attempted to increase its economic diversity through an emphasis on livestock production. This economic pursuit accelerated the rate of deforestation (Meyer 1993). This trend has been contained, at least for now, and the switch from an emphasis on cattle ranching to ecotourism can justifiably be considered a success. In this regard, Costa Rica seems to have a new industry with the potential to create an economy consistent with sustainable use of the country's most important natural assets: the forestland and its multiple products.

1.5 APPLYING THE CONCEPT: ECOTOURISM, CATTLE RANCHING AND THE ECONOMY OF COSTA RICA

Figure 1.2 is a graphical depiction of a production possibility frontier (PPF). It shows all the combinations of ecotourism services and cattle-ranching activities a society (in this case Costa Rica) can produce, given resource scarcity, using the existing technology of production in both the ecotourism and the cattle-ranching sectors of the economy. For example, Costa Rica can produce amount E_3 of ecotourism service if it chooses to use all its available resources to specialize in the production of this service and nothing else. Ecotourism service may entail conserving forestland for purposes such as bird-watching, nature appreciation and aesthetic enjoyment, preserving animal and plant species for biological prospecting, game reserves, and so on. Evidently, ecotourism is a natural resource-intensive industry, and its use as an example in this chapter is prompted by this factor alone.

Similarly, R_3 is the level of cattle-ranching activity that will be taking place if, at a point in time, all Costa Rica's available resources are used exclusively for this purpose. These are, of course, two extreme cases. The most likely scenario is represented by a mix of both economic activities. Using its available resources Costa Rica may choose to produce amounts E_1 and R_2 of ecotourism and ranching activities, respectively.

What can we learn about choice, opportunity cost and efficiency using the notion of the PPF? First, at a given point in time, we can view the production possibility curve as representing the boundary line between the feasible and infeasible product choices of a society. For example, in Figure 1.2, product (ecotourism service and cattle) combinations outside the PPF, such as M, are unattainable. On the other hand, the feasible choices represent all the product combinations inside the PPF, such as N, and all the points along the PPF curve. *In this sense, although resources are scarce, society is still confronted with an infinite number of feasible choices.* However, from a strictly economic viewpoint, there is a significant difference between output choices lying inside the PPF curve and those that are located on the PPF curve. All product combinations inside the PPF curve are regarded as *inefficient*. For example, point N is regarded as inefficient because Costa Rica could instead, by using the same amount of resources, have produced ecotourism services and cattle output combinations indicated by points A, B and C on the

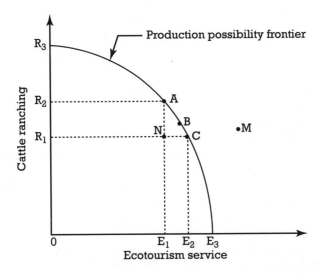

Figure 1.2 **The production possibility frontier for Costa Rica**

PPF. In so doing, Costa Rica would have been able to produce more of either the ecotourism service or cattle output (point C or A), or more of both products, as indicated by point B.

All output combinations along the PPF curve are regarded as *efficient* because, by definition, each point represents a full utilization (full employment) of all the available scarce resources at a point in time. Thus, there is no waste or idle resources. Society is still, however, confronted with an infinite number of choices, and any choice along the production possibility curve entails an *opportunity cost*. For example, in Figure 1.2, a move from A to C implies that to increase ecotourism service from E_1 to E_2 Costa Rica has to reduce (sacrifice) its output of cattle from R_2 to R_1. Thus, unless the country is using its scarce resources inefficiently (such as at point N), economic choices always entail costs in terms of alternative opportunities forgone.

Furthermore, given the normal curvature of the PPF as presented in Figure 1.2, *opportunity cost increases as more and more scarce resources are devoted to further production of a specific product.* For example, if ecotourism service is further increased from E_2 to E_3, the opportunity cost of doing this would suggest a drop of cattle production from R_1 to zero. Clearly, this cost is higher than the opportunity cost implied by an earlier move similar in magnitude when ecotourism service was increased from E_1 to E_2. Why so? This is because the increase in ecotourism is attained by the use of labor, capital and land that are progressively less suited to this particular endeavor. The reason for this is that *although resources (labor, capital and natural resources) are generally fungible, they are not easily adaptable to alternative uses.* In other words, some resources are better suited for the production of some goods than they are for other goods.

The case of Costa Rica illustrates increasing opportunity cost and its implication for resource use. In 1970s and early 1980s Costa Rica was pursuing an aggressive economic policy intended to expand its cattle-ranching sector. One of the most notable effects of this policy was the rapid transformation of forestland to pastureland. However, only 10 percent of Costa Rica's land is suitable for pastureland (Meyer 1993). Given this, continued expansion in cattle ranching could be realized only at increasing opportunity cost; that is, at incrementally faster rates of deforestation, which was the case during this period.

Furthermore, Costa Rica's deforestation problem during this period was exacerbated by other economic and institutional factors. Among others, these factors included (a) expanded use of marginal agricultural land to feed a rapidly growing population; (b) distortion of market information by the government subsidies to cattle-ranching operations (more on this in the next chapter); and (c) other institutional factors such as the land tenure system, unwarranted growth of the government sector, and misallocation of resources due to growing external debt.

What has been presented so far is a snapshot of a society's alternative feasible and efficient output choices. Furthermore, the set of feasible choices that faces a given society is subject to change as technological advances occur. The effect of technological advances is depicted by an outward shift of the PPF curve. In this way, technological change expands a society's feasible opportunity set. Several factors contribute to the expansion (growth) of the feasible combinations of goods and services that a given society can produce. Major factors include a discovery of new resources (such as a new oil deposit); an increase in the labor force; an increase in production efficiency through factor substitutions (more on this in Chapter 3); and an advance in technology representing an entirely new production technique (more on this in Chapter 3). It is through these sorts of change that a set that is infeasible at one point in time, such as point M in Figure 1.2, could become feasible at some point in the future. *Technology fosters economic growth*.

Last but not least, within this conceptual framework it is important to clearly understand the difference between economic *efficiency* and *optimality*. Efficiency simply indicates that the economy is operating on its production possibility curve; that is, resources are used to their full potential. However, as demonstrated by the use of PPF, there is no *one* unique efficient point. How, then, would society choose a point along its PPF – as it must at a particular point in time? As briefly mentioned earlier, the neoclassical economic response to this question goes as follows: The "optimal" (or best) point along a given PPF of a given country is ultimately determined by the *preferences of consumers (citizens)*. This in turn will determine the market prices for final goods and services produced in an economy at a given point in time. Given these prices, the *optimal* point along the production possibility frontier is that which yields the *maximum market value*. Thus, for example, while points A and C are equally efficient, Costa Rica may choose point A (less ecotourism and more cattle ranching) on the grounds that it is associated with a higher level of market value or vice versa. This represents the core ideological position of neoclassical economics; that is, ultimately what is "best" for a society is determined by consumers' preferences. At the same time, it also reflects the kind of value judgment economists are making in choosing a single point along a given production possibility frontier that theoretically contains an infinite set of efficient points.

1.6 CHAPTER SUMMARY

The primary objective of this chapter has been to reflect on the following "preanalytic" conceptions that neoclassical economists have of natural resources and their roles in the economic system.

- Natural resources are *scarce* and as such they should be economized.
- Natural resources are *essential* factors of production. An economy cannot produce goods and services without the use of a certain minimum amount of natural resources. However, to the extent that resources are *fungible*, natural resources need not be seen as the sole or even the primary factor in determining an economy's production capacity. For example, the economy of Costa Rica can, in principle, run without its forestland,

provided sufficient amounts of labor and other capital assets are available to offset its absence.

- Economists' view of natural resources is strictly anthropocentric; that is, from an economic point of view natural resources have no *intrinsic* value.
- The *economic value* of a natural resource is ultimately determined by consumers' preferences.
- Consumers' preferences are best expressed by a market economy, and for that reason the market system is the preferred institution for allocating resources.
- Scarcity of resources (including natural resources) is continually augmented by technological advances.
- In the human economy, as depicted in Figure 1.1, the value of natural resources is determined by the *flow* of services that these resources contribute to the economy. For example, Costa Rica's forestland is valued to the extent that it serves as a continuous source of basic resources such as hardwood, drinking water, a place to attract tourists or in which to conduct scientific experiments, and so on.
- This emphasis on the *flow* of resources rather than the *stock* of natural resources has two profound implications:

  1 The link between the flow of matter–energy in the economic process and the natural environment is simply overlooked. This fact, together with the standard anthropocentric view of natural resources, is likely to undermine the *total value* (economic plus noneconomic) of natural resources. For example, a justification for more conservation of Costa Rica's forestland (such as a move from A to C in Figure 1.2) would customarily be evaluated on the basis of its market (commercial) values. This approach, however, provides no *explicit* consideration of the fact that the forest is also home to many rare plant and animal species which are important for the ecological integrity of the forest but have little commercial value.

  2 The fact that the economic process continually depends on the natural world for both the generation of raw material "inputs" and the absorption of waste "outputs" is simply taken for granted (Georgescu-Roegen 1993).

A comprehensive understanding of the specific nature of the inter-relationships between the human economy and the natural environment requires some basic knowledge of ecology – the subject matter of Chapter 4. Students who have a strong background in economics can proceed to Chapter 4 since the two chapters in Part Two (Chapters 2 and 3) are primarily designed to offer a comprehensive review of basic economic theories and concepts relevant to environmental and resource economics.

review and discussion questions

1 Carefully review the following economic concepts and make sure you have a clear understanding of them: factors of production, opportunity cost, increasing opportunity cost, efficiency, optimality, an economy, households, a firm, product and factor markets, intrinsic value.

2 State *True* or *False* and explain why.

   (a) Resources are of economic concern only if they are scarce.
   (b) There is no such thing as a free lunch.
   (c) In the absence of technological advance, Costa Rica cannot have more of both livestock production and ecosystem service unless it was operating inefficiently initially.
   (d) The postulate that resources are *fungible* renders the problem of scarcity manageable.

3 "Resources are culturally determined, a product of social choice, technology and the workings of the economic system" (Rees 1985: 35). Do you agree or disagree with this assertion? Why?

4 In your opinion, what are some of the opportunity costs of clearing an extensive area of a topical rain forest? Do all your opportunity costs have immediately recognizable economic values? If your answer to this question is no, what does this say to you about measuring the value of a natural resource by its commercial value? Explain.

5 "Against the anthropocentric tendencies of most value theory, intrinsic values do exist apart from man's knowledge of them" (Cobb 1993: 214). Comment.

6 Nicholas Georgescu-Roegen (1993), one of the harshest critics of mainstream economists, had this to say regarding the circular flow diagram discussed in this chapter: "A glaring proof is the standard textbook representation of the economic process by a circular diagram, a pendulum movement between production and consumption within a completely closed system. . . . The patent fact that between the economic process and the material [natural] environment there exists a continuous mutual influence . . . carries no weight with the standard economist" (p. 75). Do you agree? Why, or why not? Make sure you reassess your answer to this question after reading Chapter 4.

REFERENCES AND FURTHER READING

Attfield, R. (1998) "Existence Value and Intrinsic Value," *Ecological Economics* 24: 163–8.

Cobb, J. (1993) "Ecology, Ethics, and Theology," in H. E. Daly and K. N. Townsend (eds.) *Valuing the Earth: Economics, Ecology, Ethics,* Cambridge, Mass.: MIT Press.

Georgescu-Roegen, N. (1993) "The Entropy Law and the Economic Problem," in H. E. Daly and K. N. Townsend (eds.) *Valuing the Earth: Economics, Ecology, Ethics,* Cambridge, Mass.: MIT Press.

Kohler, H. (1986) *Intermediate Microeconomics: Theory and Applications*, 2nd edn., Glenview, Ill.: Scott, Foresman.

McConnell, C. R. and Bruce, S. L. (1996) *Economics: Principles, Problems, and Policies*, 13th edn., New York: McGraw-Hill.

Meyer, C. (1993) "Deforestation and the Frontier Lands," *EPA Journal* 2, 19: 20–1.

North, D. C. (1995) "The New Institutional Economics and Third World Development," in J. Harris, J. Hunter and C. M. Lewis (eds.) *The New Institutional Economics and Third World Development*, London: Routledge.

Randall, A. (1987) *Resource Economics: An Economic Approach to Natural Resource and Environmental Policy*, 2nd edn., New York: John Wiley.

Rees, J. (1985) *Natural Resources: Allocation, Economics and Policy*, London: Methuen.

Solow, R. M. (1991) "Sustainablity: An Economist Perspective," in R. Dorfman and N. Dorfman, (eds.) *Economics of the Environment: Selected Readings*, 3rd edn., New York: W. W. Norton.

World Resources Institute (1998) *World Resources: A Guide to the Global Environment 1998–99*, New York: Oxford University Press.

part two

MARKETS, EFFICIENCY, TECHNOLOGY AND ALTERNATIVE ECONOMIC INDICATORS OF NATURAL RESOURCE SCARCITY

In Chapter 1, natural resources were recognized to be scarce and as such need to be used prudently. Furthermore, it was postulated that natural resources are owned by households and traded through market mechanisms. However, the economic process as presented by the circular flow diagram (Figure 1.1 in Chapter 1) does not go beyond this purely *descriptive* depiction of human economy. Chapters 2 and 3, in Part Two, are intended to provide the basic theoretical foundations essential for clear understanding of the neoclassical perspectives on resource scarcity and their allocation and measurement.

Chapter 2 is written with two broad objectives in mind. The first is to show how prices are formed in the market and the extent to which prices can be used as a measure of resource scarcity. The second is to provide a clear understanding of the welfare implications of the allocative efficiency of perfectly competitive markets – the so-called "invisible hand theorem." The chapter will show why mainstream economists have such deeply felt trust in the power of the market as a means of allocating scarce resources in an orderly and effective manner.

Chapter 3 is an extension of Chapter 2. In this chapter the focus is on the factor (resource) market with a special emphasis on economic variables affecting natural resource prices. The main goals of this chapter are the following: (a) To provide a clear understanding of the key economic determinants of the market value for natural resources. (b) To identify and carefully assess the relative merits of several potential candidates for measures of emerging natural resource scarcity. (c) To show the economic argument on how scarcity of natural resources can be alleviated through factor substitution possibilities and/or technological advances.

To repeat what I have already stated at the end of Chapter 1, Chapters 2 and 3 can be either skipped or skimmed over quickly by those students who have taken microeconomics beyond an introductory level. It is also possible to use the subject matter covered in these two chapters as needed. For example, Section 2.5 in Chapter 2 will be invaluable reading for students who are interested in gaining a clear understanding of the specific conditions under which a market price for a product can be consider as a "true" measure of resource scarcity. On the other hand, Section 3.6 in Chapter 3 will be most relevant to students whose interest lies in furthering their understanding of the economic arguments on how scarcity of natural resources can be alleviated through factor substitution possibilities and/or technological changes. Finally, it is important to note that this suggestion for a selective use of Chapters 2 and 3 is by no means intended to minimize the importance of the subject matter discussed in these two chapters. They provide invaluable theoretical backgrounds that are indispensable for a clear understanding of the standard economic positions on natural resource scarcity and long-term human material progress.

chapter
two

RESOURCE SCARCITY, ECONOMIC EFFICIENCY AND MARKETS:

How the Invisible Hand Works

---

learning objectives

After reading this chapter you will be familiar with the following:

- the underlying premises of an ideal market economy;
- determinants of market demand and supply of a product;
- market demand as a measure of consumers' willingness to pay;
- the law of diminishing marginal utility;
- the concepts of average and marginal costs;
- the law of diminishing marginal product;
- the concepts of short run versus long run;
- the concepts of consumers' and producers' surpluses;
- a concept of economic efficiency or Pareto optimality;
- the role of prices as measures of absolute and relative scarcity;
- price as a measure of the "true" scarcity value of a product;
- the adequacy of product price as a measure of emerging natural resource scarcity.

Markets respond to price signals. If a resource, whether it be a barrel of oil, a patch of Louisiana swamp or old-growth forest, or a breath of fresh air, is priced to reflect its true and complete cost to society, goes the argument, market will ensure that those resources are used in an optimally efficient way.

(Alper 1993: 1884)

2.1 INTRODUCTION

In Chapter 1 an attempt was made to explore the preanalytic conceptions of the neoclassical economic school on resource scarcity and the economic process. It was discovered that these preanalytic conceptions have some profound implications not only for how natural resources are used in the economic process but also for the neoclassical economics understanding of the relationships between the human economy and natural world.

This chapter and Chapter 3 systematically develop the analytical (theoretical) foundation of the neoclassical approaches to resource scarcity and the allocation and measurement of resources. This chapter deals specifically with the product markets and Chapter 3 with the factors markets.

The broader aims of the present chapter are the following: (a) to specify the conditions under which Adam Smith's notion that individuals working in their self-interest will promote the welfare of the whole of society holds good; and (b) to show formally the conditions under which market price can be used as a measure of resource scarcity. To address these two issues fully and systematically, the chapter starts by outlining the basic conditions for a model of a perfectly competitive market.

2.2 BASIC ASSUMPTIONS

As discussed in Chapter 1, consumers and producers occupy an important place in a market-oriented economy. These entities are viewed as being single-minded in their economic behavior, pursuing their own *self-interest*. For consumers, this means maximizing the level of satisfaction (utility) they attain from the consumption of final goods and services. For this reason, at least at the aggregate level, the more goods and services are available in the economy, the higher the level of satisfaction attained by the average citizen of a society. From the producers' viewpoint, self-interest implies ensuring that they earn the "highest" possible profit from the services they render to society. As we shall see shortly, producers' profit is affected by the degree of competition that exists in the market. Note that the producers' desire to enrich themselves is consistent with the consumers' desire to maximize their utility. After all, other things being equal, higher profit would enhance producers' ability to buy more goods and services, and thus increase utility. It is in this sense that economists are able to generalize about the objective of any economic agent (households): *maximize utility*. This is an important first working principle of the market-oriented economy.

In an idealized capitalist market economy, consumers' well-being is a paramount consideration. What this means is that the effectiveness of an economy is judged by how well it satisfies the material needs of its citizens – the consumers. Therefore, given that resources are scarce, an effective economy is one which is capable of producing the maximum output from a given set of basic resources (labor, capital and natural resources). Of course, as discussed in Chapter 1, this is possible if, and only if, resources are fully employed and no misallocation of resources exists. In other words, if the economy is operating on its production possibility frontier, that automatically ensures efficiency. Thus, the second working principle of a market economy is that *efficiency* is the primary criterion, if not the sole criterion, to be used as a measure of institutional performance.

The question then is, what conditions must a market system satisfy in order to be considered as an efficient institution for allocating resources? In other words, what are the conditions consistent with the ideal or perfect form of market structure? According to prevailing economic thought, a market has to satisfy the following broad conditions in order to be regarded as an efficient institutional mechanism for allocating resources:

1 *Freedom of choice based on self-interest and rational behavior* Buyers and sellers are well informed and exhibit "rational" behavior. "Rational" here refers to the notion that the behavior of a buyer or a seller is *consistent* with her or his pursuit of self-interest. It is further stipulated that these actors in the market are provided with an environment conducive to free expression of their choices. Note that as discussed in Chapter 1, choice is an inevitable by-product of resource scarcity.

2 *Perfect information* Economic agents are assumed to be provided with full information regarding any market transactions. They are also assumed to have perfect foresight about future economic events.

3 *Competition* For each item subjected to market transaction, the number of buyers and sellers is large. Thus, no one buyer or seller can single-handedly influence the terms of trade. In modern economic jargon, this means that both buyers and sellers are *price-takers*. This is assumed to be the case in both the product and the factor markets.

4 *Mobility of resources* In a dynamic economy, change is the norm. Significant shifts in economic conditions could result from a combination of several factors, namely, changes in consumer preference, income, resource availability and technology. To accommodate changes of this nature in a timely fashion, resources must be readily transferable from one sector of the economy to another. This is possible only when barriers to entry and exit in an industry are absent (or minimal).

5 *Ownership rights* All goods and services, as well as factors of production, have clearly defined ownership rights. This condition prevails when the following specific conditions are met: (a) the nature and characteristics of the resources under consideration are completely specified; (b) owners have title with exclusive rights to the resources they legally own; (c) ownership rights are transferable – that is, ownership rights are subject to market transactions at terms agreeable with the resource owner(s); and (d) ownership rights are enforceable (Randall 1987) – that is, property rights are protected by binding social rules and regulations.

When the above five conditions are met, an economy is said to be operating in a world of perfectly competitive markets. In such a setting, Adam Smith (the father of modern economics) declared over two centuries ago, the market system through its *invisible hand* will guide each individual to do not only what is in her or his own self-interest, but also that which is for the "good" of society at large. A profound statement indeed, which clearly depicts the most appealing features of the market economy in its ideal form. In the next two sections, this will be demonstrated systematically using demand and supply analysis.

2.3 AN INTERPRETATIVE ANALYSIS OF DEMAND, SUPPLY AND MARKET EQUILIBRIUM PRICE

For a given product (goods and services), the *market demand* depicts the price buyers are willing to pay in aggregate for a specified quantity provided in the market at a point in time, holding all other factors affecting demand constant. For example, as shown in Figure 2.1, if the quantity of a given product available in the market is Q_0, other things being equal, P_0 is the maximum price consumers would be willing to pay. On the other hand, if what is available in the market is Q_1, it follows that consumers would be willing to pay P_1. In general, the price–quantity relationship shows that, other things being equal, quantity demanded is inversely related to price. In other words, the market demand for a product is negatively sloped. What is the significance of the "other things being equal" assumption? Why is the demand curve for a product negatively sloped?

In the normal construction of the market demand for any product, certain variables are held constant. Some of the key variables include income, prices of related goods, the preference of consumers for the product under consideration, and the number of relevant consumers. A change in any one of these variables will be manifested by a *shift* in the entire demand curve. For example, normally, as shown in Figure 2.2, an increase in the average

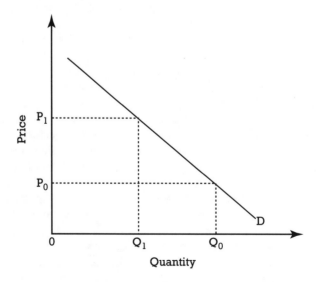

Figure 2.1 A market demand curve

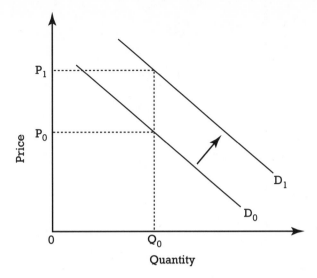

Figure 2.2 **A shift in market demand curve**

income of consumers will shift the demand curve outward from D_0 to D_1. This implies that with a rise in average income, for any given level of the product offered in the market consumers will be willing to pay a higher price. Hence, if what is offered in the market is Q_0, with an increase in average income the price consumers are willing to pay increases from P_0 to P_1.

The important lesson here is the recognition that market demand is a measure of *consumers' willingness to pay*, which depends on some key variables such as income, prices of related goods and consumer preference. The next question that we need to address is why it is that the consumers' willingness to pay declines when the quantity of a product available in the market increases.

The answer to this question requires delving into an aspect of human consumption psychology. The conventional wisdom here is that people engage in the act of consumption because, in the process of doing so, they derive satisfaction (utility). Further, if the consumption of all other products is held constant, the general tendency is for the marginal utility, the utility obtained from each additional units of a product, to decline – *the law of diminishing marginal utility*. Hence prices need to be lowered in order to entice consumers into consuming more of a given product. Thus, declining willingness to pay (price) as we move down along a given demand curve is consistent with the postulate of diminishing marginal utility.

In determining the value of any scarce resource, market demand constitutes only half of the story. The other half is market supply. Market supply shows, other things being equal, the *minimum* price that producers in aggregate are willing to accept in order to provide a given quantity of a product in the market at a given point in time. Accordingly, as shown in Figure 2.3, in order to provide level Q_0 of a product, producers will require, at the minimum, a price P_0. Similarly, to provide a larger quantity, Q_1, the

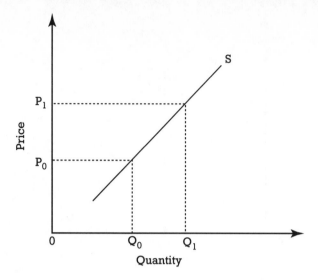

Figure 2.3 **A market supply curve**

producers' required minimum price would have to increase to P_1. The implication is that the market supply curve for a product is positively sloped. What possible explanation can we provide for this phenomenon? Before answering this question, it will be helpful to first identify the "other things being equal" assumptions regarding market supply.

In depicting the relationship between price and quantity, the supply curve assumes that certain variables are held constant. Some of the key variables held constant in the normal consideration of a supply curve include prices of factors of production (labor, capital and other basic resources), productivity of factors of production, and technology. Any change in these variables will cause the supply curve to *shift*. For example, if other factors are held constant, an increase in the price of labor (wages) will shift the supply curve to the left. That is, as shown in Figure 2.4, to provide a given level of output in the market, Q_0, after the wage increase, producers require a higher minimum price, P_1 instead of P_0. This is easy to understand, given that the ultimate effect of a wage increase, in this respect, is to increase the cost of production. The effect of a change in productivity and/or technological change on a supply curve can be demonstrated in a similar manner.

Let us now turn to the issue of why the normal shape of a supply curve for a product is positively sloped. First, it should be noted that the supply curve for a product is intimately related to the *cost of production*. If other factors affecting supply are held constant, to produce more output requires the use of more inputs (labor, capital and natural resources). Thus, a higher level of output is associated with a higher level of *total* production cost. This higher cost of production alone, however, would not have necessitated (justified) producers to increase prices, as implied by the supply curve. For example, in the case where the increase in the cost is directly *proportional* to the increase in output, the unit (average) cost of production would

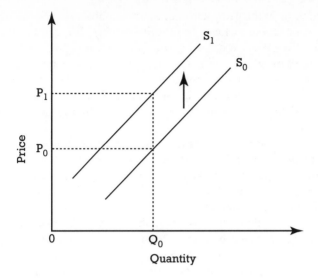

Figure 2.4 **A shift in market supply curve**

have remained constant. In other words, if the increase in cost is proportional to the increase in output, the average and marginal costs of production would be *constant*.

This can be illustrated using a simple numerical example. Suppose the total cost of production was $1,000 when the rate of output production was 20 units. In this case the cost per unit of output would be $50 ($1,000/20). Suppose now that the production of output is expanded to 60 units and, as a result of this, the total cost is increased to $3,000. What is observed here is that a tripling of the output rate causes a tripling of the total cost. As a result, it is evident that the cost per unit of output remains unchanged at $50 ($3,000/60). In this case the marginal cost, which is the addition to total cost resulting from producing one more unit of output (it is equal to the change in total cost divided by the change in output), is also $50 ($2,000/40).

Thus, in a situation where the increase in cost is proportional to the increase in output, the supply curve will be a horizontal rather than an upward-sloping curve in the price–quantity space. The implication here is that for a supply curve to be upward sloped as output increases, the increase in total cost of production must be proportionately higher than the increase in output. For this to happen, the productivity of the variable inputs must be declining as the production of output increases. What could cause this to happen?

The answer to that question depends on whether the issue under consideration is a short- or long-run supply curve. In the short run (a time period too short to allow all inputs to vary), the phenomenon of declining productivity is explained by the famous law of diminishing marginal product. This law simply states that, in a production process with at least one fixed input, variable inputs eventually encounter diminishing returns – declining marginal productivity. This is because the fixed input(s) acts as a limiting factor in the production process. To observe this, imagine a farm of ten acres producing wheat. In this simple case, it is not hard to see that after a certain point, increasing the labor of the farm owner and the application of fertilizers will not increase output (wheat) substantially because there is a limit to how much wheat ten acres of land can produce. In this case, land is the limiting factor. Hence, fundamentally, the positive slope of the short-run supply curve is explained by the law of diminishing marginal product.

In the long run, however, all inputs with the exception of technology are assumed to be variable. Thus, since there are no fixed inputs, the law of diminishing marginal product cannot be used to explain why the long-run supply curve of a product may be positively sloped. In this situation, two explanations may be given, as follows.

First, some resources may be available only in limited quantities. An example is highly skilled workers. Other things being equal, the prices for these kinds of factors of production may rise as, profit seeking, competitive firms attempt to expand their production in response to increased demand. The increase in the prices for factors of production may mean that firms are encountering rising production costs as they attempt to increase the quantity supplied of their product. The result is a long-run market supply curve that is upward sloping. It is important to note that the primary cause of the increasing unit production costs (as firms attempt to expand their output) is increase in the prices for factors of production, not declining productivity.

Second, in the long run, one way to increase the quantity supplied of a product may be by encouraging new entrants. However, not only do firms have different costs, but the expectation is that in any given industry, new entrants have higher costs than those firms already in the market. Because these new entrants have higher costs, the price must rise to make entry profitable for them. This suggests that the long-run market supply curve for a competitive industry will be positively sloping.

Now that we have discussed market demand and supply, it is time to formally demonstrate how a price is formed in the market. From the previous section, we know that market demand and supply for a product are nothing more than expressions of consumer and producer behaviors, respectively. For example, in Figure 2.5, if P_0 is the prevailing market price, consumers will purchase only amount Q_d. On the other hand, for the same price, producers will be willing to sell amount Q_s of output. This would not be a stable situation, since at P_0, producers would end up with an excess supply (unsold product), to the amount of $Q_s - Q_d$. In this situation it would be in the interest of producers to decrease price so that they could reduce their excess inventory. It would be also in the self-interest of consumers to buy more of the product, as it is offered at a lower price. These mutually reinforcing, voluntary expressions of consumers and producers will continue until a market price is reached where excess supply is eliminated. In Figure 2.5, this will be the case at the market price P_e. At this price, quantity demanded is exactly equal to quantity supplied, i.e. $Q_e = Q_d = Q_s$. Thus, a

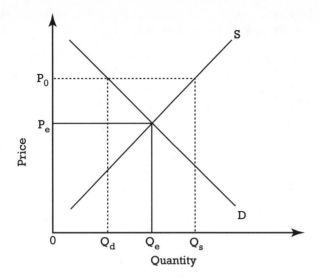

Figure 2.5 **How the market gravitates toward equilibrium**

market equilibrium price is that price which tends to equate quantity demanded with quantity supplied of a product at a point in time.

Several implications can be drawn from the above market outcome. First, the very fact that the market equilibrium price is positive entails that the product under consideration is scarce. In other words, with a positive price, acquiring this product carries with it an opportunity cost. In economic literature, this particular notion of scarcity is known as *absolute scarcity*. It is absolute in the sense that it does not go beyond simply telling us that the particular product under consideration is scarce. Second, in a situation where market prices for more than one product are available at the same point in time, market prices can be used as a measure of *relative scarcity*. For example, if the current market prices per pound of oranges and apples in Kalamazoo are $1 and $0.75 respectively, then we can conclude that oranges are scarcer than apples. This is because, on the basis of the given price information alone, in the marketplace 1.0 orange is worth as much as 1.33 units of apples. As we shall see, the notion of relative scarcity is at the heart of most economic decision-making processes. Third, the market price of a product is subject to change over time. The change could come as a result of factors affecting demand (such as income, preference, prices of related goods, etc.) and/or changes in the factors affecting supply (input prices, productivity, technology, etc.).

From the above discussion, it is evident that market prices can be used as measures of either absolute or relative scarcity of products at a point in time. At this point we need to ask: how well does a market price perform those functions? That is, is market price a *true* measure of resource scarcity? What exactly do we mean by *true scarcity*? To answer these questions adequately, we need to probe further into the operation of the market economy.

2.4 EVALUATING THE PERFORMANCE OF A PERFECTLY COMPETITIVE MARKET ECONOMY

We have so far identified a market as an institution. The performance of an institution cannot solely be based on its daily operations. A valid judgment on the performance of an institution should be based on the enduring qualities of long-term outcomes. In this regard, the claim often made by mainstream economists is this: Provided that all the assumptions of the model of perfect competition discussed in Section 2.2 are satisfied (freedom of choice and enterprise; consumers and producers as fully informed price-takers; mobility of resources; clearly defined ownership rights), in the long run the market system will tend to allocate resources efficiently. Furthermore, market prices will measure the *true* scarcity value of resources.

To demonstrate these claims in a systematic manner, let us suppose that Figure 2.6 represents the *long-run* equilibrium condition of a product produced and sold in a perfectly competitive industry. In this case, P_e and Q_e represent the market equilibrium price and quantity, respectively. It is important to note that the long-run equilibrium price is that which prevails after the existence of above-normal profits has attracted new firms to enter the industry (or below-normal profits have forced some firms to exit). It is, in other words, where all firms in that particular industry are making just *normal* profits. Normal profit means that, in the long run, firms in a given industry cannot make a return from their investment above what they would have been able to earn if they had invested in some other industry with similar operating conditions and a similar risk environment. To see the "social" significance of this long-run equilibrium situation, let us separately analyze the economic conditions of the consumers and producers.

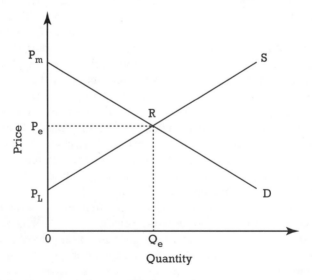

Figure 2.6 **Long-run market equilibrium price**

2.4.1 Consumers' surplus

Figure 2.7 shows the same demand function as the one in Figure 2.6. Thus, P_e and Q_e represent the long-run market equilibrium price and output. P_m is the price where the quantity demanded is zero. Thus, it can be interpreted as the maximum price consumers are willing to pay for this product rather than go without it. By focusing on the demand alone, we will now be able to demonstrate the implication of the long-run market equilibrium for the consumers' welfare.

From our earlier discussion, we know that the demand curve depicts the maximum price consumers are willing to pay for a given quantity of the product provided in the market. For example, P_m is the maximum price consumers are willing to pay rather than go without the product. On the other hand, at the market equilibrium quantity, Q_e, the consumers are willing to pay the price P_e. For quantities between 0 and Q_e, consumers will be willing to pay prices higher than P_e and lower than P_m. Note that the prices consumers are willing to pay successively decline as the quantity of a product available in the market increases. This diminishing willingness to pay is, of course, consistent with the law of demand.

To illustrate the above concept, let us assume, in a given market, that there are some eager consumers who would be willing to pay as much as $20 for a gallon of gasoline. If gasoline price in this market were more than $20, no one would buy any. If the price of gasoline were less than $20, then we can be sure that some amount of gasoline would be purchased. Suppose the actual market price is $1.50; those consumers who were willing to pay as much as $20 now essentially save $18.50 for every gallon of gasoline that they purchase. It is this kind of saving that is being conveyed by the concept of consumers' surplus.

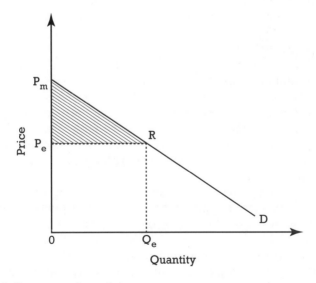

Figure 2.7 **Consumers' surplus**

Looking at demand as a measure of willingness to pay also lends itself to the interpretation of price as the *marginal* private benefit to consumers. That is, a consumer whose sole interest is to maximize utility will not purchase an additional unit of a product unless the benefit derived from the incremental unit is at least equal to the market price. The fact that the price or marginal private benefit declines as the quantity of the product increases is also consistent with the law of diminishing marginal utility.

If prices can be looked at as a measure of marginal private benefit, then, conceptually, we can compute the total private benefit by summing all the marginal benefits for a given range of the output demanded. For example, in Figure 2.7, for the market equilibrium of output, Q_e, the *total* consumers' benefit would be measured by the sum of all the prices starting from P_m all the way up to and including P_e. This is represented by the area of trapezoid $0P_mRQ_e$. In an ideal (competitive) market, in the long run this area would tend to be maximized. The reasons for this are not difficult to see. Given that both consumers and producers are price-takers and resources are freely mobile, the long-run equilibrium condition ensures that firms are operating efficiently (minimizing their costs of production). In addition, due to the free mobility of resources, firms are not able to make an above-normal profit. If this situation prevails, then the market equilibrium price, P_e, represents the lowest price firms can charge in the long run. If P_e represents the lowest price, it follows that Q_e is the largest output that could be forthcoming to the market. Thus, the trapezoid area $0P_mRQ_e$ represents the largest total consumers' benefit.

This total consumers' benefit is composed of two parts. The first part is rectangle area $0P_eRQ_e$ which represents what the consumers actually paid to acquire the market clearing output, Q_e. The second segment is the area of the triangle P_eP_mR, which represents the sum of all the prices above the equilibrium price that consumers would have been willing to pay. Since consumers did not actually pay higher prices for some units, but paid P_e for every unit up to Q_e, the sum of these prices, which is shown by the area of triangle P_eP_mR, represents *consumers' surplus*. In other words, consumers' surplus is the difference between the total willingness to pay (area $0P_mRQ_e$) and what consumers actually paid, which is represented by the area $0P_eRQ_e$. What is significant here is that in the long run consumers' surplus is maximized. This is easy to demonstrate given that the long-run equilibrium price, P_e, represents the lowest feasible price for producers. This is an important conclusion since it confirms economists' assertions that in the long run, a market economy left alone would do what is best for consumers: maximize their surpluses.

To offer a simple numerical illustration of consumers' surplus and total willingness to pay, let us suppose that the market equilibrium price and quantity in Figure 2.7 are $5 and 2,000 units, respectively. In addition, let P_m, the maximum price consumers are willing to pay for this product, be $9. Given this information, first, consumers' surplus, the shaded area in Figure 2.7, can be obtained using the formula ½ (the product of the *base* and the *height* of the relevant triangle); in this case it would be ½ (2,000 × 4), which is equal to $4,000. Second, in acquiring the 2,000 units, consumers paid a total sum of $10,000 (the product of the market equilibrium price and quantity). In Figure 2.7 this $10,000 represents the area of the rectangle $0P_eRQ_e$. On the basis of these two findings, it can be inferred that the *total* willingness to pay is $14,000 (area $0P_mRQ_e$ in Figure 2.7), since consumers have gained $4,000 in surplus while paying $10,000 for the purchase of the equilibrium quantity, 2,000 units.

2.4.2 Producers' surplus and net social benefit

Figure 2.8 is a replica of the supply curve in Figure 2.6. As stated earlier, the supply curve could be interpreted as showing the *minimum* prices producers are willing to accept to provide various levels of output in a market. For example, P_L represents the lowest price producers require before partici-pating in any production activity. Similarly, P_e is the minimum price the producers would accept to provide the last unit of the equilibrium output, Q_e. Alternatively, as discussed earlier, the supply curve is intimately related to production costs. More specifically, the supply curve represents nothing more than the mapping of the incremental (marginal) costs of production. Thus, if we employ these two interpretations of the supply curve, P_e can be understood in the following two ways. In one sense it shows the minimum price producers are willing to accept in order to bring forth the last unit of Q_e in the market. Alternatively, it represents the *marginal cost* of producing a given level of output. Note that these dual interpretations equally apply to all prices along the supply curve.

If the supply curve in fact represents the mapping of the incremental costs of production, in Figure 2.8 trapezoid area $0P_LRQ_e$ represents the total cost of production at the output level where the long-run equilibrium is

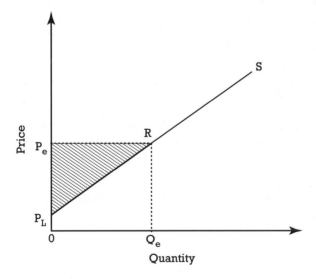

Figure 2.8 **Producers' surplus**

attained, Q_e. This area is obtained by summing the marginal costs (or the minimum acceptable prices to producers) along the relevant output range. In a competitive market setting (where producers are price-takers and resources are freely mobile), this long-run production cost is minimized and accurately reflects the opportunity costs of the scarce resources being used in the production process.

In Figure 2.8 we have already established that area $0P_LRQ_e$ represents the total cost of producing the equilibrium level of output, Q_e. However, at the equilibrium level of output and price, the total producers' receipt (revenue) is represented by area $0P_eRQ_e$. The difference between the total revenue and total production cost, triangle area P_LP_eR in Figure 2.8, is *producers' surplus*. What can this surplus be attributed to? There is no clear-cut answer to this question in the existing economic literature. For our purpose we consider producers' surplus as the cumulative payments to those producers exhibiting entrepreneurial capacity which is above that of the marginal producer (the last producer to enter the market).

To provide numerical illustrations of the concepts of producers' surplus and production cost, again let the market equilibrium price and quantity be $5 and 2,000 units, respectively. Furthermore, let P_L, the minimum price acceptable to the producers, be $2. Given this information, producers' surplus (the area of the shaded triangle in Figure 2.8) would be $3,000 (½ × 3 × 2,000). Furthermore, the total receipts (revenue) of the producers from the sale of 2,000 units would be $10,000 (5 × 2,000) or area $0P_eRQ_e$. Thus, the total production cost would be $7,000 ($10,000 – $3,000), or the area of the trapezoid $0P_LRQ_e$. This total value represents either the sum of all the minimum prices that producers are willing to accept or the sum of all the marginal costs in producing the output ranging from 0 to 2,000 units.

Finally, let us go back to Figure 2.6 to tie together what we have been discussing so far concerning the long-run equilibrium condition under a competitive market setting. In Figure 2.6 we noted that area $0P_mRQ_e$ represents the consumers' total willingness to pay (private benefit) associated with the consumption of the equilibrium level of output, Q_e. As discussed earlier, under a perfectly competitive market setting this benefit is maximized. On the other hand, area $0P_LRQ_e$ shows the cost of producing the equilibrium level of output, Q_e. As previously discussed, this cost is *minimized*. Thus, area P_LP_mR represents the net surplus, which is composed of the consumers' and the producers' surpluses. From the above arguments, it should be noted that this social (consumers' and producers') surplus is maximized – one of the hallmarks of an ideal market system.

2.4.3 Pareto optimality and the Invisible Hand Theorem

One frequently used alternative approach to arrive at the above conclusion is the notion of *Pareto optimality*. An equilibrium condition is said to be Pareto optimal if the move in any direction cannot be made without making at least one member of a society worse off. To see this, suppose in Figure 2.9 P_e and

Q_e represent the long-run equilibrium price and output, respectively. Suppose the output is increased to Q_1. What would be the effect of this increase in output from Q_e to Q_1? The answer is rather straightforward. To begin with, the increase in output from Q_e to Q_1 will require an additional production cost, as shown by the area Q_eRTQ_1 (the area under the supply curve over the relevant output range). Similarly, the benefit associated from this incremental output is measured by the area Q_eRUQ_1 (the area under the demand curve along the relevant output range). Thus, in this situation the cost outweighs the benefit by the triangle area RTU.

The curious should try to perform the following numerical exercise. Consistent with earlier examples, assume the equilibrium price and quantity in Figure 2.9 to be $5 and 2,000 units. Assume that output is now increased from Q_e to Q_1 or from 2,000 to 2,100. Furthermore, the supply price at Q_1 (point T along the supply curve) is given to be $7 and the demand price at this same level of output (point U along the demand curve) is $3. This information demonstrates the following: (a) The increase in the production cost as a result of the increase in output by 100 (from 2,000 to 2,100) which is represented in Figure 2.9 by area Q_eRTQ_1, is $600. (b) The increase in consumers' benefit resulting from a 100-unit increase in output (area Q_eRUQ_1 in Figure 2.9) is $400. Findings (a) and (b) clearly indicate that to increase output from Q_e to Q_1 would result in a net loss of $200 ($400 − $600 = −$200).

On the other hand, if output were restricted, falling from Q_e to Q_2, the forgone benefit associated with this action would be measured by the area Q_eRVQ_2. However, as a result of this reduction in output there would be a cost saving measured by the area Q_eRWQ_2. In this case the forgone benefit would outweigh the cost saving by the area of the triangle RVW. Thus, from the argument presented so far, a movement away from the equilibrium in

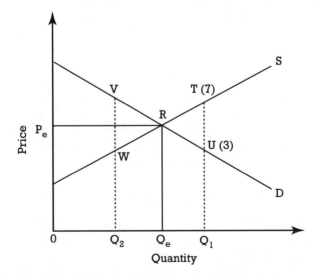

Figure 2.9 **Pareto optimality**

either direction would lead to a net loss. This clearly confirms that long-run equilibrium outcome in a setting of perfectly competitive markets is Pareto optimal. Note that Pareto optimality implies *economic efficiency* – a condition where the net benefit of producers and consumers taken together is maximized. After all, as we have seen above, any deviations from the equilibrium are associated with a reduction, not a gain, in net benefits. Indeed, this amounts to a back-handed proof of Adam Smith's Invisible Hand Theorem.

2.5 PRODUCT PRICE AS A MEASURE OF NATURAL RESOURCE SCARCITY

In this last section of the chapter, I will outline the essential roles of price in an ideal market setting, especially as a measure of natural resource scarcity. To begin this discussion, on the basis of what we have discussed so far, the following represents the key information conveyed by market price:

Price as information signal

In a market economy, one of the most basic functions of price is to provide information relevant to the culmination of transactions among buyers and sellers of a product or a resource. The demand curve provides the set of prices consumers are willing to pay for various levels of output provided in the market. Similarly, the supply curve contains the set of prices producers are willing to accept for various levels of output offered in the market. In this sense, prices are used as signals of the terms by which consumers and producers are willing to enter into a specific market transaction. For example, in Figure 2.10, if the relevant output level under consideration for transaction is Q_0, any prices between P_s and P_d are likely candidates to be observed in the market to set the negotiation between consumers and producers. Note that prices below P_s are absolutely unacceptable to producers, and prices above P_d would be rejected by consumers.

Price as market clearing signal

Price not only is used to start the negotiation process, but also serves as a means of culminating transactions. This occurs when a single price emerges that tends to equate quantity demanded and supplied of a given product at a point in time. In Figure 2.10, P_e would be such a price. In other words, this is a price that clears the market or brings about market equilibrium.

Price as a measure of resource scarcity

As we discussed earlier, since the prevailing (equilibrium) market price for a product is positive, it follows that the product under consideration is scarce. But scarce in what sense? To respond to this question adequately, let us refer to Figure 2.10 again. In this figure, the market equilibrium price is P_e given that S_0 is the relevant supply curve. From the consumers' viewpoint, this

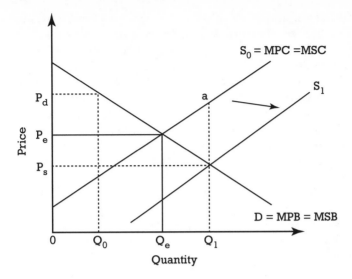

Figure 2.10 Roles of market price

price measures their willingness to pay for the last unit of the equilibrium output, Q_e. In other words, it measures consumers' *marginal private benefit* (MPB) at the equilibrium level of output. On the other hand, from the producers' perspective, the prevailing market price, P_e, measures the minimum price they are willing to accept in offering the last unit of the equilibrium output in the market. In an ideal market, where the marginal producers are just making a normal profit, this would be equivalent to the *marginal private cost* (MPC) of producing the last unit of output.

Given the above argument, in an ideal market setting the long-run equilibrium price has an implication that goes far beyond a market clearing condition. This price equates marginal private (consumers') benefit with that of marginal private (producers') costs. That is,

$$P_e = MPB = MPC$$

Furthermore, in cases where ownership rights are clearly defined, there will be no difference between private and social benefits and costs (more on this in Chapter 5). *Thus, in an ideal market condition, the long-run equilibrium price of a product is a measure of both the marginal social benefit and the marginal social cost.* That is,

$$P_e = MPB = MSB = MPC = MSC$$

It is in this context that mainstream economists base their long-standing claim that in a free competitive market, a market price tends to reflect the *true* scarcity value of a resource under consideration. True in exactly what sense? In the sense that, in the long run, market price reflects the *social cost* of using resources (land, labor, capital, etc.) to produce output at the margin.

Note that market price would fail to reflect social cost if the market price were artificially set either below or above the market equilibrium price, P_e. If either one of these situations occurs, the result will be what economists commonly refer to as a *misallocation of resources*. To see the significance of this, let us suppose that a decision is made to lower the market price from P_e to P_s in Figure 2.10. To make this possible, the supply curve needs to be shifted from S_0 to S_1, otherwise, P_s will not be a market clearing price. Suppose this is accomplished through a market intervention mechanism, such as a government subsidy (either as a tax break or a cash grant) to the firms producing the product under consideration. The question is then, how will this result in a misallocation of societal resources?

At the new and artificially established equilibrium price, P_s, the market clearing output will increase from Q_e (the socially optimal output) to Q_1. For it to do so, more resources (labor, capital and natural resources) are now allocated for the production of the output under consideration. However, for any output level beyond Q_e, the MSC (the supply prices along S_0) of using these resources exceeds the prevailing market price, P_s. Clearly, then, these resources are not being used where they benefit society the most – they are misallocated. The outcome would be similar if the market price in Figure 2.10 were raised from P_e to P_d. This could be implemented through programs such as farm price support.

As we shall see throughout this book, the concept of "resource misallocation" has widespread application in environmental and resource economics. For example, Case Study 2.1 illustrates how subsidies (in the form of investment tax credits and import duty exemptions) to ranchers by the Brazilian government obstructed important market signals that ultimately caused excessive soil loss and deforestation in the Amazon. Another way to look at this same problem, and a way that is consistent with the framework of the analysis presented in this chapter, is by assuming that, in Figure 2.10, the product of interest is hamburgers. Given this, it would be easy to see how subsidies to Brazilian ranchers could cause a shift in the supply curve of hamburgers from S_0 to S_1. Essentially, if other factors affecting supply are held constant, subsidies will lower the cost of one of the major raw materials (that is, beef) needed in the production of hamburgers. As a result, society (both Brazilian society and the societies of countries importing meat from Brazil) will have more hamburgers and at a lower price. However, as Case Study 2.1 clearly reveals, this is made possible at a human, environmental and ecological price, a situation that comes about because the price of beef, and therefore hamburgers, is not allowed to reflect the social costs of the resources used to produce it.

Price as a signal of emerging resource scarcity

Here the focus is on examining the trend of product prices over a long period of time (for example, a period of twenty to one hundred years can be used as indicator of emerging resource scarcity or abundance). For example, the price trend of a hypothetical product depicted in Figure 2.11 signals

CASE STUDY 2.1 RANCHING FOR SUBSIDIES IN BRAZIL

Theodore Panayotou

In the 1960s, the Brazilian government introduced extensive legislation aimed at developing the Amazon region. Over the next two decades, a combination of new fiscal and financial incentives encouraged the conversion of forest to pasture land. During the 1970s, some 8,000–10,000 square kilometers of forest were cleared for pasture each year. The proportion of land used for pasture in the Amazonian state of Rondonia increased from 2.5 percent in 1970 to 25.6 percent in 1985 (Mahar 1989).

It is now clear that transforming the Amazon into ranchland is both economically unsound and environmentally harmful. Without tree cover, the fragile Amazonian soil often loses its fertility, and at least 20 percent of the pastures may be at some stage of deterioration (Repetto 1988b). Indeed, cattle ranching is considered one of the foremost proximate causes of deforestation. Furthermore, ranching provides few long-term employment opportunities. Livestock projects offer work only during the initial slash-and-burn phase. Negative employment effects have been observed when income-generating tree crops such as Brazil nuts are eradicated for pasture (Mahar 1989).

Nonetheless, the incentives designed to attract ranching, which were administered by the government's Superintendency for the Development of the Amazon (SUDAM), were powerful. Fiscal incentives included ten- to fifteen-year tax holidays, investment tax credits (ITCs) and export tax or import duty exemptions . . . SUDAM evaluated projects and financed up to 75 percent of the investment costs of those that received favorable ratings using tax credit funds.

Starting in 1974, subsidized credit also played a crucial role in encouraging numerous ranching projects. The Program of Agricultural, Livestock and Mineral Poles in Amazonia (POLAMAZONIA) offered ranchers loans at 12 percent interest, while market interest rates were at 45 percent. Subsidized loans of 49–76 percent of face value were typical through the early 1980s (Repetto 1988a). . . .

The subsidies and tax breaks encouraged ranchers to undertake projects that would not otherwise have been profitable. A World Resources Institute study showed that the typical subsidized investment yielded an economic loss equal to 55 percent of the initial investment. If subsidies received by the private investor are taken into account, however, the typical investment yielded a positive financial return equal to 250 percent of the initial outlay. The fiscal and financial incentives masked what were intrinsically poor investments and served to subsidize the conversion of a superior asset (tropical forest) into an inferior use (cattle ranching). Moreover, a survey of SUDAM projects reveals that five projects received tax credit funds without even being implemented (Mahar 1989).

Source: Green Markets: The Economics of Sustainable Development, San Francisco: International Center for Economic Growth (1993). Case reproduced by permission of the author.

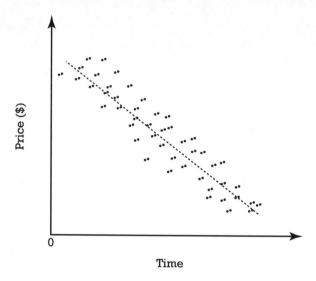

***Figure 2.11* Long-run price trend**

decreasing resource scarcity over time. That is, it shows a decline in the *aggregate* prices (or costs) of all the factors that are used in producing the product (labor, capital, natural resources, etc.)

However, this measure of resource scarcity is at an aggregate level. That is, a trend in product price of this nature would only provide us with information about what happens to resource costs over time in general. For example, suppose the specific product under consideration is electricity. In this case, Figure 2.11 would indicate a trend of falling electricity price. This declining trend in the price of electricity may be due to increasing availability (hence, lower prices) of either labor or capital or natural resources (for example, coal) which are used to produce electricity. In fact, it is quite possible for the price of a specific factor of production such as coal to be increasing while a falling trend in electricity prices is observed. In this instance, what might have happened is that the increase in the price of coal (due to its increasing scarcity) is more than offset by a decline in the prices of other factors of production (such as labor and capital) used to produce electricity. Thus, what this situation illustrates is that the possibility exists for the price of natural resources to be increasing while the price of a product is declining. Note that this observation does not take account of technological factors. For example, it is quite possible for coal to become scarcer (hence more expensive) and prices of electricity to decline over time if power plants continue to improve on the efficiency of coal burning.

In addition, another factor that needs to be considered is factor share – the percentage of a final product's price (for example, price of electricity) that is related to a specific factor of production (such as labor, capital or natural resources). Suppose the cost of coal accounts for only 2 to 5 per cent of the price of electricity. If this is the case, coal, as important as it may be in the production of electricity, is not a major component of the market (final) electricity price. Thus, the price of coal could increase significantly (for example, by 10 percent) and still have very little effect on the market price of electricity.

The implication of all this is quite clear. Even in a world of perfectly competitive markets setting, *product* price trends may not adequately signal emerging *natural resource* scarcity or abundance. This is because trends of product prices are influenced by the availability of other resources (such as labor and capital), the factor share of natural resources and technological factors. The question is, then, what alternative measures of natural resource scarcity exist? How good are these measures in signaling impending natural resource scarcity? In the next chapter, an attempt is made to address these important questions by focusing directly on the price formation (market value) of natural resources.

2.6 CHAPTER SUMMARY

The objectives of this chapter were twofold. The first aim was to clearly specify the institutional conditions under which individuals working in their self-interest will promote the welfare of the whole of society. The second was to show the various roles of prices and the extent to which product prices can be used as measures of resource scarcity.

- To address these issues fully and systematically, the following three key assumptions were made:

  1 Markets are perfectly competitive.
  2 The economy is evaluated on the basis of its long-term performance.
  3 The criteria for evaluating market performance are based on the market's ability (a) to attain *efficient* allocation of resources so that, in the long run, the aggregate social surplus is maximized, and (b) to transmit accurate signals of resource scarcity.

- It was shown that, given the above assumptions, a market system uses price information to facilitate the production and exchange of goods and services. These prices are formed by the interaction of market demand (a measure of consumers' willingness to pay) and market supply (a measure of producers' willingness to sell).

- Furthermore, when one assumes the existence of clearly defined ownership rights, market demand and supply reflect marginal social benefit (MSB) and marginal social cost (MSC), respectively. Thus, the long-run equilibrium is attained when the following condition is satisfied: P_e = MSB = MSC, where P_e is the long-run equilibrium price. This condition has the following important implications:

  1 The fact that MSB = MSC suggests that, in the long run, competitive markets allocate resources in such a way that the *net* social benefit (the sum of consumers' and producers' surplus) is maximized. This is because no reallocation can be made without adversely affecting the

net social benefit. Thus, in the long run, competitive markets are Pareto efficient.

2 Market price is a measure of the value "society" attaches to a product. That is, P_e = MSB.

3 The market equilibrium price of a product, P_e, is a measure of the "social" cost of using basic resources (labor, capital, land, etc.) to produce the desired product. That is, P_e = MSC.

4 Market price, P_e, is a "true" measure of resource scarcity because there is no discrepancy between the social value of the product (what people are willing to pay) and the social opportunity cost of the resources used to produce this product. One important implication of this observation is that market intervention through subsidies or support prices would cause distortion of important social opportunity cost(s) and in so doing lead to a misallocation of resources.

- Finally, it was observed that a secular price trend of a *final* product (such as electricity) can be used as an indicator of emerging "general" resource scarcity – general in the sense that the opportunity cost of the resources (land, labor, capital) used to produce a particular product has been either increasing or decreasing over time. However, a trend in product price may not be reliable as an indicator of emerging scarcity of a specific resource. This is an important concern, especially in natural resource economics. To what extent a trend in product price can be used as an indicator of emerging natural resource scarcity depends on factor substitutions, factor shares, technology, and the general condition of factor markets – which are discussed in the next chapter.

---

review and discussion questions

1 Briefly identify the following concepts: the invisible hand, perfectly competitive markets, willingness to pay, consumer and producer surplus, price-taker, diminishing marginal product, absolute and relative scarcity, clearly defined ownership rights, misallocation of resources, Pareto optimality, factor share.

2 State *True*, *False* or *Uncertain* and explain why.

   (a)   Decisions reached individually will be the best decision for an entire society.

   (b)   Markets are meant to be efficient, not fair.

3 In a perfectly competitive market setting, *relative price* can be viewed as a measure of opportunity cost. For example, suppose the price of Good X is $10 and the price for Good Y is $5. The price of X relative to Y indicates that the opportunity cost of X is 2Y. Does this mean that (a) the physical availability of Y must be twice that of X, or (b) the production of a unit of Y uses only half of the resources needed to produce X? Explain.

4 Answer the following question using the figure below:

Carefully show that increasing output from Q_e to Q_1 would entail a welfare loss to society as measured by the area of triangle msr.

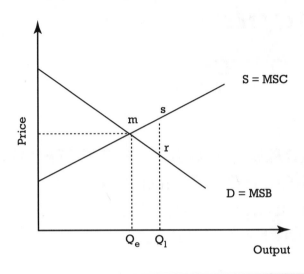

REFERENCES AND FURTHER READING

Alper, J. (1993) "Protecting the Environment with the Power of the Market," *Science* 260: 1884–5.

Mahar, D. J. (1989) *Government Policies and Deforestation in Brazil's Amazon Region*, Washington, D.C.: World Bank.

Pindyck, R. and Rubinfeld, D. (1998) *Microeconomics*, 4th edn., New York: Macmillan.

Randall, A. (1987) *Resource Economics: An Economic Approach to Natural Resource and Environmental Policy*, 2nd edn., New York: John Wiley.

Repetto, R. (1988a) *The Forest for the Trees?: Government Policies and the Misuse of Forest Resources*, Washington, D.C.: World Resources Institute.

—— (1988b) *Economic Policy Reform for Natural Resource Conservation*, Environment Working Paper, Washington, D.C.: World Bank.

chapter three

MARKET SIGNALS OF NATURAL RESOURCE SCARCITY:
Resource Price, Rent and Extraction Cost

---

learning objectives

After reading this chapter you will be familiar with the following:

- key variables affecting the demand for natural resources;
- the notion of derived demand;
- key variables affecting the supply of factors of production in general and natural resources in particular;
- market equilibrium price as a measure of social opportunity cost;
- the concepts of physical and economic scarcity of natural resources;
- alternative measures of emerging natural resource scarcity;
- the concepts of pure rent, differential rent and Ricardian scarcity;
- the concepts of factor substitution and technological advances, and their broader and varied implications for the availability of natural resources.

[I]f something is more scarce in one place than in another, or at one time compared with another, we would know this because its price is greater in the more scarce circumstance. The argument, so fundamental to economics, applies to natural resources. Natural resources are said to be growing more scarce if their relative price is rising over time.

(Brown and Field 1979: 227–8)

So price, together with related measures such as cost of production and share of income, is the appropriate operational test of scarcity at any given moment. What matters to us as consumers is how much we have to pay to obtain goods that give us particular services; from our standpoint, it could not matter less how much iron or oil there "really" is in the natural "stockpile." Therefore, to understand the economics of natural resources, it is crucial to understand that the most appropriate economic measure of scarcity is the price of a natural resource compared to some relevant benchmark.

(Simon 1996: 26)

3.1 INTRODUCTION

The main objective of this chapter is to further explore the alternative economic indicators that could be used as a measure of natural resource scarcity. In doing this, in accord with the neoclassical economics tradition, natural resources are simply viewed as factors of production. As discussed in Chapter 1, this suggests the following: First, as factors of production, natural resources are *essential* (Dasgupta and Heal 1979). That is, no good or service can be produced without the use of some positive amount of natural resources. Second, these resources are scarce and as such command positive economic prices. The questions of interest, then, are: How is the price for a natural resource determined? What exactly does the market price for a natural resource indicate? In general, what economic variables affect the price for natural resources? What kind of relationship exists between the demand (price) for natural resources and the final products that these resources are used to produce? To what extent can the market price of a natural resource be used as an indicator of scarcity? Are there alternative methods of measuring natural resource scarcity? These questions reflect to the kinds of key issue addressed in this chapter.

3.2 THE DEMAND FOR A FACTOR OF PRODUCTION: THE CASE OF NATURAL RESOURCES

The market demand for a factor of production shows the *maximum* prices producers are willing to pay for various levels of the resource available in the market at a point in time. In Figure 3.1, if the amount of coal available in the market at a point in time is C_1, r_1 indicates the maximum price producers will be willing to pay. Similarly, if what is available in the market is increased to C_0, the price that producers are willing to pay falls to r_0. This inverse relationship between the price of coal and the quantity demanded clearly suggests that the demand curve for a factor of production is negatively sloped. The economic rationale for this is rather straightforward. As more and more of a given resource is used, according to the law of diminishing marginal product (see Chapter 2) the marginal contribution of the resource in terms of output declines.

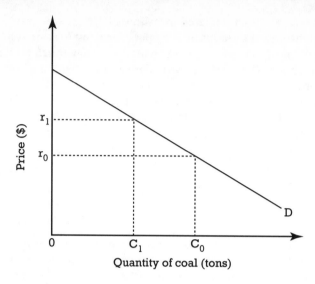

Figure 3.1 **The market demand for coal**

Suppose coal is used to produce electricity. According to the postulate of diminishing marginal productivity, as more and more coal is used to produce electricity, the marginal contribution of coal in terms of kilowatt-hours of electricity produced will tend to decline. For this reason, other things being equal, producers will be willing to buy more of a resource (such as coal) if, and only if, its price is lowered to compensate for the decline in the productivity of the resource at the margin. Note here that, unlike the market demand for a product, it is *productivity*, not *utility*, that determines the demand (value) for a factor of production.

Another significant difference between the demand for a product and the demand for a factor of production is the fact that the demand for a factor of production is viewed as a *derived demand*. That is, the demand for any factor of production is determined by the consumer demand for the goods and services that are produced using the resources under consideration (read the second of the epigraphs at the beginning of this chapter). This makes the price of the final good one of the most important factors in determining the demand for (or value of) factors of production. For example, if the primary use of coal is to generate electricity (the final product), other things being equal the demand for, and hence the price of, coal depends on the demand (price) for electricity. In general, the higher the price of electricity, the higher the demand (price) for coal will be. This situation is illustrated using Figures 3.2 and 3.3. In Figure 3.2 the initial demand and supply curves for electricity are identified by D_0 and S_0, respectively. At this point, the market equilibrium price for electricity is P_0. Similarly, in Figure 3.3 the initial demand and supply for coal are D_0 and S_0, and D_0 is constructed assuming that P_0 is the equilibrium price for electricity. Under this scenario, the market price for coal is r_0. Suppose now, as shown in Figure 3.2, the demand for electricity is increased to D_1 as a result of an increase in consumer income. In this situation, the new equilibrium price for electricity will be P_1. If other things are equal, this increase in the price of electricity will cause a shift in the demand for coal from D_0 to D_1. Thus, the increase in price of electricity ultimately resulted in an increase in the price of coal. This is shown in Figure 3.3 by the increase in the price of coal from r_0 to r_1.

In addition to product price and productivity, there are two other important factors that affect the demand for a factor of production: the prices of other factors of production, and technology. The effect of a change in either one of these two factors is manifested by a shift in the demand curve. For example, if capital and coal are considered as *substitutes* (this would be the case if, say, the use of more capital reduced the energy required to produce a unit of electricity), then a decrease in the price of capital will cause a downward shift in the demand curve for coal. Other things being equal, this will result in a decline in the price for coal. In general, therefore, decreases in the price of a factor of production that is a substitute for coal cause a reduction in the demand for, and hence the price of, coal. While this may illustrate the typical situation, it is not unusual for two factors to be *complementary* in production. In this case, other things being equal, the prices of the two relevant factors of production will move in opposite directions.

A technological change affects the demand for a factor of production in several ways. One way is through its direct effect on the productivity of the resource under consideration. For example, a technological change could enhance the productivity of coal in the production of electricity (i.e., less coal would be needed to produce a unit of electricity). This would be the case if, for example, a new chemical additive to coal were to contribute significantly to the efficient combustion (or oxidation) of coal in the production process of electricity. Other things being equal, the effect of this would be to increase the demand for, and hence the price of, coal. Another way technological change could affect the demand for a factor of production is by enhancing the productivity of substitutes. For example, if a new technology enhanced the relative productivity of natural gas (i.e., relative to coal) in the production of electricity, other things being equal this could cause a decline

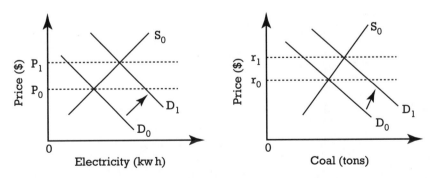

Figure 3.2 (left) **Market conditions in the electricity industry**
Figure 3.3 (right) **Market conditions in the coal industry**

in the demand for, and price of, coal. Thus, in this case the demand for coal is affected by a technological advance in the use of natural gas, which is a substitute for coal. For this reason, *factor substitution possibilities* – the degree to which a factor of production can be substituted by another input – are an important element in the analysis of a resource market. This subject is discussed at some length in Section 3.6.

To summarize this section, therefore, the demand for a factor of production is affected by several factors. Among them the most important are product price, the prices of other factors of production, and technology. It is now time to turn our attention to the factors affecting the supply of a factor of production.

3.3   KEY VARIABLES AFFECTING THE SUPPLY OF A FACTOR OF PRODUCTION: THE CASE OF NATURAL RESOURCES

In a market-oriented economy, as discussed in Chapter 1, factors of production are assumed to be owned by households (consumers). Households use factors of production as a means of generating income. This income is ultimately used to purchase final goods and services. Other things being equal, since more income means more final goods and services, it is in the best interest of households to fetch the highest possible price for the resources they own at a point in time. However, as we will see in the next section, the price that resource owners ultimately receive depends on both the demand for and the supply of the resource under consideration.

At this stage what we are interested in is to systematically identify the key variables affecting the supply for a factor of production, such as coal. To do this we first need to know what exactly the supply curve for a factor of production, such as the one shown in Figure 3.4, tells us. One viable

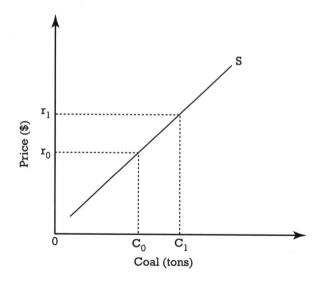

Figure 3.4 **Market supply of coal**

interpretation of the supply curve would be this: it is the locus of all possible minimum prices owners of coal mines are willing to accept for various amounts of coal offered in the market at a specified point in time. For example, to provide amount C_1 of coal in the market, owners of coal would require a minimum price of r_1. To the extent that the supply curve is assumed to be positively sloped, the minimum price that producers are willing to accept increases with an increase in quantity of coal supplied to the market. What justification can be offered to make this generalization valid?

We know that a resource such as coal has to be extracted from the ground and transported before it reaches the market. The immediate implication of this is that, in pricing coal, owners of coal mines need to account for the costs of extraction and transportation. At a minimum, owners of this resource will insist that the price they receive should cover the cost of extraction and transportation. It is for this reason that the minimum price owners of mines would require in order for them to sell a unit of coal should correspond to the cost of extracting and transporting that unit of coal. If we assume that transportation cost is negligible, a positively sloped supply curve for coal therefore implies that the extraction cost for coal is increasing. What could explain this?

One possible explanation for an increasing extraction cost of coal or any other extractive resource is that such resources are not uniformly distributed, spatially and/or in terms of quality or grade of ore (Brobst 1979). The conventional wisdom is that in a given mine, the high-grade coal is found first (Norgaard 1990). Gradually the grade tends to decline as extraction continues. Since the lower-grade coal requires further processing, other things being equal this will cause the cost of extraction to increase. Thus, according to this explanation, the rise in extraction cost has more to do with the limits imposed by nature than anything else (more on this in Chapter 17).

What remains in this section is to discuss the key factors affecting the supply of a natural resource, such as coal. In accordance with the neo-classical economic school, the factors affecting the supply of a natural resource can be divided into two broad categories – one pertaining to nature, and the other pertaining to technology.

Most economists, if not all, agree that nature plays a role in determining the availability of natural resources. At the very least, nature puts an upper limit on the reproductive (regenerative) capacity of a particular resource. Furthermore, there seems to be a growing acceptance of the notion that the supply of certain resources is *finite* for the purpose of economic consideration, given that the regenerative capacity of some natural resources (such as coal) is measured on a geological timescale. Thus, by imposing upper limits to the supply of a particular natural resource, nature does "impose a particular scarcity." In other words, the possibility of eventually exhausting a particular natural resource is real. Beyond this, however, the conventional wisdom in economic circles is that nature has only a minor role to play in determining the supply of natural resources (Barnett and Morse

1963). According to the prevailing economic view, therefore, the key factor that determines the supply of natural resources is technology.

Technology affects the supply of natural resources in a variety of ways. First, the supply of a natural resource could be enhanced through a technological improvement in the methods of resource extraction. An example of this would be the possibility of extracting a higher proportion of the useful minerals from a given rock containing some known concentration of ore. Second, the supply of a natural resource could be augmented by means of conservation through technological improvements. For example, the supply of coal could be effectively increased by means of energy-saving technology. Third, the supply of a natural resource will be affected whenever, by means of technological innovation, it is possible to find a substitute resource. For example, the supply of energy would be enhanced by a technology that significantly improved the economic feasibility of solar energy for direct use in both the residential and the industrial sectors. (More extensive discussion on factor substitution, technical change and their effects on natural resource availability is offered in Section 3.6.) A careful observation of this last point suggests that if we are interested in the supply of energy, a narrow focus on what happens to the supply of a particular resource of energy (coal, petroleum, natural gas, nuclear, solar, geothermal, etc.) could be misleading and even dangerous. For a technological optimist, which most economists tend to be, running out of a particular natural resource would not represent a major concern (Solow 1974). The notion that "nature imposes a particular scarcity but not a general scarcity" is widely held among mainstream economists (Barnett and Morse 1963).

3.4 LONG-RUN MARKET VALUATION OF A FACTOR OF PRODUCTION

So far, our discussions have centered on understanding the various factors affecting the demand and supply of a factor of production. It would be quite instructive to briefly discuss the economic interpretation of the long-run market equilibrium price for a factor of production. To show this, suppose the situation in Figure 3.5 represents long-run market equilibrium condition for coal under an ideal market setting. As discussed earlier, market demand shows producers' willingness to pay for coal at the *margin*; and the market supply depicts the *marginal* opportunity cost of extracting, refining and delivering coal to the market. Thus, at the market equilibrium, what the producers are willing to pay for the last unit of coal, r_e, is equal to the marginal opportunity cost of extracting the last unit of coal. In this sense, then, in an ideal market condition the long-run equilibrium price of a natural resource measures the marginal opportunity costs of bringing that resource to the market. Furthermore, assuming that these resources have clearly defined ownership rights, there will be no difference between *social* and *private* opportunity costs (more on this in Chapter 5). In this case market price reflects both social and private opportunity costs.

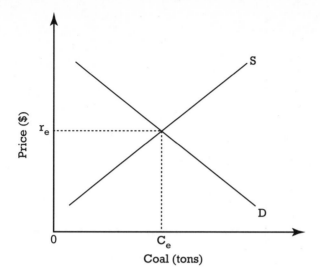

Figure 3.5 **Long-run equilibrium price for coal**

At this stage it is instructive to raise a fundamental question: What can be said about the market price of a natural resource as a measure of scarcity? As discussed above, under ideal market settings and where resources have clearly defined ownership rights, the long-run equilibrium price of a natural resource measures the marginal social opportunity cost of bringing that resource onto the market. Under this ideal condition, a positive price trend (see Figure 3.6) for a particular natural resource over a long period of time signals emerging resource scarcity. It should be noted, however, that this is a purely *economic* measure of natural resource scarcity. In other words, because of technological and demand factors that influence the market price of a resource, there may not be a perfect (one-to-one) correlation between observed price trends and the physical abundance of the natural resource under consideration. It is quite possible for the physical quantity of a natural resource to dwindle over time while the market price of this resource is showing a declining price trend. In other words, *economic scarcity* (which is measured by price) may not be the same as *physical scarcity*. The question is, then, assuming that we are interested in measuring physical scarcity, are there alternative measures of resource scarcity that are capable of measuring scarcity of this nature? The next section of this chapter considers this question.

There are several alternative ways of measuring economic scarcity other than by observing the price trend of a particular resource (see Figure 3.6). One way to do this is to compare the price of a resource (for example, coal) with the price (cost) of labor over a period of time. This price ratio serves as a measure of the opportunity cost of coal with respect to labor. Another way to measure economic scarcity is to deflate the price of coal with the price for all goods and services. This would be a measure of the *real* price of coal: the quantity of goods and services that one can purchase with a ton of coal.

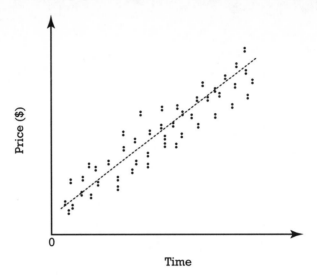

Figure 3.6 **Long-run price trend for coal**

3.5 RENT AND EXTRACTION COST AS ALTERNATIVE MEASURES OF NATURAL RESOURCE SCARCITY

One important concept that is often associated with a discussion of the supply of a particular factor of production is *rent*. As we shall see shortly, this concept can be used as an alternative measure of natural resource scarcity. In Figure 3.7 let r_e and C_e represent the market equilibrium price and quantity of coal respectively. Following an approach that we have already used in Chapter 2, area $0C_eM$ (an area under a supply curve) represents the total cost of production or extraction. In an ideal market setting, this cost would represent the opportunity costs of all factors of production (labor, capital and other resources, such as the capitalized value of land, etc.) that are used to extract the equilibrium level of coal, C_e. On the other hand, area $0r_eMC_e$ represents the total receipt (income) to the owners of the coal mines. The difference between what the owners receive as income and the cost of extraction is a rent which is represented by the area of triangle $0r_eM$. It represents the total payment to owners of a factor of production in excess of the minimum price necessary to bring the resource into the market. In other words, it is the payment above a resource owner's minimum acceptable price. To what could this payment be attributed?

Close observation would indicate that rent is a payment (value) to a resource as it exists in its natural state (with zero value-added). In other words, rent is received by owners purely for owning the resource under consideration. Owners play no part in the creation of this resource. Hence, rent is intimately related to the value of natural resources *in situ*. The implication of this is that rent can be used as a measure of physical scarcity. This is demonstrated below using a specific concept of rent known as *differential rent*.

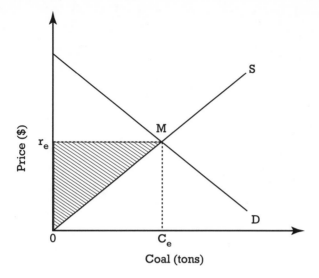

***Figure 3.7* The concept of rent**

3.5.1 Differential rent

For most extractive resources, such as coal, gold, aluminum and even agricultural land, the normal pattern tends to be to utilize or mine these resources sequentially in accordance with quality and accessibility. Mines containing higher-quality ores or agricultural land with high natural fertility are put to use first. To illustrate this point, in Figure 3.8 the supply of coal has three segments. The first segment is the horizontal line P_0–A. This supply curve relates to the amount of coal forthcoming to the market from the highest-quality and most easily accessible coal mines. Since the quality of this resource is assumed to be uniform, the horizontal supply curve, P_0, represents the constant unit production cost (extraction and transportation costs) of coal from such mines. The second segment of the supply curve is represented by another horizontal line, B–C. This parallel upward shift of the supply curve from P_0–A to B–C reflects the change in the quality of the coal mines, from mines containing high-grade ore to those whose ore is of lower grade. Thus, for the coal forthcoming from this second tier of mines, the unit cost is assumed to be uniform and higher than from the first tier of mines. The supply curve for the coal forthcoming from the third and last tier of coal mines, line E–F, can be interpreted in a similar way. What is evident from the discussion so far is the simple fact that the unit cost of production (in terms of extraction, refinement, transportation, etc.) of coal increases as mining is extended towards a fringe area containing a progressively poorer quality of ore.

How does the above discussion concern rent? To answer this, let us incorporate the demand side of the issue. In Figure 3.8, D_0, D_1 and D_2 represent three different levels of demand condition for coal. For a

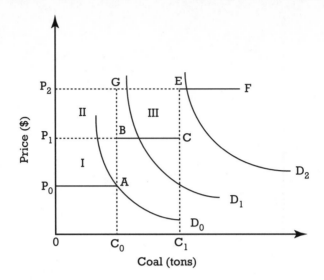

Figure 3.8 **The case of differential rent**

demand curve at or below D_0, the market price for coal will be P_0. Since the supply curve is horizontal, P_0–A, in this situation rent will be zero. This is because P_0 represents both the market price and the unit cost of coal. Thus, owners of coal mines are not receiving anything in excess of their cost of production.

However, suppose the demand for coal increases to D_1. In this situation the market price for coal will increase to P_1. Now, as a result of this development, owners of the coal mines from the first tier will start to earn rent since their production cost is still P_0, while the market price for coal is now P_1. On the other hand, owners of coal mines from the second tier will realize no rent – since there is no difference between the market price they receive and their unit cost of production, in this case P_1. Hence, from this discussion it is evident that the total rent received by the owners of coal mines from the first tier, area P_0P_1BA (or the area of the rectangle I), is attributable to differences in the quality (grade) of coal – hence the term *differential rent*.

It should be noted that differential rent increases with an increase in demand. In Figure 3.8, if the demand further rises to D_2, the rent obtained by owners from the first tier of mines also increases from area P_0P_1BA to area P_0P_2GA (or the combined areas of rectangles I and II). In addition, the owners of mines from the second tier are now able to realize rent which is measured by the area BCEG (or the area of rectangle III). Thus, as a result of the shift in demand from D_1 to D_2, the total rent has increased from area P_0P_1BA (the area of rectangle I) to area P_0P_2ECBA (or the area of rectangles I + II + III).

Another example that could have been used to illustrate the concept of differential rent is agricultural land. Agricultural land varies in its natural productive capacity – fertility. In Figure 3.8, then, the horizontal line P_0–A represents the supply curve of available farming land that is of high and uniform quality (in terms of fertility). The rent accruing from this farmland will be negligible provided the demand for farmland remains at or below D_0. This is because, over this range, the market price of a unit of farmland (P_0) is the same as the cost per unit of making the farmland available for cultivation. However, as demonstrated earlier, owners of this type of land start to earn rent as soon as the demand for farmland exceeds D_0.

Similarly, the lines B–C and E–F represent the supply curves for marginal and submarginal farmland, respectively. From Figure 3.8 it can be easily observed that rent increases as demand for farmland grows and progressively inferior land is brought into cultivation. Note here that what causes rent to increase is not, as such, the existence of *absolute scarcity* of farmland. Instead, it is the rise in the cost of harvesting resulting from the progressive decline in the quality of farmland. This phenomenon was first articulated by one of the most celebrated classical economists: David Ricardo (1772–1823). As a result of this, modern economics literature classifies this particular phenomenon as *Ricardian scarcity*.

Finally, one important implication of the above discussion is that an increase in rent is intimately associated with a growing scarcity of natural resources. Since the increase in rent is intimately associated with the physical condition (decline in quantity and/or quality) of the resource under consideration, it could in some way be taken as a measure of physical scarcity. This was shown to be the case both for coal mines and for farmland. For this reason, some economists have advocated using rent as a preferred measure of natural resource scarcity (Brown and Field 1979).

However, it is not difficult to show that rent could also be significantly affected by technological changes. What this does is to obscure or diminish the effectiveness of rent as a measure of physical scarcity. If technological elements are not carefully factored out, it is possible to observe a declining trend for rent while the physical condition of a natural resource (in terms of quality and/or quantity) is diminishing. It should also be noted that, as discussed above, rent depends on demand and supply conditions, and for that reason it is not a purely physical measure of resource scarcity. Furthermore, because of the lack of easily observable and consistent market information concerning rent, its practical value as measure of natural resource scarcity is rather limited (Brown and Field 1979).

3.5.2 Extraction cost

Finally, another possible measure of natural resource scarcity is extraction cost. In some cases, extraction costs could account for a major portion of the total value of many natural resources. In such cases, increasing extraction costs over time could be used as a signal of emerging natural resource scarcity. To some degree, compared to market price, extraction cost may be a better measure of physical resource scarcity to the extent that the rising cost indicates the degree of difficulty of extracting this resource from its original natural habitat. Furthermore, it is much easier to obtain information on extraction cost than on rent. However, even in this case, technology may bring about a distortion in the normal association between extraction cost and the ease, in physical terms, by which a natural resource is being extracted.

3.6 FACTOR SUBSTITUTION POSSIBILITIES, TECHNOLOGICAL CHANGES AND RESOURCE SCARCITY

In Sections 3.2 and 3.3, it was noted that factor substitution and changes in production technology play significant roles in the determination of both the demand for and the supply of factors of production. In Section 3.5, it was observed that while both rent and extraction cost can be used as alternative measures for detecting emerging natural resource scarcity, their ability to be used in this way depends on the extent to which these measures are sensitive to factor substitution and technological advances. In this section, therefore, an attempt will be made to carry out a systematic analysis of how factor substitution possibilities and technological change alleviate resource scarcity, with an emphasis on natural resources – a very important topic in natural resource economics.

3.6.1 Factor substitution

Suppose we let the production function of a nation be represented by the simple relationship

$$Q = f(N, K, T)$$

where Q is output; N is an input of natural resources expressed in some standard unit; K, often referred to as capital, is a composite factor of production representing all other inputs; and T represents the current techniques of production. Given this representation of an aggregate production function, factor substitution possibilities can be portrayed by using the concept of an *isoquant*. An isoquant represents the locus of all technically efficient combinations of two inputs that can be used to produce a given level of output, assuming no change in the current techniques of production (i.e. the variable T is held constant). Figure 3.9 shows three isoquant graphs which each represent a different degree of factor substitution.

Given that the isoquants are negatively sloped, in Figures 3.9a and 3.9b it is possible to substitute other factors of production (K) for natural resources (N) and still produce the same level of output. However, although both cases allow factor substitution possibilities, the nature of the substitution possibilities differs markedly. In Figure 3.9a, the straight-line isoquant implies a constant rate of factor substitution possibilities between natural resources and capital. This constant rate of factor substitution is measured by the *slope* of the isoquant curve. For example, if the constant slope of this isoquant in Figure 3.9a is –2.0, it implies that if natural resource (N) is reduced by 1 unit, capital (K) has to increase by 2 units in order to maintain

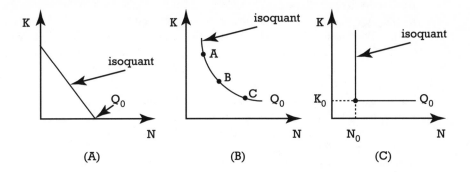

Figure 3.9 **Factor substitution possibilities**

the same level of production. This means that it takes 2 units of K to substitute for 1 unit of natural resources (N). Furthermore, this can be interpreted as saying that the *opportunity cost* of 1 unit of natural resource is twice that of capital. That is, 2 units of capital would have to be sacrificed in order to compensate for the loss of just a unit of natural resource. Note also that in this special case where the isoquant has a constant slope, the use of natural resources can be reduced to zero without raising the opportunity cost (in terms of the other inputs sacrificed). Hence, the implication is that the increasing scarcity of natural resources will not be reflected in increased opportunity cost. Although conceptually interesting, however, this case is rather unrealistic.

In the case of the isoquant shown in Figure 3.9b, natural resources can still be substituted by other factors of production but not at a constant rate. In this specific case, as natural resources are progressively substituted by other factors of production, the slope of isoquant increases monotonically. For example, as is evident from Figure 3.9b, the slope increases as we move from point C to B, and from point B to point A. Since, as discussed above, this slope is a measure of opportunity cost in terms of forgone capital (K), it can be seen that each incremental reduction in natural resource requires a progressively increasing amount of other factors of production (K) in order to maintain the same level of production, Q_0. In other words, the opportunity cost of using natural resources, in terms of other inputs sacrificed, increases at an increasing rate as natural resources become scarce. According to standard microeconomic theory, this situation is viewed as being the most plausible scenario.

Finally, the isoquant shown in Figure 3.9c represents an extreme case where factor substitution possibilities are totally absent. In this situation, natural resources, N, and other factors of production, K, are used in a predetermined *fixed proportion* to produce a given level of output. For example, as shown in Figure 3.9c, to produce Q_0 level of output, amount N_0 of natural resource and amount K_0 of other inputs are needed. Along the given right-angled isoquant, an increase in K *alone* would not precipitate a decline in the use of natural resources. That is, to produce the given level of output, Q_0, amount N_0 of natural resource is needed regardless of the level of the other inputs, K, being utilized. Therefore, one important implication of this situation is that to produce a given level of output a certain minimum level of natural resource input is needed. In our example above, to produce level Q_0 of output, at a minimum, amount N_0 of natural resources is needed. Given the current state of production technology (no change in T), any reduction in the amount of natural resources usage from this minimum will cause a decline in output, and this will be the case regardless of the amount of the other factor input used.

From the discussion thus far, we can generalize that the concern about the availability of natural resources very much depends on the assumption one makes about the nature of the rate of substitution possibilities between natural resources and other factors of production. If a natural resource is viewed as being perfectly substitutable with other factors of production, then its availability should be of little or no concern. This is the situation depicted by Figure 3.9a. On the other hand, if the substitution possibility between a natural resource and other factors of production is zero, the case demonstrated by Figure 3.9c, then a certain critical minimum of this resource will be needed to produce a given level of output. In this case, availability of natural resources would be a major concern since a decline of natural resources below this minimum would entail an automatic lowering of living standards or output.

As stated earlier, the case that is most realistic in depicting the nature of the substitution possibilities between a natural resource and other factors of production would have an isoquant with a general shape similar to the one shown in Figure 3.9b. In this situation, natural resources can always be substituted by other factors of production, but at an increasing opportunity cost. That is, successive reduction in natural resources requires an incrementally larger increase in other factors in order to maintain the production of a constant level of output. It is in this sense, therefore, that the scarcity (availability) of natural resources would become a concern.

3.6.2 Changes in production technology: technical advances

In our discussion of substitution possibilities, production technology, T, was assumed to remain constant. In other words, factor substitution possibilities were analyzed assuming no change in the current techniques (or state of the art) of production. However, in a dynamic economy, technological advance that entails a fundamental change in production techniques is a normal experience. If this is the case, it will be instructive to address the following three related questions:

1 In what specific ways does a change in production techniques affect the use of factors of production?

2 Are all factors of production equally affected by a change in production techniques?

3 What exactly are the broader implications of changes in production technology for the issue of natural resource adequacy (scarcity)?

The effect of a change in production techniques, T, is shown using two isoquants in Figure 3.10. Note that both isoquants are assumed to represent the production of the *same* level of output, Q_0. The isoquant further to the right represents the various combinations of a natural resource and other factors of production (capital) used to produce the given level of output, Q_0, prior to a change in technology. After the technological change, the same isoquant has shifted downward, implying no change in the level of output produced. What we can conclude from this is that, with technological change of this nature, the same level of output can be produced by using less factors of production. For example, as shown in Figure 3.10, before the change in technology it used to take amounts N_0 and K_0 of natural resource and other inputs, respectively, to produce the output level Q_0. With the implementation of the new techniques of production, the same level of output can be produced using amounts N_1 and K_1 of the two factors of production. Viewed in this way, technological advance in production techniques entails resource conservation.

In Figure 3.10, the isoquant is assumed to shift downward but remain parallel. Thus, along any intersection of these two isoquants and a straight line from the origin, such as points A and B, the slopes of the isoquants will be identical. As we have discussed earlier, the slope of an isoquant is a measure of substitution possibilities between two factors of production. Furthermore, it can be easily demonstrated that the slope of an isoquant is also a measure of the *relative productivity* of two inputs. To see these alternative

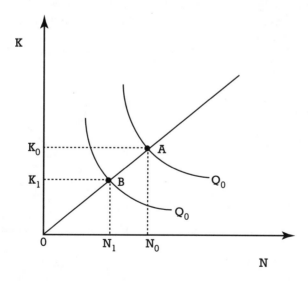

Figure 3.10 **Advances in production techniques**

interpretations of a slope of an isoquant, suppose that in Figure 3.10, at the input combination represented by point A, the slope of an isoquant is -2.0. This tells us that at this particular level of usage of natural resources and capital, it takes 2 units of capital to substitute a unit of natural resource. On the other hand, if it takes 2 units of capital to substitute a unit of natural resource, then the natural resource must be twice as productive as capital. Thus, the slope of the isoquant can be used in this way to inform us about the relative productivity of the two factors of production. In Figure 3.10 the parallel downward shift of the isoquant has no effect on the slope of the isoquant. Hence, the relative productivity of natural resource (N) and other factor inputs (K) are not affected by a technological advance of this nature. This represents a case of what economists call an unbiased (or a neutral) technological change.

However, technological changes are seldom unbiased. In other words, technical advance in production technology often enhances the productivity of one input in a disproportionate manner. When this happens, the new isoquant will not be parallel to the old.

In Figure 3.11a, the technological change is capital, K, biased. To see this, we note that as a result of the technological change, the isoquant shifted downward. But the new isoquant appears to be flatter, as compared to the isoquant before the change. Thus, the slope of the new isoquant along any given ray from the origin (i.e., constant input ratio) is smaller than the slope of the original isoquant along this same ray. For example, the slope at point R is less than that at point S. A decrease in the slope of the isoquant in this case implies a decrease in the rate at which K needs to be increased (sacrificed) in order to accommodate for a small reduction in natural resources to produce a given level of output. For example, as shown in Figure 3.11a, assume that, due to technological change, the slope of the isoquant was reduced from -3 at point S to -2 at point R. In this situation, before technological change, if the use of natural resource input (N) is reduced by a unit, the use of capital has to be increased by 3 units in order to maintain the production of the same level of output, Q_0. However, after the technological change, a

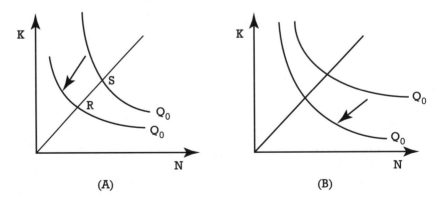

Figure 3.11 **Biased technological advances**

reduction of natural resource usage by a unit can be compensated for by only 2 (not 3) units of capital. Thus, technological change must have enhanced the productivity of K more than N. This is the reason why such a technological change would be identified as capital biased. It is important to note here that by reducing the opportunity cost of natural resources in terms of other resources, although indirectly, a capital-biased technological change has the effect of ameliorating the impact of natural resource scarcity.

Finally, using a similar argument to that above, it would not be difficult to show that the case depicted in Figure 3.11b represents a technological change that is natural resource biased. Given that the level of output produced remained unchanged at Q_0, this type of technical advance would clearly lead to conservation (less use) of natural resources. Consider, for instance, the production of technological change from the standard incandescent light-bulb. Compact fluorescent bulbs are a technological change that reduces energy (resource) use for a given amount of light. This is an improvement when compared with halogen bulbs, which use more energy to provide the same amount of light.

From the discussion in this section it should be clear that the scarcity (availability) of natural resources cannot be adequately addressed without careful consideration of technological factors such as factor substitution possibilities and technical advances in production. According to the standard economic paradigm, as will be evident from the discussion in Chapter 8, consideration of this issue is central to any attempt to assess the impacts of natural resource scarcity on future standards of living.

3.7 IMPORTANT CAVEATS

It is important to note that while the analysis presented in Chapters 2 and 3 allowed us to understand the basic elements necessary to comprehend the mainstream economic notion of resource scarcity and its measurement, it did so with several obvious limitations. The most significant of these are the following:

First, the economic analysis thus far has been strictly *static*; no time element has been considered. This is a major drawback given that natural resource economics, by its very nature, deals with the intertemporal allocation of resources – that is, how natural resources are managed over time. This particular issue will be the subject of Chapters 16 and 17: intertemporal allocations of renewable and nonrenewable resources, respectively.

Second, the economic analyses in both the product and factor markets were done assuming the existence of perfectly competitive markets. Given this institutional setting, we observed that private decision-making would actually lead to a *socially* optimal allocation of resources. Furthermore, there will be no discrepancy between the individual (private) and social assessment of benefits and costs. But what happens if the conditions for perfectly competitive markets fail to materialize? As we will see in Chapter 5, one consequence of this is to create a divergence between the social and private assessment of costs and benefits. This is crucial because evaluation of natural resource adequacy will be sufficiently addressed only when benefits and costs reflect social, not private, consideration. What this creates is a doubt concerning the effectiveness of the market system where resource allocation is solely based on private assessment of benefits and costs.

Third, in the economic analysis so far, nothing has been said about resources that have values but may not be captured through the normal operation of the market system. An example would be the value of preserving an animal species such as the northwest spotted owl. A species of this nature has very little *use value* – benefits or satisfactions received by humans from a direct utilization of the services (or amenities) – and therefore is likely to be unaccounted under the normal operation of market processes. This particular issue becomes even more serious when it is realized that market prices are formed on the basis of human preferences alone. This issue will be dealt with in Chapter 14.

Fourth, in Chapters 2 and 3 efforts were made to show how, at a point in time, prices for final products and factors of production, respectively, are determined through the free-market mechanism. To what extent information on current market prices could be used to predict future scarcity events has not been adequately addressed. More specifically, the *uncertainty* associated with predicting a future scarcity condition on the basis of past price trends has not been addressed. The position taken so far is that current resource prices are a good predictor of future scarcity events. This would be the case in a world of perfectly competitive markets where economic agents were operating with perfect foresight and costless information. Under those circumstances,

> if there is reason to judge that the cost of obtaining a certain resource in the future will be much greater than it is now, speculators will hoard that material to obtain future price, thereby raising the present price. So, current price is our best measure of both current and future scarcity.
>
> (Simon 1996: 30–1)

Fifth, up to this point our discussions about natural resources have been done in broad generality. The term *natural resource* was used to describe a heterogeneous group of resources. This is misleading, for in many cases knowledge about the crucial attributes that differentiate one group of natural resources from another is extremely important in making an economic assessment of resource adequacy. This is especially the case when the issue of *irreversibility* (the fact that beyond a certain threshold, the use of natural resources may lead to irreversible damage) is an important consideration. However, an understanding of irreversibility and other crucial properties of natural resources requires a basic grasp of ecology – the subject of the next chapter.

3.8 CHAPTER SUMMARY

- In the previous chapter, we examined how market price plays a role in signaling increasing resource scarcity. Special attention was paid to demonstrating how a secular trend of product price could be used as an indicator of emerging "general" resource scarcity. However, in some situations indicator of impending scarcity of a "particular" factor of production may be the issue of interest. An investigation of alternative economic measure to natural resources scarcity has been the focus of Chapter 3.

- In a perfectly competitive market setting, the long-run equilibrium price of a natural resource measures the marginal opportunity costs of bringing that resource onto the market. Furthermore, if the ownership rights for this resource are clearly delineated, there will be no difference between social and private opportunity costs. Thus, price reflects both social and private opportunity costs and can be used as an accurate measure of *economic* scarcity.

- However, economic scarcity may not reflect *physical* scarcity – the material abundance of the natural resource under consideration. Discrepancies between economic and physical scarcity of natural resources may arise due to technological and/or demand factors. For example, in the presence of persistent improvement in mining technology, it is possible to observe a falling price trend of an extractive natural resource such as coal in the presence of dwindling coal deposits.

- In an attempt to address the above problem, it was suggested that *rent* (the value of natural resources *in situ*) and *extraction cost* could be used as alternative measures of natural resource scarcity. These two approaches are more susceptible to the material abundance of the resources and are, therefore, more likely to reflect physical scarcity. If other factors are held constant, one expects rent and extraction cost to rise over time – indicating increasing scarcity with the passage of time. This was demonstrated using the concept of *differential rent*.

- However, other factors are not constant, especially technology. Advances in technology render both rent and extraction costs less effective as indicators of emerging physical scarcity. This is because, for example, even as finite stocks are further depleted, advances in technology could continually reduce the cost of extraction. Thus, a secular decline in extraction cost may have very little to do with the physical abundance of the resource under consideration.

- Factor substitutions and technological changes play major roles in the determination of future availability of natural resources. Both of these technological factors could provide significant opportunities to *conserve* natural resources, which, as we will see in Chapter 7, is a crucial issue in understanding mainstream economists' perspective on natural resource scarcity and its effect on economic growth.

review and discussion questions

1 Briefly explain the following concepts: derived demand, rent, differential rent, Ricardian scarcity, use value, physical scarcity, economic scarcity, isoquant, diminishing marginal rate of technical substitution, factor substitutions, technical change.

2 State *True, False or Uncertain* and explain why.

   (a) Physical scarcity *only* increases over time. This is why economic signals that suggest declining scarcity over time must be erroneous.

   (b) Technological advances in production techniques always entail resource conservation.

   (c) The notion of derived demand is an antithesis to intrinsic value.

3 "[O]ur price system provides the most effective indicator available of both absolute and relative resource scarcity. A secular increase in the price of the product of a resource industry (crude oil or wheat, for example) relative to the general price level can be regarded as a reasonably accurate indicator of resource scarcity. Similarly, a secular decline in the real price of the products of a resource sector can be regarded as an indicator of a reduction in scarcity" (Ruttan 1971: 708). Critically evaluate.

4 "[T]he analytical distinction between technological change and mere factor substitution becomes extremely difficult to maintain . . . [After all,] [t]oday's factor substitution possibilities are made possible by yesterday's technological innovations" (Rosenberg 1973: 114). Discuss.

REFERENCES AND FURTHER READING

Barnett, H. J. and Morse, C. (1963) *Scarcity and Growth: The Economics of Resource Availability*, Baltimore: Johns Hopkins University Press.

Brobst, D. A. (1979) "Fundamental Concepts for the Analysis of Resource Availability," in K. V. Smith (ed.) *Scarcity and Growth Reconsidered*, Baltimore: Johns Hopkins University Press.

Brown, G. M., Jr., and Field, B. (1979) "The Adequacy of Measures for Signaling the Scarcity of Natural Resources," in K. V. Smith, (ed.) *Scarcity and Growth Reconsidered*, Baltimore: Johns Hopkins University Press.

Dasgupta, P. S. and Heal, G. M. (1979) *Economic Theory and Exhaustible Resources*, Cambridge: Cambridge University Press.

Nicholson, W. (1998) *Microeconomic Theory*, 7th edn., Fort Worth: Dryden Press.

Norgaard, R. B. (1990) "Economic Indicators of Resource Scarcity: A Critical Essay," *Journal of Environmental Economics and Management* 19: 19–25.

Rosenberg, N. (1973) "Innovative Responses to Materials Shortages," *American Economic Review* 63, 2: 111–18.

Ruttan, V. W. (1971) "Technology and the Environment," *American Journal of Agricultural Economics* 53, 5: 707–17.

Simon, J. (1996) *The Ultimate Resources 2*, Princeton, N.J.: Princeton University Press.

Solow, R. M. (1974) "Intergenerational Equity and Exhaustible Resources," *Review of Economic Studies* 29–45.

Stiglitz, E. J. (1979) "A Neoclassical Analysis of the Economics of Natural Resources," in K. V. Smith, (ed.) *Scarcity and Growth Reconsidered*, Baltimore: Johns Hopkins University Press.

part three

ECOLOGY: THE ECONOMICS OF NATURE

One often wonders why two bright and highly regarded scholars can have diametrically opposite views and visions on the future state of the natural world. Upon a moment of reflection, however, such divergence of scholarly opinions is not so difficult to understand. It is rooted in the different sets of core assumptions scholars consciously or unconsciously hold about the very world that they are trying to analyze and, ultimately, understand. If this observation has any validity, it suggests that any effort intended to reconcile two polar views on the future states of our natural world should start with a careful scrutiny of the core assumptions held by each side.

In recent years, there seems to have been a pronounced divergence between the standard view of economists and that of ecologists concerning humans' ability to coexist with the natural world. Without a doubt, one of the most important reasons for this development can be attributed to the difference in the core assumptions that the standard practitioners of these two disciplines have concerning the natural world. In Part One, we examined in some detail the basic perception of modern economists about the natural world and how it relates to the human economy. Part Three, which consists of only one chapter, is intended to provide the reader with the assumptions vital to the understanding of the ecological perspectives of natural resources – elements crucial to the sustenance of human economy.

More specifically, in Part Three economics students are asked to venture beyond the realm of their discipline to study some basic concepts and principles of ecology. The inquiry on this subject matter is quite focused and limited in scope. The primary intent is to familiarize students with carefully selected ecological concepts and principles so that they will have, at the end, if not an appreciation, at least a clear understanding of ecologists' perspective on the natural world and its relationship with the human economy.

As will be seen in the chapters in Part Five (Chapters 6–9), the material covered in Part Three is an extremely important prerequisite for a thorough and comprehensive understanding of the seemingly perennial debate between economists and ecologists on "limits to economic growth." Furthermore, the ecological concepts and principles covered in Part Three add a good deal of insight to the analyses and discussions of what may be considered the standard economic approaches to environmental economics (Chapter 5, and Chapters 10–15) and natural resource economics (Chapters 16 and 17). For all these reasons, the position taken here is that no serious student of environmental and resource economics can afford to be ignorant of the important lessons of ecology.

chapter
four

THE CONCEPT OF NATURAL RESOURCES:
An Ecological Perspective

learning objectives

After reading this chapter you will be familiar with the following:

- ecology as a scientific field of study;
- an ecosystem and its structures and functions;
- a biocentric conception of the origin of natural resources;
- the natural law governing material recycling and energy transformation and their economic implications;
- ecodynamics: ecological succession, stability, equilibrium, resilience and complexity;
- the notion of ecological limits and their implications for the human economy;
- the ecological or biocentric view of the human economy: the economy as a subsystem of the natural ecosystem;
- a perspective on humans' historical treatment of the natural world;
- a perspective on the disciplinary ties between ecology and economics.

No serious student of environmental economics can afford to ignore the subject matter of "ecology," the widely embracing science which looks at the interrelationship between living species and their habitats.

(Pearce 1978: 31)

Natural resources could refer to all the living and non-living endowment of the earth, but traditional usages confine the term to naturally occurring resources and systems that are useful to humans or could be under plausible technological, economic, and social circumstances. Today, however, we must augment this definition to include environmental and ecological systems.

(Howe 1979: 1)

4.1 INTRODUCTION

Ecology is a branch of science that systematically studies the relationships between living organisms and the physical and chemical environment in which they live. Ecology as a scientific discipline is highly involved, as it has gone through various developmental stages extending over a period of a century. In this chapter, no attempt is made to explore the subject matter of ecology in its entirety. The main aim is to offer a preliminary exploration of ecology specifically directed at addressing the following specific objectives:

- to provide a broader and deeper understanding of the natural process by which natural resources are created and maintained;
- to understand the natural laws that impose limitations on the interaction of organisms (including humans) with their living and nonliving environment;
- to show the specific ways in which human interaction with nature has been incompatible; and
- to identify some of the important links between ecology and economics, two disciplines which are imperative for a holistic view of natural resource problems and issues.

4.2 ECOSYSTEM STRUCTURE

The hierarchical organization of biological systems often used as a starting point for an ecological study is the *ecosystem*. An ecosystem includes living organisms in a specified physical environment, the multitude of interactions between the organisms, and the nonbiological factors in the physical environment that limit their growth and reproduction, such as air, water, minerals and temperature. Viewed this way, an ecosystem practically means the house of life (Miller 1991). The definition of boundaries and the spatial scale of an ecosystem can vary. An ecosystem can be as small as a pond or as big as the entire earth. We can, therefore, refer to the ecosystem of a pond or the ecosystem of the earth in its entirety. What is important in each case is the definition of boundaries across which inputs and outputs of energy and matter can be measured (Boulding 1993).

Generally, an ecosystem is composed of four components: the atmosphere (air), the hydrosphere (water), the lithosphere (earth) and the biosphere (life). The first three comprise the *abiotic* or nonliving components of the ecosystem, whereas the biosphere is its *biotic* or living component. It is important to recognize that the living and nonliving components of an ecosystem interact with each another. The dynamic interaction of these components is critical to the survival and functioning of the ecosystem, just as breathing and eating are essential to the survival of animals. Furthermore, these components are capable of coexisting so that the ecosystem *itself* is alive (Schneider 1990; Miller 1991). For example, soil is a living system that develops as a result of interactions between plant, animal and microbial communities (living components) and parent rock material (abiotic components). Abiotic factors such as temperature and moisture influence the process of soil development.

In the ecosystem, the abiotic components serve several functions. First, the abiotic components are used as a *habitat* (space), and an immediate source of water and oxygen for organisms. Second, they act as a *reservoir* of the six most important elements for life: carbon (C), hydrogen (H), oxygen (O), nitrogen (N), sulfur (S) and phosphorus (P). These elements constitute 95 percent of all living organisms. Furthermore, the earth contains only a fixed amount of these elements. Thus, continual functioning of the ecosystem requires that these elements be recycled since they are critical to the overall welfare of the ecosystem.

The biotic (living) component of the ecosystem consists of three distinct groups of organisms: the *producers*, *consumers* and *decomposers*. The producers are those organisms capable of *photosynthesis*: production of organic material solely from solar light and carbon dioxide. This organic material serves as a source of both energy and mineral nutrients, which are required by all living organisms. Examples include terrestrial plants and aquatic plants, such as phytoplankton. The consumers are organisms whose very survival depends on the organic materials manufactured by the producers. The consumers represent animals of all sizes ranging from large predators to small parasites, such as mosquitoes. The nature of the consumers' dependence on the producers may take different forms. Some consumers (herbivores such as rabbits) are directly dependent on primary producers for energy. Others (carnivores such as lions) are indirectly dependent on primary producers. The last group of living organisms is the decomposers. These include microorganisms, such as fungi, bacteria, yeast, etc., as well as a diversity of worms, insects and many other small animals that rely on dead organisms for their survival. In their effort to survive and obtain energy they decompose materials released by plants and consumers to their original elements (C, O, H, N, S, P). This, as we shall see shortly, is what keeps material cycling within the ecosystem.

4.3 ECOSYSTEM FUNCTION

As stated above, the ecosystem itself can be viewed as a living organism. Where does life start and end in this system? What sets off, controls and regulates the material movements and transformations manifested in this system? How are the various components of the ecosystem interrelated? Is the natural ecosystem self-regulated? If so, how? In this section, an attempt will be made to answer these and other related questions, in an effort to clearly identify the general principles that govern the functioning of the natural ecosystem.

In the previous section, the structural organization (i.e., how the components and the relationships of biotic and abiotic elements of an ecosystem are organized and defined) of the ecosystem was outlined. However, for any movements or transformations of energy and matter to occur in the ecosystem, an *external* source of energy is needed. For our planet, the primary source of this energy is solar radiation: the energy from the sun. Solar energy, then, fuels the energy flow in an ecosystem.

It is through the interactions of the hydrosphere, the atmosphere and the lithosphere, activated and facilitated by solar energy, that atmospheric and water circulation (such as wind, tide, cloud, water currents and precipitation) occur. In turn, it is the impact of this atmospheric and water circulation over a long period of time that causes (a) the movements and the reshaping of the earth's crust (such as sedimentation and erosion), and (b) the formations of the flow and reservoirs of water (streams, rivers, lakes and waterfalls). Essentially, then, these types of natural and perpetual cyclical process create what we identify as natural resources (such as water, fossil fuels and soil resources, and the aesthetic values of the natural environment).

Although the previous paragraph briefly outlines the material (abiotic) cycles that are ongoing in the ecosystem, so far nothing has been said regarding biological cycles and their interrelationships with the material cycles. This is done using Figure 4.1.

The biotic component of the ecosystem relies on the ability of producers (terrestrial and aquatic plants) to directly convert solar energy to chemical or stored energy in the form of organic matter. As discussed above, this transformation of one form of energy to another is accomplished through the process of photosynthesis. Essentially, it involves synthesis of organic matter

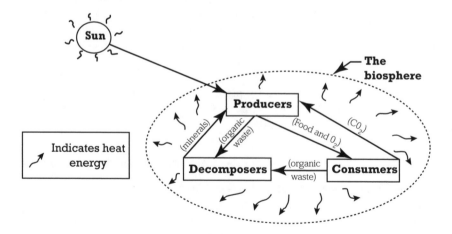

Figure 4.1 **Energy flow and material cycling in an ecosystem**

from basic elements (C, O, H, N, etc.) fueled by solar radiation. From this, it should be evident that the abiotic components of the ecosystem are linked to the photosynthetic process – the production of an energy base to support life. Also through this process, the flow of materials becomes linked to the flow of energy.

It is important to recognize that the producers are *indispensable* to the biotic component of the ecosystem. Without these organisms, it would have been impossible to create the organic matter (plant tissues) which is essential for the growth and reproduction of other organisms (consumers and decomposers). While the nature of the dependency between the producers and other forms of organisms may appear to be linear at this fundamental level (the flow of the material is from producers to consumers to the decomposers), the functioning of the ecosystem as a whole is characterized by *mutual interdependencies* among many species of organisms at each level – a food web (Miller 1991). As shown in Figure 4.1, the consumers depend on producers for energy, various nutrients and oxygen. The oxygen is the by-product of photosynthesis. The producers, in turn, depend on consumers and decomposers for carbon dioxide (CO_2) and on decomposers and abiotic processes for mineral elements (P, S, etc.). Carbon dioxide is released by all members of the biotic component through *respiration*. Finally, in the process of consuming the dead plants and animals, the decomposers convert organic compounds to inorganic minerals which plants can use. Thus, in the natural ecosystem, survival and 'proper' eco-system functioning dictate mutual interactions (interdependence) among organisms and between them and the abiotic environment (Miller 1991).

4.3.1 Materials recycling

As is evident from the above discussion, the natural recycling process starts with the formation of plant tissues through the processes of photosynthesis and biosynthesis. At this early stage, some oxygen is released into the environment. In many ecosystems, the second major stage of recycling occurs when animals, in their effort to metabolize the stored energy from plant tissue, release carbon dioxide and organic wastes. Major recycling (decomposition), however, is done by microorganisms. The micro-organisms ultimately break down dead organic matter into its simpler (inorganic) molecular components. This recycling is particularly important because the amount of mineral elements found in the ecosystem (especially N and P) is finite, and limiting to the growth and reproduction of organisms.

However, decomposition may not always be complete. The oxidation process involved in decomposition depends on the availability of oxygen and the energy circulation of a given environment. For example, oxidation takes place at a much faster pace in a tropical forest than at the bottom of a lake. Thus, in nature, material recycling is not 100 percent efficient, and some amounts of organic matter may remain, only partially decomposed. This incompletely decomposed organic matter, accumulated and aged over a period of time, forms peat, coal and petroleum – that is, fossil fuel. *This is the origin of the sources of energy so crucial to the modern human economy.* It is also a large reserve of carbon that gets released rapidly when fossil fuels are burned and contributes to global warming by releasing CO_2 to the atmosphere at an unprecedented rate.

Recycling of materials is not limited to the biological and material cycles in an ecosystem as discussed above. The well-known atmospheric cycles (such as those of carbon, nitrogen and sulfur) contribute to the circulation of these elements within the various media of the ecosystem. Furthermore, it is through atmospheric cycles that the concentration of these elements in a given environmental medium is maintained or regulated. For example, the atmosphere is composed of approximately 20 percent oxygen, 79 percent nitrogen, 0.9 percent argon (which is not significant biologically) and 0.03 percent carbon dioxide. It is very important to note, when the concern is the functioning of an ecosystem, that the atmospheric cycles cannot be viewed in isolation from other cycles (that is, geologic and biological cycles). For example, there is a large reserve of nitrogen in the atmosphere, and a variety of microorganisms are responsible for converting atmospheric nitrogen to a form that plants can use through a process called *nitrogen fixation*, whereas there is no large reserve of nitrogen in rocks. Thus, nitrogen fixation is the critical process of converting unavailable gaseous nitrogen from the atmosphere to available (inorganic) nitrogen for plants. Furthermore, physical and chemical processes associated with volcanic activities and the combustion of fossil fuels also can increase the availability of useful nitrogen to ecosystems.

In addition to the atmospheric cycles, geological processes also contribute to the constant recycling of materials in the ecosystem. For example, it is through erosion and water movement that nitrates, sulfates and phosphates in the soil, rock and sediments can be freed and reintroduced at the roots of plants. This process is particularly important for the recycling of phosphate as there is a large reserve of phosphorus in rocks and virtually none in the atmosphere. Thus, the process of converting available (inorganic) phosphorus in rock to available phosphate for plants is primarily a physical and chemical process (erosion).

Therefore, on the basis of the above discussions, the recycling process of the ecosystem is all-encompassing and demands the interaction of every facet of the ecosystem. Strictly speaking, then, the decomposition and re-circulation of materials in the ecosystem is facilitated by these *biogeochemical* cycles (Miller 1991; Pearce 1978).

4.3.2 Succession, equilibrium, stability, resilience and complexity

Ecological *succession* involves natural changes in the species composition (types of plants, animals and microorganisms) that occupy a given area over a period of time, as well as the changes that occur in ecosystem dynamics such as energy flow and nutrient cycling, discussed above. In a given area, with a specific climate and soil type, the stages of succession (typically recognized by the changes in species composition) are somewhat predictable.

The developmental stages of any ecosystem seem to adhere to the following general pattern. At the *pioneer* (or first) stage, an ecosystem is populated by only a few different species and characterized by uncomplicated inter-relationships. This stage tends to be unstable and, as such, highly vulnerable to environmental stress. Barring severe environmental disturbances, however, the system gradually continues to change in species composition and ecosystem dynamics, until it reaches what is known as the *climax* stage. At this stage, the ecosystem is stable and supports a large number of organisms with complex and diverse interrelationships. In other words, a mature ecological system is characterized by *diversity*, yet the dynamic processes of energy flow and nutrient cycling continue. This built-in diversity is what makes the ecosystem, at this last stage, quite resilient to changes in the physical environment (Holling 1997).

In the eastern United States a good example of succession is abandoned farmland. The first year after a cultivated field (such as corn) is abandoned, it tends to be populated by a few aggressive weedy plants that are sparsely distributed, allowing much of the soil to be exposed to precipitation and intense heating (and evaporation) by the sun during the day and maximum cooling at night. The rather small number of plants allows for potential removal of soil nutrients through the physical processes of erosion and/or the chemical process of leaching. If left alone for a few years, this field is likely to become a dense meadow populated by a diversity of grasses, Queen Anne's lace and/or goldenrod. Still later, woody species (shrubs) such as blackberries or sumac begin to appear. These shrubby species typically grow taller than the herbaceous weeds of the meadow and may provide more shade than some meadow species can tolerate. At the same time, these woody shrubby species do not "die back" to their roots each year, and consequently, more of the mineral nutrients in the ecosystem remain in "standing biomass" (organic material) rather than being returned to the soil through dead biomass.

After a few years, deciduous tree species can be seen emerging above some of the shrubby species and patches of open meadow. As these grow above the shrubs, they typically produce more shade than the shrubs can tolerate and the shrubs will die eventually. The larger woody stems of tree species also result in more nutrients within the ecosystem being stored in standing biomass, with less in the soil, where it may be susceptible to loss by physical or chemical processes.

In this example, at least four different successional stages have been described: (a) an abandoned "weedy" field (pioneer stage); (b) a meadow or "oldfield" stage with abundant grasses and other herbs; (c) a shrubby community; and (d) a forest. Over time, the species composition of the forest is likely to change as well. But ultimately a forest type will develop where little change will be evident over long periods of time (centuries) barring major human influence or substantial climate change (possibly associated with glaciation or global warming). Such a community type is often referred to as the climax community.

An area that is covered by a given type of climax community is often referred to as a *biome*. Much of the eastern United States is made up of the "Eastern Deciduous Forest Biome," whether it be the ancient forests of parts of the Appalachian Mountains that have never been cut or the cities of New York or Detroit which, if abandoned, eventually would most likely become deciduous forests. Other North American biomes include the "prairies" of the Midwest, the "conifer forests" of the Rocky Mountains and the deserts of the Southwest, among others.

The important lesson of succession is that an ecosystem is continually undergoing changes and the transitional time between successional changes may be considerable. The question is, then, how does the ecosystem maintain its equilibrium during this transitional period? In other words, once an ecosystem has achieved a certain developmental stage (for instance, the climax stage), how does it maintain its balance?

In the context of an ecological system, *equilibrium* refers to the apparent lack of visible changes in the biotic components of the system in spite of the many important interactions that continue to occur. As discussed above, ecological interrelationships are clear manifestations of the biological inter-dependencies among organisms. Depending on the stage of the ecological development of the given ecosystem, the biological interdependencies could be simple and represented by a *food chain* or complex and characterized by a *food web*. To offer a simple example, suppose that due to a random natural event, the population of a certain organism (for example, rabbits) starts to multiply at an above-normal rate. The immediate effect of this is an increase in the population of rabbits, which thereby creates a disturbance in the system. However, the disproportionate growth in the population of rabbits will eventually be suppressed by the limitation of food or an increase in number of their predators as more food becomes available. In general, then, in the biosphere, equilibrium is attained through the reciprocal needs of foods and other materials among organisms. In addition, as mentioned in the above discussion, elements and processes in the atmosphere, hydro-sphere and lithosphere are maintained in long-run equilibrium states through various well-known material cycles, hence they are in dynamic equilibrium. However, as will be discussed shortly, human activities can disrupt these natural processes significantly.

In this subsection, so far we have covered some key ecological concepts such as succession, diversity, stability, resilience and equilibrium. These are interrelated concepts of major significance in understanding the limits or in defining the boundaries of human coexistence with nature. Thus, it would be instructive to have a clearer understanding of each one of these concepts and how they are related to each other. This also will help us discover and understand the nature of some important controversial ecological issues such as biodiversity.

Earlier, succession was defined as the changes that occur naturally in the species composition of an ecosystem over time. Generally, the time span is measured in terms of tens and hundreds of years. It was also postulated that succession will eventually lead to a climax community. This last stage of succession is characterized by diversity: complex and wide-ranging interrelationships among multitudes of species. Accordingly, at the climax stage both the interrelationships and the number of species are near a maximum. Furthermore, increasing diversity was considered an important factor in ecological stability, especially in the climax stage. The intuitive explanation for this is that the more an ecosystem is characterized by wide-ranging interrelationships among a large number of species, the lesser the effect of loss of a single species on the overall structure and functioning of that ecosystem (Holling 1997).

Stability, as defined here, refers to the ability of a natural ecosystem to return to its original condition after a change or disturbance. A system at a dynamic equilibrium inherently tends to be more stable than one in which disequilibrium exists. The resilience of a system refers to the *rate* at which a perturbed system will return to its original state (Holling 1997). The conventional wisdom seems to be that as succession proceeds there tends to be an increase in stability, resilience, diversity and complexity.

However, the seeds of many ecological controversies seem to sprout from the lack of universal agreement about these generalizations (Holling 1997). These controversies are fueled by different conclusions resulting from manipulated experiments versus natural field studies. The differences are exacerbated even further by the argument that the more interconnected the components of the system are, the less stable the system is likely to be. There can be major impacts on closely connected species, initiating a "ripple effect" through the system. Another case that can be made is that diversity does not always lead to stability. Some of the more resilient ecosystems – the Arctic tundra, for example – are actually very simple. Suffice it to say that considerably more research is necessary before these controversies can be resolved. An important consideration in this discussion is that not only do we not understand clearly how these factors are related, we have relatively little knowledge of the kinds or magnitudes of environmental changes that might lead to major ecosystem disruptions (Holling 1997). This important point is particularly salient with regard to actual and potential anthropogenic perturbations such as deforestation and global warming. Our inability to predict what changes might occur as a result of such human activities is cause for major concern. The fear is further compounded when the scientific uncertainty of the long-term effects of certain environmental problems such as global warming is used to justify inaction. For example, an economic study by Nordhaus (1991) argued for a modest program of international abatement of carbon dioxide on the basis that many of the long-term effects of global warming are still uncertain.

4.4 THE LAWS OF MATTER AND ENERGY

In the discussion so far, we have briefly examined the crucial role energy plays in the functioning of the natural ecosystem. The availability of the chemical energy that supports all forms of living organisms and the main-tenance of material circulation within the ecosystem – which are essential in the revitalization of the natural ecosystem – requires a continuous flow of energy from an external source or sources. For our planet, this external source of energy has been the radiation from the sun.

Why is it that the natural ecosystems need to have a continuous flow of energy from an external source? An adequate response to this question demands a discussion of the laws governing the transformation of matter and energy. As a working definition, *matter* may be identified as anything that occupies a space and has mass; and *energy* may be viewed as an entity that lacks mass but contains the capacity for moving and/or transforming an object(s) – capacity to do work.

A living ecosystem is characterized by a continuous transformation of matter and energy. The flow and transformation of matter and energy are governed by several laws of physics. Of these, there are two laws especially relevant to our understanding of the functioning of the natural ecosystem. These two laws (the laws of thermodynamics) deal with energy, and their respective implications are discussed below.

The *first law of thermodynamics* refers to the principle of conservation of matter and energy. This law states that matter and energy can neither be created nor destroyed, only transformed. The ecological implication of this law is rather straightforward. It clearly suggests that in the natural ecosystem we can never really throw matter away, or that "everything must go somewhere." This same principle holds for energy as well. This is clearly apparent in Figure 4.1, which shows how energy is released at each ecological path. However, the first law dictates that the energy lost in one process must equal the energy gained by the surrounding environment. Therefore, in terms of *quantity*, the total energy is always *constant*. This is why at times the first law is referred as the law of conservation of matter–energy.

The *second law of thermodynamics* deals with energy transformations and with the concepts of energy quality (useful versus useless energy). Energy can exist in a number of different "states." For example, light is a form of energy, as are various types of fossil fuels, wind, nuclear power sources (fuels), gunpowder and electricity, among others. Energy from fossil fuels can be converted to heat energy to boil water and produce steam that can turn a turbine to produce electricity that can be converted to make a lightbulb work or run an electric motor. We may consider each of these forms of energy to be useful since they can be used to do work (turn a turbine, move an automobile) or provide light by which to see. The second law of thermodynamics states that each time useful energy is converted or transformed from one state (or form) to another, there always is less useful energy available in the second state than there was in the first state. Therefore, in accordance with the "first law of thermodynamics" (which deals with energy conversion), the "second law" says that in every energy conversion some useful energy is converted to useless (heat) energy (Georgescu-Roegen 1993; Miller 1991). In the case of an incandescent lightbulb, electrical energy is converted to "useful" light energy as well as some useless heat which you can detect by touching a lightbulb that has been turned on for a few minutes. Similarly, the energy of fossil fuel used to do the work of moving an automobile generates a substantial amount of useless heat that must be dissipated through the "cooling system" (i.e., radiator and water pump), or it will ruin the motor. Therefore, in any transformation of energy, in terms of energy quality (useful energy), there is an apparent loss of available energy. This phenomenon is often referred to as the principle of energy degradation or *entropy*, and it is universally applicable (Georgescu-Roegen 1993).

The significant implications of the second law are the following:

1 Energy varies in its quality or ability to do work.
2 In all conversion of energy to work, there will always be a certain waste or loss of energy quality. Thus, we shall never be able to devise a "perfect" energy conversion system, or perpetual motion.
3 Since energy moves unidirectionally, from high to low temperature, it follows that a highly concentrated source of energy (such as the available energy in a piece of coal) can never be reused. *We can never recycle energy.* This clearly explains, then, why the natural ecosystem requires continual energy from an external source.

Taken together, what points 2 and 3 convey is the existence of biophysical limits to technology and terrestrial energy resources (see Exhibit 4.1).

EXHIBIT 4.1 PERPETUAL MOTION, A SORT OF "ORIGINAL SIN" IN SCIENCE

Garrett Hardin

Perpetual motion is an anti-Epicurean notion. Derek Price argues that it was probable, though not certain, that the pursuit of perpetual motion did not become a "growth industry" until after A.D. 1088, when "some medieval traveler . . . made a visit to the circle of Su Sung" in China. At this place there was exhibited a marvelous water clock that seemed to run forever without any motive force being required to replenish the elevated water supply. "How was the traveler to know that each night there came a band of men to turn the pump handles and force the tons of water from the bottom sump to the upper reservoir, thus winding the clock for another day of apparently powerless activity?"

Such may have been the historical origin of what Price calls "chimera of perpetual motion machines . . . one of the most severe mechanical delusions of mankind." The delusion was not put to rest until the late nineteenth century when explicit statements of the conservation of matter and energy were advanced by physicists and accepted by scientists in general. It should be noted that a comparable advance was made in biology at about the same time when Pasteur (and others) demolished the supposed evidence for the spontaneous generation of living organisms. Modern public health theory is based on, and committed to, the belief that Epicurus was right: there is indeed a "need of seeds," for disease germs to appear in this world of ours.

The "conviction of the mind" that limits are real, now firmly established in the natural science, has still to be made an integral part of orthodox economics. As late as 1981 George Gilder, in his best-seller *Wealth and Poverty*, said that "The United States must overcome the materialistic fallacy: the illusion that resources and capital are essentially things which can run out, rather than products of the human will and imagination which in freedom are inexhaustible." Translation: "Wishing will make it so."

Six years later at a small closed conference two economists told the environmentalists what was wrong with their Epicurean position. Said one: "The notion that there are limits that can't be taken care of by capital has to be rejected." (Does that mean that capital is unlimited?) Said another: "I think the burden of proof is on your side to show that there are limits and where the limits are." Shifting the burden of proof is tactically shrewd: but would economists agree that the burden of proof must be placed on the axiom, "There's no such thing as a free lunch"?

Fortunately for the future progress of economics the wind is shifting. The standard ("neoclassical") system of economics assumes perpetual growth in a world of no limits. "Thus," said economist Allen Kneese in 1988, "the neoclassical system is, in effect, a perpetual motion machine." The conclusion that follows from this was explicitly laid out by Underwood and King: "The fact that there are no known exceptions to the laws of thermodynamics should be incorporated into the axiomatic foundation of economics." But it will no doubt be some time before economics is completely purged of the covert perpetual motion machines that have afflicted it from the time of Malthus to the present.

Source: Living within Limits: Ecology, Economics, and Population Taboos (1993: 44–5). Copyright © 1993 by Oxford University Press, Inc. Used by permission.

4.5 THE BASIC LESSONS OF ECOLOGY

Several lessons can be drawn from the above discussions of ecology. Among them, the following are most pertinent to the study of natural resource economics:

1 The substances that we often identify as natural resources (air, water, food, minerals, valleys, mountains, forests, lakes, watersheds, waterfalls, wilderness, etc.) evolved from a multitude of complex interactions of living and nonliving organisms that are powered by the energy of the sun over a period measured on a geological timescale. Viewed this way, the term *natural resource* refers to all of the elements that constitute the biosphere. In other words, natural resources include all the "original" elements that comprise the earth's natural endowments or the life-support systems: the lithosphere, the hydrosphere and the atmosphere, together with the solar radiation from the sun. Furthermore, even from a purely anthropocentric perspective, some of the services of nature's ecosystem would include the items presented in Table 4.1. An important implication of this is that it would be wrong to conceive of natural resources as just factors of production that can be directly used in the production and consumption processes of the human economy (see Chapter 1).

2 The interactions among the elemental components of the biosphere are governed by three basic principles. The first principle is that all matter in the ecosphere is mutually linked (Miller 1991). Furthermore, since

everything is related to everything else, survival of the biosphere requires recognition of the mutual interdependencies among all the elements that constitute the biosphere. Strictly from an ecological viewpoint, then, the human economy cannot be viewed in isolation from the natural eco-system or biosphere as depicted by the circular diagram, Figure 1.1 in Chapter 1 (Georgescu-Roegen 1993). Instead, the economy is a *subsystem* of the environment, both as a source of raw material inputs and as a "sink" for waste output as shown in Figure 4.2 (Boulding 1993). As will be further explored in Chapters 8 and 9, this vision of the human economy as a subsystem of the biosphere has very profound implications; especially for the issue of "optimal" *scale* (the size of human economy relative to the natural ecosystem).

The second principle deals with the fact that *material recycling* is essential for the growth and revitalization of all the components of the ecosphere (Miller 1991). In every natural ecosystem, what is a by-product (waste) for one organism is a resource for another. In this sense there is no such thing in nature as waste. Furthermore, in nature, materials are continuously circulated through the biosphere by a combination of atmospheric, geologic, biologic and hydrologic cycles. These cycles are essential for maintaining the long-run equilibrium of the elements in the atmosphere, hydrosphere and lithosphere.

The third principle essential to the understanding of the functioning of the biosphere deals with the recognition that the various components of the biosphere (the ecosystems) go through developmental stages. A mature ecosystem supports a large diversity of species with a web of inter-relationships. These diverse interrelationships in turn make the ecosystem quite resilient to changes in the physical environment. Thus, according to what seems to be the conventional wisdom, in nature it is through diversity that a particular ecosystem maintains stability.

3 The biosphere cannot escape the fundamental laws of matter and energy. By the first law of thermodynamics, the biosphere is composed of a constant amount of matter. In this sense, what typifies the activity in nature is not the creation but the transformation of matter. *No activity in the biosphere creates matter* (Georgescu-Roegen 1993). The first law clearly instructs us that natural resources are *finite* (Boulding 1993; Georgescu-Roegen 1993). Furthermore, it informs us that in the process of transformation of matter, we cannot get rid of anything. An important implication of this is that *pollution* is an inevitable by-product of any transformation of matter–energy (including, of course, the human economy).

The biosphere also operates within another restriction stemming from the second law. For any activities (i.e., transformation of matter) to occur in the biosphere, a continual flow of energy from an external source is required. As discussed earlier, this is because the second law states that energy cannot be recycled. Furthermore, the fact that energy cannot be recycled raises an important issue about the use of terrestrial energy resources, such as fossil fuels. These terrestrial resources are not only finite, but also nonrecyclable. As will be shown in Chapters 8 and 9, these are core concepts essential to the understanding of ecological economics and the argument for sustainable economic development.

Table 4.1 **Nature's ecosystem services**

Raw materials production
   (food, fisheries, timber and building materials, nontimber forest products,
   fodder, genetic resources, medicines, dyes)
Pollination
Biological control of pests and diseases
Habitat and refuge
Water supply and regulation
Waste recycling and pollution control
Nutrient cycling
Soil building and maintenance
Disturbance regulation
Climate regulation
Atmospheric regulation
Recreation, cultural, educational/scientific

Source: *Worldwatch Institute*, State of the World 1997, p. 96. Copyright © 1997. Reprinted by permission.

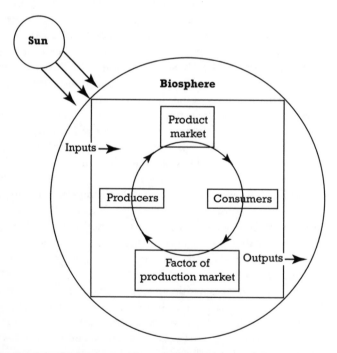

Figure 4.2 **Ecologically enlightened economic view (full world scenario)**
Source: Reproduced with permission from J. Collett and S. Karakashian (eds.) *Greening the College Curriculum*, copyright © Island Press (Washington, D.C., 1996), p. 77.

4.6 HUMANITY AS THE BREAKER OF CLIMAXES

Where does humankind fit into the above scheme of ecological events? From a purely ecological viewpoint, humans are a part of nature, and occupy no special place. Like any other living organisms, their livelihood and survival depend on the stored energy and minerals (plants, animals, soil, etc.) found in the biosphere. Thus, in an environment where mutual coexistence among living organisms was the rule, at any point in time humans' use of the stored wealth of nature would only be commensurate with their needs for survival. However, one distinguishing feature of humans has been their ability to manipulate nature through technological means (Georgescu-Roegen 1993; Hardin 1993). In particular, ever since humankind acquired technology in the form of fire, the pace of its dominance and exploitation of nature has been dramatic. In general, the consequences of continuous and rapid harvesting and mining of natural resources by humans have been twofold:

1 *Simplification of the ecosystem* As a whole, human actions can be looked at as efforts to simplify the biological relationships within the ecosystem to their own advantage (Miller 1991). By clearing land and planting crops or orchards, a complex and mixed flora of wild plants, which once extended over a wide area, is now replaced by a single kind of plant – *monoculture* (see Exhibit 4.2). To increase yield, fertilizers are applied to the soils, disrupting natural nutrient cycles. Competition by other organisms (insects, weeds and disease pests) is reduced or eliminated through ecological poisoning, such as the use of insecticides, herbicides and fungicides.

2 *Creation of industrial pollution (waste)* No organism can function without creating waste. In a natural ecosystem, the normal amount of waste created by organisms poses no problem because, as stated earlier, one organism's waste is another's food. In this sense, in a well-functioning ecosystem there is no such thing as waste. In general, in their natural settings, ecosystems are self-repairing, self-maintaining and self-regulating (Miller 1991). One could therefore infer from this that ecosystems are well prepared to handle a major environmental stress caused by humankind. Why, then, are human-generated wastes a problem for ecosystems? Two explanations can be offered to this question. First, as humankind has asserted its dominance by the rapid increase of its population, the amount of waste created by humans has been increasing at an alarming rate. Impacts from these increased volumes of waste have been further intensified by continued human efforts to simplify the natural ecosystem, which have the undesirable effect of reducing the number of decomposers. Furthermore, beyond certain thresholds, increased waste could cause the total collapse of or irreversible damage to an ecosystem (more on this in Chapter 8). Second, with advances in technology, humanity started to introduce wastes that were new to natural ecosystems (Commoner 1974). These human-made wastes, such as synthetic chemicals, large doses of radiation, etc. – for which there exist few, if any, decomposers – continue to cause serious stresses on natural ecosystems. In other cases, relatively nontoxic wastes such as CO_2 may be produced in

such large quantities that they cannot be handled by normal ecosystem processes and they may begin to accumulate (in this case potentially causing global warming and the altering of climate). The ultimate effect of such environmental stresses has been to lessen the *productivity* and *diversity* of natural ecosystems. For example, Exhibit 4.3 shows how in Thailand waste resulting from a recent boom in commercial shrimp farming is causing ecological havoc. In this sense, purely from an ecological viewpoint, the natural disposition of the technological human has been to act as the breaker of climaxes. Such an act is clearly inconsistent with the sustainability of natural ecosystems.

EXHIBIT 4.2 THE IRISH POTATO FAMINE

Catharina Japikes

More than a million Irish people – about one in every nine – died in the Great Potato Famine of the 1840s. To the Irish, famine of this magnitude was unprecedented and unimaginable . . .

When the famine hit in 1845, the Irish had grown potatoes for over 200 years – since the South American plant had first arrived in Ireland. During this time, the lower classes had become increasingly dependent on them. Potatoes provided good nutrition, so diseases like scurvy and pellagra were uncommon. They were easy to grow, requiring a minimum of labor, training, and technology – a spade was the only tool needed. Storage was simple; the tubers were kept in pits in the ground and dug up as needed. Also, potatoes produce more calories per acre than any other crop that would grow in northern Europe.

To increase their harvest, farmers came to rely heavily on one variety, the lumper. While the lumper was among the worst-tasting types, it was remarkably fertile, with a higher per-acre yield than other varieties. Economist Cormac O Grada estimates that on the eve of the famine, the lumper and one other variety, the cup, accounted for most of the potato crop. For about 3 million people, potatoes were the only significant source of food, rarely supplemented by anything else.

It was this reliance on one crop – and especially one variety of one crop – that made the Irish vulnerable to famine. As we now know, genetic variation helps protect against the decimation of an entire crop by pests, disease or climate conditions. Nothing shows this more poignantly than Ireland's agricultural history.

In 1845, the fungus *Phytophthora infestans* arrived accidentally from North America. A slight climate variation brought the warm, wet weather in which the blight thrived. Much of the potato crop rotted in the fields. Because potatoes could not be stored longer than 12 months, there was no surplus to fall back on. All those who relied on potatoes had to find something else to eat.

The blight did not destroy all of the crop; one way or another, most people made it through winter. The next spring, farmers planted those tubers that remained. The potatoes seemed sound, but some harbored dormant strains of the fungus. When it rained, the blight began again. Within weeks the entire crop failed.

Although the potatoes were ruined completely, plenty of food grew in Ireland that year. Most of it, however, was intended for export to England. There, it would be sold – at a price higher than most impoverished Irish could pay. In fact, the Irish starved not for lack of food, but for lack of food they could afford.

The Irish planted over two million acres of potatoes in 1845, according to O Grada, but by 1847 potatoes accounted for only 300,000 acres. Many farmers who could turned to other crops. The potato slowly recovered, but the Irish, wary of dependence on one plant, never again planted it as heavily. The Irish had learned a hard lesson – one worth remembering.

Source: EPA Journal Vol. 20, Fall 1994, p. 44 Reprinted by permission.

EXHIBIT 4.3 THAILAND'S SHRIMP BOOM COMES AT GREAT ECOLOGICAL COST

John McQuaid

Ban Lang Tha Sao, Thailand – Two years ago, Dulah Kwankha was toiling his life away in a rice paddy on the outskirts of his village, supporting his wife and three children with the $400 he earned each year. Then, in a story worthy of Horatio Alger, he became an entrepreneur and started earning six times that much. Dulah, 46, rode the economic wave that has swept up and down the Thai peninsula during the 1980s and '90s: shrimp farming.

With a $12,000 bank loan, backed by a Thai company, he converted his rice paddy into a shrimp pond that produces three crops a year, earning him $2,400. He now spends most of his time supervising the two villagers he pays to feed the shrimp, maintain the water flow and circulation, and harvest the black tiger prawns when they reach full size.

The succulent prawns, produced cheaply by farms like Dulah's, have flooded the US market in the past ten years and continue to gain popularity. To cash in, Thailand, Ecuador, China, Taiwan and other developing countries have thrown billions of dollars into shrimp farms. The shrimp-farming craze illustrates the power of the global marketplace to alter people's lives on opposite sides of the world, often for the worse.

Farmed shrimp has undercut the price of wild shrimp caught in the Gulf of Mexico, helping send a once-vital industry spiraling into economic decline. And it has brought the forces of capitalism to the doorsteps of subsistence farmers and fishers for the first time in history. Aquaculture has turned thousands of square miles of coastline in Thailand and other countries into humming engines of shrimp production.

But the price of this newfound wealth has been high. Cultures and values have been altered, often with devastating consequences. And in many places, the delicate ecologies that millions of people depend upon for their living are being ravaged by a headlong rush to collect on the world shrimp boom.

Every shrimp crop produces a layer of black sludge on the bottom of the pond – an unhealthy combination of fecal matter, molted shells, decaying food and chemicals. It must be removed somehow – by bulldozer, hose or shovel – before the next crop cycle can begin.

There's no place to put it. So it is piled everywhere – by roadsides, in canals, in wetlands, in the Gulf of Thailand, on the narrow spits of land between the ponds. When it rains, the waste drains into the watershed, causing health problems. All along the coast, fishers say, the sludge, along with untreated or poorly treated shrimp farm waste water, has killed fish close to shore. Over time, a buildup of waste products from the ponds often renders them useless. When that happens, neither shrimp nor rice farming is possible.

The farms have other costs too, which may not become apparent for years. Nearly every tree in the shrimp farm zone has been uprooted or killed by polluted water. Many of those that remain are dying. There is literally nothing holding the land in place, and coastal erosion has increased dramatically in the past 10 years, residents say. The intrusion of salt water has ruined rice paddies where they still exist.

Source: Kalamazoo (MI) Kalamazoo Gazette/Newhouse News Service, Nov. 1996. Copyright © The Times-Picayune Publishing Corporation. Reprinted by permission.

4.7 CHAPTER SUMMARY

- In this chapter it is observed that the subject matter of ecology deals with the study of the interrelationships between living organisms and their habitat, the physical environment. Since the key issue is always interrelation, the concept of system is fundamental in any serious ecological study. Using the *ecosystem* as a framework, ecologists try to explain the general principles that govern the operation of the biosphere.
- The basic lessons of ecology are several; and from a purely biophysical perspective, the most pertinent ones are:

  1 No meaningful hierarchical categorizations can be made between the living and nonliving components of an ecosystem because the physical environment and the living organisms are mutually interdependent.
  2 Energy is the lifeblood of an ecosystem.
  3 The operation of the natural ecosystems is characterized by the continuous transformation of matter and energy. This may be manifested in several forms, such as production, consumption, decomposition and the processes of life themselves.
  4 Any transformation of matter–energy is governed by certain immutable natural laws, two of which are the first and second laws of thermodynamics. The first law informs us that there are finite stocks of resources; the second law reminds us that the continuing operation of any system requires a flow of energy from an external source.
  5 The species composition of a natural ecosystem undergoes gradual and evolutionary changes (succession). A mature ecosystem supports a great number of interdependent species.
  6 Ecosystems, however, are also systems of discontinuous changes. Disruptions resulting from external environmental factors (such as global warming) which affect extensive areas could have significant detrimental effects on species composition and the structure and functioning of the ecosystem.

- Furthermore, in this chapter attempts were made to highlight some of the important links between ecology and economics. Among them are:

1 Economics and ecology deal with common problems. That is, both disciplines deal with transformation of matter and energy. This interpretation is quite consistent with the meaning of the common prefix of these two disciplines – that is, the Greek word "eco," which literally means the study of households.

2 However, this means that, like that of the natural ecosystem, the operation of the human economy is characterized by continuous transformation of matter and energy. For this reason, the human economy must depend on the earth's ecosystems for its basic material and energy needs. The dependence of the economic system on the natural ecosystems is so complete that the human economy can rightfully be regarded as nothing more than a subsystem of the entire earth's ecosystem (Georgescu-Roegen 1993; Boulding 1993).

- Beyond this, on the basis of the materials discussed in this chapter, we were able to infer the following:

1 Natural resources are finite. In this regard, the human economy is "bounded" by a nongrowing and finite ecological sphere. The implication of this is that nature cannot be exploited without limits.

2 Pollution is an inevitable by-product of any economic activity.

3 There are definite limits to technology.

4 Throughout history, the tendency of humanity has been to act as the breaker of climaxes, by either a simplification of the ecosystem and/or the introduction and disposal of industrial wastes.

---

review and discussion questions

1 Briefly describe the following ecological concepts: ecosystem, primary producers, consumers, decomposers, photosynthesis, nitrogen fixation, ecological succession, biodiversity, ecological resilience, pioneer stage, climax stage, the first and second laws of thermodynamics, entropy, monoculture.

2 State *True*, *False* or *Uncertain* and explain why.

    (a) Energy is the ultimate resource.

    (b) A climax ecosystem is complex, diverse, resilient and, as such, stable.

    (c) In principle, an ecosystem can function without the presence of consumers.

    (d) Ecology and economics deal with production and distribution of valuable resources among complex networks of producers and consumers. Energy and material transformations underlie all these processes, and therefore both ecology and economics must comply with the fundamental constraints imposed by thermodyamics.

3   In his classic article "The Historical Roots of Our Ecological Crisis", (1967) Lynn White, Jr., asserted that "we shall continue to have a worsening ecological crisis until we reject the Christian axiom that nature has no reason for existence save to serve man." Do you agree or disagree? Explain your position.

4   "Economists are fond of saying that we cannot get something for nothing. The entropy law teaches us that the rule of biological life and, in man's case, of its economic continuation is far harsher. In entropy terms, the cost of any biological or economic enterprise is always greater than the product. In entropy terms, any such activity necessarily results in a *deficit*" (Georgescu-Roegen 1993: 80). Provide a brief explanation of the essential message(s) conveyed by this remark.

REFERENCES AND FURTHER READING

Commoner, B. (1974) *The Closing Circle: Nature, Man and Technology*, New York: Bantam Books.

Boulding, K. E. (1993) "The Economics of the Coming Spaceship Earth," in H. E. Daly, and K. N. Townsend (eds.) *Valuing the Earth: Economics, Ecology, Ethics*, Cambridge, Mass.: MIT Press.

Georgescu-Roegen, N. (1993) "The Entropy Law and the Economic Problem," in H. E. Daly, and K. N. Townsend (eds.) *Valuing the Earth: Economics, Ecology, Ethics*, Cambridge, Mass.: MIT Press.

Holling, C. S. (1997) "The Resilience of Terrestrial Ecosystems: Local Surprise and Global Change," in R. Costanza, C. Perrings and C. J. Cleveland (eds.) *The Development of Ecological Economics*, London: Edward Elgar.

Howe, C. W. (1979) *Natural Resource Economics*, New York: John Wiley.

Miller, T. G., Jr. (1991) *Environmental Science*, 3rd edn., Belmont, Calif.: Wadsworth.

Nordhaus, W. D. (1991) "To Slow or Not to Slow: The Economics of the Greenhouse Effect," *Economic Journal* 6, 101: 920–37.

Pearce, D. W. (1978) *Environmental Economics*, 3rd edn., London: Longman.

Schneider, S. H. (1990) "Debating Gaia," *Environment* 32, 4: 5–9, 29–30, 32.

White, L., Jr. (1967) "The Historical Roots of Our Ecological Crisis," *Science* 55: 1203–7.

part four

FUNDAMENTALS OF THE ECONOMICS OF ENVIRONMENTAL RESOURCES

Parts One and Three discussed the economics and ecological perspectives of natural resources and their implications for the economic and the natural world, respectively. In many respects, viewed separately and in abstract, the differences between these two perspectives may appear to be irreconcilable. However, pragmatic considerations require the recognition that both perspectives have relevance when the issue at hand deals with the coexistence of humanity with nature. This is most vividly observed in the economics of the environment – the subject matter of Part Four.

Part Four consists of one chapter, Chapter 5. It deals with the economics of using the environment for the disposal of waste products from human activities – the economics of pollution. This is a relevant economic issue because the environment has a *limited* though not necessarily fixed capacity to self-degrade waste – which is subject to the natural biological processes of decomposition. This means that the problem of environmental pollution cannot be adequately addressed without a sound understanding of the economics and ecological dimensions of the problem. This need for an integrative approach to ecology and economics should be apparent in the discussions of Chapter 5. In this respect, this chapter provides a first look at how ecological and economic concepts can be jointly used to help us understand and resolve resource problems of vital social concern.

The discussions in Chapter 5 are limited to the fundamental elements of a subject commonly known as "environmental economics." The emphasis is on understanding the following two points: (a) the key ecological and technological factors that are essential in understanding the trade-off between increased economic activities and environmental degradation; and (b) the reasons why a system of resource allocation that is guided on the basis of individual self-interest (hence, private markets) fails to account for the social costs of environmental damage and what can be done to remedy this omission. Concepts like assimilative capacity of the environment, common property resources, public goods, externality, transaction costs, market failure and environmental taxes are discussed. Chapter 5 also briefly discusses the macroeconomic effects of environmental regulations – measures taken to remedy pollution problems.

chapter
five

THE MARKET, EXTERNALITY, AND THE "OPTIMAL" TRADE-OFF BETWEEN ENVIRONMENTAL QUALITY AND ECONOMIC GOODS

---

learning objectives

After reading this chapter you will be familiar with the following:

- the waste assimilative (absorptive) capacity of the natural environment;
- economic, ecological and technological factors affecting the waste assimilative capacity of the natural environment;
- conditions for clearly defined ownership rights;
- common property resources and the economic problem;
- the concept of transaction cost;
- the concept of externality;
- the root causes and economic consequences of environmental externality;
- market failure;
- the optimal trade-off between economic goods and environmental quality;
- using environmental tax to correct environmental externality;
- the macroeconomic effects of environmental regulations.

Most environmental problems are traceable to the common property nature of environmental resources. Common property ownership of resources such as the atmosphere has traditionally meant no ownership at all and free access to all users. Environmental degradation of such resources has occurred when the demand has risen to overwhelm their limited capacity to absorb wastes. Individual maximizing behavior becomes perversely inefficient when property rights to resources are held in common and government assertion of public property rights is required to assure efficient resource allocation.

(Seneca and Taussig 1984: 103)

5.1 INTRODUCTION

Although it may be objectionable to some, the conventional wisdom in environmental and resource economics is to view the natural environment as a commodity or an asset with a multitude of qualitative attributes (Tietenberg 1992). Let us consider a river flowing along a wooded area as an example. To avid anglers, this river is a valuable asset because it serves as a constant source of fish. To a group of nature lovers, the value of this river may be primarily spiritual. Moreover, for these individuals, the river may not be viewed in isolation from its surroundings. To yet another group, the river may serve as a dumping ground for industrial waste.

This example shows that the environment is a multifaceted asset or commodity. It can be used as a spiritual object, aesthetic consumption goods, a source of renewable resources such as fish, and/or a dumping ground for waste. In this chapter the primary focus will be on the economic management of the natural environment (in the form of either water, air or landmass) in terms of its potential service to degrade or store waste. A "proper" management of the environment to this end requires the following two considerations. First, there should be a good understanding of the nature of the waste-absorptive capacity of the environment under consideration. Second, there should be a mechanism by which to identify the costs (degradation of environmental quality) and the benefits resulting from the use of the natural environment to an economic end (the production of more goods and services). In other words, the trade-off between economic goods and environmental quality or degradation needs to be carefully assessed, taking into consideration the opportunity costs for all alternative uses of the environmental asset in question.

To address these issues thoroughly and systematically, in the next section an attempt is made, using a simple model, to explain the relationship between economic activities (production and consumption of goods and services) and the waste-absorptive capacity of the natural environment. The primary objective of this model is to identify certain key ecological and technological factors that are essential in understanding the trade-off between increased economic activities and environmental degradation. These are the kinds of fundamental knowledge essential for providing clear and adequate responses to the questions raised at the end of Exhibit 5.1. The answer to question 1 should be evident after reading Section 5.2. Questions 2 and 3 anticipate issues addressed in Section 5.3.

EXHIBIT 5.1   WHAT IS THE MOST DESIRABLE LEVEL OF POLLUTION?

Recently, the "Society for Zero Pollution" sponsored a panel discussion on the topic "Is Zero Pollution Viable?" The panelists included a well-known environmental economist and a very famous ecologist.

Probably to the dismay of their sponsor, both the economist and the ecologist agreed that zero pollution is neither viable nor desirable. On the other hand, both panelists were quite complimentary about the society's efforts to initiate a timely and well-conceived public debate on general issues concerning the environment, and the genuine concern the society has shown for the growing deterioration of our environment.

In discussing his view against zero pollution, the ecologist stated that we must not forget that the environment has a limited ability to process waste. The concern for environmental pollution arises only when we emit wastes into the environment beyond its assimilative capacity. In his view, therefore, the socially desirable level of waste discharge (pollution) is that which is consistent with the assimilative capacity of the environment. In other words, waste emission should not exceed the renewable assimilative capacity of the environment.

In her turn, the economist disputed the assertion made by the ecologist by stating that it is quite consistent and rational for society to discharge waste (pollute) above and beyond the assimilative capacity of the environment in so far as society collectively values the benefit from the excess pollution (the extra value of the goods and services produced) at more than the cost of the damage to the environmental quality. Hence, the *optimal* (socially desirable) level of pollution is attained when the marginal social cost (MSC) of waste reduction – in terms of extra output and services sacrificed – is equal to the marginal social benefit (MSB) of waste reduction – in terms of the psychic and tangible benefit society may attain from improved environmental quality.

1 Do you agree that zero pollution is neither viable nor desirable? Why? Be specific.
2 How would you reconcile the views expressed by the ecologist and the economist? If you think they are irreconcilable, why so? Explain.
3 Recently, the Environmental Protection Agency proposed to ban the use of EDB (ethylene dibromide) to spray on domestically produced citrus fruits. Would this be consistent with either one of the above two views? Why, or why not?

5.2   THE ECONOMIC PROCESS AND THE ASSIMILATIVE CAPACITY OF THE NATURAL ENVIRONMENT

We all want to protect the purity and vitality of our air and water, and the natural landscape. However, despite our desire to do so, as long as we are engaged in transforming material inputs (land, labor, capital and raw materials) into economic goods, we cannot avoid creating residuals (the second law of matter and energy). This residual of the economic process is commonly referred to as *pollution*. Pollution is, then, an inevitable by-product of economic activities.

Furthermore, by the first law of matter and energy, we know that this residual has to go somewhere. That "somewhere" consists of various media of the natural environment – air, water and/or the landscape. It is in this way that the natural environment is used as a repository of wastes generated through the economic process. In general, however, disposal in this way should pose no problem if done in moderation. This is because, as noted in Chapter 4, the natural environment has a decomposer population which, given adequate time, will transform the waste into harmless material, and/or return it as a nutrient to the ecosystem. This self-degrading ability of the natural environment is commonly referred to as its *assimilative capacity*. It should not be surprising, then, that from the viewpoint of environmental management, the *quality* of a particular environmental medium (air, water, land) is determined by the extent of its capacity to assimilate (degrade) waste.

In further discussing the assimilative capacity of the natural environment, the following important factors should be noted. First, like anything else in nature, the assimilative capacity of the environment is *limited*. Thus, the natural environment cannot be viewed as a bottomless sink. With respect to its capacity to degrade waste, the natural environment is, indeed, a *scarce* resource. Second, the assimilative capacity of the natural environment depends on the flexibility of the ecosystem and the nature of the waste. That is, the natural environment will not degrade any and all waste with equal efficiency (Pearce 1978). For example, the natural environment can deal with *degradable* pollutants, such as sewage, food waste, papers, etc., with relative ease. On the other hand, it is quite ineffective in dealing with *persistent* or *stock* pollutants, such as plastics, glass, most chemicals, and radioactive substances. For most of these waste elements there are no biological organisms in existence that can accelerate the degradation process. Thus, a very long period of time is required before these wastes can be rendered harmless. Third, the *rate* at which the waste is discharged greatly affects the ability of the environment to degrade residuals. The implication of this is that pollution has a cumulative ecological effect. More specifically, pollution reduces the capacity of an environmental medium to withstand further pollution (Pearce 1978).

The obvious lesson is that, in managing the natural environment, it is crucial to give careful consideration to the *quality* of the waste, its *quantity* and the *rate* at which it is disposed of into the environment. To understand the significance of this point, the following simple model can be used. It is assumed that a linear relationship exists between waste and economic activity. Furthermore, this relationship is expected to be positive – that is, more waste is associated with increasing levels of economic activity. Mathematically, the general form of the functional relationship between waste emission into the environment and economic activity can be expressed as

$$W = f(X, t) \tag{5.1}$$

Or, in explicit functional form, as

$$W = ßX \qquad (5.2)$$

where W is the level of waste generated and X is the level of economic activity. The variable t in equation (5.1) represents technological and ecological factors. Equation (5.2) depicts the simple linear relationship we assumed between waste and economic activity, holding the variable t at some predetermined level. In equation (5.2), ß represents the slope parameter, and is assumed to be positive. Also, the fact that the above linear equation has no intercept term suggests that only waste generated from economic activity, X, is considered relevant in this model. The relationship shown in equation (5.1) can be presented graphically, as shown in Figure 5.1. In this figure, the x-axis shows the level of economic activity (in terms of production of goods or services) and the y-axis represents the quantity (volume) of waste disposed into the environment in some unspecified unit. The broken horizontal line, W_0, represents an additional assumption that was made to complete the basic framework of this simple model. This line is assumed to represent the total amount of waste that the environment could assimilate at a given point in time. Note also that to the extent that W_0 is positive, strictly speaking this model deals with degradable pollutants only. What general conclusions can be reached from this simple model?

First, given that the assimilative capacity is invariant at W_0, X_0 represents the maximum amount of economic activity that can be undertaken without materially affecting the natural environment. The waste generated at this level of economic activity will be completely degraded through a natural process. Thus, from this observation we can draw the general observation that a certain *minimum* amount of economic goods, such as X_0 in Figure 5.1, can be produced without inflicting damage to the natural environment. Thus, X_0 indicates an *ecological threshold* of economic activity.

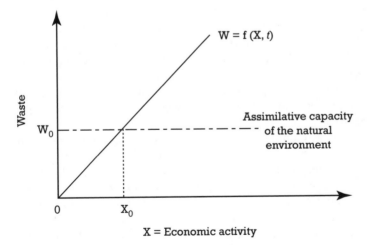

Figure 5.1 A simple relationship between economic output and waste discharge

Second, increased economic activity beyond X_0 would invariably lead to an accumulation of unassimilated waste in the natural environment. Although it may not be fully captured by the above simple model, the effect of this accumulated waste on environmental quality (damage) will be progressively higher because, as indicated earlier, pollution reduces the capacity of an environment to withstand further pollution. In Figure 5.1, the ultimate impact of this dynamic ecological effect would be to shift the assimilative capacity of the environment – the broken horizontal line – downward. Note, that if other factors are held constant, this kind of shift will have the effect of lowering the ecological threshold of economic activity to less than X_0.

The third point that can be conveyed using the above model is how technological factors may affect the ecological threshold of economic activity. The effect of technological change could take the following two forms: (a) Through technology the decomposition process may be accelerated. Note that in our simple model, this type of change is captured by the variable, t. For example, the decomposition process of municipal waste can be accelerated by adding activated charcoal in a sewage treatment facility. This amounts to an artificial enhancement of the assimilative capacity of the environment. Therefore, in Figure 5.1 the effect of this type of technological change would be to shift the dotted line upward, indicating an increase in the assimilative capacity of the environment. Other factors remaining equal, this would have the effect of increasing the ecological threshold of economic activity to something greater than X_0. (b) A change in technology may also alter the relationship between the level of economic activity, X, and the rate at which waste is discharged into the natural environment. In our simple model this would be indicated by a change in the slope parameter, ß. For example, a switch from high to low sulfur content coal in the production of electricity would lower the amount of sulfur emitted into the environment per kilowatt-hour of electricity produced, X. In this case the ultimate effect would be to lower the value of the slope parameter, ß. This entails a clockwise rotation of the line depicting the relationship between waste and economic activity. Again, if other factors are held constant, the overall effect of this type of technological change is to increase the ecological threshold of economic activity. Thus, the implication here is that we can, to a certain degree, augment the ecological threshold of the natural environment by means of technology. As discussed above, the technological improvement could be triggered by either an improvement in waste processing or input switching.

However, as Commoner (1971) warned us, technological solutions to environmental problems can have harmful side effects (more on this in Chapter 6). For example, at the local level, the problem of acid deposition (acid rain in dry form) arising from sulfur dioxide emission can be substantially alleviated by increasing the height of factory smokestacks. The intended effect of this is to emit a good share of the pollutants into the higher strata of the atmosphere. This would amount to solving the problem of pollution through *dilution*. However, as it turns out, what this does is to change the local pollution problem into a transboundary acid rain problem.

The important lesson here is that technological projects intended to address environmental concerns should not be implemented without careful consideration of their potential side effects.

The final point that should be noted is that, as discussed earlier, the natural environment will not degrade all waste with equal efficiency. In some instances the assimilative capacity of the natural environment could be, if not zero, highly insignificant. In Figure 5.1, this situation would dictate that the broken horizontal line representing the assimilative capacity of the natural environment would be closer to, or could even coincide with, the x-axis. In this situation, the ecological threshold of economic activity, X_0, would, for all practical purposes, be zero.

We can draw several lessons from the discussion in this section. First, we observed that the natural environment has a limited capacity to degrade waste. The implication of this observation is that, in purely physical (not necessarily economic) terms, the waste assimilative capacity of the natural environment is a *scarce* resource. Second, a certain minimum amount of economic goods can be produced without causing damage to the natural environment. Thus, *zero* pollution not only is a physical impossibility, but even on purely ecological considerations, it is an unnecessary goal to pursue. Third, although this is not adequately captured by the simple model, the cumulative effect of waste discharge into the natural environment is nonlinear. This is because pollution tends to reduce the capacity of an environment to withstand further pollution. Last but not least, we observed that the ecological threshold of economic activity (X_0 in Figure 5.1) can be augmented by technological means.

The above observations are made through a simple but careful conceptual analysis of the various factors affecting the relationships between the level of economic activity and the damage this action inflicts on the natural environment. However, so far nothing specific has been said about the trade-off between economic activity (the production of goods and services) and environmental quality. This issue becomes relevant when the level of economic activity extends beyond a certain ecological threshold (for example, X_0 in Figure 5.1). After this point, any additional use of the environment has to be made with careful considerations of its benefits and costs. This is, indeed, a key issue that will occupy much of the next section.

5.3 COMMON PROPERTY RESOURCES, EXTERNAL COSTS AND MARKET FAILURE

One important lesson that we have learned from the discussion so far is that the natural environment has a limited capacity to degrade waste. To that extent, then, the natural environment is a *scarce* resource. Given this, it would be in the best interest of any society to manage its natural environment *optimally*. As discussed in Chapter 2, this entails that, as for any other scarce resource, the services of the natural environment as a repository of waste should be considered taking full account of *all* the *social* costs and benefits. Could this be done through the normal operations of the market system? A complete response to this question, first and foremost, requires a clear understanding of certain complications associated with assignment of *ownership rights* to environmental resources. This is the subject matter of the next subsection.

5.3.1 Common property resources and the economic problem

In Chapter 2, it was established that under a perfectly competitive market setting, resource allocation through a private market economy would lead to what is considered to be a socially optimal end. It was also demonstrated that the allocation of any scarce resource is *socially* optimal when, for the last unit of the resource under consideration, the marginal social benefit is equal to the marginal social cost (MSB = MSC).

How could a market economy that is primarily instigated by decisions of private actors seeking to promote their own self-interest lead to a socially optimal result? In other words, what is the magic at work in transforming self-interest to social interest? To Adam Smith, as discussed in Chapter 2, this magic is "invisible" yet real, provided the actors in the market have indisputable rights to the use and disposal of all the resources that they are legally entitled to own. In other words, for Adam Smith's "invisible hand" to operate, resource ownership must be *clearly defined*.

What *exactly* do we mean by a clearly defined ownership right? From the perspective of resource allocation, the ownership of a resource is said to be clearly defined if it satisfies the following conditions (Randall 1987): First, the ownership rights of the resource are *completely specified*. That is, its quantitative and qualitative features as well as its boundaries are clearly demarcated. Second, the rights are *completely exclusive* so that all benefits and costs resulting from an action accrue directly to the individual empowered to take actions. Third, the ownership rights of the resource are *transferable*. In other words, resources can be exchanged or simply donated at the "will" of their owners. Finally, ownership is *enforceable*. That is, ownership of resources is legally protected. When these four criteria are met, it can be shown that reliance on the self-interest-based behavior of individuals will ensure that resources are used where they are *most valued*.

An example of a resource that satisfies the above four criteria is the ownership of a private car. The ownership manual, together with the car registration, completely specifies the contents, model, color and other relevant characteristics of the car. On the car's registration document, the owner's exclusive legal right to the car is confirmed by the authority of the state. Therefore, no one else is allowed to use this car without proper permission from the owner. Once an exclusive ownership is attained, it is in the owner's interest to adhere to a regularly scheduled maintenance program for the car since failure to do so would cost no one else but the owner. Last but not least, the owner of the car can enter into voluntary trade or exchange of her or his car at any point in time. Furthermore, should the owner decide to sell the car, it would be in her or his best interest to sell it at the highest possible price. The ultimate effect of this process is to assure that ownership of a car will gravitate toward those individuals who value it the most (or are willing to bid the highest price).

In the real world, not all resources satisfy the above ownership specifications. For example, a lake shared by all residents living in the surrounding area will not satisfy the second and third of the conditions set out above. In this case, the lake is a resource that is owned in common by all users living within a given geographic boundary line. Another example is the ambient air of a certain locality or region. In this case, none of the above four conditions could be completely satisfied. Thus, the ambient air is a common property owned by everyone, and on practical grounds it is owned by no one – a clear case of *res nullius*. As you can see from these two examples, environmental resources, such as the ambient air and water bodies (lake, rivers, ocean shorelines, etc.), tend to be common property resources. By their very nature, the ownership of these resources cannot be clearly defined.

The question then is, what happens to private markets as a medium for resource allocation in situations where ownership rights of a resource(s) cannot be clearly delineated? We will analyze the implications of this question by using the following hypothetical situation:

Assume for a moment that you are a resident of a small island nation with a population of only 150,000. The families of this nation are economically well off and most of them own at least one car. The nation hardly uses public transportation. Now, imagine that one morning you wake up at your usual time, around 6:30 a.m., and you hear on the radio that the government has passed a law that completely revokes the private ownership of a car. The public announcement also states that the government has issued a master key that will run any car on the street, and such a key is to be found on the doorstep of each individual household. Of course, your first reaction would be to think that this is just a dream. However, the public announcement is so incessant and firm that it leaves you no chance of ignoring the event, of taking it as just a dream.

As shocking and disturbing as this event may be, let us assume that the people of this nation are so nonviolent that no visible disturbance occurs as a result of this Draconian action. Instead, the people, perhaps grudgingly, make the necessary efforts to deal with the prevailing situation. What is the situation? First, people still need a car to go to work, to shop, to visit friends and relatives, etc. Second, the citizens of this nation have no access to public transportation. Third, by government decree every citizen has free access to the cars that currently exist on the island. What will happen to the use and maintenance of cars in this society under these circumstances?

At first, people will start by driving a car that is within easy reach of them. Once they reach their destination, they will leave the car knowing full well that the same car may not be available for their next use. For how long would this pattern of car use continue? Not for long. This is because people would not have any incentive to properly maintain the cars. Who would fill a car with gasoline knowing that any amount left unused from a one-way trip might never be recouped? What would happen to cars should they run out of gas in the middle of a highway? Furthermore, who would have the incentive to pay for regularly needed maintenance, such as oil changes, tune-ups, etc.? What would happen to the cars that simply ceased running because of mechanical problems? The answer to all these questions is that in a short while, in this island nation, cars would be transformed from being commodities of great value to valueless debris scattered all over the traffic arteries of the nation. Of course, the root cause of this undesirable end is the treatment of cars as common property with free access for all. As Garrett Hardin (1968: 1244) elegantly puts it, "Ruin is the destination toward which all men rush, each pursuing his own best interest in a society that believes in the freedom of the commons. Freedom in a commons brings ruin to all." Clearly, from the perspective of environmental and natural resource management, the implications of this conclusion are quite significant. After all, what is at stake is the vitality and integrity of the global commons: the ambient air, most rivers, the sea, the shorelines, the oceans, etc.

A closer look at the above analysis brings the following *two* important points into focus. First, for the *commons*, economic pursuit on the basis of individual self-interest would not lead to what is best for society as a whole. In other words, the principle of Adam Smith's "invisible hand" (see Chapter 2) would be violated. Second, if tragedy is to be averted, the use of commons needs to be regulated by a "visible hand" (Hardin 1968). The next sub-section will further explore this using the environment as the case in point.

5.3.2 Environmental externalities and their economic consequences

We noted above that Adam Smith's fundamental theorem of the "invisible hand" will fail when resource ownership is defined in such a way that individuals cannot take account of the full *benefits* or *costs* of their actions. This will happen not because the costs or benefits are not real. Instead, in this situation, the costs and benefits would be treated as incidental or external. A technical term used to describe this situation is *externality*. Formally, we define externalities as conditions arising when the actions of some individuals have direct (negative or positive) effects on the welfare or utility of other individuals, none of whom have direct control over that activity. In other words, externalities are incidental benefits (costs) to others for whom they are not specifically intended. Two classic examples of externality are described by the following cases. One is represented by the action of an avid gardener who invests in the beautification of her or his own property and, in so doing, raises the property values of the surrounding houses. A second example is represented by a fish hatchery plant that has to bear the cleanup costs for wastes discharged by a paper mill located up-stream. In the first example, the neighbors are gaining *real* external benefits (positive externalities) without sharing the costs of the actions that yielded the beneficial result(s). In the second case, the cleanup cost to the hatchery is external (negative externality) because it is the result of an action imposed by a third party, in this case the paper mill.

What are the main sources of externalities? Let us use the above two classic examples to answer this question. In the first example, no assumption is made that the benefits to the neighbors have resulted from a benevolent act by the gardener. On the contrary, the assumption is that the gardener's investment, in terms of both time and monetary outlays in the beautification of her or his property, is done on the basis of cost–benefit calculations which are consistent with any investor's self-interest. However, the fruit of this investment is an "aesthetic enhancement" or "environmental amenity" which has peculiar characteristics when viewed as an economic commodity. This commodity is *nonrival* in consumption. That is, once it is produced, the consumption of this commodity, say by the neighbors or any passers-by, would not reduce the utility of the gardener. Therefore, when such a commodity is produced, it makes no economic sense to exclude anyone from the use (consumption) of such an activity. Of course, in our simple example, the gardener, if she or he wishes, could exclude the neighbors by building a tall concrete wall around the house. However, this would not be achieved without additional cost. The most commonly used economic jargon to describe the costs associated with *internalizing* (remedying) externalities is *transaction cost*. In broad terms, transaction cost includes any outlay expended for the purpose of specifying properties, excluding nonusers and enforcing property rights. This would be the intended effect if, in fact, the gardener in our example decided to erect a concrete wall around her or his clearly identified property line.

To summarize, the basic lesson that we can draw from the first example, a private garden, is that an externality arises when the use of a property (resource) is difficult to *exclude*. This difficulty may result from one of two possible sources. First, the resource by its very nature may be *nonrival* in consumption, and hence subject to *joint consumption*. Second, for either natural or technical reasons, the *transaction cost* of internalizing the externality may be excessively high (Coase 1960).

In the second example, the river, externality arises from the fact that the owners of the hatchery plant do not have the legal right to stop the operators of the paper mill from dumping their industrial wastes in the river. For that matter, since the river is viewed as a common property, no one can be excluded from using it. Thus, similarly to our first example, the nonexclusive use of the river is what causes an externality to persist. The only difference is the source of nonexclusiveness. In the first case, non-exclusiveness resulted from the fact that the resource under consideration is nonrival, and thus subject to joint consumption. In our second example, nonexclusiveness resulted from the fact that the ownership of the resource under consideration (the river) was not clearly defined – that is, it is common property. Hence, from these two examples we can generalize that, in the final analysis, *lack of excludability* (nonexclusiveness) is the root cause of externality (Randall 1983). Most, if not all, environmental resources are externality-ridden for this very reason.

What is the economic consequence of an externality? Given what we have discussed so far, this is a simple question to answer. In the presence of real externalities, there will be a divergence between private and social evaluations of costs and benefits (Turvey 1963). In general, we can expect the following relationships to hold:

(a)   In a situation where a *positive externality* is present (example 1 above):

Social benefits = Private benefits + External benefits

and

External benefits > 0

Therefore,

> **Social benefits > Private benefits**

(b)   In a case where *negative externality* prevails (example 2 above):

Social costs = Private costs + External costs

and

External costs > 0

Therefore,

> **Social costs > Private costs**

What we infer from the above series of relationships is that, in the presence of an externality, we expect to observe a clear *divergence* between social and private benefits and social and private costs. Under these conditions, resource allocation through a market mechanism – that is, one solely based on consideration of *private* costs and benefits – would be inefficient when viewed from the perspective of society at large. This constitutes a clear case of *market failure* because the market, if left alone, lacks any mechanism by which to account for external costs and/or benefits.

Equipped with a clear understanding of the factors contributing to market failure, we are now in a position to examine why the allocation of environmental goods and services through market mechanisms leads to suboptimal results. This will be demonstrated using the hypothetical case of not just a single paper mill, but the firms of a paper mill industry in their entirety. It is assumed that all firms in this industry are located along river banks and use rivers as a means of disposing of their industrial waste.

In Figure 5.2, curve D represents the market demand for paper. As discussed in Chapter 2, a demand curve such as D represents the marginal private benefit to consumers, MPB. Furthermore, in a situation where external benefit is zero (i.e., there are no positive externalities), a demand curve represents both the marginal private and the social benefits. This is assumed to be the case in Figure 5.2 (D = MPB = MSB).

The complication arises when considering the supply curve of paper. For the paper industry, the supply curve, S, represents the marginal private costs of producing varying levels of paper. These costs represent the firms' expenditures on all priced inputs (i.e., labor, capital, raw materials, and the

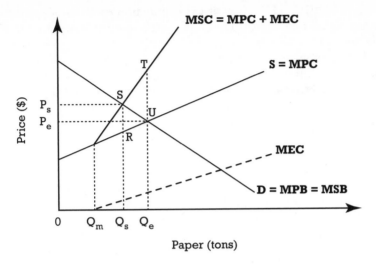

Figure 5.2 **Social optimum in the presence of externality: the case of the paper industry**

services of any resources owned by the owners of the firms in this industry). However, in the process of producing paper, firms are assumed to use rivers to dispose of their production waste *at no cost*. Thus, no such cost appears in the balance sheets of the firms in this hypothetical paper industry, and therefore no disposal cost forms part of the firm's supply curve, S, in Figure 5.2.

However, as explained in Section 5.2, the discharge of waste to a river would cause damage costs beyond a certain threshold level (see X_0 in Figure 5.1). In Figure 5.2, this damage cost is represented by the broken curve labeled MEC – marginal external cost. This cost represents the monetary value of pollution damage imposed on society by the paper mill industry.

At this stage it is important to note the following two important features about the MEC curve in Figure 5.2. First, the marginal external costs do not start to materialize until the paper industry reaches a production level of Q_m. This is because, consistent with our earlier discussion, a certain minimum amount of output can be produced by the paper industry without materially affecting the quality of the environment (the river). Second, the marginal external cost curve, as shown in Figure 5.2, is expected to be positively sloped. That is, beyond Q_m, further increases in the production of paper (hence, more waste discharge) would be associated with external costs that tend to increase at an increasing rate. This is because, as discussed earlier, pollution reduces the capacity of an environment to withstand further pollution.

As shown in Chapter 2, efficiency in resource allocation, or *Pareto optimality*, requires the equating of MSC and MSB. In Figure 5.2 this condition would be met when the level of paper production was Q_s. Note that the marginal social cost curve (MSC) in Figure 5.2 is obtained by the *vertical* summation of the marginal private and marginal external cost curves (i.e., MPC + MEC). However, if the production decision of paper were made through a freely operating market mechanism, the optimal level of production would have been Q_e, where MPB = MPC. Clearly, then, the market solution would *fail* to achieve the level of paper production that is consistent with what is considered to be socially optimal. More specifically, *the tendency would be for the market to produce more paper than is socially desired.* This can be explained by showing that society would stand to gain if, in fact, the production of paper were curtailed from Q_e to Q_s. In other words, the market solution is *not* Pareto optimal.

If the production of paper were reduced from Q_e to Q_s, the total cost savings as a result of this move would be represented by the area under the social marginal cost curve, $Q_e TSQ_s$. This total social cost is composed of the total private costs as represented by the area under the marginal private cost curve, $Q_e URQ_s$, and the total external costs as indicated by the area UTSR. On the other hand, in reducing the production of paper from Q_e to Q_s society would incur a loss in benefits. The forgone benefits to society as a result of this particular move would be measured by the area $Q_e USQ_s$ – the area under the marginal social benefit curve. Stated differently, this represents the forgone *consumers' benefit* resulting from a reduction of paper production from Q_e to Q_s. Clearly, then, in reducing the production of paper from Q_e to Q_s, the total cost saving, area $Q_e TSQ_s$, exceeds the total forgone benefit area $Q_e USQ_s$. Thus, the final outcome of this move represents a *net* cost saving measured by the area of the triangle UTS. Furthermore, since a move away from the market solution represents a clear gain to society, the market solution, Q_e, is *not* Pareto optimal. Note that the market's inability to deliver the socially optimal solution arises from the fact that it has no automatic mechanism to account for the external costs. In Figure 5.2 area UTSR represents the total external costs that would be unaccounted for by the market. *This cost is a measure of the imputed value for the additional environmental service (river) required if the production of paper is expanded from Q_s to Q_e.*

What exactly is the implication of the above analysis in terms of environmental quality? The answer is rather straightforward. Assuming the amount of waste dumped in the river is directly proportional to the amount of paper produced (see Figure 5.1), the market solution, Q_e, would be associated with a higher level of pollution than the socially optimal level of output, Q_s. *What this suggests is that the market, if left alone, would lead to a lower environmental quality.*

At this stage it will be instructive to see what general conclusions we can draw from the analysis presented thus far. In the presence of an externality, resource allocation through the guidance of a free-market system would lead to inefficiency. More specifically, because the market lacks a mechanism by which to account for external costs, *it tends to favor more production of goods and services from industries inflicting damage to the natural environment.* Thus, the presence of real externality creates a misallocation of societal resources.

The question, then, is what can be done to correct the misallocation of resources created by environmental externalities? Does this require a minor or a major modification of the market system? In responding to these questions, the key issue at hand is finding the most effective way(s) of internalizing the externality. Some argue that, on the whole, there are no *technical* solutions to environmental externalities (Hardin 1968). In other words, externalities cannot be effectively internalized through voluntary private negotiation among the parties involved. Thus, according to this view, the only way to resolve environmental externalities effectively is through coercive methods (Hardin 1968). Among others, such methods include opting for public ownership of environmental resources, imposing environmental taxes or setting emission standards. These measures may entail direct or indirect interference with the operation of a free private market economy. For that reason, they are not generally favored by mainstream economists. Most economists would take the position that environmental externalities are effectively remedied provided property rights are clearly defined. Thus, the role of a public agent (government) is to assign rights to someone when a property lacks ownership. Once this is accomplished, the "invisible hand" will guide the market to allocate resources efficiently (Coase 1960). According to this view, then, internalization of environmental externalities requires a minimal and very indirect government involvement.

An extensive analysis of the various alternative methods of internalizing environmental externalities is carried out in Chapters 11 and 12. In the meantime, in the next section an attempt will be made to show how a tax on the output of a pollution-generating firm could be used to correct the market distortion resulting from environmental externalities. This will be demonstrated using the paper industry again.

5.4 INTERNALIZING EXTERNALITY USING THE PIGOUVIAN TAXES APPROACH

Figure 5.3 is a replica of Figure 5.2 with one important exception that will soon be evident. In this figure, Q_e represents the market equilibrium quantity of paper. However, as discussed earlier, this output level would not be optimal because the firms in this industry are not paying for using rivers to discharge their industrial waste. Of course, this happened because rivers are treated as common property resources. Suppose now that legislation was passed providing the central government with complete authority to regulate the use of all rivers. In this capacity the government's role would be to make sure that all rivers were used in a manner consistent with the public interest at large. For our simple example, public interest may dictate subjecting the paper industry to produce output consistent with what is considered to be socially optimal. As shown in Figure 5.3, this would be achieved at output level Q_s. Thus, to achieve the socially optimal level of paper production, the output needs to be reduced from Q_e to Q_s. One way for the central government to attain this goal could be to impose a tax per unit of paper produced. In Figure 5.3, this is accomplished by imposing a tax, t. The common name for taxes that are imposed to internalize environmental

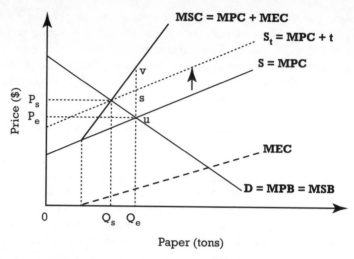

Figure 5.3 Social optimum through a tax on output

externalities is Pigouvian taxes, after economist Arthur Pigou (1877–1959). In this chapter, a specific type of Pigouvian tax is discussed, a tax levied on a unit of output of goods and services causing pollution or environmental damage. As shown in Figure 5.3, imposing a tax of this nature would shift the supply curve from S to S_t. This new supply curve intersects the demand curve at the output level Q_s, the socially desirable level of output.

Why would this method work? It would work because paper producers view the tax as a payment for their use of rivers for dumping waste. In other words, *the tax forces producers of paper to internalize the cost of using rivers.* Hence, the service of rivers is no longer viewed as a free good. In this way, therefore, a Pigouvian (or more generally environmental) tax corrects a market distortion, namely the externalities arising from an excessive use of environmental services (more on this in Chapters 11 and 12).

While it is easy to show how a Pigouvian tax would work to internalize externality in this simple case, the task is much harder in a real-world situation. For one thing, how would the government decide on the right level of tax? What would be the distributional effects of such a tax? In other words, how is the burden of the tax to be shared between the consumers and producers? What would be the costs to the government of monitoring and collecting the tax? That is, how high are the transaction costs of specifying and enforcing property rights? Does this method lead to unnecessary government intrusion into the business affairs of private enterprises? These questions suggest that a careful evaluation of Pigouvian taxes is needed, and it is done below.

One of the major advantages of a Pigouvian tax that is based on output is that it is relatively easy to implement and monitor the tax collection. This is because the tax is based on final output, which can be easily verified by cross-checking the various accounting reports that firms are legally required to prepare. Once the level of output is verified, assessment of the tax does not require more than knowledge of the tax rate, which is at the discretion of the regulators. In this respect, then, a Pigouvian tax may be favored since the transaction cost of implementing and monitoring such a procedure is relatively low. Despite this advantage, however, a tax of the above nature has several serious drawbacks.

1   The purpose of implementing the tax is to improve environmental quality. However, to the extent that the tax is based on the amount of *output*, rather than the volume of *waste discharged*, it may fail to bring about the socially desired level of environmental quality. To see this, let us begin by briefly enumerating some of the factors that need to exist in order for a method that relies on tax per unit of output to yield a result that would be consistent with a socially optimal level of environmental quality. First, we need to have a precise knowledge of how output and waste are related. That is, we need to know exactly how much waste is discharged per unit of output produced. In addition, we need to assume that this technical relationship between output and waste conversion is relatively stable. Without such knowledge, it is difficult to establish a direct correspondence between tax per unit of output and cost per unit of waste discharged. In regulating the firm's behavior in relation to waste disposal, the latter is perhaps the most important. A type of Pigouvian tax that is based on the number of units of pollution emitted is discussed in Chapter 12.

2   If the environmental tax is to be effective in attaining the socially optimal level of environmental quality, the entire tax burden should fall on the firms responsible for the pollution – the *polluter-pays* principle. This principle is based on the notion that firms do not have sufficient incentive to reduce the production of output (hence, releasing waste) to the level that is regarded as socially optimal if they can somehow find a way of shifting the tax burden onto some other members of the society.

3   Since the penalty to the firms is based on output rather than the waste discharged, a public policy based on a Pigouvian tax that is based on output would provide *no incentive* to firms to search for improved methods of waste disposal.

4   An environmental tax is also to be criticized on the basis of a noneconomic factor. Some economists argue that, by definition, an environmental policy based on *tax* tends to provide too much empowerment to public authorities. The main objection here is not the mere transfer of money from private to public hands, but rather it is the fear that public intervention through its bureaucratic mismanagement may lead to market distortion, hence misallocation of resources. In this sense, *government failure* is a real possibility.

5   Last but not least, as shown in Figure 5.3, a unique tax rate (line segment u–s) is needed to realize the optimal level of output, Q_s, or the optimal environmental quality that corresponds to this output. Thus, as Baumol and Oates (1992) have indicated, the implication of this is that a prior knowledge of the optimal output is needed in order to levy the appropriate level of tax rate. For example, the tax rate would have been

higher (the vertical line u–v instead of u–s) if the tax were determined using the output lever prior to the environmental regulation (Q_e in Figure 5.3). The ultimate effect of this would have been a lower level of paper output (or a higher level of environmental quality) than is socially optimal. The real issue here is the need to know the optimal output, Q_e, prior to imposing the tax, which, because of the additional technological and economic information needed, could be quite costly (more on this in Chapter 12).

5.5 THE MACROECONOMIC EFFECTS OF ENVIRONMENTAL REGULATIONS: AN OVERVIEW

So far we have observed that, if not corrected, environmental externalities will cause a misallocation of resources. More specifically, from a societal viewpoint too many resources (labor, capital and raw materials) will be devoted to the production of goods and services (such as paper, cars, lawn mowers, television sets, restaurants, laundromats, etc.) and not enough resources to the preservation or protection of the environment (such as the atmosphere, the hydrosphere, wilderness areas, animal and plant species, etc.). This is generally recognized as the microeconomic effect of environmental externalities. As discussed above, one way of correcting (internalizing) this is by imposing a penalty on those who are directly responsible for polluting the environment. The Pigouvian type of tax discussed above is one example. For our purposes here, the exact nature of the environmental regulation is not important (an exhaustive study of the various policy instruments used to protect the environment is deferred to Chapters 11 and 12).

However, policies used to internalize environmental externalities could have economy-wide effects. For example, as shown in both Figures 5.2 and 5.3, the socially optimal level of paper is associated with higher price (P_s instead of P_e) and lower level of output (Q_s instead of Q_e). If this is to be viewed as an economy-wide phenomenon, the implication would be that environmental policies may contribute to *inflation* (an increase in the aggregate price of goods and services) and *unemployment* (since less output means less use of labor and capital). These are the possible impacts of environmental regulations on macroeconomic performance. This can be a very serious consideration indeed during an inflationary and/or recessionary period such as the 1970s. A number of economic studies were conducted to offer an empirical estimate of the macroeconomic impacts of environmental regulations (Gary 1987; Portney 1981; Crandall 1981; Denison 1979). In general, the results of these studies were inconclusive. For a recent empirical study of this topic see Case Study 5.1. This case study offers preliminary analyses of the macroeconomic impacts of the Clean Air Act amendments of 1990.

Indeed, an environmental regulation may have the effect of reducing output (hence, increasing unemployment) in the sectors of the economy that are directly affected by the regulation. For example, other factors remaining equal, a tax imposed on the automobile industry for the purpose of protecting the environment is likely to raise the price of cars and perhaps lead to an increase in industry-wide unemployment. However, because the ultimate purpose of the tax is to improve environmental quality, the sectors of the economy that are involved in the cleanup of the environment are likely to be expanding. Thus, the economy-wide effect of environmental regulation on unemployment is unclear since a decrease in employment in a certain sector of an economy could be offset by a gain in other sectors. Some economists even go as far as to claim that cleaning up the environment creates more jobs than it destroys (Hamrin 1975; Sullivan 1992). The reason for this is that, in general, pollution control is relatively more labor-intensive. Others argue that environmental regulations have negative effects on productivity (hence, on aggregate output – GNP) for a variety of reasons. For example, it is argued that pollution control expenditures displace investment in new plant and equipment, and require firms to use some inputs for compliance, hence adversely affecting the rate of increase in labor productivity (Crandall 1981). Furthermore, regulation is believed to increase the uncertainty climate of private industry, hence adversely affecting the level of industry-wide investment.

At least in theory, the *price* or the inflationary effect of environmental regulation seems to be indisputable. This is because environmental policy forces society to take into account costs that would have otherwise been neglected. However, what is not clear is the magnitude of the inflationary effect of environmental regulation. In the United States, several empirical studies seem to suggest that this effect has been very minimal (e.g., Portney 1981). The main reason for this is that the aggregate expenditure on pollution control relative to GNP is quite small. However, for a given sector of the economy, the price effect of environmental regulation may be quite significant. For example, environmental regulation of the textile industry may require a significant increase in the price of textile products while having minimal effect on the aggregate price of goods and services taken as a whole.

To add to the above controversies, more recently Porter has (1990, 1991) hypothesized that strictly enforced environmental policy could have the effect of forcing firms to adopt more efficient production technologies. In the long run, the effect of this would be a reduction in production costs and a further stimulus to the economy (for actual evidence of what is now known as the "Porter hypothesis" see World Resources Institute 1992).

CASE STUDY 5.1 THE ECONOMIC IMPACT: THE 1990 CLEAN AIR ACT AMENDMENTS

Keith Mason

In the recent debate in Congress and the media over a stronger Clean Air Act, questions about the economic implications of the proposed amendments figured prominently. Opinions were aired concerning the costs of the amendments, their potential impacts on employment, and possible ramifications for US industry in international competition.

In large part, the economic debate was triggered by the costs of expanded air-pollution control programs. EPA [the Environmental Protection Agency] and the President's Council of Economic Advisors estimate that the new Clean Air Act will cost approximately $12 billion per year by 1995 – and approximately $25 billion per year when fully implemented in the year 2005. This is in addition to an already extensive level of air-pollution control: EPA estimated that expenditures for air-pollution control were approximately $27 billion annually in 1988.

Considered as a lump sum, this cost is enough to give anyone pause. In fact, however, economic impacts will be widely dispersed over the entire US economy and gradually incurred over a 15-year time period, and when the new requirements are fully phased in, the estimated cost per day will be around 24 cents per person.

However, as with any cost estimate associated with a complicated piece of legislation that must be implemented over an extended period, uncertainty is the rule rather than the exception. Part of the difficulty lies in predicting future methods of pollution control. Air-pollution control technology and the cost of that technology change over time.

Given this, it is even more difficult to predict how increased pollution-control expenditures will affect such economic indicators as employment, growth, productivity and trade. In terms of an approximate $7 trillion economy in the year 2005, $25 billion represents much less than 1 percent of the size of that economy.

Real economic growth and productivity impacts are likely to be small, according to the Council of Economic Advisors. To the extent that productivity gains are decreased slightly, the impact is likely to be transitional and not permanent. The Council has said that some temporary unemployment will result from the act (such as with high-sulfur coal miners), but the new law is not likely to have significant permanent negative effects on aggregate US employment.

Moreover, expenditures on pollution control bolster a growing US industry. The pollution-control industry is an important part of our economy. Expenditures on pollution control create domestic high-skilled jobs (some estimates are that for every $1 billion of air-pollution control expenditure, between 15,000 and 20,000 jobs are created). As an added benefit, the reduced air-pollution levels lead to improvements in worker health and productivity.

As for impacts on international trade, exact studies concerning the impact of the new act on competitiveness have not been completed. However, a preliminary comparison of selected industries among major trading partners indicates that other countries with strong national economies and trade surpluses have relatively greater degrees of air-pollution control for some industries than will be required in the United States under the new Clean Air Act. For instance, sulfur dioxide and nitrogen oxide emission control requirements that will apply to US power plants are less stringent than the controls already in place in Germany. The notion that additional environmental protection necessarily endangers international trade is to date unsubstantiated.

What have been substantiated are the enormous trade opportunities for pollution-control equipment and expertise. The Soviet Union's recent $1 billion order of General Motors pollution-control equipment is just one example.

Source: EPA Journal Vol. 17, Jan./Feb. 1991, pp. 45–7. Reprinted by permission.

5.6 CHAPTER SUMMARY

- This chapter has dealt with concepts and principles fundamental to understanding standard environmental economics.
- It was postulated that the assimilative capacity of the environment (i.e., the ability of the natural environment to degrade waste arising from an economic activity) is in effect *scarce*, and is affected by a number of ecological and technological factors.
- It was observed that, for degradable pollutants such as most municipal wastes, a certain minimum amount of economic goods can be produced without causing damage to the natural environment. The exception to this is the emission of a highly toxic and persistent chemical compound such as DDT. In such a case, a zero level of pollution may be justified – like the ban on DDT in the United States.
- However, given that most economic activities extend beyond the ecological thresholds necessary to keep the integrity of the natural environment intact (beyond X_0 in Figure 5.1), trade-offs between increased economic activity and level of environmental quality become unavoidable.
- It was noted that the search for the "optimal" trade-off between economic and environmental goods requires full consideration of all the relevant *social* costs and benefits. Unfortunately, for environmental resources, this cannot be done through the normal market mechanism for the reasons outlined below:

  1 Environmental resources, such as the atmosphere, all large bodies of water and public lands, are common property resources, and access to them has traditionally been open to all users.
  2 Consequently, environmental resources tend to be prone to *externalities* – incidental costs imposed by a third party.
  3 In the presence of externalities, economic pursuits on the basis of individual self-interest (hence, the private market) do not lead to what is best for society as a whole. This is because a freely operating private market has no automatic mechanism to account for *external costs*. Thus, scarce environmental resources are treated as though they are free goods.
  4 When external costs are unaccounted for, the production of economic goods and services is in excess of what is socially optimal, and the quality of the environment is compromised.

- Alternatively, the above problem could be viewed this way. In the presence of an externality, market prices fail to reflect "true" scarcity value. Price is a measure of "true" scarcity when the market equilibrium price, P_e, is equal to both marginal social cost and marginal social benefit (i.e., P_e = MSC = MSB). However, in the presence of an externality, the market equilibrium price, P_e, is equal to marginal private cost but not the marginal social cost (P_e = MPC < MSC). This is because the market simply ignores the external component of the social cost (MSC = MPC + MEC). Thus, since P_e < MSC, market price fails to reflect "true" scarcity value.

- Once this is understood, a possible solution to this type of externality problem is to find a mechanism which will account for external costs and correct the price distortion.

- A Pigouvian tax – a tax on the output of pollution-generating firms – is an example of such a mechanism. At the socially optimal level of output, P_s = MSC = MPC + t*, where t* is the optimal tax rate and a measure of marginal external cost. Thus, market prices again reflect "true" scarcity. However, finding the optimal tax rate is not an easy matter; and the Pigouvian approach to environmental regulation has several flaws.

- Finally, it was shown that regulating the market to take into account environmental externalities is accompanied by a decline in economic goods and an increase in price. Therefore, one often-raised concern is the *macroeconomic effect* of environmental regulations. In general, environmental regulations are suspected to have a negative effect on the economy for two reasons. First, they increase the private costs of firms. Second, they reduce the productivity of the economy because resources are diverted from the production of goods and services to investment in pollution control. Despite this claim, studies of the effects of environmental policies on macro variables such as GNP, inflation, productivity and unemployment have been inconclusive.

review and discussion questions

1   Briefly identify the following concepts: persistent pollutants, ecological threshold, common property resources, transaction cost, joint consumption, externality, market failure, the "polluter-pays" principle, internalizing externality, government failure, the Porter hypothesis.

2   State *True*, *False* or *Uncertain* and explain why.
   (a) "Everybody's property is nobody's property."
   (b) Waste emission should not exceed the renewable assimilative capacity of the environment.
   (c) While most taxes distort incentives, an environmental tax corrects a market distortion.
   (d) Environmental regulation creates more jobs than it destroys.

3 It makes no sense whatsoever to talk about the "optimal" trade-off between economic goods and environmental quality when this outcome requires a prior knowledge of a *precise* level of tax to be levied on polluters. Comment.

4 In some instances, consideration of "transaction costs" alone could make internalizing an externality (positive or negative) economically indefensible. Can you provide three concrete examples of this nature?

5 Due to concern about "global warming," imagine that the United States is considering doubling its federal tax rate on gasoline. The intent of this bold legislative measure is, of course, to drastically curtail the emissions of greenhouse gases, especially carbon dioxide.

(a) Do you think the measure will succeed? Why or why not?

(b) How would you evaluate this policy measure on the basis of "fairness?" That is, is the effect of the tax neutral with regard to different income groups? If not, what income group(s) do you think will end up paying most of the taxes? Explain.

(c) A member of the United States Congress arguing against the gasoline tax remarked, "It is stupid on our part to think that unilateral action by our country will remedy a global pollution problem." Another congressman countered this argument by saying, "We are the richest nation on the face of the earth. Furthermore, we emit substantially more greenhouse gases than any other nation in the world. It is, therefore, incumbent upon us to take a lead in this noble endeavor to save humanity." Are these two views reconcilable? Why, or why not?

REFERENCES AND FURTHER READING

Baumol, W. and Oates, W. (1988) *The Theory of Environmental Policy*, 2nd edn., Cambridge: Cambridge University Press.

—— (1992) "The Use of Standards and Prices for Protection of the Environment," in A. Markandyna and J. Richardson (eds.) *Environmental Economics: A Reader*, New York: St. Martin's Press.

Coase, R. (1960) "The Problem of Social Cost," *Journal of Law and Economics* 3: 1–44.

Commoner, B., Corr, M. and Stamler, P. J. (1971) "The Causes of Pollution," in T. D. Goldfarb (ed.) *Taking Sides: On Controversial Environmental Issues*, 3rd edn., Sluice Dock, Conn.: Guilford.

Crandall, R. W. (1981) "Pollution Controls and Productivity Growth in Basic Industries," in T. G. Cowing and R. E. Stevenson (eds.) *Productivity Measurement in Regulated Industries*, New York: Academic Press.

Denison, E. P. (1979) *Accounting for Slower Economic Growth: The United States in the 1970s*, Washington, D.C.: Brookings Institution.

Gary, W. (1987) "The Cost of Regulation: OSHA, EPA and Productivity Slowdown," *American Economic Review* 5: 998–1006.

Hamrin, R. (1975) "Are Environmental Regulations Hurting the Economy?," *Challenge* May–June: 29–38.

Hardin, G. (1968) "The Tragedy of the Commons," *Science* 162: 1243–8.

Pearce, D. W. (1978) *Environmental Economics*, 3rd edn., London: Longman.

Porter, M. A. (1990) *The Competitive Advantage of Nations*, New York: Free Press.

—— (1991) "America's Green Strategy," *Scientific American* 168.

Portney, P. (1981) "The Macroeconomic Impacts of Federal Environmental Regulation," in H. M. Peskin, P. R. Portney and A. V. Knees (eds.) *Environmental Regulation and the U.S. Economy*, Baltimore: Johns Hopkins University Press.

Randall, A. (1983) "The Problem of Market Failure," *Natural Resource Journal* 23: 131–48.

—— (1987) *Resource Economics: An Economic Approach to Natural Resource and Environmental Policy*, 2nd edn., New York: John Wiley.

Seneca, J. J. and Taussig, M. K. (1984) *Environmental Economics*, 3rd edn., Englewood Cliffs, N.J.: Prentice-Hall.

Sullivan, T. (1992) *The Greening of American Business*, Rockville, Md.: Government Institutes.

Tietenberg, T. H. (1992) *Environmental and Natural Resource Economics*, 3rd edn., New York: HarperCollins.

Turvey, R. (1963) "On Divergence between Social Cost and Private Cost," *Economica*, August: 309–13.

World Resource Institute (1992) *World Resources 1992–93*, New York: Oxford University Press.

part five

THE PERENNIAL DEBATES ON THE BIOPHYSICAL LIMITATIONS TO ECONOMIC GROWTH

In Part Three, we observed that, from a purely physical viewpoint, natural resources are finite. Furthermore, we learned that the transformation and regenerative capacity of these resources are governed by certain immutable natural laws. For example, the flow of energy is always unidirectional. That is, energy resources cannot be recycled. Another example of these laws is the transformation of matter–energy, which always increases entropy. Hence, pollution is an inevitable by-product of any economic activity. Furthermore, Part Four also showed the formidable economic problems associated with environmental issues. From these two examples alone, it is not hard to envision a situation where, in a finite world, economic growth can be adversely affected (or limited) by either emerging scarcity of terrestrial energy resources or excessive pollution of the natural environment. In other words, there could be ecologically imposed limits to economic growth.

In Part Five, we will systematically explore the association of ecological limits and economic growth. The main questions I would like to address are: Can we expect unlimited economic growth in a world endowed with "finite" resources? If ecological limits are important factors in determining future trends of economic growth, what steps or precautions should be taken in order to avoid transgressing these biophysical limits? Clearly, the key issue here is *scale* – the size of human economy relative to the natural environment. To that extent, the focus is *not* on efficiency but on sustainability.

In the academic world, the nature and the extent of the relationship between economic growth and biophysical limits have been a subject of controversy for well over a century. In the next four chapters, the essence of this controversy is thoroughly and systematically examined. In Chapters 6, 7 and 8, three alternative perspectives to biophysical limits to economic growth are explored, namely the Malthusian viewpoint, the neoclassical approach and ecological economics. In Chapter 9 the economics of sustainable development is presented.

The issue of scale is given a very inadequate treatment in most standard textbooks of environmental and resource economics. In general, topics that relate to this specific issue are placed toward the last section of the text and discussed matter-of-factly. In this book, not only are four chapters devoted to this particular issue, but also, this subject is thoroughly discussed before we embark on serious analyses of and reflections on matters dealing with environmental and resource policy issues relevant to the long-term survival of humanity.

chapter
six

BIOPHYSICAL LIMITS TO ECONOMIC GROWTH:
The Malthusian Perspective

---

learning objectives

After reading this chapter you will be familiar with the following:

- the simple Malthusian economic growth model: population growth, resource scarcity and limits to economic growth;
- modern variations of the Malthusian growth model;
- population and its adverse impact on resource utilization and environmental quality;
- per capita consumption and its influence on resource depletion and environmental quality deterioration;
- the Malthusian perspective on technology and its influence on the population–resource–environment interrelationship;
- the basic policy implications of the Malthusian economic growth model;
- the relevance of the Malthusian growth model to the population, resource and environmental problems facing the contemporary world.

If the present growth trends in world population, industrialization, pollution, food production, and resource depletion continue unchanged, the limits to growth on this planet will be reached sometime within the next one hundred years. The most probable result will be a rather sudden and uncontrollable decline in both population and industrial capacity.

(Meadows *et al.* 1974: 29)

6.1 INTRODUCTION

The designation "Malthusian" here refers to a particular perspective on the association of resource scarcity and the prospect for long-run human economic growth. This perspective has a long history and traces its origin to the original work of an English economist, Thomas R. Malthus (1766–1834) – hence the word Malthusian. The basic postulates of the Malthusian doctrine of resource scarcity and economic growth are as follows:

1 Resources are scarce in absolute terms. That is, humanity is endowed with a *finite* amount of material resources.
2 If uncontrolled, the tendency of human populations is to grow exponentially.
3 Technology should not be perceived as the "ultimate" escape from the problem of resource scarcity.

Given this reality, the Malthusians argue, economic activity cannot be expected to grow indefinitely unless the rates of population growth and/or the rate of resource utilization are effectively controlled. Limits to economic growth could come through either the depletion of key resources and/or large-scale degradation of the natural environment (Meadows *et al.* 1974).

This chapter offers a detailed examination of this so-called Malthusian growth doctrine as it has evolved over time. In the next section, using a simple model the essential elements of the Malthus's original contributions to this doctrine are examined.

6.2 THE SIMPLE MALTHUSIAN GROWTH DOCTRINE: POPULATION AND RESOURCE SCARCITY

The earliest attempt to explain systematically the effect of biophysical limits on human aspirations to improve living standards was manifested by a historical association of population growth and the availability of food and other basic necessities of life. In 1798 Malthus published his book *An Essay on the Principle of Population as It Affects the Future Improvement of Mankind*, possibly the first formal theoretical underpinning for concern with the human population problem. In expounding his population–resource theory, Malthus made the following three postulates: (a) The total amount of land available for agriculture (arable land) is immutably fixed. (b) The growth of population is limited by the amount of food available for subsistence. (c) Human population will invariably increase where the means of subsistence increase.

He then stated that if not prevented by some checks, the tendency is for the population to grow *geometrically* (2, 4, 8, 16, etc.) while the means of subsistence grows *arithmetically* (1, 2, 3, 4, etc.). Unless this tendency of ever-increasing imbalance between the growth rates in population and the means of subsistence is resolved by moral restraints (negative checks such as the postponement of marriage, abstinence from sex, etc.), in the long run vice and misery (positive checks) will ultimately repress the superior power

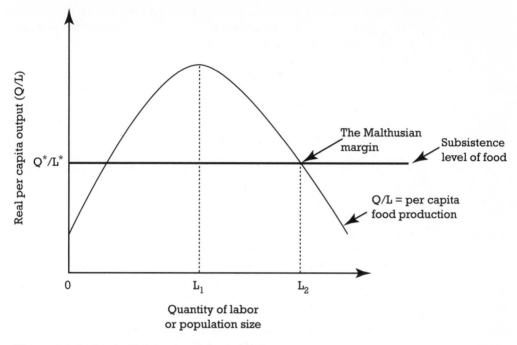

Figure 6.1 **A simple Malthusian growth model**

of a population to a level consistent with the means of subsistence. In other words, population growth, if left unchecked, would lead to the eventual downfall of living standards to a point barely sufficient for survival. This has been called the "dismal doctrine" of Malthus, or, more formally, Malthus's iron law of wages.

The essence of this doctrine can be further captured using a simple graphical approach as shown in Figure 6.1. If we assume that quantity of labor, L, can be used as a proxy for population size and *real* output, Q/L, as a measure of per capita income, Figure 6.1 can be viewed as depicting the relationship between population size and per capita income. This relationship is constructed assuming *fixed* amounts of resource (i.e., land) and technology. Since the intent here is to offer an alternative explanation to the simple Malthusian model discussed above, let output, Q, represent agricultural or food products in general.

In Figure 6.1, per capita food output, Q/L, was initially rising with an increase in population. This positive association between population and per capita food production continued until the population size (labor force) reached L_1. Beyond this point, however, farm labor productivity (measured in terms of output per unit labor service) started to decline with each successive addition of labor service in accordance with the law of diminishing marginal product. Since fertile land is assumed to be fixed in supply, more labor applied to a given plot of a homogeneous quality of land or to a successively less fertile plot of land yields a proportionately smaller return (see Chapter 2 and the discussion on Ricardian rent in Chapter 3). Hence, as the population increases and, accordingly, so does the demand for food and fiber, the production of any additional units of farm output requires progressively larger quantities of labor.

In Figure 6.1, Q^*/L^* – the thick horizontal line – represents the output per unit of labor (or real wage rates) barely sufficient for survival, i.e., the *subsistence* level of food. Thus, when the labor force (i.e., the population) has increased to a level L_2, the Malthusian margin is attained. This will be a stable long-run equilibrium, because for a population below L_2, unless enforceable public policy measures are taken to limit population growth (i.e., negative checks), according to Malthus the natural tendency of the human population is to continue growing as long as the per capita food exceeds the minimum food required for a subsistence life – Q^*/L^*. On the other hand, any increase of population beyond L_2 would be prevented by positive checks, or, to use Malthus's terms, by "vice and misery." Thus, in the long run, disease, malnutrition and famine will bring growth to a halt at L_2. Finally, one interesting feature of the simple model above is its suggestion of an optimum population size (labor force). In Figure 6.1, the *optimum* population size is attained at L_1, where the per capita food level is at its maximum.

Of course, the Malthusian population–resource theory has been subjected to criticism from the very beginning for being too simplistic in several respects. First, it ignores the *institutional factors* that affect population growth. Humans do not just multiply like rabbits. There are social and economic factors that induce humans to check their own population growth under adverse conditions (Cole *et al.* 1973; Simon 1996).

Second, the Malthusian theory simply overlooks the very important role that *technology* plays in ameliorating resource scarcity (Cole *et al.* 1973; Ausubel 1996; Simon 1996). For example, according to the traditional Malthusian view, at a given point in time the amount of land available for food is perceived as fixed (or scarce in absolute terms). But through improvements in farming technology (for example, finding new crop varieties with genetic engineering), it may be possible to produce more food from the same amount of land. In addition, technology may make farming possible in an area where it was impossible before. In Figure 6.1, the effect of a technological change, either through a discovery of new land or through improvement in farming, would be to shift the average product curve (Q/L) outward. Hence, this would move the "Malthusian margin" to the right. *In a sense, then, the effect of technological change is to make the Malthusian margin a moving target.* However, this fact alone will not be sufficient to contradict Malthus's main assertion that, in the long run, humanity is predestined to the attainment of subsistent life (Hardin 1993).

Third, Malthus's model is considered to be *ecologically* naive. That is, it does not go beyond recognizing the existence of absolute limits to natural resources (land), and thereby fails to explain the effect of economic growth on the natural ecosystem and its inhabitants as a whole. Thus, the simple Malthusian theory on population and resource is viewed as incomplete from economic, technological and ecological perspectives.

Despite its simplicity, however, Malthus's theory on population and resources and, in particular, its gloomy prediction about the long-run economic destiny of humankind have remained an issue of vigorous contention even to this day. On the one hand, it would be easy to dismiss the theory and its predictions on the ground that almost two hundred years have passed since the formal pronouncement of Malthus's gloomy prophecy, and yet our experience has been characterized by a rapid growth in resource uses and population growth, along with significant improvements of material standards of living on a per capita basis. On the other hand, it is difficult to completely discredit Malthus since the main thrust of his dismal forecast is still applicable and of major concern to most developing and under-developed nations of the world. In this sense, after two hundred years, the Malthusian specter is still with us (for some recent evidence see Exhibit 6.1).

EXHIBIT 6.1 FEEDING THE WORLD: LESS SUPPLY, MORE DEMAND AS SUMMIT CONVENES

Charles J. Hanley

Decade by decade, the land has provided – wheat fields, rice paddies, bulging silos of corn keeping pace with a growing world population. But now the grain harvests have leveled off, the people have not, and the world is left to wonder where next century's meals will come from. The blip in the upward slope of grain production in the 1990s has ready explanations: Economics, politics and weather conspired to hold down global output.

But some specialists believe longer-range forces, from the Kansas prairie to China's river deltas, are also at work – and the outlook is troubling. Troubling enough, in Africa particularly, for the Food and Agriculture Organization to hold a global summit in Rome this week to search for new approaches to help poor nations grow, buy or otherwise get more food.

"We are in a crisis situation," said FAO chief Jacques Diouf. His UN agency projects world agricultural production must expand by 75 percent by 2025 to match population growth. It's not off to a good start. New FAO figures show that the global grain harvest – forecast at 1,821 million tons for 1996–97 – will have increased by 2.3 percent since 1990, while population was growing 10 percent. . . . Because of this lag in production, grain prices rose and the world's buffer stocks of wheat, rice and other grains were drawn down. Reserves now stand at 277 million tons – some 40 million below what is needed to meet emergencies. A mix of factors helped stunt the decade's crops.

Lester Brown of Washington's Worldwatch Institute maintains that fertilizers and high-yield grain varieties have been pushed to their limit in many places. . . . [In addition] Worldwatch sees China as a huge problem. Shrinking croplands, rising incomes and a growing appetite for meat – an inefficient means for passing along the calories of grain – have combined to turn China, almost overnight, into the world's No. 2 grain importer, behind Japan. "It is only a matter of time until China's grain import needs overwhelm the export capacity of the United States and other exporting countries," Brown contends.

On the broader, global point, the World Resource Institute, a Washington think tank, finds some agreement among major studies that birth rates may slow enough to allow a plodding agriculture to keep up with "effective" demand – the demand from consumers with the money to buy. But that projection comes with asterisks attached: In Africa and other poor regions without that money, hundreds of millions will remain underfed.

To Luther Tweeten, the outcome is far from clear. Looking ahead to 2030, the Ohio State University agricultural economist stacked the global trend in per-acre yield – rising ever more slowly – up against UN population projections. The yields lose out. "I don't want to take a Lester Brown approach on this," Tweeten said, but the world cannot be complacent. "It's daunting."

The FAO estimates 800 million people are undernourished worldwide, at a time when high prices have undercut international food aid, slicing it in half since 1993 to today's 7.7 million tons of grain a year. The summit will try to encourage increased aid, stepped-up research and pro-agriculture policies in Africa and other food-short regions.

But Brown sees another solution – population control. "I think we're now in a new situation where the primary responsibility for balancing food and people lies with family planners, rather than fishermen and farmers," he said. "And I don't think the world has quite grasped that yet."

Source: Kalamazoo (MI), *Kalamazoo Gazette/The Associated Press*, November 10, 1996. Copyright © 1996 The Associated Press. Reprinted by permission.

6.3 MODIFIED MALTHUSIAN MODELS: POPULATION, RESOURCE USE AND ENVIRONMENTAL QUALITY

Over time, the Malthusian theory on population and resources has undergone several refinements. Responding to the criticisms raised by both economists and ecologists, neo-Malthusians have been able to develop conceptual models that incorporate the effects of technology and human institutions on their considerations of both population growth and resource availability (Ehrlich and Holdren 1971; Commoner *et al.* 1971). In this section, the essence of these models is illustrated by using a general conceptual framework that is hereafter referred to as the *Ehrlich–Commoner Model*. The primary purpose of using this model is to develop, inasmuch as possible, the basic elements essential for understanding the causal relation-ships between population growth, resource depletion and pollution – which are believed to be the ultimate causes for limits to economic growth. This is done in an effort to consider technological factors explicitly. It is important to note that while the model bears the joint name of two highly distinguished environmentalists, it is wrong to think that these scholars share a common view on the adverse impacts of population growth on resource use and the environment. On the contrary, their positions on this issue are markedly different.

The Ehrlich–Commoner model starts with the postulate that all human activities modify the natural environment to some extent (Ehrlich and Holdren 1971). In its simplest form, this model can be mathematically expressed as follows:

$$I = P \times F \qquad (6.1)$$

where the variable I represents the *total* environmental effect or damage measured in some standard unit, P is a variable representing population size in terms of head count, and F is an index that measures the per capita impact (or damage) to the environment.

Equation (6.1) formally states that, at any given point in time, the total environmental impact of human activities is a product of the underlying population size, P, and the per capita damage to the environment, F. In other words, total environmental impact equals total population multiplied by the average impact that each individual person has on the environment. However, this function does not tell us what factors determine the per capita impact, F, or whether or not population size and per capita impact are interrelated. In other words, a good deal of complexity is masked in the above model. Thus, to make this simple model more revealing and of some practical value, we need to further examine the per capita impact as a separate function that is affected by several key variables as expressed below:

$$F = f[P, c, t, g(t)] \qquad (6.2)$$

where c indicates per capita consumption or production, t represents technology and g refers to the composition or the mix of material inputs or output used in an economy.

Thus, when we take equations (6.1) and (6.2) together, we see that the total environmental impact, I, of human activities depends on total population, P, and a host of other interrelated variables affecting the *per capita* damage function. Given this, the challenge before us is to explain, in a systematic fashion, the relative significance of the key variables indicated in these two equations in terms of their contributions to the total environmental impact, I. For example, is population the major contributor to environmental degradation? To what extent would an increase in per capita consumption of resources adversely impact the environment? In what ways can technology be used to ameliorate the environmental impact of economic activities? Can technology contribute to further environmental deterioration? In the next two subsections attempts are made to address these specific questions.

6.3.1 Population and its impact on resource utilization and environmental quality

According to Paul Ehrlich, population plays a *primary* role in explaining the impact human activities have on the environment and resource use. He argues that when population grows, the total impact, I, increases for two reasons. First, the size of the population, P, will increase. Second, for reasons to be explained below, per capita impact, F, increases with successive additions to population, P. Therefore, according to equation (6.1), the total impact increases since both P and F grow with expansions in population. This is illustrated in Figure 6.2.

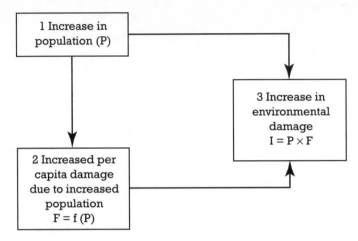

Figure 6.2 **Ehrlich's model: the impact of population on the environment**

Why is the per capita damage, F, an increasing function of population? Ehrlich gave the law of diminishing marginal returns as a plausible explanation to this phenomenon. He argued that most of the developed nations' economies are already operating at high levels of production capacity. These nations are, therefore, on the diminishing returns part of their production activities. Furthermore, the same argument can be made for the agricultural sectors of most developing countries. For most of these nations the agricultural sector accounts for a significant percentage of their economy, and diminishing returns would be encountered because of the limited availability of farmland.

Under these circumstances, if other factors are held constant, successive addition of people would require increased use of resources, such as energy, water, fertilizer, pesticides, and other renewable and nonrenewable resources. Thus, as a population continued to grow, the per capita impact, in terms of resource depletion and environmental deterioration, would increase successively.

The major weakness of the above position advanced by Ehrlich is that many of the factors already identified as having an effect on per capita impact, F, such as per capita consumption of resources, technology and product mix, are held *constant*. Furthermore, no explanation is given as to why these factors should have neutral and insignificant effects on per capita damage, F. This is evident in Figure 6.2 since per capita impact, F, is shown to be a function of only population. Thus, in the next subsection an attempt will be made to examine the validity of Ehrlich's theory on population and the environment when explicit consideration is given to changes in per capita consumption. This will be followed by a consideration of technology.

6.3.2 Per capita consumption and its influence on the population–resource–environment interrelationship

Per capita consumption, c, refers to the amount of goods and service consumed per person, per unit of time – generally a calendar year. At the aggregate level, consumption can be viewed as being equivalent to production. Thus, per capita consumption may be used as a measure of the well-being or affluence of the average person. Would a change in per capita consumption, c, directly and significantly affect the per capita impact, F? This is really an empirical question, but let us first provide a general explanation of the expected relationship between per capita consumption, c, and per capita impact, F.

If population, consumer preference and technology are held constant, an increase in per capita consumption, c, could only result from increased use of resources. Increased resource utilization implies increased production, and in the absence of technological progress this would translate into increased pollution and perhaps resource depletion. Thus, in general, we would expect that *an increase in per capita consumption would be associated with increased per capita damage, F* (see Figure 6.3). This observation has a number of interesting implications.

First, suppose that as proposed by Ehrlich, the per capita damage, F, is an increasing function of population, P. Then, an increase in per capita consumption, c, *reinforces* the negative impact that a population increase has on per capita damage to the environment. In this case, because population, P, and per capita consumption, c, affect the per capita damage function, F, in the *same* direction (see Figure 6.3), it would be difficult to isolate the *independent* effects of these two variables (P and c) on the per capita damage function, F, without undertaking a full-blown empirical test. This poses a serious challenge to Ehrlich's unequivocal assertion that population growth

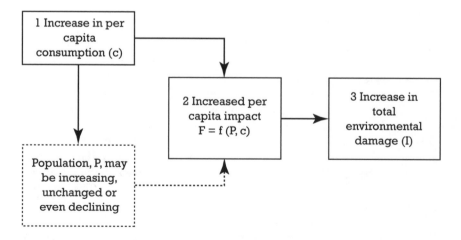

Figure 6.3 **Per capita consumption and its effect on the environment**

is the single most dominant factor in explaining the total environmental impact, I. *In other words, one cannot relegate the impact of per capita consumption, c, to a minor role, as Ehrlich seems to have done, without solid empirical evidence.*

Second, as stated above, if an increase in per capita consumption, c, leads to an increase in per capita damage to the environment, F, *it is easy to envision a situation where the total environmental impact, I, may be increasing while population, P, remains unchanged or even declining.* In other words, in equation (6.1), P and F may move in opposite directions, causing uncertainty in the direction of the total impact, I. This supports the argument often made by some scholars that the main culprit of environmental deterioration and resource depletion is *overconsumption* (Durning 1992). If this has any validity, it suggests that some of the most serious global environmental problems have been caused by the phenomenal growth in per capita resource consumption in the developed nations (more on this in Chapter 18).

6.3.3 Technology and its influence on the population–resource–environment interrelationship

Let us now turn to examining how changes in technology, t, may affect human impact on the natural environment – a variable that has been held constant in the analysis so far. Technological changes have relevance here to the extent that they can be used to conserve resources in the following two specific ways: (a) *economies of scale*, which can be attained through efficient, combined use of production and organizational capacities; and (b) *technical progress*, which implies the use of entirely new techniques in production. How do changes of this nature affect the population–resource–environment interrelationship?

Economies of scale

Formally, economies of scale are present when a simultaneous increase in inputs (all inputs) leads to a more than proportionate increase in output; for example, doubling all inputs more than doubles outputs. Evidently, *the advantage of scale is best exploited with an increase in output production.* Basically, the idea is that population growth, by increasing demand for output, allows these economies of scale to be exploited (Simon 1996). Where this holds true, an increase in population (labor force) would be accompanied by increasing gains in production efficiency. Under these circumstances, if other factors remain constant, *an increase in population could lead to a decrease in the per capita environmental impact, F.* That is, when economies of scale are present, successive additions of people to the labor force (population) require less of all resources on a per capita output basis. If the resource savings from economies of scale are significant, *it is possible to observe a decrease in the total impact of the environment, I, when population is actually increasing.* That is, in equation (6.1), an increase in population, P, could be more than offset by the decrease in the per capita impact, F, resulting from economies of scale.

Here again, Ehrlich's pronouncement that population growth causes a disproportionate negative impact on the environment and resource utilization is, if not invalidated, put in doubt. Yet Ehrlich is not entirely invalidated, because economies of scale are realized within a limited scope. As Meade (1967: 235) puts it:

> It is not sufficient merely that there should still be scope for increasing returns to scale for a rise in the population in itself to lead to a rise in output per head. There are increasing returns to scale if a 1% increase in every factor input – in land and natural resources and in capital equipment as well as in labor – would cause more than 1% increase in total output; but this does not ensure that a 1% increase in labor alone will cause a more than 1% increase in total output; the scope for increasing returns to scale will have to be very marked for this to be so.

Thus, unless the size of population is an irrelevant issue, a country may not be in a position to increase its population indefinitely in equal proportion to all its resources or vice versa. If this is the case, sooner or later, as Ehrlich anticipated, diminishing returns will take effect.

Technical progress

For our purposes, technical progress specifically refers to scientific discovery and its technical application to industry and management. Technical progress is generally attained through changes in input and output mixes, but not necessarily changes to the *scale* of operations. Economies of scale are neither a necessary nor a sufficient condition for technical progress to occur (Nicolson 1998). Thus, the fact that productivity can be enhanced through technical progress without any consideration of *scale* means that technical progress is the method by which diminishing returns could be overcome. What should be obvious from this discussion is that technical progress, in general, refers to the kinds of advancement by which productivity is enhanced. That is, less inputs are used to produce the same level of output (see Chapter 3). Viewed this way, the impact of technical progress on the population–resource–environment interrelationship would be similar to our discussion above regarding economies of scale. That is, *the possibility exists that even with an increase in population, technical progress could lead to a decrease in per capita damage, F.* Note that this decrease in per capita damage would be realized because the productivity increase due to technical progress would be accompanied by potential resource savings. *If the magnitude of this per capita impact is significant, it would be possible to observe a decrease in the total negative impact on the environmental quality, I, while population is still increasing.*

Unfortunately, the effect of technical progress on resource utilization and the environment does not end with this positive note. In some intellectual circles, modern technology is viewed as being the main source of environmental problems emanating from the developed nations. Barry Commoner has been the leading advocate of this position. Commoner's position against modern technology has to be differentiated from that of Ehrlich, however. Ehrlich has little faith in "technological fixes" because he believes that most industrial nations are already on the diminishing returns part of their economic activities. In other words, technological fixes suffer from a limitation of certain key resources. On the other hand, Commoner *views modern technology as being ill-conceived and not wisely applied in the production of goods and services.* Why is Commoner taking this position? What evidence does he rely upon?

In order to understand Commoner's antitechnological position, it is important to understand that technical progress is often attained by changing the compositions, or mix, of inputs and outputs for an economy. According to Commoner, the decision to change the composition of economic inputs and outputs is made purely on the basis of profit motives. Therefore, input and output decisions are made on the basis of technical efficiency (increased per capita production), rather than the impacts these decisions may possibly have on the environment (see Chapter 5). To illustrate this, consider how Commoner (1971: 101) depicted the outcomes of technical progress in industrial nations. In their rush to increase productivity, industrial nations have been engaged in excessive use of "synthetic organic chemicals and the products made from them, such as detergents, plastics, synthetic fibers, rubbers, pesticide and herbicide, wood pulp and paper products; total production of energy, especially electric power; total horsepower of prime movers, especially petroleum-driven vehicles; cements; aluminum; mercury used for chlorine production; petroleum and petroleum products." This suggests that changes in the composition of material inputs and outputs, variable $g(t)$ in equation (6.2), have the effect of increasing the per capita damage to the environment, F. Thus, according to Commoner, technological responses to population pressure (increase in P) invariably lead to increased *total* environmental damage, I (since $I = P \times F$). Furthermore, to Commoner, the most significant portion of total environmental damage in contemporary industrial nations arises not from population increases, P, but from increases in per capita impact, F, resulting from changes in the mix of inputs and outputs, $g(t)$.

This is indeed a serious indictment of modern technology, and it requires an empirical justification. Aware of this, Commoner made a serious effort to substantiate his thesis on technology and the environment using data from the United States for the period 1946–68. On the basis of this data analysis, he reached the conclusion "the predominant factor in our industrial society's increased environmental degradation is neither population, nor affluence (per capita consumption), but the increasing environmental impact per unit of production due to technological changes" (Commoner *et al.* 1971: 107). Moreover, Commoner *et al.* made the following general observations:

On these grounds it might be argued as well that the stress of a rising human population on the environment is especially intense in a country such as the United States, which has an advanced technology. For it is modern technology which extends man's effects on the environments for air, food, and water. It is technology which produces smog and smoke; synthetic pesticide, herbicides, detergent, plastics; rising environmental concentrations of metals such as mercury and lead; radiation, heat; accumulating rubbish and junk.

(ibid.: 97)

Of course, the above quotation is somewhat dated, and for this reason its relevance for our current situation may be questioned. However, even at the present time there exists a widely held belief that modern technology has been more successful in *shifting* the environmental impact than in removing it. Indeed, over the past two decades most industrial nations have been able to ameliorate some of their environmental problems, especially at the local and regional levels. No doubt, stricter environmental regulation and advances in emission control technologies have played a major part in making such environmental improvements possible. However, in some cases a closer look at some of the technological solutions that brought relief to local pollution problems seem to have caused pollution problems that cross regional and international boundaries. For example, requiring coal-burning electric power plants in the Midwest to install smoke stacks might alleviate local pollution problems, but improvement in the local environment would be achieved at the expense of increased acid precipitation in the northeastern United States and in Canada (Soroos 1997). In essence, then, in the new era, the scope of environmental and resource concerns is becoming increasingly global, as are issues like ozone holes, global warming, tropical deforestation and depletion of well-known commercial fish species.

6.3.4 The basic lessons of the Ehrlich–Commoner model

One of the major lessons that we have learned from the discussion so far is that *it is very difficult to delineate the population–resource–environment inter-relationship clearly*. Despite this, using a simple conceptual framework we have been able to identify some elements critical in tracing the adverse effects of population growth on resource utilization and the quality of the environment.

First, we observed that population, through its size and growth, has adverse impacts on resource utilization and the environment. This statement seems to be supported by a number of empirical studies (Allen and Barnes 1995; Repetto and Holmes 1983; Rudel 1989). For example, in his empirical investigation on the causes of deforestation, Thomas K. Rudel (1989: 336) reported the following as one of his findings: "The analysis provides empirical support for the Malthusian idea that population growth contributes to high rates of deforestation both directly (by increasing the population which clears the land) and indirectly (by increasing the demand for wood products in a country)." In spite of this, there seems to be no complete agreement on the relative magnitude of the negative impact(s) that growing population may have on the condition of natural resources, in both quantitative and qualitative terms. For instance, Ehrlich and his followers would contend that rising human population is a predominant factor for accelerating pollution and other resource problems in both the developed and the developing nations of the world. On the other hand, to Commoner and his associates, population growth plays only a minor role in explaining the environmental and resource condition of the modern era, especially in the economically advanced regions of the world.

Second, even in the presence of a stable population, increases in per capita consumption could lead to rapid resource depletion and the deterioration of the environment (more on this in Chapter 18).

Third, the assortment of economic activities pursued by a nation, and the resulting composition of production and consumption in response to population pressure, could significantly intensify the resource and environmental problems for a country. This would be especially true for countries where the institutions for effective environmental regulations are not well developed or simply lacking (see Chapter 5). According to Commoner, this is the primary cause for rapid increase of pollution in the United States and other industrial nations.

Last but not least, as Exhibit 6.2 suggests, the application of technology to solve environmental and resource problems arising from population pressure should be subjected to careful scrutiny. Applications of ill-conceived technology could do harm, rather than solve environmental and resource problems.

EXHIBIT 6.2   BEYOND SHIVA

Garrett Hardin

If, as European folk wisdom has it, each new mouth brings with it a pair of hands, how are we to view the fantastic changes brought about by the industrial–scientific revolution of the past two hundred years or so? Have we not now reached a stage at which each new mouth comes into the world with more than a single pair of hands? The woolgathering mind may recall statues of the Indian god Shiva, with his many (most commonly four) lively arms and busy hands.

If scientists were inclined to take up new gods (which they are not), Shiva would be a fine one for representing science and technology ("custom" in Bacon's language). Even before Malthus, technology began to increase the output of human hands (through such inventions as the wheelbarrow), but the change did not catch people's attention for a long time. Everyone is aware of it now. Especially in the developed world it has become obvious that material income per capita has increased greatly. The Shiva of Western technology is indeed a many-handed god.

As the beneficiaries of more than two centuries of rapid growth of science and technology, the masses cannot easily be persuaded that they should be worried about the future of population and the environment. Yet we would do well to remember that the Hindus' Shiva is a god of both creation and destruction. It is not without reason that we perceive a many-handed god as uncanny and frightening.

Source: Living within Limits: Ecology, Economics, and Population Taboos (1993: 100–1). Copyright © 1993 by Oxford University Press, Inc. Reprinted by permission.

6.4 HAS MALTHUS BEEN DISCREDITED?

Even in such a revised version of the simple Malthusian model, where the impacts of technology and human institutions are considered explicitly, the long-run prospects of the human predicament remain unaltered and gloomy. Malthusians of all stripes are of one mind in their belief that *biophysical limits* to economic growth are real, and they continue to support this hypothesis through numerous studies.

In the early 1970s, using a computer simulation, the authors of a highly controversial book, *The Limits to Growth* (Meadows *et al.* 1971), clearly demonstrated the various scenarios under which the industrial world would encounter limits. The basic conclusion of the book was used as the epigraph to this chapter. To repeat it, "If the present growth trends in world population, industrialization, pollution, food production, and resource depletion continue unchanged, the limits to growth on this planet will be reached sometime within the next one hundred years. The most probable result will be a rather sudden and uncontrollable decline in both population and industrial capacity" (p. 29). Although controversial, the frightful warning of the book was taken seriously, as it reflected the consensus view of a group of influential scientists and world leaders. A decade later, in response to the energy crisis of the late 1970s, a study was commissioned by the administration of President Carter in order to conduct a thorough and comprehensive assessment of global resource adequacy. The final outcome of this study was published under the heading *The Global 2000 Report to the President* (Council on Environmental Quality and Department of State 1980: 1). The major conclusions of this report read as follows:

If present trends continue, the world in 2000 will be more crowded, more polluted, less stable ecologically, and more vulnerable to disruption than the world we live in now. Serious stresses involving population, resources, and environment are clearly visible ahead. Despite greater material output, the world's people will be poorer in many ways than they are today.

For hundreds of millions of the desperately poor, the outlook for food and other necessities of life will be no better. For many it will be worse. Barring revolutionary advances in technology, life for most people on earth will be more precarious in 2000 than it is now – unless the nations of the world act decisively to alter current trends.

Clearly, this report basically echoed the conclusion pronounced a decade earlier by *The Limits to Growth*. In addition, there are a number of other recent empirical studies that reinforce the general conclusions reached by *The Global 2000 Report to the President*. In particular, it is worth mentioning the various publications periodically issued by the Worldwatch Institute – an independent nonprofit environmental resource organization. These publications include the annual *State of the World*, which is now published in twenty-seven languages; *Vital Signs*, an annual compendium of global trends of key environmental and natural resource variables; the Environmental Alert book series; *World Watch* magazine; and the Worldwatch Papers series. The Worldwatch Institute is guided by its able and energetic leader, Lester Brown, and the primary aim of this private establishment's publications is to provide in-depth quantitative and qualitative analysis of the major issues affecting prospects for a sustainable society.

How should we deal with this seemingly perennial Malthusian specter? To most scholars of a Malthusian persuasion, the problem cannot be adequately addressed until we fully recognize the existence of biophysical limits on continued improvements to material living standards. Once this fact is acknowledged, the remedy to this age-old problem will be quite apparent. Specifically, economic growth that is sustainable far into the future will necessitate the design and implementation of social and technological conditions that ensure both environmental and economic stability concurrently (Meadows *et al.* 1974). More on this in Chapter 9: "The Economics of Sustainable Development."

In terms of policy options, Malthusians would prescribe strict control on population growth and environmental pollution, and advocate adjusting the per capita consumption of goods and services to a level consistent with "basic" material needs. Furthermore, since resource scarcity with the passage of time is taken for granted, Malthusians require the current generation to make a material sacrifice so that the well-being of succeeding generations is not unduly compromised.

Generally, Malthusians have a tendency to perceive that both the population and the pollution problems involve the use of scarce resources that are held in common by everyone in society. These commonly owned resources include the atmosphere, all large bodies of water, and a large number of publicly owned lands. In the case of population the problem is viewed as "taking something out of the commons"; that is, extracting or harvesting resources from the commons to feed, clothe and house a growing number of humans. On the other hand, the problem of pollution is viewed as "putting something in" the commons, such as industrial, agricultural and household wastes (Hardin 1993). Thus, the resolution to both the population and the environmental problems requires the use of effective mechanisms to deal with real external costs or benefits.

For this reason, generally, Malthusians have a skeptical view of the market. Their skepticism is based on the general tendency of the private market, as discussed in Chapter 5, toward overexploitation and degradation of common property resources. On the other hand, Malthusians do not rule out the using of "coercive" methods as a means of controlling population growth or ameliorating environmental degradation (Hardin 1993). This could include formal and effectively enforced legal sanctions such as fines or imprisonment.

6.5 CHAPTER SUMMARY

- This chapter has dealt with analyses of the Malthusian perspective on "general" resource scarcity and its implications for the long-term material well-being of humanity.
- This perspective has a long history and it starts with the premise that natural resources are *finite* and, therefore, will eventually limit the progress of the human economy.
- This conclusion is further reinforced by the observation that, historically, human population and per capita resource consumption have grown *exponentially*. The key feature of exponential growth is that it seems to start slowly and then continues fast. Malthusians, therefore, stress the danger of exponential growth (Ehrlich and Holdren 1993).
- Malthusians typically manifest their concerns in terms of the eventual depletion of some key, but conventionally identified, natural resource (such as oil, gas, arable land, uranium, etc.).
- Malthusians are generally skeptical about the ability of technology to circumvent biophysical limits for two reasons:

  1 They believe that technological progress is subject to diminishing returns.
  2 They are mindful of the long-run costs of technological cures. Some even take the position that malign technologies are the major culprit in the modern environmental crisis.

- In searching for solutions, Malthusians favor tightly regulated demand management – a reduction in the demand for resources. This includes population control and a reduction in per capita resource consumption.
- In general, Malthusians tend to emphasize *population control* as a key policy variable. They believe that if human society fails to address the population problem effectively, the future outlook is bleak.
- For Malthusians, concern for the well-being of future generations is paramount. This requires abandonment of our long-held "exponential-growth culture, a culture so heavily dependent upon the continuance of exponential growth for its stability that it is incapable of reckoning with problems of nongrowth" (Hubbert 1993: 125).

review and discussion questions

1 Briefly identify the following concepts: negative and positive checks to population growth, exponential growth, the Malthusian margin, the Malthusian notion of subsistence survival, real per capita output, technical progress, economies of scale.

2 State *True*, *False* or *Uncertain* and explain why.

(a) The connection between population growth and environmental damage is undeniable. More people cause increasing damage to the environment.

(b) It is inadequate to identify the "optimal" level of population solely in terms of its correspondence to the maximum real per capita output (such as L_1 in Figure 6.1).

(c) Economies of scale are neither a necessary nor a sufficient condition for technical progress to occur.

3 Malign technology, not population growth or affluence, has been primarily responsible for today's global population problems. Critically comment.

4 The isolated and sporadic instances of hunger that we continue to witness in parts of our contemporary world do not support the Malthusian theory. These events are caused not by population pressure but by poor global distribution of resources. Do you agree? Why, or why not?

5 Garrett Hardin (1993: 94) wrote, "[even though] John Maynard Keynes had the highest opinion of his contributions to economics, Malthus continues to be bad-mouthed by many of today's sociologists and economists. The passion displayed by some of his detractors is grossly disproportionate to the magnitude of his errors. A conscientious listing of the explicit statements made by Malthus would, I am sure, show that far more than 95 percent of them are correct. But for any writer who becomes notorious for voicing unwelcome 'home truths' a correctness score of 95 percent is not enough." In your opinion, is this a convincing and substantive defense of Malthus? Discuss.

REFERENCES AND FURTHER READING

Allen, J. C. and Barnes, D. F. (1995) "The Causes of Deforestation in Developed Countries," *Annals of the Association of American Geographers* 75, 2: 163–84.

Ausubel, J. H. (1996) "Can Technology Spare the Earth?," *American Scientist* 84: 166–77.

Cole, H. S. D., Freeman, C., Jahoda, M. and Pavitt, K. L. R. (1973) *Model of Doom: A Critique of the Limits to Growth*, New York: Universe Books.

Commoner, B., Corr, M. and Stamler, P. (1971) "The Causes of Pollution," in T. D. Goldfarb (ed.) *Taking Sides: Clashing Views on Controversial Environmental Issues*, 3rd edn., Sluice Dock, Conn.: Guilford.

Council on Environmental Quality and the Department of State (1980) *The Global 2000 Report to the President: Entering the Twenty-first Century, 1980*, Washington, D. C.: U.S. Government Printing Office.

Durning, A. T. (1992) *How Much Is Enough?*, Worldwatch Environmental Alert Series, New York: W. W. Norton.

Ehrlich, P. R. and Holdren, J. P. (1971) "Impact of Population Growth," *Science* 171: 1212–17.

Hardin, G. (1993) *Living within Limits: Ecology, Economics, and Population Taboos*, New York: Oxford University Press.

Hubbert, K. M. (1993) "Exponential Growth as a Transient Phenomenon in Human History,"in H. E. Daly and K. N. Townsend (eds.) *Valuing the Earth: Economics, Ecology, Ethics*, Cambridge, Mass.: MIT Press.

Meade, E. J. (1967) "Population Explosion, the Standard of Living and Social Conflict," *Economic Journal* 77: 233–55.

Meadows, D. H., Meadows, D. L., Randers, J. and Behrens, W. W. III (1974) *The Limits to Growth: A Report for the Club of Rome's Project on the Predicament of Mankind*, 2nd edn., New York: Universe Books.

Nicolson, W. (1998) *Microeconomic Theory*, 7th edn., Fort Worth: Dryden Press.

Repetto, R. and Holmes, T. (1983) "The Role of Population in Resource Depletion in Developing Countries," *Population and Development Review* 9, 4: 609–32.

Rudel, T. K. (1989) "Population, Development, and Tropical Deforestation: A Cross-national Study," *Rural Sociology* 54, 3: 327–37.

Simon, J. L. (1996) *The Ultimate Resource 2*, Princeton, N.J.: Princeton University Press.

Soroos, M. S. (1997) *The Endangered Atmosphere: Preserving a Global Commons*, Columbia: University of South Carolina Press.

Worldwatch Institute (1997) *Vital Signs 1997*, New York: W. W. Norton.

chapter
seven

BIOPHYSICAL LIMITS TO ECONOMIC GROWTH:
The Neoclassical Economic Perspective

---

learning objectives

After reading this chapter you should be familiar with the following:

- fundamental premises of the neoclassical economic perspective of natural resource scarcity;
- why neoclassical economists are skeptical about the gloom-and-doom prophecies of the Malthusian variations;
- why the finiteness or absolute scarcity of natural resources should not be viewed as an ultimate deterrent to continued economic growth;
- the significance of differentiating between "general" and "specific" natural resource scarcity;
- the empirical evidence against the classical doctrine of increasing resource scarcity over time;
- some of the major criticisms of the neoclassical economists' empirical evidence for increasing natural resource abundance and their unguarded optimism concerning continued rapid resource-saving technical progress;
- the neoclassical perspectives of population and environmental problems.

The existence of a finite stock of a resource that is necessary for production does not imply that the economy must eventually stagnate and decline. If there is continual resource augmenting technical progress, it is possible that a reasonable standard of living can be guaranteed for all time. But even if we postulate an absence of technical progress we must not overlook substitution possibilities. If there are reasonable substitution possibilities between exhaustible resources and reproducible capital, it is possible that capital accumulation could offset the constraints on production possibilities due to exhaustible resources.

(Dasgupta and Heal 1979: 197)

7.1 INTRODUCTION

As is evident from Chapters 1–3, the neoclassical economic perspective of natural resource scarcity, allocation and measurement is based on the following distinguishing postulates: (a) Nothing rivals the market as a medium for resource allocation. (b) Resource valuation depends only on individual "preferences" and initial endowments as determinants of prices. (c) For privately owned resources, market prices are "true" measures of resource scarcity. (d) Price distortions arising from externalities can be effectively remedied through appropriate institutional adjustments. (e) Resource scarcity can be continually augmented by technological means. (f) Human-made capital (such as machines, buildings, roads, etc.) and natural capital (such as forests, coal deposits, wetland preserves, wilderness, etc.) are *substitutes*.

On the basis of these fundamental premises, most neoclassical economists have traditionally maintained a strong skepticism toward gloom-and-doom prophecies pertaining to the future economic condition of humanity. In fact, from the perspective of neoclassical economics it is tautological and therefore uninteresting to say that resources are becoming increasingly scarce given that resources are assumed to be available in geologically fixed quantity while population continues to grow (Rosenberg 1973). Instead, the real issue of significance should be to understand the circumstances under which technological progress will continue to ameliorate resource scarcity. And this should be done with a belief that, under the right circumstances, technology will continue not only to spare resources but also to expand our niche (Ausubel 1996). Indeed, this view is in sharp contrast to the characteristically gloomy Malthusian position on technology and resource scarcity.

This chapter consists of the neoclassical economics *responses* to the Malthusian perspective on limits to economic growth. For them, the fundamental issue to be addressed in this is not so much the existence of *biophysical limits*, but rather how, through technological progress and appropriate institutional arrangements, such limits can be overcome. To understand the essence of this position, this chapter starts by questioning the fundamental assumptions of Malthusians regarding human wisdom, resource scarcity and technology.

7.2 RESOURCE SCARCITY, TECHNOLOGY AND ECONOMIC GROWTH

As already stated, most neoclassical economists have maintained a strong tradition of skepticism concerning gloom-and-doom prophecies pertaining to the future economic condition of humanity. The belief has been that while economic fluctuations (or business cycles) are a normal occurrence in a dynamic economy, the overall economic trend of the past two centuries, worldwide, has been nothing but upward. Thus, even during the early 1970s, when the concern for energy and the environment was intense, the call for drastic and fundamental changes in our economic institutions to adjust for an impending resource crisis was not taken seriously by neo-classical economists. This is because, as discussed in Chapters 2 and 3, mainstream economists hold an unshakable belief in human ability to make adjustments in technology, resource substitution and consumption habits to overcome potential natural resource limits on economic growth.

Basically, mainstream economists provide the following two explanations for the gloomy Malthusian disposition. First, Malthusians are generally predisposed to view humankind as having a natural propensity for self-destruction. As a result of this, they tend to underestimate human wisdom and instinctive capability for self-preservation (Cole *et al.* 1973; Simon 1980). Second, scholars of a Malthusian persuasion have the strong tendency to lump all resources together without regard to their importance, ultimate abundance or substitutability (Simon 1996). When these factors are considered, what matters is not that terrestrial resources are finite – *absolute scarcity* (for an expanded discussion on this issue read Exhibit 7.1). Malthusians simply do not comprehend the possibility of there being an infinite amount of resource substitutability, even in a world with a finite resource endowment (Goeller and Weinberg 1976).

EXHIBIT 7.1 RESOURCES, POPULATION, ENVIRONMENT: AN OVERSUPPLY OF FALSE BAD NEWS

Julian Simon

The supplies of natural resources are finite. This apparently self-evident proposition is the starting point and the all-determining assumption of such models as *The Limits to Growth* [Meadows *et al.* 1974] and of much popular discussion.

Incredible as it may seem at first, the term "finite" is not only inappropriate but downright misleading in the context of natural resources, from both the practical and the philosophical points of view. As with so many of the important arguments in this world, this one is "just semantic." Yet the semantics of resource scarcity muddle public discussion and bring about wrongheaded policy decisions.

A definition of resource quantity must be operational to be useful. It must tell us how the quantity of the resource that might be available in the future could be calculated. But the future quantities of a natural resource such as copper cannot be calculated even in principle, because of new lodes, new methods of mining copper, and variations in grades of copper lodes; because copper can be made from other metals, and because of the vagueness of the boundaries within which copper might be found – including the sea, and other planets. Even less possible is a reasonable calculation of the amount of future services of the sort we are now accustomed to get from copper, because of recycling and because of the substitution of other materials for copper, as in the case of the communications satellite.

With respect to energy, it is particularly obvious that the earth does not bound the quantity available to us; our sun (and perhaps other suns) is our basic source of energy in the long run, from vegetation (including fossilized vegetation) as well as from solar energy. As to the practical finiteness and scarcity of resources – that brings us back to cost and price, and by these measures history shows progressively decreasing rather than increasing scarcity.

Why does the word "finite" catch us up? That is an interesting question in psychology, education and philosophy; unfortunately there is no space to explore it here.

In summary, because we find new lodes, invent better production methods and discover new substitutes, the ultimate constraint upon our capacity to enjoy unlimited raw materials at acceptable prices is knowledge. And the source of knowledge is the human mind. Ultimately, then, the key constraint is human imagination and the exercise of educated skills. Hence an increase of human beings constitutes an addition to the crucial stock of resources, along with causing additional consumption of resources.

Source: *Science* Vol. 268, 1980, pp. 1435–6. Copyright © American Association for the Advancement of Science, 1980. Reprinted by permission.

Thus, if human wisdom and resource availability are taken in their proper perspective, the possibility of exhausting a particular resource (or set of resources) should not be a cause for alarm, since as a resource(s) becomes less abundant (or scarce), its price relative to other resources will start to increase. If this situation persists, the search for a substitute resource will be activated. The theoretical justification of this line of reasoning is provided by Harold Hotelling's (1931) groundbreaking work on optimal natural resource depletion. The basic tenet of this theory is that in a perfectly competitive market environment, the expectation is that increasing resource scarcity will be accompanied by a steady increase in price that will eventually lead to appropriate substitutions (more on this in Chapter 17). Thus, through this process markets will automatically determine the optimal rate of resource exploitation.

Furthermore, mainstream economists offer abundant empirical evidence of where scarcity of a particular resource has been averted (or ameliorated) through technological progress, especially during the past two centuries. The earliest attempt of this nature was made in a book published in 1963, *Scarcity and Growth: The Economics of Natural Resource Availability*. The authors of this book, Barnett and Morse, were members of President Truman's Commission on Materials Policy whose mission was to investigate the validity of a widespread public perception of future material shortage in the United States following the Second World War. This study was a carefully and ingeniously designed statistical trend analysis for the United States, and it encompasses the period dating from the Civil War (1870) to 1957. Barnett and Morse used these data to test the validity of a core principle of the Malthusian doctrine: the inevitability of "increasing resource scarcity with a passage of time."

7.3 THE CLASSICAL DOCTRINE OF INCREASING RESOURCE SCARCITY: THE EMPIRICAL EVIDENCE

In their analysis Barnett and Morse defined increasing scarcity as increasing *real cost*, which is measured by the amount of labor and capital required to produce a unit of extractive resources. They put forward the following hypothesis:

> The real cost of extractive products per unit will increase through time due to limitations in the available quantities and qualities of natural resources. Real cost in this case is measured in terms of labor (man-days, man-hours) or labor plus capital per unit of extractive output.
>
> (Barnett 1979: 165)

Barnett and Morse refer to this postulate as the *strong* hypothesis of increasing economic scarcity. It suggests that increasing resource scarcity will be evident if, over time, an increasing trend of labor and capital per unit of extractive output, $(aL_E + bK_E)/Q_E$, is observed (see Figure 7.1). Note that L_E and K_E represent the labor and capital used in the extractive sectors of the economy, and Q_E represents the aggregate output of the extractive sectors (which include agriculture, fishing, forestry and mining). The parameters a

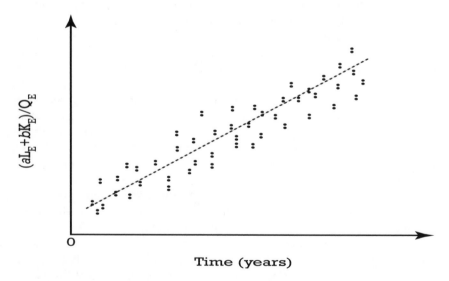

Figure 7.1 **The strong hypothesis of increasing natural resource scarcity**

and *b* are the weight factors of labor and capital, respectively. Note that the "real cost" as defined here is very similar to the Ricardian rent, discussed in Chapter 3. In both instances the idea is to find a *physical* measure of resource scarcity.

Using the above model specification, Barnett and Morse proceeded with their extensive statistical trend analysis, and concluded the following:

> The U.S. output in extractive sectors (which includes agriculture, forestry, fishing, and mining) increased markedly from the Civil War to 1957, yet the statistical record fails to support, and in fact is contradictory to, the classical hypothesis. Real costs per unit of extractive goods, measured in units of labor plus capital, did not rise. They fell, except in forestry (which is less than 10% of extraction). In fact, the pace of decline in real cost . . . accelerated following World War I, compared with the preceding period.
>
> (Barnett 1979: 166)

How can a rapidly developing nation such as the United States, that has experienced strong economic and population growth, not yet experienced increasing economic scarcity of natural resources? This should not be totally surprising because of the rapid technological progress experienced during the period under consideration. Specifically, there was increased efficiency of resource use, in particular energy (see Exhibit 7.2), substitution of more plentiful resources for the less plentiful ones, improvements in transportation and trade, and improvements in exploration techniques and the discovery of new deposits, as well as increased recycling of scraps.

EXHIBIT 7.2 ENERGY

Jesse H. Ausubel

Energy systems extend from the mining of coal through the generation and transmission of electricity to the artificial light that enables the reader to see this page. For environmental technologists, two central questions define the energy system. First, is the efficiency increasing? Second, is the carbon used to deliver energy to the final user declining?

Energy efficiency has been gaining in many segments, probably for thousands of years. Think of all the designs and devices to improve fireplaces and chimneys. Or consider the improvement in motors and lamps. About 1700 the quest began to build efficient engines, at first with steam. Three hundred years have increased the efficiency of generators from 1 to about 50 percent of the apparent limit, the latter achieved by today's best gas turbines. Fuel cells can advance efficiency to 70 percent. They will require about 50 years to do so, if the socio-technical clock continues to tick at its established rate. In 300 years, physical laws may finally arrest our engine progress.

Whereas centuries measure the struggle to improve generators, lamps brighten with each decade. A new design proposes to bombard sulfur with microwaves. One such bulb the size of a golf ball could purportedly produce the same amount of light as hundreds of high-intensity mercury-vapor lamps, with a quality of light comparable to sunlight. The current 100-year pulse of improvement . . . will surely not extinguish ideas for illumination. The next century may reveal quite new ways to see in the dark. For example, nightglasses, the mirror image of sunglasses, could make the objects of night visible with a few milliwatts.

Segments of the energy economy have advanced impressively toward local ceilings of 100 percent efficiency. However, modern economies still work far from the limit of system efficiency because system efficiency is multiplicative, not additive. In fact, if we define efficiency as the ratio of the theoretical minimum to the actual energy consumption for the same goods and services, modern economies probably run at less than 5 percent efficiency for the full chain from primary energy to delivery of the service to the final user. So, far from a ceiling, the United States has averaged about 1 percent less energy to produce a good or service each year since about 1800. At the pace of advance, total efficiency will still approach only 15 percent by 2100. Because of some losses difficult to avoid in each link of the chain, the thermodynamic efficiency of the total system in practice could probably never exceed 50 percent. Still, in 1995 we are early in the game.

Source: *American Scientist* Vol. 84, 1996, pp. 166–76. Copyright Sigma Xi, the Scientific Research Society 1996. Reprinted by permission.

However, on the basis of what has been discussed thus far, what is not clear is the impact of technology on the extractive sector, *relative* to the nonextractive sector. Intuitively, the inclination would be to assume that, due to stringent resource constraints imposed by nature, the extractive sector would encounter diminishing returns at a much lower output level than the nonextractive sector. If this is the case, one would expect the impact of technological growth on the extractive sectors to be less than for the nonextractive sectors of the economy. Or, as Barnett (1979: 170) put it:

> While the tendency for real costs of extractive output to rise as a result of increasing scarcity is more than offset by the dynamic forces in the economy, nonetheless, the resulting rate of decline in real costs of extractive goods may be less than the rest of the economy.

The above statement constitutes what Barnett and Morse referred to as the *weak* hypothesis of increasing economic scarcity. Given this postulate, then, increasing scarcity can be empirically tested by examining the trend of the ratio of labor and capital per unit of the extractive sector, and labor and capital per unit of the nonextractive sector of the economy – that is, $[(aL_E + bK_E)/Q_E] /[(aL_N + bK_N)/Q_N)]$. (Note that the subscript N denotes the nonextractive sector of the economy.) Therefore, if the weak hypothesis is valid, then the trend of the unit cost of extractive goods relative to non-extractive resources will resemble that shown in Figure 7.2.

However, contrary to this expectation, Barnett and Morse concluded that "the weak hypothesis fails in all extraction, agriculture, and minerals. Costs per unit of output in these sectors decline no less rapidly than in the economy at large. Only in forestry is the weak scarcity hypothesis

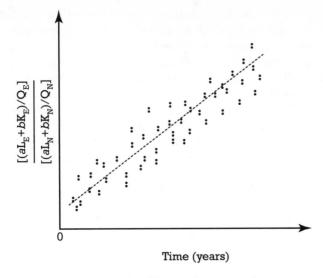

Figure 7.2 **The weak hypothesis of increasing natural resource scarcity**

supported." In fact, in most instances, the rate of decline in unit costs was more pronounced in the extractive sectors than for the economy as a whole (that is, the reverse of the expected trend that is depicted in Figure 7.2).

Thus, according to this study, both the strong and the weak hypotheses are consistent in contradicting the classical doctrine of increasing scarcity with the passage of time; the only exception is forestry. In fact, the empirical evidence in both the strong and weak hypotheses is suggestive of decreasing resource scarcity. It is important, however, to note that this conclusion is strictly applicable to the United States and at a specific moment in its history. As such, it would be inappropriate to generalize global resource conditions from the results of this case study. Despite its limited scope, this study occupies a special significance in setting a framework for analyzing general resource scarcity through empirical means.

7.4 EMERGING RESOURCE SCARCITY OR ABUNDANCE: THE RECENT EVIDENCE

In terms of public awareness of ecological limits and its various implications, in many ways the 1970s were watershed years. Fittingly, the 1970s are often referred to as the environmental decade. The first Earth Day was celebrated in April 1970. This event was significant since it clearly marked the beginning of environmental awareness throughout the world. During that same year, the United States instituted a new government agency, the Environmental Protection Agency (EPA). This agency, with a cabinet-level status, was established with the primary mandate of protecting the ambient environment of the nation. During the 1970s a number of books and articles were published warning the public about impending natural resource scarcity in the not too distant future. The most influential of these publications was *The Limits to Growth*, first published in 1971 (see Meadows *et al.* 1974). Although controversial, the frightful warning of the book was taken seriously because the study was supported by the Club of Rome, which is composed of a large group of well-reputed scientists from around the world. Of course, both the Arab oil embargo of 1973 (a result of the Arab–Israeli War) and the 1978 energy shortage (a result of a unilateral decision by OPEC, the Organization of Petroleum Exporting Countries, to limit petroleum supply) clearly demonstrated the vulnerability of the industrial nations' economies to a prolonged shortage of a key, but finite resource: petroleum.

Among standard economics practitioners, the events of the 1970s brought a renewed interest in the Barnett and Morse approach for empirically testing the evidence of alleged emerging global resource scarcity. In the late 1970s several attempts were made to empirically study recent trends of resource scarcity. Manely Johnson *et al.* (1980) updated the original findings of Barnett and Morse and reexamined the strong and weak hypotheses by extending the period under consideration from the Civil War up to 1970. Kerry Smith (1979) analyzed the United States data from 1900 to 1973, using a more sophisticated statistical technique. While Smith was somewhat critical of Barnett and Morse's work on purely methodological grounds, the overall results and conclusions of the above studies were very much consistent with the findings of Barnett and Morse, namely, that the United States' experience is still indicative of decreasing resource scarcity with passage of time. But, again, these studies are confined to the economic performance of one nation. The question that still remains unanswered is: Can the United States' experience be generalized to other nations?

In 1978, Barnett, using the published time series data from the United Nations, made similar studies for various nations of the world. For each specific nation, on the basis of the available data, the trend analysis failed to support the strong hypothesis of increasing scarcity for minerals, and the weak hypothesis, too, is not supported in most cases by the evidence. In fact, all the results pertaining to the strong hypothesis are consistent with the opposite hypothesis: that is, increasing resource availability. However, as Barnett (1979: 185) himself suggested, "these international results should be regarded as preliminary, since the series involved are only available for short periods (since post World War II) and, in several of the cases, of questionable quality."

Again, in 1982, Barnett *et al.* examined data through 1979. At this time, there was some evidence of increasing scarcity in the 1970s, but this was attributed to the changing market structure in general and the OPEC cartel in particular.

The overall implication of the above studies is that aggregate global and United States economic trends are improving. Thus, the bad news of the 1970s (pollution, energy crises, acceleration in the rates of soil erosions, desertifications, deforestations, etc.) was not indicative of emerging resource scarcity. If anything, such events have to be taken as a temporary setback. Common beliefs assert that these problems, if envisioned properly, would be solved through institutional adjustments and technological means. To use the old adage, "necessity is the mother of invention." This particular belief is reaffirmed in a controversial book written in the early 1980s by Julian L. Simon and Herman Kahn, *The Resourceful Earth: A Response to Global 2000*:

> We are confident that the nature of the physical world permits continued improvement in humankind's economic lot in the long run, indefinitely. Of course there are always newly arising local problems, shortages and pollution, due to climate or to increased population and income. Sometimes temporary large-scale problems arise. But the nature of the world's physical conditions and the resilience in a well-functioning economic and social system enable us to overcome such problems, and the solutions usually leave us better off than if the problem had never arisen; that is the great lesson to be learned from human history.
>
> (Simon and Kahn 1984: 3)

The Resourceful Earth, as indicated by its subtitle, is written as a critical response to *The Global 2000 Report to the President* (Council on Environmental Quality and Department of State 1980). As discussed in Chapter 6, the conclusions of this neo-Malthusian report were very frightening. Simon and Kahn's response to such gloomy conclusions was quite drastic. In most parts, relying on statistical trend analyses similar to those developed by Barnett and Morse, their general conclusion was that "for the most relevant matters we have examined, aggregate global and U.S. trends are improving rather than deteriorating." In addition, in response to the specific conclusions reached by *The Global 2000 Report*, Simon and Kahn (1984: 1) asserted:

> If present trends continue, the world in 2000 will be less crowded (though more populated), less polluted, more stable ecologically, and less vulnerable to resource-supply disruption than the world we live in now. Stresses involving population, resources, and the environment will be less in the future than now. . . . The world's people will be richer in most ways than they are today. . . . The outlook for food and other necessities of life will be better . . . [and] life for most people on earth will be less precarious economically than it is now.

Under this worldview, then, distributional concerns, especially those relating to intergenerational equity, would not be warranted. As William J. Baumol, a prominent economist, wrote, "in our economy if past trends and current developments are any guide, a redistribution to provide more for the future may be described as a Robin Hood activity stood on its head – it takes from the poor to give to the rich. Average real per capita income a century hence is likely to be a sizeable multiple of its present value. Why should I give up part of my income to help support someone else with an income several times my own?" (Baumol 1968: 800).

Finally, while the empirical studies of Barnett and Morse and several others are vividly suggestive of decreasing scarcity with the passage of time, can we generalize from these studies about impending scarcity of natural resources in the foreseeable future? Contrary to these cornucopian views, the answer to this question is quite uncertain for the following four reasons.

First, the very idea that long-run scarcity of natural resources can be empirically assessed by looking at economic indicators is logically flawed (see Norgaard 1990). Also, an updating of the original work by Barnett and Morse (1963) using new models of resource scarcity appears to suggest reconsideration of their original conclusions (Hall and Hall 1984). Clearly, then, both the conceptual basis and the robustness of the empirical findings of models of the Barnett and Morse variety are questionable.

Second, studies based on statistical trends do not make explicit environmental quality considerations. This is because the prices for environmental goods might have been significantly undervalued due to externalities. Thus, because of this omission, one might argue that – over the past half-century – the changes in the patterns of extraction have increased the effective supply of the material input components of natural resources (i.e., natural resource commodities), while reducing the amenity and life-support services of these same resources. That is, the greater degree of technological substitution possibilities that has been evident in the past might have come from the increasing replacement of priced goods and services for unpriced goods, services and amenities (Brown and Field 1979).

Third, during the period when the above-mentioned empirical studies were conducted, major transformations in the use of energy had occurred. More specifically, higher-quality fuels displaced the use of lower-quality fuels – first coal replaced wood, and then oil and natural gas replaced coal. According to Culter Cleveland (1991), it was this type of substitution of high-quality fuels that reduced the labor–capital costs of extractive sectors in the United States as depicted in the Barnett and Morse study. In other words, the decline in real costs of resource extraction observed by empirical studies of the Barnett and Morse type was not due to technological changes *per se*, but rather due to the substitution of higher-quality energy resources for labor and capital in the extraction of resources.

To verify this, Cleveland conducted an empirical study analogous to that of Barnett and Morse. More specifically, he calculated the quantities of direct and indirect fuels used to produce a unit of resource in the United States extractive sectors (mining, agriculture, forest products and fisheries industries) using this approach: $Q/(E_d + E_I)$, where Q is the total extractive output and E_d and E_I are the direct and indirect energy used to extract the resource in question. Thus, a general trend that showed a decline in the output per unit of energy input (i.e., the productivity of energy input) would indicate an increase in physical scarcity or an increase in energy cost per unit of output. This is because as high-quality resources were depleted, more energy would be needed to further extract a unit resource. For most recent years, between 1970 and 1988, the results of Cleveland's empirical findings indicated increasing scarcity in the metal mining, energy extraction, forestry and fishery sectors of the United States economy. The exception to this has been the nonmetal industry.

Fourth, as will be discussed in the next chapter, the laws of thermodynamics impose certain limits on the substitution of human capital for natural resources. This implies that there is a physical limit to the ability of technological change to offset the depletion or degradation of energy (see Exhibit 7.3).

Furthermore, the pace of technical progress over the past has been uneven. In fact, "a disproportionate fraction of technological improvements during the past 5000 years has been concentrated over the last 300 years or so" (Dasgupta and Heal 1979: 206). Given this, it would be dangerous to use past evidence and merely extrapolate into the future. If this point is taken seriously, *rapid* resource-saving technical progress of the kind experienced in the past two hundred years does not necessarily imply continued technical progress in the future.

7.5 ECONOMIC GROWTH, THE ENVIRONMENT AND POPULATION: THE NEOCLASSICAL PERSPECTIVE

So far, little, if anything, has been said about the environment specifically. To what extent is continued economic growth consistent with maintaining a healthy environmental quality? Should not increased economic activities that accompany economic growth generate an increased level of pollution, and hence greater environmental stress? The standard response of neoclassical economists to these equations is straightforward. They argue that significant improvements in environmental quality are fully compatible with economic growth for the following reasons:

First, one of the benefits of economic growth is an increase in per capita income. Higher per capita income will increase the demand for improved environmental quality. This means increased expenditures on environmental cleanup operations.

Second, continued improvement in pollution abatement technology will not allow the cost of environmental cleanup to grow without bound. That is, in a healthy and growing economy, growth in pollution abatement expenditures will be continually moderated by technological advances. Furthermore, even if this is not the case, increase in pollution cleanup expenditure need not be a major concern unless it is a large proportion of the GNP. In general, expenditures on pollution abatement are a very small portion of GNP.

According to the above arguments, therefore, economic growth is more likely to be good than bad for the environment. Furthermore, this hypothesis has been supported by a general empirical observation on the relationship between per capita income and environmental quality (Grossman and Krueger 1996). The specific claim has been that increase in per capita income is initially encountered by worsening environmental conditions up to a certain point, which is then followed by improvement in environmental quality – a relationship that is graphically portrayed by an "inverted U." Taken at its face value, what this suggests is that a country has to attain a certain standard of living before it starts to respond to its concern for improved environmental quality. The "inverted U" is sometimes referred to as the "environmental Kuznets curve" because of its similarity to the relationship between per capita income and income inequality first postulated by Simon Kuznets (1955).

Recently, the "inverted U" or the so-called "environmental Kuznets curve" hypothesis has been criticized for a number of reasons (Rothman and de Bruyn 1998; Torras and Boyce 1998). The main arguments raised against the hypothesis have been most effectively summarized by Rothman and de Bruyn (1998: 144) as follows: (a) The inverted-U curve has been found for only a few pollutants, mainly those that have local health effects and can be dealt with without great expense. (b) The existing empirical work focuses on the relationship between income and emissions, or concentration of pollution, which, due to the stock nature of many environmental problems, does not fully account for environmental impacts. For example, ecological dimensions such as carrying capacities and ecosystem resilience capacities have been ignored (Arrow *et al.* 1995). (c) Not all current empirical studies support the hypothesis. (d) No good explanations have been given as to the reasons why pollutants ease downwards after a certain income level has been reached. In this regard, a recent empirical study by Torras and Boyce (1998), which includes more explanatory variables than income alone, found that social factors such as income equality, wider literacy and greater political liberties tend to have a significant positive effect on environmental quality, especially in the low-income countries.

The above deficiencies do not in themselves discredit the "inverted U" hypothesis. They caution us, however, against viewing economic growth as the prescribed remedy to environmental problems in developing nations.

What about the population problem? The neoclassical economists also believe that economic growth is not only good for the environment, but also a cure for a nation's population problem. This contention is supported by what is commonly known as the theory of demographic transition. This theory is based on an empirical generalization and it claims that, as nations develop, they eventually reach a point where the birth rate falls (Leibenstein 1974). In other words, in the long run, the process of industrialization is accompanied by a sustained reduction in population growth. This is because the increase in income of the average family in the course of industrialization reduces the desire for more children.

This empirically observed negative relationship between household income and family size is supported by systematic microeconomic explanations. The microeconomic theory of human fertility specifically deals with the issue of how parents make decisions about childbearing, and how this choice is influenced by the family's income (Becker 1960). (See Chapter 18 for more extensive discussions of both the theory of demographic transition and the microeconomic theory of human fertility.)

In general, the following reasons are given for the negative association between increases in a nation's average income and the rate of its population growth:

1 As a nation advances economically, it can afford to provide its people with improved health care facilities. The effect of this is to reduce infant mortality. With a decline in infant mortality people are less likely to have a desire for a big family.

2 As families become increasingly wealthier, their needs for using children as a hedge for old age security become less important.

3 Continued economic progress provides increased opportunities for mothers (and, in general, for females) to work for income. It also increases the need for more highly educated citizens. Thus, considerations of both the increase in the opportunity cost of the mother and the cost of educating a child cause families to desire a smaller number of children (see Exhibit 7.3).

EXHIBIT 7.3 FALLING BIRTH RATES SIGNAL A DIFFERENT WORLD IN THE MAKING

Michael Specter

Stockholm, Sweden – Mia Hulton is a true woman of the late twenieth century. Soft-spoken, well educated and thoughtful, she sings Renaissance music in a choral group, lives quietly with the man she loves and works like a demon seven days a week.

At 33, she is in full pursuit of an academic career. Despite the fact that she lives in Sweden, which provides more support for women who want families than any other country, Hulton doesn't see how she can possibly make room in her life for babies – someday maybe, but certainly not soon.

"There are times when I think perhaps I will be missing something important if I don't have a child," she said slowly, trying to put her complicated desires into simple words. "But today women finally have so many chances to have the life they want – to travel and work and learn. It's exciting and demanding. I just find it hard to see where the children would fit in."

Hulton would never consider herself a radical, but she has become a cadre in one of the fundamental social revolutions of the century.

Driven largely by prosperity and freedom, millions of women throughout the developed world are having fewer children than ever before.

They stay in school longer, put more emphasis on work and marry later. As a result, birthrates in many countries are now in a rapid, sustained decline.

Never before – except in times of plague, war and deep economic depression – have birthrates fallen so low, for so long.

There is no longer a single country in Europe where people are having enough children to replace themselves when they die. Italy recently became the first nation in history where there are more people over the age of 60 than there are under the age of 20. This year Germany, Greece and Spain probably will cross the same eerie divide.

The effects of the shift will resonate far beyond Europe. Last year Japan's fertility rate – the number of children born to the average woman in a lifetime – fell to 1.39, the lowest level it has ever reached.

In the United States, where a large pool of new immigrants helps keep the birth rate higher than in any other prosperous country, the figure is still slightly below an average of 2.1 children per woman – the magic number needed to keep the population from starting to shrink.

Even in the developing world, where overcrowding remains a major cause of desperation and disease, the pace of growth has slowed almost everywhere.

Since 1965, according to United Nations population data, the birthrate in the Third World has been cut in half – from 6 children per woman to 3. In the last decade alone, for example, the figure in Bangladesh has fallen from 6.2 children per woman to 3.4. That's a bigger drop than in the previous two centuries.

Source: *Kalamazoo Gazette/New York Times*, July 10, 1998. Copyright © 1998 by The New York Times. Reprinted by permission.

The upshot is clear. According to neoclassical economists, it is more, not less, economic growth that is needed to ameliorate both the population and the environmental problems that nations are facing. However, what is missing here is explicit consideration of biophysical limits based on a global perspective. Can the world resource base and the environment in particular support indefinite economic growth on a global scale? The idea that this may not be possible is the reason behind the recent revival in ecological economics and sustainable development – the subjects of the next two chapters.

7.6 CHAPTER SUMMARY

- In this chapter we discussed the neoclassical economic perspective on "general" resource scarcity and its implications for the long-term material well-being of humanity.
- Neoclassical economists do not reject outright the notion that natural resources are *finite*. However, unlike the Malthusians, they do not believe that this fact implies that economic growth is limited. Neoclassical economists uphold this position for five reasons:

  1 They believe that technology – by finding substitutes, through discovery of new resources, and by increasing the efficiency of resource utilization – has almost no bounds in ameliorating natural resource scarcity.
  2 They differentiate between "general" and "specific" natural resource scarcity. To them, general or absolute scarcity (that is, the awareness that there is "only one Earth" and that it is a closed system with regard to its material needs) is tautological, therefore uninteresting. What is relevant is scarcity of specific resources, or relative scarcity.
  3 However, relative scarcity does limit growth, due to the possibility of factor substitution.
  4 In sharp contrast to the Malthusians, neoclassicists believe that economic growth, through increases in per capita income and improvements in technology, provides solutions to environmental and population problems.
  5 Neoclassical economists believe in the effectiveness of the market system to provide signals of emerging resource scarcity in a timely

fashion. Price distortions arising from externalities simply require a minor fine-tuning of the market.

- Given that societal resources are allocated by a smoothly functioning and forward-looking market, the key resource for continued human material progress is *knowledge*. It is through knowledge that human technological progress (a necessary ingredient for circumventing biophysical limits) will be sustained indefinitely.
- Thus, the best inheritance to leave to posterity is knowledge in the form of *education* (stored information about past discoveries) and *physical capital*.
- This is done without concern about the nature of the capital inherited by future generations, because for the neoclassical paradigm, human-made capital (roads, factories and so on) and natural capital (forest, coal deposits, wilderness, etc.) are substitutes. Much human progress, especially that of the past two centuries, has stemmed from the substitution of human-made for natural capital.
- According to the neoclassical growth paradigm, this process will continue into the future. Therefore, future humans' material progress will be determined primarily by the pace of technological growth. Given the evidence of the past two centuries, the expectation is for a brighter future. Furthermore, this prognosis is independent of the fact that natural resources are finite.

---

review and discussion questions

1 Briefly identify the following concepts: absolute scarcity, extractive resources, real cost, the strong and weak hypotheses of increasing natural resource scarcity, the "inverted U" hypothesis, the environmental Kuznets curve, the theory of demographic transition.

2 State *True*, *False* or *Uncertain* and explain why.

    (a) Since resources have substitutes, "nature imposes *particular* scarcities, not an inescapable *general* scarcity."

    (b) Rising per capita income will ultimately induce countries to clean up their environment. Thus, economic growth can be prescribed as the remedy to environmental problems.

    (c) Improved social and economic status for women is the key to controlling population growth.

3 "The major constraint upon the human capacity to enjoy unlimited minerals, energy, and other raw materials at acceptable price is knowledge. And the source of knowledge is the human mind. Ultimately, then, the key constraint is human imagination acting together with educated skills. This is why an increase in human beings, along with causing additional consumption of resources, constitutes a crucial addition to the stock of natural resources" (Simon 1996: 408). Do you agree? Why, or why not?

4   Do you see a parallel between the concept of Ricardian rent discussed in Chapter 3 and real cost of extractive resources as defined by Barnett and Morse in the present chapter? Explain.

5   Studies of long-run scarcity of natural resources of the Barnett and Morse variety are primarily criticized for the following two reasons: (a) They fail to make explicit consideration of environmental quality concerns. (b) They fail to account for the substitution of high-quality energy resources for labor and capital that has been taking place in the extraction sectors. Are these valid criticisms? Explain.

REFERENCES AND FURTHER READING

Arrow, K., Bolin, B., Costanza, R. *et al.* (1995) "Economic Growth, Carrying Capacity, and the Environment," *Science* 268: 520–1.

Ausubel, J. H. (1996) "Can Technology Spare the Earth?," *American Scientist* 84: 166–77.

Barnett, H. J. (1979) "Scarcity and Growth Revisited," in K. V.Smith (ed.) *Scarcity and Growth Reconsidered*, Baltimore: Johns Hopkins University Press.

Barnett, H. J. and Morse, C. (1963) *Scarcity and Growth: The Economics of Natural Resource Availability*, Baltimore: Johns Hopkins University Press.

Barnett, H., Van Muiswinkel, G. M. and Schechter, M. (1982) "Are Minerals Costing More?" *Resource Manag. Optim.* 2: 121–48.

Baumol, W. J. (1968) "On the Social Rate of Discount," *American Economic Review* 58: 788–802.

Becker, G. (1960) "An Economic Analysis of Fertility," in National Bureau of Economic Research, *Demographic and Economic Changes in Developing Countries*, Princeton, N.J.: Princeton University Press.

Brown, G., Jr., and Field, B. (1979) "The Adequacy of Measures of Signalling the Scarcity of Natural Resources," in K. V. Smith (ed.) *Scarcity and Growth Reconsidered*, Baltimore: Johns Hopkins University Press.

Cleveland, C. J. (1991) "Natural Resource Scarcity and Economic Growth Revisited: Economic and Biophysical Perspective," in R. Costanza (ed.) *Ecological Economics: The Science and Management of Sustainability*, New York: Columbia University Press.

Cole, H. S. D., Freeman, C., Jahoda, M. and Pavitt, K. L. R. (1973) *Models of Doom: A Critique of the Limits to Growth*, New York: Universe Books.

Council on Environmental Quality and Department of State (1980) *The Global 2000 Report to the President: Entering the Twenty-first Century*, Washington, D.C.: US Government Printing Office.

Dasgupta, P. S. and Heal, G. M. (1979) *Economic Theory and Exhaustible Resources*, Cambridge: Cambridge University Press.

Goeller, H. E. and Weinberg, A. M. (1976) "The Age of Substitutability: What Do We Do When the Mercury Runs Out?" *Science* 191: 683–9.

Grossman, G. M. and Krueger, A. B. (1995) "Economic Growth and the Environment," *Quarterly Journal of Economics* 110: 353–77.

—— (1996) "The Inverted U: What Does It Mean?" *Environmental and Development Economics* 1: 119–22.

Hall, D. C. and Hall, J. V. (1984) "Concepts and Measures of Natural Resource Scarcity with a Summary of Recent Trends," *Journal of Environmental Economics and Management* 11: 363–79.

Hotelling, H. (1931) "The Economics of Exhaustible Resources," *Journal of Political Economy* 39: 137–75.

Johnson, M. and Bennett, J. T. (1980) "Increasing Resource Scarcity: Further Evidence," *Quarterly Review Economics and Business* 20: 42–8.

Johnson, M., Bell, F. and Bennett, J. (1980) "Natural Resource Scarcity: Empirical Evidence and Public Policy," *Journal of Economic and Environmental Management* 7: 256–71.

Kuznets, S. (1955) "Economic Growth and Income Inequality," *American Economic Review* 45: 1–28.

Leibenstein, H. (1974) "An Interpretation of the Economic Theory of Fertility: Promising Path or Blind Alley?," *Journal of Economic Literature* 22: 457–79.

Meadows, D. H., Meadows, D. L. Randers, J. and Behrens, W. W. III (1974). *The Limits to Growth: A Report for the Club of Rome's Project on the Predicament of Mankind*, 2nd edn., New York: Universe Books.

Norgaard, R. B. (1990) "Economic Indicators of Resource Scarcity: A Critical Essay," *Journal of Environmental Economics and Management* 19: 19–25.

Rosenberg, N. (1973) "Innovative Responses to Materials Shortages," *American Economic Review* 63: 111–18.

Rothman, D. S. and de Bruyn, S. M. (1998) "Probing into the Environmental Kuznets Curve Hypothesis," *Ecological Economics* 25: 143–5.

Simon, J. L. (1980) "Resources, Population, Environment: An Oversupply of False Bad News," *Science* 208: 1431–7.

—— (1996) *The Ultimate Resource 2*, Princeton, N.J.: Princeton University Press.

Simon, J. L. and Kahn, H. (1984) *The Resourceful Earth: A Response to Global 2000*, Oxford: Basil Blackwell.

Smith, K. V. (1978) "Measuring Natural Resource scarcity: Theory and practice," *Journal of Environmental Economic Management* 5: 150–71.

—— (1979) "Natural Resource Scarcity: A Statistical Analysis," *Review of Economic Statistics* 61: 423–7.

—— (1981) Increasing Resource Scarcity: Another Perspective," *Quarterly Review of Economics and Business* 21: 120–5.

Solow, R. M. (1974) "The Economics of Resources or the Resources of Economics," *American Economic Review* 24: 1–14.

Torras, M. and Boyce, J. K. (1998) "Income, Inequality, and Pollution: A Reassessment of the Environmental Kuznets Curve," *Ecological Economics* 25: 147–60.

chapter eight

BIOPHYSICAL LIMITS TO ECONOMIC GROWTH:
The Ecological Economics Perspective

---

learning objectives

After reading this chapter you will be familiar with the following:

- ecological economics and its distinguishing features;
- the historical development of ecological economics;
- the argument for ecological limits to economic growth;
- energy as a limiting factor to economic growth;
- biophysical and moral/ethical arguments for why the neoclassical economic growth paradigm is untenable;
- the steady-state economy (SSE);
- the biophysical, economics and ethical dimensions of the SSE;
- the qualitative difference between economic growth and economic development;
- the SSE and its policy implications;
- the practical problems of operationalizing the SSE.

The environmental resource base upon which all economic activity ultimately depends includes ecological systems that produce a wide variety of services. This resource base is finite. Furthermore, imprudent use of the environmental resource base may irreversibly reduce the capacity for regenerating material production in the future. All of this implies that there are limits to the carrying capacity of the planet.

(Arrow *et al.* 1995)

The closed economy of the future might similarly be called the "spaceman" economy, in which the earth has become a single spaceship, without unlimited reservoirs of anything, either for extraction or for pollution, and in which, therefore, man must find his place in a cyclical ecological system which is capable of continuous reproduction of material form even though it cannot escape having inputs of energy.

(Boulding 1966)

8.1 INTRODUCTION

In Chapter 6, we saw that the Malthusian arguments on limits to economic growth are primarily based on the fear of depleting some key natural resources, including the natural environment's capacity to assimilate waste. In Chapter 7, we learned that this fear has been vigorously challenged by mainstream economists on the basis of resource substitution possibilities and other technical advances. That is, to the extent that resource substitution is possible, exhaustion of a particular resource need not cause major alarm (Solow 1974). Furthermore, if the possibility of infinite substitution of natural resources by human-made capital and labor is to be taken seriously, the existence of *absolute limits* to economic growth would become rather meaningless (Rosenberg 1973; Goeller and Weinberg 1976). Unfortunately, even under this extreme case, absolute limits could be ignored only for certain extractive mineral resources such as aluminum bauxite, copper ore, etc. When considerations of limits are made on the basis of the availability of energy and/or the resilience of the natural ecosystems, denial of limits based on technological possibilities *per se* would not be adequate. In fact, they could be misleading and even dangerous (Georgescu-Roegen 1986). Such is the ecological economic perspective of natural resource scarcity – the subject of this chapter. In the next section, the distinguishing features of ecological economics are highlighted.

8.2 ECOLOGICAL ECONOMICS: NATURE AND SCOPE

Ecological economics deals with a comprehensive and systematic study of the linkages between ecological and economic systems. Its basic organizing principles include the idea that ecological and economic systems are complex, adaptive, living systems that need to be studied as integrated, co-evolving systems in order to be adequately understood (Costanza *et al.* 1993). In this sense, ecological economics attempts to reintegrate the academic disciplines of ecology and economics – two areas of study that have been going their own separate ways for over a century.

The ecological economics approach to economic studies is different from that of neoclassical economics in several ways:

First, in ecological economics the human economy is viewed as a subsystem of the natural ecosystem (see Figure 4.2, Chapter 4). The nature of the exchanges of matter and energy between the ecosystem and economic subsystem is the primary focus of ecological economics (Ayres 1978; Pearce 1987).

Second, given the above premise, in ecological economics, production (which is essentially a transformation of matter and energy) is viewed as a starting point in economic activity (Ayres 1978). The basic factors of production are taken as being raw materials, energy, information flows, and the physical and biological processes within the ecosystem that are essential to sustaining life. Thus, except for information, the natural ecosystem is the *ultimate* source of all material inputs for the economic subsystem. In this sense, then, *nature* can rightfully be regarded as the ultimate source of wealth. Furthermore, in ecological economics there exists a clear recognition of limits on both the regenerative and the assimilative capacities of the natural ecosystem arising from the physical laws that govern the energy and matter transformation (Georgescu-Roegen 1993). Thus, natural resources cannot be conceived as boundless.

Third, to the extent that production (transformation of matter and energy) is the focus, ecological economists use thermodynamics and ecological principles in order to delineate the "proper" role of natural resources in the economic process. Since all transformations require energy and there is no substitute for energy, the ecological economics approach tends to significantly elevate the importance of *energy* resources to the economic process and the ecosystem as a whole (Odum and Odum 1976; Costanza 1980; Mirowski 1988).

Fourth, another central theme of ecological economics is the *complementarity* of factors of production. All inputs in a production process are viewed as complements rather than substitutes. The main message here is that since neither capital nor labor physically creates natural resources, depletion of natural resources cannot be resolved through endless substitutions of labor and capital for natural resources. This fact, together with the laws of thermodynamics, challenges the optimistic "technological assumptions" of neoclassical economics production analysis.

Last but not least, the ecological economics approach stresses the importance of the issue of *scale*. Here, scale refers to the size of a human economic subsystem relative to the total global natural ecosystem (Daly 1992). Ecological economists believe that, under present conditions, the size of the human economy relative to the global ecosystem is large enough to cause significant stress on the limited capacity of the natural ecosystem to support the economic subsystem (Goodland 1992). As evidence of this, they cite some of the major environmental and resource concerns which have made the headlines since the early 1980s: the alarming increase in the rate of generation of toxic wastes; the rapid acceleration of deforestation in the tropical rain forests; the rather compelling evidence of the rapid trend of species (animals and plants) extinction; the increasing evidence of stratospheric ozone depletion; the unrestrained exploitation (both for waste dumping and resource extraction) of the ocean; and the growing evidence for global warming.

Thus, according to the ecological economics school of thought, the search for an "optimal" scale first and foremost requires the recognition of *biophysical limits* to economic growth (Daly 1996). This has to be the case because the growth of the economic subsystem is "bounded" by a non-growing and finite ecological sphere. This requires throughput (low-entropy matter–energy) reduction, which has far-reaching implications, given that conventionally, economic growth is pursued through increased used of throughput. In fact, as will be observed shortly, this may necessitate a fundamental modification to the conventional "dogma of economic growth" in such a way that the "ethos of sustainability" is taken quite seriously.

In ecological economics this is viewed as requiring fresh approaches to economic analysis in the following specific ways:

1 The performance of an economy should not be judged by *efficiency* considerations alone. Explicit consideration should be given to distributional and ethical concerns of both intertemporal and intergenerational varieties (Daly 1973). Furthermore, to ensure that the well-being of non-human beings is protected, resource values should not be assessed on the basis of human preference alone.

2 To the extent that the human economy is viewed as a subsystem of the natural ecosystem and the interactions of these two systems are perceived as complex, economic problems should be analyzed using a *system framework* (which uses nonlinear mathematics, general systems theory and nonequilibrium thermodynamics) and with an *interdisciplinary* focus (Norgaard 1989; Costanza *et al.* 1993). This is in contrast to static or comparative static equilibrium analyses – the most widely applied analytical techniques in standard economics.

3 Uncertainty should be assumed to be fundamental to long-term economic assessment of natural resource availability since problems of this nature involve interactions of complex systems that are subject to *irreversible* processes (Arrow *et al.* 1995). Serious consideration of this warrants *caution* in introducing technology and species, pollution control measures, and protection for rare, threatened or endangered ecosytems and habitats. In other words, what is being proposed here is a precautionary approach to natural resource management. As McGinn (1998) put it, in general the precautionary principle "holds that society should take action against certain practices when there is potential for irreversible consequences or for severe limits on the options for future generations – even when there is as yet no incontrovertible scientific proof that serious consequences will ensue" (p. 57).

The application of the precautionary principle has already been shown to have very profound policy implications. For example, Cline's study (1992) on global warming, which was largely constructed on the basis of risk aversion (hence the precautionary principle), concluded that the resolution to the problem requires undertaking an aggressive program with international cooperation to significantly and effectively reduce the greenhouse effect. On the other hand, Nordhaus's study (1991) of this same subject matter but using a standard cost–benefit analysis approach (Cline's and Nordhaus's studies will be further discussed in Chapter 10) recommended policy actions that were far too modest. The precautionary principle is gaining increasing application in resource management, as will be evident from the discussions in Chapters 10, 15 and 16.

8.3 THE DEVELOPMENT OF ECOLOGICAL ECONOMICS: A BRIEF HISTORICAL SKETCH

Ecological economics in its modern version is a relatively new field. However, it would be entirely wrong to consider ecological economics a new subdiscipline. Its historical roots can be traced as far back as the preclassical Physiocrats – the economists of the French school of the mid-seventeenth century (Cleveland 1987; Martinez-Alier 1987). One of the fundamental premises of the Physiocratic school of thought was that all economic surplus derived from the productive power of "land," or its modern equivalent, of natural resources. In this sense, then, natural resources were regarded as the ultimate source of material wealth. It is to underscore this point that Sir William Petty (1623–83), one of the most celebrated economists of the Physiocratic school, stated that "land is the mother and labor is the father of wealth." This treatment of land as the ultimate resource was also prominent in the literature of classical economics. For example, David Ricardo referred to land as the "original and indestructible powers of the soil." During both the Physiocratic era and the era of classical economics, land was viewed as a limiting factor. Thus, understanding the "natural laws" that govern this resource was considered a key factor to any effort seeking to address the fate of the human economy in the long run. To this end, Ricardo's discovery of the *law of diminishing returns* was of considerable significance.

Another turning point in the historical development of biophysical economics occurred with the formulation of the laws of thermodynamics in the early nineteenth century. This discovery contributed to a clear understanding of the physical laws governing the transformations of matter and energy. Immediately afterwards, thermodynamic laws were used to explain the "natural limits" relevant to the transformations of natural resources into final goods and services.

Within the economic discipline, the laws of thermodynamics have been used for two distinctive purposes. First, using the relationship between energy flow and economic activity, thermodynamic laws have been used to help in the understanding of an economy's workings and its interaction with the natural ecosystem. This led to a clear understanding of the *biophysical foundations* of economics. Some of the major lessons drawn from closer examinations of the laws of thermodynamics are the complementarity of factor inputs, the limits to technology, the limits to the regenerative and assimilative capacities of the natural environment, and, in general, the existence of biophysical limits to economic growth. These issues are further explored later using the works of Georgescu-Roegen.

Second, in the late nineteenth century several physical scientists and economists started to advocate the use of energy as a basis for a unified *value* theory. All transformations require energy; its flow is unidirectional; and there is no substitute for it. It therefore makes sense to use energy as a *numeraire* – a denominator by which the value of all resources is weighed (Odum and Odum 1976). This is equivalent to attempting to express the value of economic activities in terms of their embodied energy (Costanza 1980). Even to this day, there are a number of scholars who strongly advocate what appears to be an "energy theory of value."

The most recent breakthrough in the development of ecological economics has occurred since the Second World War and the emergence of the space age. In particular, the 1960s were, in many ways, watershed years in the revival of interest in ecological economics. This decade marked the beginning of heightened public awareness of ecological limits. Several events were responsible for this occurrence. Of these, two factors are especially worthy of brief mention. First, as human society entered the space age, the idea that "Planet Earth" is a finite sphere became conventional wisdom. Second, until the publication of *Silent Spring* (1962) by Rachel R. Carson, public awareness of ecological damage(s) was extremely low. By alerting the world community to the damage resulting from pesticide misuse, this classic book was responsible for starting the modern environmental movement in the United States and elsewhere. In addition, the book's impact was not limited merely to increasing public awareness of ecological ills; it also changed the nature of the scholarly debate on growth, resources and the environment.

In the mid-1960s, Kenneth Boulding's classic "The Economics of the Coming Spaceship Earth" ushered in the modern revival of ecological economics. During the 1970s, Nicholas Georgescu-Roegen and Herman Daly, two unorthodox economists, were responsible for the development of some of the most insightful ideas in ecological economics. The essential message of these three economists' works was that limits to economic growth could no longer be argued solely on the basis of the possibility of running out of conventional resources – the traditional Malthusian approach. Nor could technology be viewed as the ultimate means of circumventing ecological limits – as neoclassical economists would like to advocate. Instead, availability of high-quality energy and the loss of *ecosystem resilience* were recognized as two key limiting factors in humanity's pursuit for a material nirvana. As is evident from the discussion in Exhibit 8.1, ecosystem resilience is an emerging concern of considerable significance. It involves problems of the following nature: ecological stress from prolonged environmental pollution, the effect of which is a sudden loss of biological productivity; irreversible changes such as desertification and loss of biodiversity; and uncertainty associated with environmental effects of economic activities.

Where is ecological economics today? As the world has gradually but surely shifted from a relatively "empty world" to a relatively "full world," the relevance of ecological economics for addressing global environmental

EXHIBIT 8.1   CARRYING CAPACITY AND ECOSYSTEM RESILIENCE

K. Arrow, B. Bolin, R. Costanza *et al.*

The environmental resource base upon which all economic activity ultimately depends includes ecological systems that produce a wide variety of services. This resource base is finite. Furthermore, imprudent use of the environmental resource base may irreversibly reduce the capacity for generating material production in the future. All of this implies that there are limits to the carrying capacity of the planet. . . .

Carrying capacities in nature are not fixed, static or simple relations. They are contingent on technology, preferences, and the structure of production and consumption. They are also contingent on the ever-changing state of interactions between the physical and the biotic environments. A single number for human carrying capacity would be meaningless because the consequences of both human innovation and biological evolution are inherently unknowable. Nevertheless, a general index of the current scale or intensity of the human economy in relation to that of the biosphere is still useful. For example, Vitousek *et al.* calculated that the total net terrestrial primary production of the biosphere currently being appropriated for human consumption is around 40 per cent. This does put the scale of the human presence on the planet in perspective.

A more useful index of environmental sustainability is ecosystem resilience. One way of thinking about resilience is to focus on ecosystem dynamics where there are multiple (locally) stable equilibria. Resilience in this sense is a measure of the magnitude of disturbance that can be absorbed before a system centered on one locally stable equilibrium flips to another. Economic activities are sustainable only if the life-support ecosystems on which they depend are resilient. Even though ecological resilience is difficult to measure and even though it varies from system to system and from one kind of disturbance to another, it may be possible to identify indicators and early-warning signals of environmental stress. For example, the diversity of organisms and the heterogeneity of ecological functions have been suggested as signals of ecosystem resilience. But ultimately, the resilience of systems may only be tested by intelligently perturbing them and observing the response with what has been called "adaptive management."

The loss of ecosystem resilience is potentially important for at least three reasons. First, the discontinuous change in ecosystem flips from one equilibrium to another could be associated with a sudden loss of biological productivity, and so to a reduced capacity to support human life. Second, it may imply an irreversible change in the set of options open to both present and future generations (examples include soil erosion, depletion of groundwater reservoirs, desertification and loss of biodiversity). Third, discontinuous and irreversible changes from familiar to unfamiliar states increase the uncertainties associated with the environmental effects of economic activities.

If human activities are to be sustainable, we need to ensure that the ecological systems on which our economies depend are resilient. The problem involved in devising environmental policies is to ensure that resilience is maintained, even though the limits on the nature and scale of economic activities thus required are necessarily uncertain.

Source: *Science* 268, 1995, pp. 520–1. Copyright © American Association for the Advancement of Science (AAAS). Reprinted by permission.

and resource concerns has been widely recognized (Cleveland 1987). The resurgence of interest in ecological economics has been particularly dramatic over the past decade. In 1988, the International Society for Ecological Economics (ISEE) was officially inaugurated. Presently, it has a membership in excess of ten thousand; and it is truly international in both its missions and membership composition.

What effects, if any, have the recent renewal of interest in ecological economics had on the economic profession at large? On the whole, the influence of ecological economics on mainstream economic thinking has been insignificant. By and large, mainstream economists continue to resist any suggestions made by ecological economists demanding a shift in the neoclassical growth paradigm (Young 1991). For that matter, there are considerable numbers of economists who simply consider the works of influential ecological economists such as Boulding, Georgescu-Roegen and Daly (these are going to be discussed in the next section) interesting, but nothing more than a new spin on the old-fashioned neo-Malthusian way of thinking.

Despite this skepticism there are a growing number of economists who do not necessarily identify themselves as ecological economists, but are making serious, scholarly efforts to find ways of incorporating the implications of ecological limits into the general framework of mainstream economic analysis. This is especially evident in the field of environmental and resource economics – a subfield of economics that has gained increasing popularity since the 1970s. No serious textbooks in environmental and resource economics written over the past decade have failed to contain some discussion of concepts such as the material balance approach (referring to the first law of thermodynamics); the second law of thermodynamics; limits to the absorptive capacity of the natural environment; and carrying capacity – to mention only a few.

8.4 BIOPHYSICAL LIMITS AND THEIR IMPLICATIONS FOR ECONOMIC GROWTH: AN ECOLOGICAL ECONOMIC PERSPECTIVE

In this section an attempt will be made to discuss in some detail the actual nature of the biophysical limits relevant to human concerns for continued increases in material standard of living. This is done using the pioneering works of three highly distinguished economists, namely Kenneth Boulding, Nicholas Georgescu-Roegen and Herman Daly. A common feature of the scholarly works of these three economists is their use of thermodynamics and ecological principles to demonstrate the existence of ecological limits on "economic growth." In the process of doing this, they fiercely challenge the basic tenets of the neoclassical growth paradigm. Furthermore, these three unorthodox economists argue for an economy that is ecologically sustainable. Herman Daly would even go so far as to propose his own brand of growth paradigm.

8.4.1 Kenneth Boulding (1909–93): ecological limits

Kenneth Boulding's article "The Economics of the Coming Spaceship Earth" (1966) represents one of the earliest attacks from an ecological perspective on modern economists' preoccupation with economic growth. His article is a true classic written in a style that allows economists to understand and appreciate ecological arguments that are relevant to economics. In this regard, one could safely claim that this is the first article to have sparked interest in ecology among mainstream economic scholars.

The main messages of the article are rather straightforward. Boulding starts the article by reminding us that our past is characterized by a *frontier mentality*: that is, the strongly held belief that there is always a new place to discover "when things got too difficult, either by reason of the deterioration of the natural environment or a deterioration of the social structure in places where people happened to live" (p. 297). The Earth is, therefore, viewed as an open system or illimitable plane. Boulding uses the metaphor "the cowboy economy" to describe the economic system that is compatible with this resource availability scenario. In this situation, where resource availability is taken for granted, both consumption and production are regarded as good things. Accordingly, nature is recklessly exploited with little or no concern. Moreover, the success of an economy is measured by the amount of throughput (matter and energy) used to produce the desired goods and services, without regard to depletion or pollution. Thus, according to Boulding, reckless exploitation of nature – which is consistent with cowboy-like behavior – represents our past.

Boulding, however, views the future quite differently. Specifically, he alerts us to the fact that we are now in a transition from the *open* to the *closed* Earth. We were able to fully realize this rather recently when we entered into the space age and vividly observed that the Earth is a finite sphere. Thus, the

> earth has become a single spaceship, without unlimited reservoirs of anything, either for extraction or for pollution, and in which, therefore, man must find his place in a cyclical ecological system which is capable of continuous reproduction of materials even though it cannot escape having inputs of energy.
>
> (Boulding 1966: 303)

According to Boulding, this new reality has significant economic implications. The economy of the future, which he referred to as the "spaceman" economy, requires economic principles which are different from those of the open Earth of the past:

> In the spaceman economy, throughput (matter and energy) is by no means a desideratum, and is indeed to be regarded as something to be minimized rather than maximized. Hence, the essential measure of the success of the economy is not production and consumption, but

the nature, extent, quality, and complexity of the total capital stock, including the state of the human bodies and minds included in the system.

(ibid.: 304)

Boulding then goes on to argue that mainstream economists still have a difficult time accepting the above implications of the spaceman economy because the suggestion that both production and consumption are bad things rather than good things works against the natural instinct of mainstream economists.

With this in mind, Boulding's messages are quite clear. First and foremost, for all practical purposes the Earth is a closed ecological sphere. When human population was small and its technological capabilities were not overpowering, viewing the Earth as an illimitable plane might have been, if not right, certainly understandable and admissible. However, current human conditions with respect to population, technology and habits of consumption and production warrant a fresh look at our social values and economic systems. We need to espouse social values and erect economic systems that reinforce the idea that – in a material sense – more is not necessarily better. In the final analysis, Boulding's message is simply this: *The future of humankind depends on our ability to design an economic system that regulates the flow of throughput with full recognition of ecological limits to establish a sustainable economy.*

8.4.2 Nicholas Georgescu-Roegen (1906–94): energy as a limiting factor

Another highly acclaimed economist, who is even harsher in his criticisms of standard economics than Boulding, is Nicholas Georgescu-Roegen. Georgescu-Roegen's contributions to economics are numerous and varied. His works in consumer choice and utility theory, measurability, production theory, input–output analysis and economic development are fairly well recognized and contribute a good deal to the mainstream economics literature in these areas. His major contributions to standard economics literature are reflected in his book *Analytical Economics* (1966). Paul Samuelson in his preface to *Analytical Economics* referred to Georgescu-Roegen as "a scholar's scholar, an economists' economist" (Daly 1996).

Georgescu-Roegen's insightful but revolutionary contributions to resource economics were forcefully articulated in his book *The Entropy Law and the Economics Process* (1971). This seminal work represents a vigorous, insightful and critical appraisal of the standard economics paradigm of resource scarcity and economic growth. He did this by using fundamental principles from thermodynamics – the natural laws that govern the transformation of energy–matter. In so doing he introduced a new and revolutionary conceptual framework in the economic analysis of the interactions between ecological and economic systems. To Georgescu-Roegen, from a purely physical viewpoint both the human economy and the natural ecosystems are characterized by continuous "exchange" of matter and energy; and careful analysis of this energy and material flow is paramount to the understanding of the physical limits to the economic process. It is for this reason that he went on to declare thermodynamics as the "most economic of all physical laws." However, he was truly baffled and disappointed by the complete lack of attention given to this fundamental idea in the standard economic analysis of resource allocations.

Georgescu-Roegen observed that epistemologically the neoclassical school of economics still follows the mechanistic dogma that it inherited from "Newtonian mechanics." For this reason economic analysis is based on a conceptual framework that is rather simplistic and unidirectional. As proof of this, Georgescu-Roegen cited the standard economics textbook representation of the economic process by a circular flow diagram (see Chapter 1, Figure 1.1). From a purely physical viewpoint, this diagram represents a circular flow of matter–energy between production and consumption within a completely closed system. Alternatively, the circular flow of matter–energy is replaced by an immaterial flow of dollars as costs and revenues. This flow of matter–energy or dollars, as the case may be, is assumed to be regulated not by any natural or supernatural being, but by *utility* and *self-interest* (see Chapter 2). Clearly, then, no explicit link was made between the flow of matter–energy in the economic process and the physical environment. In other words, the economic process is treated as an "isolated, circular affair," independent of the natural environment from which materials are extracted. According to Georgescu-Roegen, to conceptualize the economic process in this manner is not only simplistic, but quite misleading and dangerous for the following three reasons.

First, it makes economists focus on *economic value* alone. Consequently, this leads to a blatant disregard of the physical flows of matter–energy (biophysical foundation) of the economic process. To counter, Georgescu-Roegen, using the second law of thermodynamics, reminds us that "from a purely physical viewpoint, the economic process only transforms valuable natural resources (low entropy) into waste (high entropy)" (1971: 265). This qualitative difference between what goes into the economic process and what comes out of it should be enough to confirm that "nature, too, plays an important role in the economic process as well as in the formation of economic value" (ibid.: 266). Note that Georgescu-Roegen is not claiming here that economic value is solely determined by nature. He is an astute economist who realizes that economic value is determined by both demand (utility) and supply (technology and nature). To confirm this, he argued that

> the true economic output of the economic process is not a material flow of waste, but an immaterial flux: the enjoyment of life. If we do not recognize the existence of this flux, we are not in the economic world. Nor do we have a complete picture of the economic process if we ignore the fact that this flux – which, as an entropic feeling, must characterize life at all levels – exists only as long as it can continually feed itself on environmental low entropy.

(ibid.: 80)

Thus, according to Georgescu-Roegen, low entropy is a necessary but not a sufficient condition for economic value. However, this in no way should justify the blatant disregard of the key role that low-entropy matter–energy plays in the formation of economic value.

Second, it causes standard economists to overlook the role that *energy* plays in the economic process. Using the second law of thermodynamics, Georgescu-Roegen forcefully argued for the significance of energy as a limiting factor not only to the growth of material standards of living, but also ultimately to the economic process itself. He argued that

> environmental low entropy is scarce in a different sense than Ricardian land. Both Ricardian land and the coal deposits are available in limited amounts. The difference is that a piece of coal can be used only once. The economic process is solidly anchored to a material base which is subject to definite constraints. It is because of this constraint that the economic process has a unidirectional irrevocable evolution.
>
> (ibid.)

Third, by failing to acknowledge the natural constraints to the economic process, mainstream economists become first-rate technological optimists. The belief that any material problem(s) humanity faces can be solved by technological means started to be taken for granted by economists, but this is wishful thinking for the following reasons:

1 According to the second law of thermodynamics, it is impossible to discover a self-perpetuating industrial machine. In the ordinary transformation of matter and energy – which the economic process is subjected to – there can never be "free recycling as there is no wasteless industry" (ibid.: 83) In other words, there are absolute minimum thermodynamic requirements of energy and materials to produce a unit of output that cannot be augmented by technical change.

2 As was later expounded by Ayres (1978), the laws of thermodynamics place limits on the substitution of human-made capital for natural capital (low-entropy matter and energy) and, therefore, the ability of technological change to compensate for the depletion or degradation of natural capital. In fact, in the long run, *natural and human-made capital are complements because the later requires material and energy for its production and maintenance*. This is indeed a rejection of one of the important core principles of the neoclassical growth paradigm: the notion of infinite substitution between human-made and natural capital.

However, it is important to note that both Georgescu-Roegen and Boulding are not against the very idea of technology or technological advancement. In this particular case, their concerns are twofold. First, we need to acknowledge that there is a *limit to technological advancement*. Second, technology can be abused or misused. On the other hand, used prudently, technology could be a blessing. For example, a technological advance that decreases the need for throughput, while maintaining a material standard of living at some desired level, is indeed to be sought after.

On the other hand, if technological advance is directed toward producing more goods and services with no limit in sight, such a strategy is highly questionable from the viewpoint of long-term sustainability. Thus, a prudent use of technology requires the recognition of the ultimate constraints imposed by nature – natural limits.

Georgescu-Roegen and Boulding can rightly be thought of as the two economists who were mainly responsible for establishing the conceptual and theoretical foundation of the modern variation of ecological economics. However, in terms of offering a concrete alternative paradigm to traditional economics growth, no one rivals Herman Daly – a student of Georgescu-Roegen.

8.4.3 Herman Daly: the steady-state economy

Herman Daly is a visionary scholar who is particularly known for his insistent and forceful attack on the neoclassical economics growth paradigm. He worked for the World Bank for several years at the time when the bank was making serious attempts to correct the ecological contradictions of its development plans. Presently, he is a professor at the University of Maryland School of Public Affairs.

Daly is particularly recognized for his effort to articulate a viable alternative to the neoclassical growth paradigm, namely the steady-state economy (SSE). Herman Daly's conceptual model of the SSE is not a totally new idea since it shares common themes and concerns with John Stuart Mill's vision of a "stationary state" of over a century ago. Daly's model is different to the extent that it explicitly incorporates additional resource constraints – the ecological and physical realities articulated by Boulding and Georgescu-Roegen. In fact, one could safely state that the SSE is a theoretical economic "growth" model that explicitly attempts to incorporate the biophysical limits and ethical considerations proclaimed by Georgescu-Roegen and Boulding.

The means and ends spectrum

Daly (1993) began his argument by declaring that the neoclassical economic growth paradigm is untenable because it is not based on sustainable bio-physical and moral considerations. He explains this contention by using a simple scheme of a means and ends spectrum (ordering), as presented in Figure 8.1.

According to Daly, standard economic growth models ignore the *ultimate means* by which the growth of material standards of living are attainable. Here, ultimate means refers to the low-entropy matter–energy of the ecosphere. The fact that the ultimate means are scarce in absolute terms or that these basic resources are constrained by natural laws is considered irrelevant by mainstream economists. Instead, because of their blind faith in technology, mainstream economists exclusively focus on the availability of *intermediate means*: labor, capital and conventional natural resources (raw

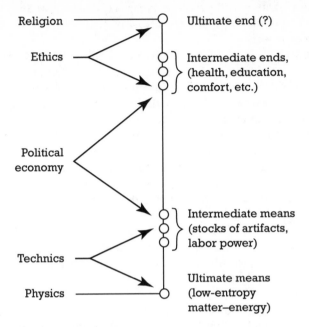

Religion ——————○ Ultimate end (?)

Ethics ——————○
                 ○ } Intermediate ends,
                 ○   (health, education,
                     comfort, etc.)

Political
economy ——————

Intermediate means
(stocks of artifacts,
labor power)

Technics ——————

Ultimate means
(low-entropy
matter–energy)

Physics ——————

***Figure 8.1* Ends–means spectrum**
Source: Reprinted by permission from V. K. Smith, *Scarcity and Growth Reconsidered*,
copyright © Resources for the Future (Washington, D.C., 1979), p. 70.

materials). In the process, the fact that the availability of intermediate means ultimately depends on the availability of ultimate means seems to have escaped standard economic thinking. For this reason, focusing on intermediate means, economists discuss relative scarcity and prices, on the basis of which resources are allocated to alternative societal uses (see Chapters 2 and 3).

Given this biophysical reality, it is no wonder that standard economists are so infatuated with continual growth in *intermediate ends*: market-valued goods and services. This seemingly sacred goal in economics is pursued not only without regard to biophysical limits, but also without consideration of both intra- and intergenerational equities. In other words, how the total quantity of goods and services produced in a given calendar year is distributed among the people of the current generation (intragenerational), and how current economic activities may affect the well-being of future generations (intergenerational), are simply not considered. This is not to suggest that standard economists are in denial of the existence of mal-distribution of income among the current generation, or that they are insensitive to the possible adverse effects of current production (such as pollution) on the well-being of the distant generations. Rather, as discussed in Chapter 7, the main position of standard economists has been that sustaining a moderate to high rate of growth is the single most effective panacea for current and future economic and ecological ills. In some scholarly circles, this view is known as *growthmania*.

A position taken by Daly and others is that, when viewed realistically, it would be dangerous to pursue the ideals of growthmania for at least the following two reasons.

First, human aspiration is not limited to accumulating material wealth. Humans are social beings with feelings and ideals that are purely social, psychological and/or spiritual. Furthermore, humans are biological beings with instincts for survival. These are the elements that define and shape the relationships of humankind over time, space and other ideals – like their relationship with the physical or spiritual world. The extent to which humans care about future generations, then, depends on the totality of these nonmaterial based ideals. Daly called these the *ultimate ends*. According to Daly, mainstream economists have failed to consider the ultimate ends because of their undue preoccupation with the material world.

Second, growthmania, if pursued blindly, could have abrupt and catastrophic economic and ecological consequences. Therefore, the argument against growthmania is not to avoid the "inevitable extinction of humankind," but to safeguard humanity from sudden economic and ecological collapse; hence the imperative for a precautionary approach to resource management.

To summarize Daly's position: neoclassical economists have ignored both ultimate means and ultimate ends by advocating continual economic growth. The ultimate means are forgotten because of the strong and persistent belief that resource scarcity can always be ameliorated through technology. The ultimate ends are ignored because of the standard economists' preoccupation with the material world. Therefore, as shown in Figure 8.1, economic concern occupies only the middle portion of the means–ends spectrum. That is, the neoclassical growth paradigm concentrates on intermediate means (such as labor, capital and raw materials) and on intermediate ends: the attainment of market-valued goods and services. Thus, given such a narrow and incomplete perspective of material and nonmaterial reality, it is not difficult to see why mainstream economists are so eager to believe in the prospect of boundless economic growth.

If the above growth paradigm is to be rejected on the basis of its incomplete material and ethical considerations, what alternative model(s) could be proposed? Herman Daly's response to this question is the steady-state economy (SSE). What is the SSE? And in what ways does it differ from the neoclassical growth model?

The biophysical, economic and ethical dimensions of the steady-state economy

From the beginning, Daly defines the SSE as "a constant stock of physical wealth and people (population)." Note that, in this way, the SSE is intentionally defined in a *purely biophysical* context which suggests that the total inventory of all the intermediate means and ends, including human population, is frozen at some "desirable" constant. In other words, in quantitative terms the material requirements to run an economy are held constant at all times. Thus, in the SSE the primary focus is on what Daly identified as *stock maintenance*: maintaining a constant inventory of inter- mediate means and ends. From now on the term *stock* will be used in reference to this constant inventory of intermediate means and ends.

But, in an entropic world, stock maintenance can never be achieved without *cost*: constant withdrawal of finite ultimate means. The question, then, is not how should we avoid this cost, but what can we do to minimize it? Daly suggests that this can be done through vigorous pursuit of *maintenance efficiency*, which is composed of a ratio of two key factors: the constant stock and throughput (stock/throughput). *Throughput* refers to the flow of low- entropy matter–energy that needs to be used to replace the periodical depreciation of stock. Given that stock is held constant, this ratio can be maximized by minimizing throughput. Thus, in the SSE, maintenance efficiency is attained in the following two ways: (a) *durability* – producing artifacts (intermediate ends) which are long-lasting; and (b) *replaceability* – producing products which are easy to replace or recycle. Technology can play a key role in the realization of these two components of maintenance efficiency. Hence, the SSE is not antitechnology, but insists that technology should be used in certain ways. As a general rule, any technological change that results in the maintenance of a given stock with a lessened throughput is clearly to be encouraged. Case Study 8.1 offers an excellent account of how a company, in this case the Xerox Corporation, using common sense and technology was able to establish an equipment and parts recycling program in which durability and replaceability are emphasized.

CASE STUDY 8.1 ASSET RECYCLING AT XEROX

Jack Azar

In the industrial society, the proliferation of solid waste in the face of diminishing landfill space continues to be a major concern. Reacting to this challenge, in some countries legislation is in the works that could significantly affect marketplace demands. In Germany, legislation has been proposed that would require manu- facturers and distributors to take back and recycle or dispose of used electronic equipment. The European Community is considering similar legislation. In Canada, too, interest in such legislation has been expressed. And in Japan, a 1991 regulation issued by the Ministry of International Trade and Industry promotes not only the use of recycled materials in certain durable items but also the recyclability of those items themselves.

In response to what seems to be a future trend in worldwide movement toward recycling, in 1990 Xerox began a corporate environmental strategy that encompasses equipment and parts recycling. The cornerstone of this strategy is the *Asset Recycle Management* program. As the name implies, it entails treating all products and components owned by the company – whether out on rental or on the company's premises – as physical "assets."

The key feature of the Asset Recycle Management program at Xerox is the emphasis on a rather "unconventional" approach that machines should be *designed* from concept with the remanufacturing process and the recapture of parts and materials in mind. This meant getting the company's design and manufacturing engineers to bring an entirely new perspective to their work. To facilitate this the company instituted an Asset Recycle Management organization. The principal charge of this organization is to continually identify areas where significant opportunities to optimize the use of equipment and parts, even for existing products, could be captured.

Early on, it was recognized that company engineers needed design guidelines to enhance remanufacturing and materials recycling. . . . Specifically, the guidelines reflect the following design criteria: extended product and component life – i.e., use of more robust materials and design to make asset recovery practical; selection of materials that are relatively easy to recycle at the end of product life; simplification of materials to facilitate recycling; easy disassembly as well as easy assembly; remanufacturing convertibility, meaning that a basic product configuration is convertible to a different use – e.g., a copier to an electronic printer; and use of common parts to enable future reuse in different models and configurations.

Xerox's first environmental design to reach the market was a customer-replaceable copy cartridge, which has many of the characteristics of a complete xerographic copier. Designed for use in the company's smaller convenience copiers, the copy cartridge contains the main xerographic elements critical to the copying process: photoreceptor, electrical charging devices and a cleaning mechanism.

Copy cartridges designed for older convenience copiers posed a special challenge. They had not been designed for recycling. In fact, their plastic housings were assembled by ultrasonic welding. The company had to break them open to get at the components within, thereby destroying the plastic housings. While it was usually possible to reclaim the photoreceptor-transport assemblies, all that could be done with the housings was to grind them down for reuse as injection-molding raw materials.

The new 5300 series of convenience copiers has a new design: a cartridge that is assembled with a few fasteners. It is totally remanufacturable, a process that costs far less than building one with all new parts, and more than 90 percent of the material is recoverable. It also meets all product quality specifications and carries the same warranty as newly manufactured cartridges.

To date, the Asset Recycling Program at Xerox has been a big success from the standpoint of both environmental and business considerations. On the business side, the company saved a total of $50 million the first year in logistics, inventory and the cost of raw materials. These savings are to increase greatly as design-for-environment Xerox products enter the market. In addition, only a minimal amount of material has been scrapped compared with previous years.

Source: EPA Journal Vol. 19, 1993, pp. 15–16. Reprinted with permission.

Thus far, the SSE has been described in terms of its biophysical attributes. However, as Georgescu-Roegen would like to remind us, the economic world is defined not only by material flow or transformation of matter–energy, but by "an immaterial flux: the enjoyment of life." How does the SSE address this important dimension of the economic world?

As the architect of the SSE, Daly postulated that the primary goal of an economy is to *maximize service* subject to the constraint of constant stock. Service is defined as the satisfaction (utility) obtained when wants are satisfied. Or, in more general terms, "the final benefit of all economic activity." It is important to note that only stock (the inventory of inter-mediate means and ends) is capable of generating utility. Under this condition, how best can service (utility) be maximized? According to Daly, this objective can be achieved through what he calls *service efficiency*, which is identified as the ratio of service to the constant stock (service/stock). Maximization of this ratio amounts to finding ways of making the numerator larger while keeping the denominator constant. Daly identified two specific ways of doing this: allocative and distributive efficiencies.

Attainment of *allocative efficiency* requires that two specific conditions be fulfilled. First, the production of goods and services should use the least amount of intermediate means (labor, capital and natural resources) possible – *production efficiency*. Second, the goods and services that are produced should be the ones that provide the most satisfaction to people. These are efficiency factors which are primarily if not exclusively empha-sized in standard economics. Considering this, over the past fifty years standard economists have made a significant stride in developing the conceptual framework and in articulating the criteria necessary to achieve these types of efficiency requirements (see Chapter 2).

On the other hand, *distributive efficiency* requires that the distribution of the constant stock (intermediate means and ends) should be done in such a way "that the trivial wants of some people do not take precedence over the basic needs of others." It is important to note that this requirement is not motivated by ethical considerations alone. If the postulate of *diminishing marginal utility* is accepted (see Chapter 2), then distributive efficiency would lead to increased total social welfare (utility).

Furthermore, it is important to note that distributive efficiency is not limited to equity issues among existing generations – *intragenerational equity*. Another equally important issue to consider is *intergenerational equity*. That is, it is important to ensure that current generations are not enriching themselves at the expense of future generations. In general, the issue of equity is difficult to discern because it deals with the difficult issues of fairness or justice, which require value judgments. It becomes even more challenging as the issue stretches in time and space. Nevertheless, while generally accepted standards of fairness or justice do not exist with reference to intergenerational equity issues, one criterion that is gaining popularity (Rawlsian justice) declares that "at a minimum, future generations should be left no worse off than current generations."

Therefore, in the SSE, it is expected that the general principle of maximum total satisfaction (service) from a constant stock should be pursued with full consideration of *fairness* and *justice* both in time and space. As shown in Figure 8.1, this requires a formulation of ethical principles linking intermediate and ultimate ends. A matter of such importance is not even peripherally addressed in standard economics, where the prevailing attitude is to treat intergenerational equity as, basically, a nonissue. Accordingly, the general sentiment is "What has posterity ever done for me?" Furthermore, as discussed in Chapter 7, the empirical evidence over the past two centuries clearly indicates improved material standards of living in each succeeding generation – strong evidence that makes concern about future generations unnecessary.

To summarize the above discussion, there are, conceptually, three general principles which govern the operation of the SSE. First, the SSE requires the use of throughput (low-entropy matter–energy) to be minimized at all times. This suggests that in the SSE, as much as is feasible, all possible technological avenues must be pursued to produce goods and services that are long-lasting and easily recyclable – attainment of *maintenance efficiency* (see Case Study 8.1). Second, in the SSE, service (utility) is to be maximized. This should be done through a combination of both *production efficiency* (production of more goods and services from a given resource) and *distributive efficiency* (fair or equitable distribution of goods and services produced).

Finally, and most importantly, the SSE requires that *stock* (the total inventory of intermediate means and ends) should be held constant because in a world endowed with finite resources (low-entropy matter–energy), equity considerations in both time and space make the requirement of constant stock an essential prerequisite of the SSE.

Practicality of the steady-state economy

Does the SSE imply economic stagnation? This is a natural question, given that in the SSE, the quantities of the physical stock (intermediate means and ends, including human population) are held constant. Nevertheless, Daly's response to this question is a definite "no." To explain his position, Daly differentiated between "economic growth" and "economic development." Economic growth means the production of more goods and services to satisfy ever-increasing human wants, or, as Daly put it, "the creation of ever more intermediate means (stocks) for the purpose of satisfying ever more intermediate ends" (1993: 21). Because stocks are held constant, economic growth is impossible in SSE. This, however, should not be a cause for concern since an economy can grow *qualitatively* without necessitating a corresponding *quantitative* growth in its physical dimensions. How?

First, while physical stocks are held constant in the SSE, the stress should be on measuring economic improvements in terms of nonphysical goods: services and leisure. Second, emphasis should be placed on technological progress that increases leisure activities (such as growing appreciation of environmental amenities, friendships, meditation, etc.) which are far less material-intensive than the production of physical outputs. With these adjustments, economic growth, measured in terms of an increasing level of satisfaction (utility) from a given level of resource stocks, is quite possible. Daly referred to this qualitative growth in economic well-being as "economic development." *Accordingly, in the SSE it is possible to develop even in the total absence of traditional economic growth.*

No doubt, in terms of both its biophysical and its ethical requirements, the SSE is radically different from the neoclassical growth models. The question is: is the SSE practicable? The viability of any theoretical model largely depends on the pragmatic issues that need to be overcome to make the model workable. In this case, the actual implementation of the SSE requires the establishment of several social institutions that may be considered quite revolutionary and, in some ways, impractical.

First, in the SSE, stocks are required to be held constant. How should the constant stocks be determined? Is this going to be done solely by govern-ment decree? If so, would that be acceptable in a democratic society where the political quest is to minimize the role of government in the economic affairs of the citizens? Would the market have any role in rationing the constant stocks once their level is determined? Herman Daly's response to these questions is rather simple. He proposed *depletion quotas* as a strategy for controlling the flow of aggregate throughput. Behind this strategy is the idea that controlling the rate of depletion would indirectly limit both pollution and the size of throughput – the flow of low-entropy matter–energy. Initially, the government would auction the limited quota rights to many resource buyers. Afterwards, the resource is expected to be allocated in its best use under a competitive market setting.

Second, in the SSE, population is held at constant level with low birth and death rates. How would one determine the *optimal* level of population? What social and technological means are used to control population? Can population control measures be effectively and uniformly implemented in an ideologically and culturally pluralistic society? Daly's proposed solution to the population problem is *transferable birth licenses*. Again this is a strategy that combines both a government fiat and the market. Here, the government would issue every woman (or couple) with a certain number of reproduction licenses that correspond to replacement fertility; that is, 2.1 licenses. These birth licenses are transferable so that those who want more than two children can sell them at the going market price. Since population is allowed to grow at a rate no greater than the replacement fertility rate, the total population would thereby remain constant.

Third, and finally, in the SSE institutions are required to regulate the distribution of income and wealth. This is important because, as discussed earlier, even without equity consideration, income redistribution is one avenue by which total social welfare can be increased. However, is it practical to envision an institution that imposes limits on income and wealth? After all, what is the difference between such an institution and communism? Daly has offered no tangible proposal to resolve the redistribution problem.

On practical grounds the SSE is extremely difficult to defend. Nevertheless, this should not in any way suggest that Daly's specific policy recommendations are erroneous or misguided. It only means that we, as a society, are not yet ready to make the political, moral and psychological adjustments necessary to effect the suggested institutional changes. At this stage of its development, therefore, the strength of the SSE lies solely in confronting us with the inescapable biophysical limits to human economy. It warns that we cannot continue with an attitude of "business as usual." Instead, we need to develop new social and ethical awareness so that improvement in the material well-being of the present generation is not pursued at the risk of impoverishing future generations. Certainly this could not be accomplished automatically or without sacrifices. To be sure, it would require adopting some institutional measures that might have the effect of limiting our individual freedom in respect of some economic and reproductive decisions. But even if we do not agree with the specific solutions he proposed, establishing a clear link between biophysical limits and individual freedom of choice is one of Daly's major contributions.

8.5 CHAPTER SUMMARY

This chapter has discussed the ecological perspective on "general" resource scarcity and its implications for the long-run material well-being of humanity.

- In contrast to neoclassical economics, the ecological economic perspective seems to be rather cautious. In large part, this caution is a result of looking at biophysical limits from a broader context.
- Ecological economists do not view the human economy as being isolated from natural ecosystems. In fact, the human economy is regarded as nothing but a small (albeit important) subset of the natural ecosystem. Furthermore, since these two systems are considered to be interdependent, ecological economists focus on understanding the linkages and interactions between economic and ecological systems.
- From such a perspective, the *scale* of human activities (in terms of population size and aggregate consumption of resources) becomes an important issue. Furthermore, in ecological economics the consensus view seems to be that the scale of human development is already approaching the limits of the finite natural world – the full-world view. This has several implications. Among them are:

1 It is imperative that limits be put on the *total* resources used for either production and/or consumption purposes – stock maintenance.
2 "The essential measure of the success of the economy is not production and consumption at all, but the nature, extent, quality, and complexity of the total capital stock, including the state of the human bodies and minds included in the system" (Boulding 1966: 304).
3 As far as possible, the use of throughput should be minimized, which implies the production of goods and services that are long-lasting and

easily recyclable. Technology could play a significant positive role in this regard.

- On the other hand, technology will not be able to circumvent fundamental energy, pollution and other natural resource constraints for two reasons: first, natural and human-made capital are *complements*; second, availability of natural resources will be a limiting factor to continued economic growth.
- Thus, according to the ecological economic perspective, it is imperative that human society make every effort to ensure that the scale of human activities is ecologically *sustainable*. This necessitates careful consideration of biophysical limits, and intergenerational equity. These concerns extend beyond humanity, to the future well-being of other species and the biosphere as a whole.
- In many respects, one of the major contributions of ecological economics has been to shift the focus of the debates on natural resource scarcity from limits to economic growth to sustainable development – the subject matter of the next chapter.

---

review and discussion questions

1 Briefly identify the following concepts: throughput, growthmania, the "cowboy" economy, the "spaceman" economy, intermediate means, intermediate ends, ultimate means, ultimate ends, the steady state economy, irreversibility, complementarity of factor of production, the precautionary principle, intergenerational equity.

2 State *True*, *False*, or *Uncertain* and explain why.

- Consideration of "ultimate ends" is beyond economics – which is not a moral science.
- In general, complementarity of factors of production implies the existence of *limits* to factor substitution possibilities.
- A steady-state economy is a theoretical model with no practical significance.
- An economy can "develop" without experiencing "growth."

3 It is argued that all transformations require energy; energy flow is unidirectional; and there is no substitute for energy. It therefore makes sense to use energy as a *numeraire* – a denominator by which the value of all resources is weighed. That is, energy is the *ultimate* resource. Critically comment.

4 Why is uncertainty an important consideration in ecological economics?

5 Nicholas Georgescu-Roegen labeled "steady-state" a "topical mirage" and pointed out its logical snags: "The crucial error consists in not seeing that . . . even a declining [growth] state which does not converge toward annihilation, cannot exist forever in a finite environment. . . . [Thus], contrary to what some advocates of the stationary state claim, this state does not occupy a privileged position vis-à-vis physical law." Is this a fair criticism of the steady-state economy? Explain.

REFERENCES AND FURTHER READING

Arrow, K., Bolin, B., Costanza, R. *et al.* (1995) "Economic Growth, Carrying Capacity, and the Environment," *Science* 268: 520–1.

Ayres, R. U. (1978) "Application of Physical Principles to Economics," in R. U. Ayres (ed.) *Resources, Environment, and Economics: Applications of the Materials/Energy Balance Principle*, New York: John Wiley.

Ayres, R. U. and Nair, I. (1984) "Thermodynamics and Economics," *Physics Today* 37: 63–8.

Boulding, K. E. (1966) "The Economics of the Coming Spaceship Earth," in H. Jarrett (ed.) *Environmental Quality in a Growing Economy*, Washington, D.C.: Johns Hopkins University Press.

Burness, S., Cummings, R., Morris, G. and Paik, I. (1980) "Thermodynamics and Economic Concepts Related to Resource-Use Policies," *Land Economics* 56: 1–9.

Carson, R. M. (1962) *Silent Spring*, Boston: Houghton Mifflin.

Cleveland, C. J. (1987) "Biophysical Economics: Historical Perspective and Current Research Trends," *Ecological Modelling* 38: 47–73.

Cline, W. R. (1992) *The Economics of Global Warming*, Washington, D.C.: Institute for International Economics.

Costanza, R. (1980) "Embodied Energy and Economic Valuation," *Science* 210: 1219–24.

Costanza, R., Wainger, L. and Folke, C. (1993) "Modeling Complex Ecological Economic Systems: Toward an Evolutionary, Dynamic Understanding of People and Nature," *BioScience* 43, 8: 545–53.

Daly, H. E. (1973) "Introduction," in H. E. Daly (ed.) *Toward a Steady-State Economy*, San Francisco: W. H. Freeman.

—— (1987) "The Economic Growth Debate: What Some Economists Have Learned but Many Have Not," *Journal of Environmental Economics and Management* 14: 323–36.

—— (1992) "Allocation, Distribution, and Scale: Towards an Economics That Is Efficient, Just, and Sustainable," *Ecological Economics* 6: 185–93.

—— (1993) "Valuing the Earth: Economics, Ecology, Ethics," in H. E. Daly and K. Townsend (eds.) *Valuing the Earth: Economics, Ecology, Ethics*, Cambridge, Mass.: MIT Press.

—— (1996) *Beyond Growth*, Boston: Beacon Press.

Georgescu-Roegen, N. (1966) *Analytical Economics*, Cambridge, Mass.: Harvard University Press.

—— (1971) *The Entropy Law and the Economic Process*, Cambridge Mass.: Harvard University Press.

—— (1986) "The Entropy Law and the Economic Process in Retrospect," *Eastern Economic Journal* 12: 3–25.

—— (1993) "The Entropy Law and the Economic Problem," in H. E. Daly and K. Townsend (eds.) *Valuing the Earth: Economics, Ecology, Ethics*, Cambridge, Mass.: MIT Press.

Goeller, H. E. and Weinberg, A. M. (1976) "The Age of Substitutability: What Do We Do When the Mercury Runs Out?," *Science* 191: 683–9.

Goodland, R. (1992) "The Case That the World Has Reached Limits," in R. Goodland, H. E. Daly and S. El Sarafy (eds.) *Population, Technology and Lifestyle: The Transition to Sustainability*, Washington, D.C.: Island Press.

McGinn, A. P. (1998) "Rocking the Boat: Conserving Fisheries and Protecting Jobs," Worldwatch Paper 142, Washington, D.C.: Worldwatch Institute.

Martinez-Alier, J. (1987) *Ecological Economics: Energy, Environment, and Society*, Cambridge, Mass.: Basil Blackwell.

Mirowski, P. (1988) "Energy and Energetics in Economic Theory: A Review Essay," *Journal of Economic Issues* 22: 811–30.

Nordhaus, W. D. (1991) "To Slow or Not to Slow: The Economics of the Greenhouse Effect," *Economic Journal* 6, 101: 920–48.

Norgaard, R. B. (1989) "The Case for Methodological Pluralism," *Ecological Economics* 1: 37–57.

Odum, H. and Odum, E. (1976) *Energy Basis for Man and Nature*, New York: McGraw-Hill.

Pearce, D. W. (1987) "Foundation of Ecological Economics," *Ecological Modelling* 38: 9–18.

Rawls, J. (1971) *A Theory of Justice*, Cambridge, Mass.: Harvard University Press.

Rosenberg, N. (1973) "Innovative Responses to Materials Shortages," *American Economic Review* 63, 2: 111–18.

Solow, R. M. (1974) "The Economics of Resources or the Resources of Economics," *American Economic Review* 64, 2: 1–14.

Young, J. T. (1991) "Is the Entropy Law Relevant to the Economics of Natural Resource Scarcity?" *Journal of Environmental Economics and Management* 21: 169–79.

chapter
nine

THE ECONOMICS OF SUSTAINABLE DEVELOPMENT

learning objectives

After reading this chapter you will be familiar with the following:

- the link between biophysical limits and economics of sustainable development;
- sustainable development as defined by the Brundtland Commission report;
- the problem of defining sustainable economic development;
- sustainability and the nature of the relationship between human and nature capital;
- trade-offs between intergenerational efficiency and equity;
- the Hartwick–Solow approach to sustainability;
- the ecological economic approach to sustainability;
- the safe minimum standard (SMS) approach to sustainability;
- sustainable national income account.

Issues of sustainability are ultimately issues of limits. If material economic growth is sustainable indefinitely by technology, then all the environmental problems can (in theory at least) be fixed technologically. Issues of fairness, equity and distribution (between sub-groups and generations of our species and between our species and others) are also issues of limits. We don't have to worry so much about how an expanding pie is divided, but a constant or shrinking pie presents real problems. Finally, dealing with uncertainty about limits is the fundamental issue. If we are unsure about future limits then the prudent course is to assume they exist. One does not run blindly through a dark landscape that may contain crevasses. One assumes they are there and goes gingerly and with eyes wide open, at least, until one can see a little better.

(Costanza *et al.* 1997: xix–xx)

The problem of ecological sustainability needs to be solved at the level of preferences or technology, not at the level of optimal prices. Only if the preferences and production possibility sets informing economic behaviour are ecologically sustainable can the corresponding set of optimal and intertemporally efficient prices be ecologically sustainable. Thus the principle of "consumer sovereignty" on which most conventional economic solutions are based, is only acceptable to the extent that consumer interests do not threaten the overall system – and through this the welfare of future generations.

(Costanza *et al.* 1997: xv)

9.1 INTRODUCTION

A careful reading of the above two epigraphs tells us the following: First, issues of sustainability are about *biophysical limits*. Therefore, there will be a natural overlap between issues addressed in this chapter and those considered in the previous three chapters.

Second, the economics of sustainability goes far beyond the neoclassical focus on the *efficient allocation* of scarce environmental resources. It requires that issues of fairness, equity and distribution be explicitly considered. These issues have a time dimension (and often involving several human generations), and they include considerations of the well-being of species other than humans.

Third, the problem of ecological sustainability requires careful scrutiny of our *technological choices*, and it also demands reexaminations of our *social* and *value systems* – to the extent that they affect human preferences. This questions the usual treatment of preferences as an exogenously determined variable.

Fourth, the economics of sustainable development deals with the decision-making process under extremely *uncertain circumstances*. Uncertainty is a vital consideration in the economics of sustainability because over time it is expected that changes will occur in technology, income and people's preference(s). Technology may change enormously in response to changing relative scarcities and knowledge. Income will not be constant and preferences will differ across generations. The problem is not that changes will occur, but rather that we do not know for sure how and when these changes will occur (i.e., the changes will be, from our prospect viewpoint, random in nature) and we do not know what the implications of these changes will be for future resource availability. Furthermore, in the economics of sustainability, attention is given to the uncertain effects of the current level and pattern of human enterprise on the integrity of the natural ecosystem (Krutilla 1967; Perrings 1991). In this particular context, one issue of significance is *irreversibility*. That is, beyond a certain threshold, continued human exploitation of nature or economic growth may cause irreversible damage to certain vital components of a natural ecosystem (such as forestland, wetland preserves, etc.).

This chapter provides a systematic analysis of the above four key issues, namely physical limits, intergenerational equity and economic efficiency, technological options and social values, and intertemporal management of natural resources under conditions of uncertainty and irreversibility. These four broad categories of issues are analyzed by assuming that the overriding social goal is progress toward sustainable economic development.

In recent years, there seems to have been a heightened interest among academicians and public policy-makers on the general issue of sustainable development. Since sustainability assumes explicit recognition of bio-physical limits as potential constraints to long-run economic growth, the debate on "limits to economic growth" (a topic that occupied much of our attention in Chapters 6–8) is rendered fruitless. In other words, the very existence of biophysical limits is no longer an issue of significant contention. However, this in no way suggests that no controversial issues are involved in the economics of sustainable development. On the contrary, controversies exist, and primarily arise from the way sustainability is conceptualized.

In this chapter, sustainable development is examined using three different conceptions of sustainability, namely Hartwick–Solow sustainability, eco-logical economics sustainability and safe minimum standards (SMS) sustainability. Hartwick–Solow sustainability basically represents the neo-classical perspective on the economics of sustainable development, and one of its defining characteristics is the assumption that human capital (basic economic infrastructure, such as machines, buildings, highway systems, knowledge, etc.) and natural capital (stock of environmentally provided assets such as soil, forest, wetland preserves, water, fishing grounds, etc.) are *substitutes*. Thus, natural capital may not be considered as an absolute necessity or a nonbinding constraint to sustainability. For this reason, the Hartwick–Solow approach is viewed as being equivalent to *weak sustain-ability*. By contrast, the ecological economics sustainability presumes that the sustainability of ecological systems is a prerequisite to sustainable economic development; and it views human and natural capital as com-plements. *Strong sustainability* is an alternative phrase often used to describe the ecological economics sustainability approach. Finally, SMS, the third approach to sustainability, has as its central theme the uncertainty associated with irreversible environmental damage and its implications for long-term resource management. Thus, the main focus is not so much on whether human and natural capital are substitutes or complements, but rather on resource management decisions under conditions of uncertainty and irreversibility.

Before further consideration of these three approaches, it is important to give a clear meaning to sustainable development. As will be evident from the discussions in the next section, this will not be easy. The aim of this effort is rather modest. It is not so much to establish a consensus on the definition of sustainable development, as to pinpoint certain key features of sustainable development so that the essential elements of the concept are clearly featured and understood. The hope is that this could help ameliorate some of the existing confusion on the subject.

9.2 SUSTAINABLE DEVELOPMENT: A HELPFUL TERM OR A VAGUE AND ANALYTICALLY EMPTY CONCEPT?

Since the early 1980s, the term *sustainable development* has been used widely and rather indiscriminately. The phrase started to gain its popularity when it became increasingly fashionable to use it as a way of responding to global environmental concerns (such as global warming, biodiversity, ozone depletion, etc.). The unintended outcome of this has been to render the concept somewhat broad and vague. In fact, some scholars (including economists) have even gone so far as to claim that the concept of sustainable development is too vague and, as such, is void of analytical content. Of course, this is a rather extreme position to take. However, this outcry of academicians does justifiably indicate the need for a sharper definition and understanding of sustainable development.

It was with this in mind that the World Commission on Environment and Development, a UN agency, commissioned a study on the subject of sustainable development. This culminated in the publication of the Brundtland Commission Report, *Our Common Future* (World Commission on Environment and Development 1987). This report defined sustainable development as "development which meets the needs of the present without sacrificing the ability of the future to meet its needs." This definition not only is well known, but is, in many instances, accepted as the standard definition of sustainable development.

There are several key features of the above definition that are worth pointing out. First, the definition clearly establishes sustainable development as an *equity* issue. As such, it conveys that the economics of sustainable development has principally a normative goal. Second, the Brundtland Report's definition of sustainable development offers a rather specific ethical criterion: the needs of the present are not to be satisfied at the expense of future needs (well-being). It therefore deals with equity across generations: intergenerational equity. Third, the Brundtland Report, by emphasizing equity, raises a question concerning the validity of standard economic analysis based exclusively on efficiency.

Indeed, the Brundtland Report's definition of sustainability has been quite helpful in establishing a clear consensus that sustainable development is principally an ethical issue. Yet a number of important features of sustainable development that were discussed in the first section of this chapter are not explicitly captured by the Brundtland Report definition. The purpose of discussing these missing features is not to indicate weaknesses in the report, however, because no one definition can realistically be expected to capture all the essential elements of a seemingly dialectic concept like sustainable development.

First, the Brundtland Report's definition of sustainable development is not explicit about the physical and technological dimensions of the resource constraints required for sustainability. In other words, what is the specific nature of the resource constraints required for sustainability? Is human capital considered a substitute for or a complement to *natural capital*? What are the assumptions about the role of technology in ameliorating or circumventing resource scarcity? How should the various resource constraints be measured – that is, in physical or in monetary terms?

Second, it is not clear from the Brundtland Report definition, what the term "development" implies or how it is (should be) measured if it is going to be used as an indicator of intergenerational "well-being." Does development refer to the conventional conception of economic growth: an increase in the quantity of goods and services? Or does it refer to the kind of qualitative economic growth discussed in Chapter 8 in conjunction with Herman Daly's notion of the steady-state economy? Is development measured using the conventional national accounting system (gross national product, GNP)? Does it matter how the depreciation of human versus natural capital stocks is treated?

Third, the Brundtland Report definition does not make clear the exact nature of the trade-offs between equity and efficiency. The report simply emphasizes the importance of equity in any considerations of sustainable development. Yes, this signals a departure from economic analyses that are based on the premises of the neoclassical economic paradigm, but does this mean that the efficiency consideration is irrelevant? Figure 9.1 is used to illustrate the significance of this question. This figure is constructed assuming a number of simplifying conditions. The curve represents a production possibility frontier, similar to that presented in Chapter 1 but measured in terms of GNP – the monetary value of all goods and services produced. In other words, GNP is used as a measure of well-being (more on this in Section 9.6). This production possibility frontier is constructed for given tastes, technology and resource endowments, across two generations. It also assumes that market prices reflect "true" scarcity values, and that markets exist for all goods and services (see Chapter 2).

What can be said about the trade-offs between efficiency and equity from Figure 9.1? Let us assume that our starting point is point G. Clearly, this point is inefficient because it is located inside the production possibility frontier. A move to point J or I or any point between these two would lead to a Pareto optimal outcome. That is, such a move would benefit at least one of the generations without affecting the well-being of the other generation. The discussion so far seems to suggest that efficiency (which is reflected by points along the production possibility frontier) is desirable. However, what if a move were made from point G to H? Clearly, point H is efficient since it is on the production possibility frontier. But the move to point H makes the future generation worse off. Thus, equity considerations may preclude such a move. The point that needs to be stressed is this: If equity is an important issue in considering sustainable development, not all efficient points are sustainable.

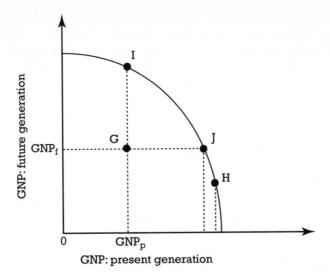

Figure 9.1 **Trade-offs between intergenerational efficiency and equity**

The upshot of the above discussion is clear. Despite the gallant effort of the Brundtland Report, it is, if not impossible, very difficult to define sustainable development in ways that are both unambiguous and comprehensive enough to include all the key attributes essential to a clear understanding of the full implication(s) of the concept. However, as indicated in the above discussions, the concept of sustainable development has far-reaching implications that go beyond making a statement about the significance of intergenerational equity. These include careful considerations of the exact nature of the resource (capital) constraints; technological options and their limits; economic efficiency; intergenerational equity; and aspects of human values and institutions consistent with sustainable development. To the extent that a conscious effort is made to do this, even if we cannot come up with an analytically precise definition, our definition will be descriptively rich enough to provide us with a clear picture of the essential elements necessary to understand the full implications of sustainable development.

In this section an attempt was made to identify the elements essential to understanding the primary goals of sustainable development. That done, it is now time to begin to explain and evaluate the three alternative approaches to sustainability referred to in Section 9.1. It is important to note that the term "sustainability" is used in a very specific context – that is, as condition(s) for sustainable "economic development."

9.3 THE HARTWICK–SOLOW APPROACH TO SUSTAINABILITY

To begin with, in the Hartwick–Solow approach, sustainability is defined in terms of maintaining a constant real consumption (of goods and services) over an indefinite period of time while recognizing the constraints imposed by a given set of resource endowments. The constraint of exhaustible resources is particularly stressed in this approach. In fact, the core problem of sustainability is initially envisioned in terms of how consumption of goods and services could be sustained over several generations given that some resources are potentially exhaustible.

The above notion of consumption is then related to an equivalent concept of a net income by using Hicks's (1946: 172) definition of income:

> The purpose of income calculations in practical affairs is to give people an indication of the amount which they can consume without impoverishing themselves. Following out this idea, it would seem that we ought to define a man's income as the maximum value which he can consume during a week, and still expect to be as well off at the end of the week as he was at the beginning. Thus when a person saves he plans to be better off in the future; when he lives beyond his income he plans to be worse off. Remembering that the practical purpose of income is to serve as a guide for prudent conduct, I think it is fairly clear that this is what the central meaning must be.

Thus what Hicks has in mind is *sustainable net income*: the amount that can be spent on a regular basis without causing impoverishment in some future period. Viewed this way, sustainability has the following two important implications:

First, due to depreciation of capital assets (buildings, machines, highways, etc.) and the degradation of the natural environment, sustainable economic development would require maintenance of a nondeclining capital stock – composed of natural and human capital. That is, maintenance of an "appropriate level" of constant capital stock is a crucial component of the definition of sustainability. It should be noted also that the replacement of the depreciated capital assets requires constant withdrawal of both renewable and exhaustible resources from nature (for clear distinctions between renewable and exhaustible resources refer back to the Introduction to the book).

Second, sustainability requires that the conventional method of national income accounting be reexamined. According to the conventional income accounting system, net national product (NNP), which is used as a proxy for measuring the aggregate well-being of a given society, is obtained by subtracting the depreciation of human capital (machines, buildings, roads, etc.) from the gross national product (GNP). *What is not accounted for in this procedure is the depreciation or depletion of natural capital assets* (forest, fisheries, mineral deposits, etc.) that have been used up to support the production and consumption activities of an economy. Thus, for a sustainable *net* national product, GNP must be modified to account for the depreciation of natural capital in the same way that net national income is equal to gross national income less estimated depreciation on human-generated capital. (Section 9.6 provides a comprehensive treatment of this topic.)

Such an adjustment to the conventional method for the accounting of national income should not be taken lightly as it has a very important implication for how economic growth is perceived and defended. For example, as Dieren (1995: 189) points out,

> In the majority of developing countries . . . proceeds from mining natural resources have been treated as income. The faster the depletion, the more prosperous the country would seem to be and the more rapid its apparent economic growth. The fact that such prosperity would be ephemeral, and that the apparent growth was misleading, did not seem to worry most economists who continued to base their country analysis and policy prescriptions uncritically on the erroneously reckoned national accounts.

A distinguishing feature of Hartwick–Solow sustainability is its conception of the capital stocks. In this regard, it adheres to the neoclassical perspectives of natural resources discussed at some length in Chapter 7. More specifically, it assumes that natural and human capital are *substitutes*. This is a critical assumption since it has the far-reaching implication of making natural resources a nonbinding constraint to sustainability. This is because, as discussed in Chapter 7, if human and natural capital are substitutes, depletion of exhaustible resources and large-scale degradation of environmental quality need not be a major source of concern. According to this view, sustainable development simply requires the maintenance of constant capital stock, but the composition of the capital stock is not considered relevant. For this reason the Hartwick–Solow criterion for sustainability is sometimes referred to as the *weak sustainability* criterion – weak in the sense that it does *not* render natural capital an absolute must for continued economic growth. Given this, the relevant issue is then whether "adequate" compensatory investments are made to protect the interests of future generations.

This is clearly an ethical question, and it is partially addressed by an application of a simple *sustainability rule* developed by Hartwick (1977). This rule simply states that maintaining a constant real consumption of goods and services or real income (in the Hicksian sense) is possible even in the face of exhaustible resources provided that the rent (see Chapter 3) derived from "an intertemporally efficient use" of these resources is reinvested into renewable capital assets. *Thus, the focus of concern is on the prudent use of the returns or savings from exhaustible resources rather than the fact of the depletion of these resources* (see Exhibit 9.1).

EXHIBIT 9.1 WHAT WILL HAPPEN TO SAUDI ARABIA WHEN ITS OIL RESERVES ARE EVENTUALLY EXHAUSTED?

It is widely accepted that Saudi Arabia possesses the largest share of the total known petroleum reserves in the world. This is also a nation whose people's livelihood depends solely on this one commodity. The revenue from petroleum exports accounts for a significant share of the country's GNP. This is because most of Saudi Arabia is primarily a desert and unsuitable for conventional agricultural pursuits. Furthermore, Saudi Arabia has an insignificant amount of other mineral deposits apart from petroleum. There is therefore good reason for Saudi Arabia to be concerned about what happens when the petroleum is exhausted.

This is a fundamental concern that goes beyond Saudi Arabia. It pertains to the sustainability of an economy that depends solely on an exhaustible mineral resource(s). If a fundamental concern of this nature is addressed within the context of the Hartwick–Solow sustainability approach, the following will be the course of action that Saudi Arabia may need to take in order to assure a reasonable standard of living for its citizens beyond the petroleum age:

First, the extraction rates of the country's petroleum deposits are determined in such a way as to maximize the present value of the rent from the intertemporal use of its total petroleum deposits. In general, this intertemporally efficient use of resources is consistent with maximizing current extraction rates, and as such dictates that certain principles of resource conservation be observed (more on this in Chapter 17). Thus, Saudi Arabia cannot simply pump more oil at any price just to raise the standard of living of the current generation.

Second, sustainability requires that the rent derived from the current extraction of petroleum be reinvested into other forms of renewable capital assets. For example, in the case of Saudi Arabia, this may entail investing in large-scale water desalination projects. If successful, this may allow Saudi Arabia to irrigate its land and produce agricultural products in sufficient amounts to feed its people and even export on a sustainable basis. This is just one of many options that Saudi Arabia has to use an exhaustible resource, petroleum, without jeopardizing the well-being of its future citizens.

The clear message is that the people of Saudi Arabia can sustain a reasonable standard of living into the indefinite future provided they are able to use their rich deposits of petroleum efficiently at all times. Of course, this will not occur automatically or without some difficulty. It requires prudent long-term planning, self-discipline and astuteness in using the proceeds from oil.

However, Hartwick derived the above "sustainability rule" primarily to trace the optimal intertemporal sustainable path (or course of actions). The derivation of this rule is based on several assumptions. Among others, preferences and resource ownership are exogenously determined; and market prices are assumed to reflect the true social value of resources over time, which literally implies the existence of a complete set of competitive markets from now to eternity. Strictly speaking, then, *this rule is more of a condition of intergenerational efficiency than it is for sustainability*.

In addition, to the extent that intergenerational efficiency deals with comparing the welfare of people across generations, the issue of *discounting* cannot be ignored. The notion of discounting refers to people's preference for present consumption (benefit) relative to future consumption (benefit). In general, it is assumed that people have *positive* time preference. That is, other things remaining equal, people prefer their benefit (consumption) now rather than later. Given this, people would be willing to trade or substitute present consumption for consumption at a future date only at a *premium* or by discounting the future. In other words, to sacrifice a dollar's worth of present consumption people would require compensation exceeding a dollar in future consumption. For example, sacrificing $1 worth of present consumption may require $1.10 in future consumption. This suggests that the general tendency is for people to *discount* future consumption, meaning that they value it less. The rate at which this is done is called the *discount rate*, and indicates the rate at which present consumption is substituted or traded for consumption in future date. For example, the simple numerical example given above implies a discount rate of 10 percent (more on this in Chapter 15).

Why do people discount the future? The standard reply is that people tend to discount the future because they are either myopic or uncertain (or both) about the future. In general, individuals are seen as selfish and shortsighted. They seem to be mostly concerned with their own welfare in the present or in the very near future, assigning little importance to a benefit (or cost) that might be forthcoming in the future. *The implication of this is that people, in general, would prefer to consume more at the present than in the future.* This will be the case provided the discount rate is greater than zero.

Furthermore, the general expectation is that the future will be discounted more heavily by private individuals than by a society at large. This is because individuals (or private concerns) will not view the future the same way as a society, which represents the collective concerns of individuals. Society is likely to be less shortsighted and uncertain about the future than the individual (more on this in Chapter 15).

Thus, the *choice* of the discount rate (private versus social) is crucial. As discussed above, any positive discount rate would automatically imply a desire to consume more at present than in the future. To such an extent the very idea of discounting becomes an ethical issue since the decision made by the current generation on the basis of this rate affects the well-being of future generations – a lower discount rate generally favoring the future generations. *Nevertheless, in the Hartwick–Solow approach to sustainability this is not considered a serious problem since the effect of a positive discount rate could be offset by a rate of growth in technical progress.* Accordingly, there is nothing intrinsically wrong or immoral in using a positive discount rate.

What remains now is to briefly discuss some of the major weaknesses of the Hartwick–Solow sustainability approach. First, this approach assumes that, in the main, human-generated and natural capital are substitutes. As we observed in Chapter 8, this assumption has been a source of lively dispute between neoclassical and ecological economists. Ecological economists believe that at the current level and pattern of human economic activity, it is more appropriate to view human and natural capital as *complements*, not substitutes. The implication of this assumption for sustainability is far-reaching, as will be evident in our discussion in the next section.

Second, as discussed above, intergenerational efficiency requires that the prices of all goods and services (including environmental goods) should reflect their social values. However, the practical problems of arranging this are not explicitly addressed (see Chapter 5). In other words, price distortions due to environmental externalities are either simply ignored or assumed to be remedied with little or no difficulty.

Third, some economists and ecologists would argue that the very idea of positive discounting is wrong (Perrings 1991). For this reason alone they view Hartwick–Solow sustainability as being insufficiently concerned with the well-being of future generations and as such ethically questionable.

Fourth, in the Hartwick–Solow approach the determination of the sustainable constraints (the actual size of the nondeclining capital stock) is assumed to be independent of the current level and pattern of human economic development (Daly 1996). Should the current level (initial position) of aggregate resource consumption of goods and services be subject to a downward adjustment? What this suggests is that the Hartwick–Solow approach to sustainability does not explicitly consider *scale* (the size of the existing human economy relative to natural ecosystems) as an issue (Daly 1996).

In this regard, as we will see in the next section, ecological economists argue that the standard economic approach to sustainability is based on a rather narrow vision of the natural environment. In fact, the role that natural resources could play in the economic process is conceptualized without a clear understanding of the complex interactions between the economic and the ecological systems. To such an extent, the Hartwick–Solow conceptualization of sustainability is incomplete. It only refers to economic sustainability or *the sustainability of an economic system*. However, the fact that the sustainability of an economic system may be linked with or influenced by the ecological system (which the economic system is only a part of) does not seem to be formally acknowledged by the Hartwick–Solow model.

Sixth, the Hartwick–Solow approach to sustainability is specifically criticized for its inadequate treatment of the nature of the uncertainty associated with long-term natural resource assessment and management. The fact that beyond a certain threshold the scale of human economic activities could cause irreversible damage to the natural environment (ecosystem) is not recognized. This could be a serious omission since the cost may entail the irrevocable loss of human life support systems or major reductions in the quality of human life (such as increase in cancer incidence due to the depletion of ozone from the upper strata of the atmosphere). Uncertainty associated with irreversible environmental damage and its implications for long-term resource management will be the central theme of the discussions in Section 9.5, which deals with the safe minimum standard approach to sustainability.

9.4 THE ECOLOGICAL ECONOMIC APPROACH TO SUSTAINABILITY

Most of the basic ideas of the ecological economic approach to sustainability and its drawbacks have already been addressed in Chapter 8 in conjunction with the discussion of Herman Daly's steady-state economy (SSE) model. Therefore, to avoid unnecessary repetition, in this section the discussion of ecological sustainability will be brief and limited in its scope. The focus will be on clarifying the key differences between the sustainability concepts of neoclassical economics (Hartwick–Solow) and ecological economics.

The ecological economics approach to sustainability starts with a worldview that the natural world is not only finite, but also nongrowing and materially closed. Furthermore, it is postulated that the general capacity of this finite natural world is starting to be strained by the size of the human economy, as measured by the aggregate use of throughput – low-entropic matter–energy. Proponents of this so-called "full-world view" insist that this new reality demands a shift in our vision of how the human economic system is related to the natural world. What has become increasingly evident is the unsustainability of "economic growth," especially if it is based on increasing use of throughput from the natural ecosystem. Why is that so?

In the "full-world" scenario, natural and human capitals can no longer be viewed as substitutes. In fact, the more realistic way to view the future relation between these two components of capital is as *complements*. What this suggests is that a combination of both types of capital assets is needed in the production process. *Thus, contrary to what has been suggested by the Hartwick–Solow approach to sustainability, an economy cannot continue to function without natural capital.* Furthermore, it is expected that natural capital will be the *limiting factor* in the future. That is, fishing will be limited not by the number of fishing boats but by remaining fish stocks; petroleum use will be limited not by refining capacity but by geologic deposits and by atmospheric capacity to absorb carbon dioxide. Most important of all, human-made capital (machines, buildings, etc.) cannot be substituted for scarce terrestrial energy without limit because a certain minimum energy is required in any transformation of matter or performance of work (Dieren 1995). *To that extent, then, natural capital is the key factor in any consideration of sustainability.* Thus, because natural capital is viewed as a limiting factor to future economic growth, the ecological economic approach to sustainability is sometimes referred to as the *strong sustainability* criterion.

Accordingly, the ecological economics approach defines sustainability in terms of a nondeclining (constant) "natural" capital. A consideration of inter-generational equity is the underlying reason for this specific requirement. If viewed as a problem of an intertemporal efficient allocation of resources, the ideal size of the constant natural capital constraint would be kept at a level that would be adequate to ensure that, at a minimum, future generations will be left no worse off than current generations.

However, the above ethical concern is rather narrow to the extent that it tends to be human centered or anthropocentric in its perspective. It is argued that ecological sustainability needs to go beyond human interests. At least in principle, the ecological economics approach to sustainability involves concerns extending beyond the human species: the well-being of ecological systems in their entirety. For this reason, the ecological approach to sustainability is broadly defined and has both economic and ecological dimensions. Thus, the level at which the nondeclining natural capital stock is set is expected to be consistent not only with economic sustainability but also with the ability of the ecosystem to withstand shocks: ecological resilience (see Case Study 9.1). The ultimate effect of all this will be to provide greater allowance for natural resource preservation for the purpose of safeguarding future generations against large-scale, irreversible ecological damage (such as biodiversity loss, global warming, etc.).

From a public policy perspective, the sustainability rules often advocated by the proponents of the ecological economics approach to sustainability are of the following nature:

1 The rate of exploitation of renewable resources should not exceed the regeneration rate.
2 Waste emission (pollution) should be kept at or below the waste-absorptive capacity of the environment. For flow or degradable wastes the rate of discharge should be less than the rate at which the ecosystem can absorb those wastes. For stock or persistent wastes (such as DDT, radioactive substances, etc.) the rates of discharges should be zero since the ecosystem has no capacity to absorb these wastes.
3 The extraction of nonrenewable resources (such as oil) should be consistent with the development of renewable substitutes. This is equivalent to the compensatory investment rule advocated by Hartwick.

CASE STUDY 9.1 SUSTAINABLE FOREST MANAGEMENT PRACTICE: THE CASE OF THE MENOMINEE INDIAN RESERVATION

The Menominee Indian Reservation of Wisconsin is a federally recognized sovereign "nation." The reservation was established in 1854. It occupies 234,000 acres, about 95 percent of which is covered with mixed hardwood/coniferous forests. Today, the population of the Menominee community is about 8,000 and half of them live on the reservation. About 25 percent of the workforce make their living on jobs directly related to the management, harvesting and processing of timber.

The Menominee Indians claim that they have been practicing sustainable forestry since the birth of their reservation more than 140 years ago. In fact, sustainable forest management practice is part of the present-day Menominee Constitution. In general, sustainable forestry is defined as harvesting trees at a rate within the forests' capacity to regrow (more on this in Chapter 16). Furthermore, the Menominee sustainable forestry practice refers "not only to forest products and social benefits, but also to worldlife, site productivity, and other ecosystem functions" (Menominee Tribal Enterprises 1997: 9).

To assure this, the Menominee Indians follow forestry management principles that rely on both their strong traditional beliefs as the stewards of nature and state-of-the-art forestry technology. The "annual allowable cut" from the reservation forest is determined on the basis of a 15-year cutting cycle with 150-year planning horizon, employing various methods including selective cutting, shelterwood, and small-scale clear-cutting only when it can improve stand quality and diversity. Up-to-date information on change in timber volume and growth is provided through the use of the continuous forest inventory (CFI) method.

The production, marketing and product distribution aspects of the tribe are handled by the Menominee Tribal Enterprise (MTE). MTE claims that silviculture, not market forces, determines how much wood is cut. It is estimated that when the reservation was established, it contained 1.2 billion feet of timber. Since then, 2 billion feet have been cut, and 1.5 billion feet are standing today. The standing timber volume inventory now is greater than at the time when the reservation was created in 1854.

Although several efforts including a gaming (casino) operation are under way to diversify the economic basis of the Menominee community, the forest with its multiple products continues to be one of the major sources of employment and income. While the Menominee forest is one of the most intensively managed tracts of forest, it still remains the best example of biodiversity in the Great Lakes Regions. From the air, it has been described as "a big green postage stamp," or "an island of trees in a sea of farmland." The contrast can be seen from space, and entering the reservation along Highway 55 has been described as entering a "wall of trees." In this respect, although on a small scale, the Menominee Reservation has provided a successful model of sustainable development for the twenty-first century. During the Earth Day celebration of 1995 the United Nations formally recognized the exemplary achievements of the MTE in its forest-based sustainable development practices. A year later, Vice President Al Gore presented the Menominee with the President's Award for Sustainable Development.

In fact, these may be considered very vague operational rules for several reasons. First, nothing specific is said about the regenerative (or natural growth) rate of renewable resources. For example, in the case of fish, as will be shown in Chapter 16, there can be an infinite number of *sustainable* harvests (where annual harvest equals to the annual growth in fish population or biomass), depending on the underlying fish population. In this case, society has to make a decision regarding the "optimal" sustainable harvest rate. The above general rule does not address this important issue. Second, the rule that states "waste emission should be kept at or below the waste-absorptive capacity of the environment" totally ignores economic considerations. As discussed in Chapter 5, the "optimal" level of pollution can be in excess of the absorptive capacity of the environment. Third, in general, the above rules are only stated in biophysical terms without much economic content and institutional context. To that extent their usefulness as a guide to public policy may be somewhat limited.

9.5 THE SAFE MINIMUM STANDARD (SMS) APPROACH TO SUSTAINABILITY

The idea of a safe minimum standard traces its origin to the work of Ciriacy-Wantrup (1952) and Bishop (1978). It started as a practical guide to natural resource management under the condition of extreme uncertainty; for example, the preservation of individual species such as the Pacific northwest spotted owl. For problems of this nature, it is argued that irreversibility becomes a key issue to consider. That is, beyond a certain threshold (or critical zone), the exploitation of natural resources may lead to irreversible damage. For example, the Pacific northwest spotted owl would be declared extinct if its population dropped beyond a certain minimum; and this minimum is greater than zero. Therefore, in managing natural resources of this nature, it is highly important to pay serious attention to not extending resource use beyond a certain safe minimum standard (SMS). Otherwise, the social opportunity cost of reversing direction might become "unacceptably large." However, it is important to note that considerable uncertainty exists regarding both the cost and the irreversibility of particular human impacts on the natural environment. Thus, it is in this sense that uncertainty is central to the concept of safe minimum standard.

What specific relevance does the SMS approach to resource management have to sustainability? The answer to this question lies in understanding the implications of irreversibility and the potential social opportunity cost associated with it. In situations where human impacts on the natural environment are regarded as uncertain but may be large and irreversible, *the SMS suggests that human and natural capital cannot be safely assumed to be substitutes*. That is, when viewed from a long-run resource management perspective, the nature of the substitution possibilities between natural and human capital is uncertain. In this respect, then, *sustainability warrants maintenance of nondeclining natural capital*.

Understood this way, the SMS approach to sustainability does not totally invalidate the standard economics approach to resource assessment and management, or even the concept of sustainability. It simply narrows the scope and the applicability of the standard economics conception of sustainability by restricting its relevance to human impacts on the natural environment where the potential consequences are regarded as being small and reversible. In this situation, Hartwick's compensatory investments could be applicable, and social opportunity costs could be assessed using standard cost–benefit analysis (see Chapter 15).

It is also obvious that, to some degree, the SMS and the ecological approaches to sustainability share common features. Both approaches adhere to the notion of limits in the substitution possibilities between human and natural capital. However, these two approaches provide different explanations for *limits* in factor substitutions. The SMS uses irreversibility while the ecological economics approach relies on all-encompassing physical laws (of which ecological irreversibility is only a part).

In many respects, then, the SMS approach to sustainability can be perceived as a hybrid between the standard and the ecological economic approaches to sustainability. It does not attempt to reject the basic tenets of the standard economics approach to sustainability and resource assessment and management philosophies. At the same time, in broad terms it collaborates with the ecological economics notion that nature in some ways imposes limits to factor substitutions (see Case Study 9.2).

Finally, it is important to note that the operational rule of SMS is quite straightforward. When the level of uncertainty and the social opportunity of current activities (such as global warming, ozone depletion and protection for rare, threatened or endangered ecosystems and habitats) are both high, the

CASE STUDY 9.2 HABITAT PRESERVATION OF ENDANGERED FISH SPECIES IN THE VIRGIN RIVER SYSTEMS: AN APPLICATION OF THE SAFE MINIMUM STANDARD APPROACH

This case study is based on an article that appeared in the *Journal of Land Economics* (Berrens *et al.* 1998). This article dealt with two regional case studies from the south-western United States, the Colorado and Virgin River systems. The primary objective of these studies was to analyze the regional and subregional economic impacts of the US Federal Court order for the preservation of endangered fish species in the designated areas. The rules for this court order were based on the provisions of the Endangered Species Act of 1973. These rules are consistent with the safe minimum standard (SMS) approach. Individual areas can be excluded from the designation of critical habitat, and therefore extinction of species is allowed if, and only if, the economic impacts of preservation are judged to be extremely severe or intolerable.

For brevity, only a summary of the economic impact analyses of the Virgin River study area is presented. This study area involved two counties: Clark County, Nevada, and Washington County, Utah. The problem stemmed from a precipitous decline in the fish populations observed in this area. The declines were caused by physical and biological alterations of the Virgin River systems primarily resulting from extended uses of water for agricultural, municipal and industrial purposes. The critical habitat designation was considered in order to restore the Virgin River systems to conditions that would allow the recovery of the endangered fish species.

The implementation of the above consideration will result in less diversion of the river water for commercial or human uses. The economic consequences of this were measured in terms of changes in output and employment. This in turn was done by comparing the economic activity with and without taking the needs of the endangered fish species into account. For the Virgin area study, the study covered a time horizon of over forty-five years (1995–2040) and the economic impact analyses were performed using input–output (I–O) models.

The overall economic impact of critical habitat designation was found to be negative but insignificant. The present value of the lost output was estimated to range between 0.0001 and 0.0003 percent from the baseline – the regional economic development scenario over the study's time span in the absence of the federal court order for habitat preservation on behalf of the endangered fish species. In terms of employment, the reduction was estimated to range between nine and sixty jobs. Subregional variations were observed in both the output and employment impacts. To put this into proper historical perspective, between 1959 and 1994 the regional economy in the Virgin study area grew on average by 3.01 percent.

Overall, the economic impacts of critical habitat designation were found to be far below the recommended threshold for exclusion, which was 1 percent deviation from the baseline projection of the aggregate economic activity. As a result, on the basis of regional economic impacts no sufficient ground could be established to recommend exemption from fish species protection in the Virgin River area.

prudent course entails erring on the side of the unknown. This is, in fact, identical to the precautionary principle discussed in Chapter 8. In the end, the important message conveyed by this rule is the social imperative for safeguarding against large-scale, irreversible degradation of natural capital.

9.6 SUSTAINABLE NATIONAL INCOME ACCOUNTING

As mentioned in Section 9.2, sustainable economic development requires a modification of the conventional national accounting concepts of income, in particular the gross national product (GNP). The key issue has been that a nation's income as measured by GNP does not account for *all* the resource costs that are attributable to the production of goods and services during a given accounting period, and as such cannot reflect a level of income (economic activities) that is sustainable indefinitely (El Serafy 1991; Daly 1996). The relevant question is, then, in what way(s) can the national accounting concepts of GNP be modified so that sustainability of income or economic activity is assured?

As discussed earlier, fundamental to sustainability is the requirement that a nondeclining (constant) capital be maintained. Capital is one of the primary factors that determines the productive capacity of a nation. This requirement for keeping capital intact can be achieved if, and only if, proper accounting is done for capital consumption or depreciation. In other words, given that capital is one of the primary determining factors of a nation's productive capacity, maintenance of a sustainable income – a level of income that a nation can receive while keeping its capital intact – requires setting aside a sufficient amount of current income to preserve capital so that the ability to generate future income is not adversely affected. From the viewpoint of a national income measurement, the implication of this is rather straightforward. An income accounting system that attempts to keep capital intact needs to explicitly account for capital depreciation (El Serafy 1997). Thus, the relevant income measurement is the net (not the gross) national income.

Traditionally, the above concern has been met by recognizing the depreciation of human capital (machines, buildings, inventories, etc.) as a legitimate deduction from gross income or product (income):

$$NNP = GNP - DHC \qquad (9.1)$$

where NNP is net national product (income) and DHC is the depreciation allowance of human capital. However, although widely used, adjustments of this nature are still incomplete to the extent that they fail to account for the depreciation of natural capital – environmental costs of current production and consumption activities (El Serafy 1997). These environmental costs can be grouped into two broad categories.

The first category consists of the monetary costs of net degradation and depletion of natural assets (forest, air and water qualities, fisheries, oil, etc.) directly attributable to current production and consumption activities (Daly 1996). The basic argument here is that to keep environmental capital intact, provision should be made for its degradation in the same way as for depreciation of human capital. However, how to reflect the charges in the stock of available natural resources (both renewable and nonrenewable resources) brought about by economic activity in national accounting measurements is still a controversial issue. Despite this, for our purpose here, the key issue is the recognition that natural assets are depreciable (degradable), and any effort to measure the *net* proceeds from an economic activity should account for this cost (Repetto 1992). This is how, in physical terms, the stark reality of this cost is depicted by Georgescu-Roegen (1993: 42):

> Economists are fond of saying that we cannot get something for nothing. The entropy law teaches us that the rule of biological life and, in man's case, of its economic continuation is far harsher. In entropy terms, the cost of any biological or economic enterprise is greater than the product. *In entropy terms, any such activity necessarily results in a deficit.*

The second category of environmental costs that needs to be considered is defensive expenditures (Daly 1996; Pearce 1993). Defensive expenditures are *real* costs incurred by society to prevent or avoid damage to the environment caused by the side effects of normal production and consumption activities (Daly 1996). Examples of this type of expenditure are extra expenditures on health care for problems due to air pollution; extra expenditures on cars to equip them with catalytic converters; and extra costs incurred in offshore water cleanup of oil spills. In the ordinary calculation of GNP, defensive expenditures of this nature are treated as part of the national income. But this is erroneous, given that defensive expenditures actually represent a loss of income that cannot be spent once again for consumption or investment but can be spent only to repair or prevent environmental damage caused by normal economic activities (Daly 1996). In fact, an environmentally defensive expenditure actually represents "a real income transfer from the human production system to the environment." Thus, if the goal is to estimate a measure of true net income, environmentally defensive expenditures should be deducted (not added, as is normally done) from GNP. These are not only real costs, but also could be significant relative to the total GNP.

Consequently, to arrive at an environmentally adjusted national income, equation (9.1) needs to be reformulated as follows:

$$SNI = NNP - DNC - EDE \qquad (9.2)$$

where SNI is sustainable national income, DNC is the depreciation of natural capital – the monetary value of the diminution of the natural resource stocks and the deterioration and degradation of the environment – and EDE represents the environmentally defensive expenditures. It should be noted that since national income is a flow measure, only those aspects of DNC and EDE that are relevant to the current accounting period should be considered (El Serafy 1997). At this stage, it is important to recognize that conceptually, assuming no change in technology, SNI represents the maximum amount of income that can be expended for current consumption without impairing the future productive capacity of a nation (i.e., keeping capital stock intact). This is the case because, at least conceptually, the depreciation costs for capital (including natural capital) are fully considered. Furthermore, explicit consideration of the environmentally defensive expenditures would avoid counting some environmental quality maintenance costs as income. However, while conceptually straightforward, environmentally adjusted national income like SNI would involve estimation of DNC and EDC, in equation (9.2), in monetary terms. In recent years, a great deal of work has been done on developing methodologies for valuing natural resources and the environment in monetary terms (Lutz 1993). Nevertheless, because of the subjective elements involved in the economic valuation of the environment, there appears to be no consensus among national income accountants on how best to make the appropriate adjustments for the environment. Thus, the income accounting approach proposed in this section, namely SNI, is just one of several methods currently in use by national accountants throughout the world to arrive at an environmentally adjusted net national income.

Since the mid-1980s much work has been done in the field of natural resources and environmental accounting (Lutz 1993). The pioneering work by Repetto *et al.* (1989) of the World Resources Institute includes important case studies for Costa Rica and Indonesia. The United Nations and the World Bank have conducted several joint studies which culminated in the publication of *Towards Improved Accounting for the Environment* (Lutz 1993). This publication includes case studies for Papua New Guinea and Mexico. In its 1993 revision, the United Nations' System of National Accounts (SNA) has officially advocated the use of an environmentally adjusted national income accounting or what is popularly known as "green

Table 9.1 **How green is your country?**

Country	GNP	Green NNP	% fall on GNP
	($ per capita 1993)		
Japan	31,449	27,374	−13
Norway	25,947	21,045	−18.9
United States	24,716	21,865	−11.5
Germany	23,494	20,844	−11.3
South Korea	7,681	7,041	−8.3
South Africa	3,582	2,997	−16.3
Brazil	2,936	2,579	−12.2
Indonesia	732	616	−15.8
China	490	411	−16.1
India	293	242	−17.4

Source: Nature Vol. 395, 1998, p. 428. Copyright © 1998 Macmillan Magazines Ltd. Reprinted by permission.

accounting." These are indeed important beginning steps in the effort to develop more refined and comprehensive methods of environmental accounting for sustainable development (see Table 9.1). In some important ways these efforts also reflect the increasing awareness of the global community that the natural environment is a *scarce* resource (not a free good) that needs to be managed prudently.

Let me conclude this section by pointing out one implication of green accounting with considerable national and international significance. Traditionally, gross domestic product (GDP) is used for international comparisons, and for measuring economic growth. Higher GDP and higher rate of growth in GDP are often identified as being clear signals of the strong and robust economic performance of a nation. However, this could be misleading if, for example, a country were deriving its prosperity largely from depleting its natural capital stocks. In this case, the current level of income would be unsustainable unless proper allowance were made for the liquidation (depreciation) of the natural capital assets. This is how this particular message was conveyed in *Taking Nature into Account* (Dieren 1995: 188–9), a book published as a report to the Club of Rome:

> To the extent that the depletion allowance was correctly estimated, and exploitation was carried out in the private sector, the national accounts came out right. In the majority of developing countries, however, where natural resources have been worked in the public sector, proceeds from mining natural resources have been treated as income. The faster the depletion, the more prosperous the country would seem to be and the more rapid its apparent economic growth. The fact that such prosperity would be ephemeral, and that the apparent growth was misleading, did not seem to worry most economists, who continued to base their country analysis and policy prescriptions uncritically on the erroneously reckoned national accounts.

9.7 CHAPTER SUMMARY

In this chapter, three alternative conceptual approaches to sustainable development were discussed: the Hartwick–Solow, ecological economics and the safe minimum standard (SMS).

- Careful examination of the above approaches to sustainability reveals that they share the following common features:

  1 In principle, there appears to be a tacit recognition of *biophysical limits* to economic growth.
  2 Sustainable economic development is envisioned as a viable and desirable option.
  3 A nondeclining capital stock (composed of natural and human capital) is regarded as a prerequisite for sustainability.
  4 Sustainability requires consideration of both efficiency and equity.

- However, the three approaches also differ in two *very* important ways:

  1 They differ in the way they perceive the relationships between human-made and natural capital. In the Hartwick–Solow approach, these two categories of capital are viewed as *substitutes*. This implies that the composition of the capital stock to be inherited by future generations is irrelevant. The ecological and the SMS approaches, in contrast, regard human-made and natural capital assets as *complements*.

  2 Differences exist in the degree of emphasis placed on equity relative to efficiency. In the Hartwick-Solow approach to sustainability the emphasis is on intertemporal efficiency: efficient allocation of societal resources over time. In the ecological approach, the emphasis is on intergenerational equity. The SMS approach emphasizes equity to the extent that present actions are suspected to cause irreversible harmful effects on future generations.

- All three approaches presented in this chapter are plagued by the difficulty associated with obtaining the information necessary to determine the "appropriate" size of the nondeclining capital stock.

- The determination of the "appropriate" capital stock size requires, at minimum, the following: price information extending over a long period of time; estimation of shadow prices (extramarket values) for nonmarket environmental goods; decisions on social discount rate; reexamination of the national accounting system; and the establishment of social, legal and political institutions intended to effectively operationalize the concept of sustainable development.

- Progress toward sustainable development may be slowed considerably because of unreasonably large administrative, information and legal costs.

- Another practical consideration that tends to hamper the implementation of sustainable development programs is concern for intragenerational equity (concern for the poor living today). In considering sustainability, the emphasis has been on intergenerational equity: the well-being of future generations. Given this, sustainability stresses *investment* in long-term projects at the expense of current *consumption*. However, concern about the currently poor entails adopting a policy that leads to increased current consumption, rather than increased investment.

- Despite the above-cited practical difficulties, the recent popularity among economists of sustainable development has contributed to increased academic interest in the following two important issues:

  1 *Intergenerational equity*. The key issue here is the ethical legitimacy of discounting.

  2 *Sustainable national income accounting*. In recent years, an increasing level of attention has been given to ways in which the conventional national accounting system might be overhauled in such a way that environmental defensive expenditures and depreciation of natural capital are accurately reflected.

review and discussion questions

1 Briefly identify the following concepts: intergenerational equity, the weak and strong sustainability conditions, private discount rate, social discount rate, depreciation of natural capital, environmental defense expenditures, net national income (NNI), sustainable national income (SNI).

2 State *True, False* or *Uncertain* and explain why.

(a) Not all efficient points are sustainable.

(b) GNP, however distributed, may be more an index of cost than of benefit.

(c) The main difference between the Hartwick–Solow and the ecological economics approaches to sustainability is the size at which the nondeclining capital stock is predetermined.

3 Sustainability should require considerations of both efficiency and equity. Discuss.

4 Sustainable development ultimately implies a static population size. Do you agree? Why, or why not?

5 Intergenerational fairness justifies no discounting at all. Comment.

6 "National accounting cannot be all-comprehensive, and accounting for environmental change will always be partial. Much environmental change will remain difficult or even impossible to value meaningfully in money terms, and this should be accepted" (Dieren 1995: 1991). Discuss.

REFERENCES AND FURTHER READING

Berrens, R. P., Brookshire, D. S. McKee, M. and Schmidt, C. (1998) "Implementing the Safe Minimum Standard Approach: Two Case Studies from the U.S. Endangered Species Act," *Land Economics* 2, 74: 147–61.

Bishop, R. C. (1978) "Endangered Species and Uncertainty: The Economics of a Safe Minimum Standard," *American Journal of Agricultural Economics* 60: 10–18.

Casler, E. N., Berrens, R. P. and Polasky, S. (1995) "Lecture in Economics: The Economics of Sustainability," Oregon State University Graduate Faculty of Economics Lecture Series No. 8.

Ciriacy-Wantrup, S. (1952) *Resource Conservation: Economics and Policy*, Berkeley: University of California Press.

Common, M. and Perrings, C. (1992) "Towards an Ecological Economics of Sustainability," *Ecological Economics* 6: 7–34.

Costanza, R., Perrings, C. and Cleveland, C. J. (1997) "Introduction," in R. Costanza, C. Perrings and C. J. Cleveland (eds.) *The Development of Ecological Economics*, London: Edward Elgar.

Daly, H. E. (1996) *Beyond Growth: The Economics of Sustainable Development*, Boston: Beacon Press.

Dieren, W. (ed.) (1995) *Taking Nature into Account: A Report to the Club of Rome*, New York: Springer-Verlag.

El Serafy, S. (1997) "The Environment as Capital," in R, Costanza, C. Perrings and C. J. Cleveland (eds.) *The Development of Ecological Economics*, London: Edward Elgar.

Georgescu-Roegen, N. (1993) "The Entropy Law and the Economic Problem," in H. E. Daly and K. N. Townsend (eds.), *Valuing the Earth: Economics, Ecology, Ethics*, Cambridge, Mass.: MIT Press.

Hanley, N., Shogren, J. F. and White, B. (1997) *Environmental Economics: In Theory and Practice*, New York: Oxford University Press.

Hartwick, J. M. (1977) "Intergenerational equity and the investing of rents from exhaustible resources," *American Economic Review* 67: 972–4.

—— (1978) "Substitution among exhaustible resources and intergenerational equity," *Review of Economic Studies* 45: 347–54.

Hicks, J. R. (1946) *The Value of Capital*, 2nd edn., Oxford: Oxford University Press.

Krutilla, J. V. (1967) "Conservation Reconsidered," *American Economic Review* 57, 4: 787–96.

Lutz, E. (ed.) (1993) *Towards Improved Accounting for the Environment*, Washington, D. C.: World Bank.

Menominee Tribal Enterprises (1997) *The Menominee Forest Management Tradition: History, Principles and Practices*, Keshena, Wis.: Menominee Tribal Enterprises.

Pearce, D. W. (1993) *Economic Values and the Natural World*, Cambridge, Mass.: MIT Press.

Perrings, C. (1991) "Reserved Rationality and the Precautionary Principles: Technological Change, Time, and Uncertainty in Environmental Decision Making," in R. Costanza (ed.) *Ecological Economics: The Science and Management of Sustainability*, New York: Columbia University Press.

Repetto, R. (1992) "Accounting for Environmental Assets," *Scientific American* 266: 94–100.

Repetto, R., McGrath, W., Wells, M., Beer, C. and Rossini, F. (1989) *Wasting Assets: Natural Resources in the National Accounts*, Washington, D.C.: World Resources Institute.

Solow, R. M. (1974) "The Economics of Resources or the Resources of Economics," *American Economic Review* 64: 1–14.

—— (1986), "On the intertemporal allocation of natural resources," *Scandinavian Journal of Economics* 88: 141–9.

—— (1993) "Sustainability: An Economist's Perspective," in R. Dorfman and N. Dorfman (eds.) *Selected Readings in Environmental Economics*, 3rd edn., New York: W. W. Norton.

World Bank (1992) *World Development Report 1992: Development and the Environment*, New York: Oxford University Press.

World Commission on Environment and Development (WCED) (1987) *Our Common Future*, New York: Oxford University Press.

part
six

THE ECONOMICS OF
ENVIRONMENTAL RESOURCES:
PUBLIC POLICIES AND
COST–BENEFIT ESTIMATIONS OF
ENVIRONMENTAL DAMAGE

Part Six is an extension of Part Four. It primarily covers topics relating to the economics of the natural environment with specific reference to the use of the environment for the disposal of waste products from human activities. The primary issue here is public policy. Theories are discussed to the extent that they are relevant to the understanding of environmental policy issues.

Part VI is composed of six chapters (Chapters 10–15). Chapter 10 develops theoretical models and economic conditions that can be used as a guide to control environmental pollution. In Chapters 11 and 12 a number of pollution control policy instruments are thoroughly discussed and evaluated. Chapter 13 focuses on pollution problems with transboundary and global dimensions; more specifically, acid rain, the depletion of ozone and global warming. Chapters 14 and 15 deal with economic valuation of the environment. Some of the key concepts and issues addressed in these two chapters include the various techniques used to measure environmental damage (benefits), cost–benefit analysis, time preference, discount rate and intergenerational equity.

The chapters in Part Six, together with Chapter 5, cover topics normally included in standard texts on "environmental economics."

However, while the general approaches used in these chapters have the appearance of following the standard treatment of these subjects in economics, a careful reading of each chapter reveals a departure of some significance from the norm. This difference stems from the conscious efforts to interject ecological perspectives relevant to the main topics addressed in each chapter. These efforts are not made casually, either. In general, the approach taken is first to present the topic under consideration using the standard economic treatment, and then to follow this with critical appraisals of the main conclusions on the basis of their conformity or departure from what would have been realized if sufficient reflection had been given to the ecological perspectives on this same subject matter.

chapter

ten

THE ECONOMIC THEORY OF POLLUTION CONTROL
The Optimal Level of Pollution

---

learning objectives

After reading this chapter you will be familiar with the following:

- the main features of the pollution control (abatement) cost function;
- the main features of the pollution damage cost function;
- the trade-off between pollution control and pollution damage costs;
- the optimal level of pollution;
- how a change in consumers' preference for environmental quality affects the optimal level of pollution;
- how a change in technology affects the cost of pollution control and the optimal level of pollution;
- an alternative explanation of market failure and its policy implications;
- the optimal pollution strategy: an ecological appraisal.

Pollution cleanup is better than doing nothing, but pollution prevention is the best way to walk more gently on the earth.

(Miller 1993: 15)

10.1 INTRODUCTION

In Chapter 5 an attempt was made to address the issue of environmental quality by looking at the trade-off society has to make between economic goods and improved environmental quality. In addition to merely recognizing the existence of this trade-off, in the same chapter an attempt was made to formally establish the *necessary* condition for attaining the level of output (economic goods) that would be consistent with the socially optimal level of environmental quality. This is an indirect approach, because the volume of waste emitted, which ultimately determines the quality of the environment, is presumed to be managed through output adjustment. This would pose no problem if there existed a stable and predictable relationship between waste emission and output, and if changes in market conditions did not have an independent effect on output. However, these are technical and economic considerations that can hardly be taken for granted.

For these reasons, this chapter will discuss an alternative approach to the management of environmental quality by looking *directly* at the nature of waste disposal costs. Viewed this way, the economic problem will be to determine the volume of waste (not output as in Chapter 5) that is consistent with the socially optimal level of environmental quality; that is, the *optimal* level of pollution. This approach, as will be seen shortly, provides a good many helpful new insights as well as a thorough evaluation of all the economic, technological and ecological factors that are considered significant in assessing pollution prevention (abatement) and pollution damage costs.

10.2 MINIMIZATION OF WASTE DISPOSAL COSTS

As discussed in Chapter 4, two principles, the first and second laws of thermodynamics, inform us that pollution is an inevitable by-product of any economic activity. Furthermore, as discussed in Section 5.2 of Chapter 5, a certain minimum amount of economic activity can be pursued without causing damage to the natural environment. This is because the natural environment has the capacity, albeit a limited capacity, to degrade waste, although for persistent pollutants (such as DDT, mercury, radioactive waste and so on) the assimilative capacity of the environment may be, if not zero, quite insignificant.

Clearly, then, economic consideration of waste (pollution) becomes relevant when the amount of waste disposed exceeds the assimilative capacity of the environment. When this critical threshold is exceeded, what becomes immediately apparent is the trade-off between environmental quality and pollution. That is, further pollution beyond this threshold could occur only at the cost of reduced environmental quality. In other words, pollution occurs at a cost. This is, then, the rationale for pollution control strategy or environmental management.

From a purely economic perspective, the management of environmental quality or pollution control is easily understood if the problem is viewed as minimizing *total* waste disposal costs. Broadly identified, waste disposal costs originate from two distinct sources. The first component is *pollution control* (abatement) cost: the cost which arises from society's cleanup effort to control pollution using some kind of technology. The second element is the *pollution damage* cost, which results from damage caused by untreated waste discharged into the environment. Thus

Total waste disposal cost = Total pollution control (abatement) cost
+ total pollution damage cost.

Hence, the economic problem of interest is to minimize the total disposal cost, with full recognition of the implied trade-off between its two components: control and damage costs. *This is because, from an economic viewpoint, any amount of investment (expenditure) on pollution control technology will make sense if, and only if, society is compensated by the benefits to be realized from the avoidance of environmental damage, resulting directly from this specific investment.* A good understanding of this economic logic requires, first of all, a clear and in-depth understanding of the nature of these two types of waste disposal costs, to which we now turn.

10.2.1 Pollution control (abatement) costs

Pollution control (abatement) costs represent direct monetary expenditures by a society for the purpose of procuring resources to improve environmental quality or to control pollution. Expenditures on sewage treatment facilities, smokestacks, soundproof walls and catalytic converters on passenger cars are just a few examples of pollution control costs. These expenditures may be incurred exclusively by private individuals, such as expenditures on soundproof walls by residents living in close proximity to an airport. In contrast, sewage treatment facilities may be undertaken as a joint project by local and federal government agencies. In this case the expenditures are shared by two government bodies. In some situations a project may be undertaken by a private firm with some subsidy from the public sector. Thus, as these examples illustrate, the bearers of the expenditures on pollution control projects may vary, and in some instances are difficult to trace. Despite this possible complication, the conventional wisdom is to view pollution control cost in its entirety. To this extent the specific source of the expenditure is irrelevant. What is relevant is that all components of the expenditures attributable to a specific project are fully accounted for, regardless of the source of the funds.

In general, we would expect the *marginal* pollution control cost to increase with increased environmental quality or cleanup activities. This is because incrementally higher levels of environmental quality require investments in technologies that are increasingly costly. For example, a certain level of water quality could be achieved through a primary sewage treatment facility. Such a facility is designed to screen out the solid and visible material wastes, but nothing more. If a higher level of water quality is desired, an additional expenditure on *secondary* or *tertiary* treatment may be required. Such additional treatments would require implementation of new and costly technologies designed to apply either chemical and/or biological treatments to the water. Graphically, we can visualize the marginal control cost (MCC) as follows.

Figures 10.1a and 10.1b are two alternative ways of representing the marginal pollution control cost in graph form. Before we proceed any further, it is very important to understand the exact reading of these two curves. First, as will be evident shortly, the two graphs convey the same concept, but have different labels on their *x*-axes. In Figure 10.1a, the *x*-axis represents units of untreated waste emitted into the environment, and in Figure 10.1b the same axis represents the units of treated waste or cleanup. Second, in Figure 10.1a, the marginal cost of the twentieth unit of waste is indicated to be zero. This number represents the benchmark or total number of units of waste that is being considered for treatment. Third, the curves in both figures measure *marginal* cost. For example, in Figure 10.1a, the cost is $200 when the unit of waste emitted is 5. What exactly does this cost measure? It measures the cost of cleaning up or controlling the fifteenth unit of waste. This is because given a benchmark of 20 units of waste, emission of only 5 units means a cleanup of 15 units (20 − 5). In fact, this result is easily confirmed by looking at Figure 10.1b since the marginal control cost of treating the fifteenth unit of waste is $200. This clearly shows that Figures 10.1a and 10.1b are two different ways of looking at the same thing. Finally, it is important to note that in both cases, the marginal pollution control cost increases at an *increasing rate* as a higher level of cleanup or environmental quality is desired. The numerical example in Figure 10.1b clearly illustrates this. The marginal cost to control (or treat) the tenth unit of waste is indicated to be $50. However, the marginal cost is increased to $200, a fourfold rise, to treat the fifteenth unit of waste.

At this stage it is important to specify certain important technological factors that determine the position of any marginal pollution control cost curve. More specifically, it is important to note that the marginal pollution control cost curves are constructed by holding constant such factors as the technology of pollution control, the possibility of input switching, residual

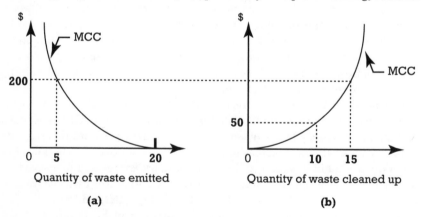

Figure 10.1 **Marginal pollution control cost**

recycling, production technology, etc. A change in any one of these pre-determined factors will cause a shift in the entire marginal pollution control cost curve. For instance, a power company that uses coal as its primary source of input could reduce pollution (sulfur) emission by switching from coal with a high sulfur content to low-sulfur coal. In this particular case, the effect would be to shift the marginal pollution control cost downward. Similar results would occur if there were a significant improvement in pollution control technology, such as the development of a new and more efficient catalytic converter for automobiles.

Finally, since pollution control costs are *explicit* or out-of-pocket expenditures, it is assumed that no apparent market distortion occurs as a result of a third party effect – that is, an *externality*. In other words, for pollution control costs, there will be no difference between private and social costs. However, this is not to suggest that market distortion in the assessment of pollution control costs cannot exist as a result of either market imperfection (power) or government intervention.

As stated earlier, pollution control cost accounts for only one side of the total social costs of pollution. Let us now turn to a detailed examination of the second component of the total pollution disposal costs, namely pollution damage costs.

10.2.2 Pollution damage costs

Even if it is technologically feasible to get rid of all pollutants from a given environmental medium, such an undertaking may be difficult to justify on the basis of cost considerations. However, as discussed in Chapter 5, when the volume of waste discharged exceeds the assimilative capacity of the environment, and is left untreated, it can contribute to a deterioration in environmental quality. The total *monetary* value of all the various damages resulting from the discharge of untreated waste into the environment is referred to as *pollution damage cost*.

Such damage to environmental quality may be manifested in a variety of ways, largely depending on the amount and the nature of the untreated waste. For example, when biodegradable pollutants, such as sewage, phosphate-containing detergents and feedlot waste are emitted into a lake, they can lead to the development of a process known as *eutrophication*. Over time, the outcome of this process is to cover a substantial portion of the lake with green substances composed mainly of algae and weeds. One immediate effect is the reduction of the scenic appeal of the lake. In addition, there is a negative impact on the population of aquatic organisms, because the ability of a body of water to support fish and other organisms depends on how much dissolved oxygen it contains. Thus, if biodegradable pollutants were discharged into a lake and left untreated, the damage to environmental quality would be identified in terms of reduced scenic attraction and decreased population of certain aquatic organisms, such as fish. The monetary value of these adverse environmental effects constitutes pollution damage cost.

The identification and estimation of pollution damage costs are even more complicated in the case of *persistent* pollutants. Examples of such pollutants include toxic metals, such as lead and mercury, radioactive wastes, and inorganic compounds such as some pesticides and waste products produced by the petrochemical industry. What is particularly significant about these types of pollutants is not the mere fact that they are patently dangerous to living organisms and the ecosystem as a whole, but the fact that because of their very slow decomposition process they tend to persist in the environment for a very long period of time. In other words, their adverse environmental effects transcend present action. For example, radioactive elements leaking from nuclear power plants today will have detrimental effects over several generations. This makes the estimation of damage costs arising from persistent pollutants extremely difficult.

In general, then, pollution damage costs are identified in terms of the losses of or damage to plants and animals and their habitats; aesthetic impairments; rapid deterioration to physical infrastructures and assets; and various harmful effects on human health and mortality. *In order to estimate damage costs, however, we need to go beyond the physical account of damage. More specifically, the damage identified in physical terms needs to be expressed in monetary terms as much as possible* (see Case Study 10.1).

CASE STUDY 10.1 ECONOMIC EFFECTS OF POOR INDOOR AIR QUALITY

Curtis Haymore and Rosemarie Odom

Poor indoor air quality (IAQ) takes its toll in a variety of ways. It damages our health and our possessions; it lowers our productivity at work; and it diverts resources to diagnosing and solving problems that result from it. Although the economic costs of some of these damages are fairly tangible and easy to quantify, a large portion are hidden. The cumulative impact can easily reach into the billions of dollars.

The cost of diagnosing, mitigating and litigating IAQ problems is evidenced by the burgeoning number of businesses providing these services. A recent EPA survey indicated that over 1,500 firms specialize in IAQ services, a 25 percent increase from 1988. The median price for evaluating and balancing ventilation systems ranges from $250 to $1,500. The median for duct-cleaning services is about $500 and for asbestos abatement and construction/renovation, about $5,000. Costs can be as high as $50,000 for some of these services.

In addition, the cost of fee, awards and settlements is also growing as an increasing number of IAQ-related cases are being litigated. Although most IAQ complaints are resolved through settlements, enormous sums of money have to be invested in investigations, testing and expert testimony, in addition to legal fees. The settlements themselves are often in the hundreds of thousands to millions of dollars.

The economic costs of poor IAQ also include the actual damages to property caused by contaminants. Indoor air pollutants can damage metals, paints, textiles, paper and magnetic storage media and can cause increased soiling, deterioration of appearance and reduced service life for furniture, draperies, interiors, and heating, ventilation and air conditioning (HVAC) equipment.

Some objects and materials are "sensitive populations" and are particularly susceptible to damage. For example, antique leather-bound books and fine art are particularly vulnerable to a number of contaminants. Electronic equipment, which is particularly susceptible to corrosion, represents a large investment at risk from poor IAQ.

Injury to people represents an even larger cost of poor IAQ. EPA [the Environmental Protection Agency] ranks IAQ problems as one of the largest remaining health risks in the United States. Health effects range from the mildly irritating, such as headaches and allergies, to the life threatening, such as cancer and heart disease. Medical costs due to excess cancer cases caused by indoor air contaminants are estimated to range from $188 million to $1.375 billion nationwide. Heart disease caused by exposure to environmental tobacco smoke can equal another $300 million. One study indicated that for every 100 white-collar workers, poor IAQ would cause an extra 24 doctor visits per year. This amounts to another $288 million.

One of the "invisible" costs of poor IAQ is the lost productivity of workers who experience headaches, eye irritation and fatigue, among other symptoms. Productivity drops as employees are less effective at their task, spend more time away from their work stations, or require more frequent breaks. Even a seemingly minor activity such as taking a pain reliever or opening a window can disrupt productivity. In more severe cases, increased absenteeism and plummeting morale result. One study found that 14 minutes are lost per 8-hour day due to poor IAQ. In addition, for every 10 workers, poor IAQ causes an additional six sick days per year. If this is true, the resulting cost of the lost productivity for the United States is $41.4 billion.

Source: *EPA Journal* Vol. 19, No. 4, 1993, pp. 28–9. Reprinted by permission.

As the above discussions indicate, the estimation of pollution damage costs is a formidable task and requires a good deal of imagination and creative approaches. Furthermore, other factors being equal, the more persistent the pollutants, the harder the task of evaluating damage costs. In fact, as we will see in Chapter 14, some aspects of pollution damage are simply beyond the realm of economic quantification. Regardless of these difficulties, pollution damage does occur. Hence, as a society striving for a better life, we need to develop a procedure that will provide us with a framework designed to enhance our understanding of pollution damage costs.

Conceptually, Figures 10.2a and 10.2b are two alternative representations of the general characteristics of the marginal pollution damage cost (MDC). As with the MCC curves, the only difference between these two figures is in the labeling of the *x*-axis. A basic assumption in the construction of these curves is that damage cost is an *increasing* function of pollution emissions. In other words, the damage caused by a unit of pollution increases

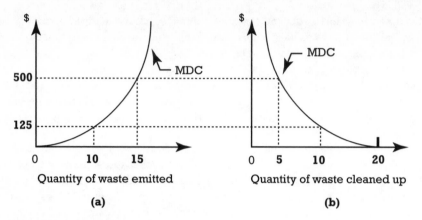

Figure 10.2 **Marginal pollution damage cost**

progressively as the amount of pollution (untreated waste) emitted increases. As the numerical example in Figure 10.2a indicates, the marginal damage cost increases from $125 (the cost of the tenth unit of waste) to $500 (the cost of the fifteenth unit of waste) as the amount of waste emissions increases from 10 to 15 units. This is, of course, in accord with the ecological principle discussed in Chapters 4 and 5 of a cumulative (nonlinear) effect of pollution on the environment.

It is also important to note that these two alternative presentations offer different interpretations regarding the damage cost curve. In Figure 10.2a, as discussed above, the damage cost curve measures the social cost of the damage to the environment in monetary terms, resulting from each additional unit of waste emission. This cost increases as the volume of waste emitted increases. On the other hand, the damage cost curve represented by Figure 10.2b depicts the amount society is *willing to pay to avoid damage* (or cleanup) at the margin. In other words, it measures society's willingness to pay for improved environmental quality on an incremental basis, or the *demand* for environmental quality.

To gain a clearer understanding of this concept, let us assume, as we did earlier, a benchmark of 20 units of waste that needs to be treated or cleaned up. This unit is shown in Figure 10.2b, and the marginal damage cost is zero at this level of treatment. That is, no damage is done given that all the 20 units are treated. Now, suppose the amount of waste treated is reduced to 5 units – which is equivalent to saying that 15 units of untreated waste are charged into the environment. With this in mind, the $500 value of marginal damage cost indicated in Figure 10.2b can be interpreted in the following two alternative ways. (a) The $500 is a measure of the marginal damage cost of the fifteenth unit of untreated waste. This is *identical* to the interpretation given to this dollar amount in Figure 10.2a. (b) The $500 is a measure of what society is *willing to pay* to clean up the fifth unit waste. When viewed this way the MDC curve represents society's demand for environmental quality. Furthermore, as shown in Figure 10.2b, society's willingness to pay declines as higher levels of environmental quality (more cleanup) are sought. For example, society's willingness to pay for the cleaning up of the tenth unit of waste is $125, which is less than what society is willing to pay for the fifth unit, $500 – indeed an observation consistent with the law of demand (see Chapter 2).

Several factors affect the *position* of the marginal pollution damage cost curve. These include changes in people's preference for environmental quality; changes in population; discovery of new treatment(s) to damage caused by environmental pollution – such as a medical breakthrough in a treatment of a certain cancer; or a change in the nature of the assimilative capacity of the environment. Alterations in any one of these factors will cause the marginal pollution damage costs to shift. With other factors held constant, a preference for a higher level of environmental quality will shift the marginal damage cost curves in Figures 10.2a and 10.2b upward. That is, in Figure 10.2a the cost curve will shift to the left, and in Figure 10.2b the shift will be to the right. This is rather straightforward once it is understood, as shown in Figure 10.2b, that the marginal pollution damage cost curve actually represents what people are willing to pay to avoid damage. It makes sense, then, that a preference for higher environmental quality is consistent with an increase in society's willingness to pay to avoid damage.

One last issue of considerable significance to be discussed is the fact that *pollution damage costs are externalities*. By definition these are costs incurred by members of a society *after* the pollution damages have already occurred. This is an important factor in the determination of the optimal level of pollution – the subject matter of the next section.

10.3 THE OPTIMAL LEVEL OF POLLUTION

At the outset of this chapter it was stated that the management of environmental quality is easily understood if the problem is viewed as the minimization of total disposal costs. It was also made clearer that the *total* disposal costs are composed of two parts: pollution control and pollution damage costs. In subsections 10.2.1 and 10.2.2 we made a considerable effort to understand the nature of these two components. Equipped with this information, we are now in a position to formally specify what exactly is meant by an *optimal* level of pollution and how it is associated with the minimization of total disposal cost.

In Figure 10.3 the marginal damage cost (MDC) and the marginal control cost (MCC) curves are drawn on the same axes. From this graph it is evident that if a pollution control measure is not undertaken, the total amount of waste discharged would be W^*. However, the socially optimal level of waste discharge is W_k, where the usual *equimarginal* condition is satisfied – that is, MDC is equal to MCC. At this level of waste discharge, the *total* control cost is represented by the area W^*SW_k (the area under the MCC curve) and the *total* damage cost is depicted by the area $0SW_k$ (the area under the MDC curve). The *total* disposal cost, which is the sum of these two costs, is shown by area $0SW^*$. The question, then, is how do we

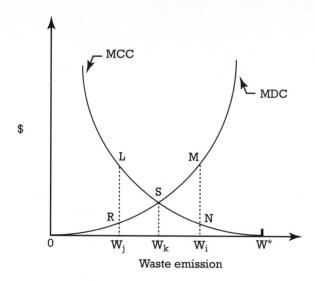

Figure 10.3 **Optimal level of pollution**

know that this total cost represents the minimum? Or, stated another way, how do we know that W_k represents the Pareto optimal level of waste emission?

As discussed in Chapter 2, we can easily demonstrate that W_k is Pareto optimal by showing that any attempt to set the level of waste emission either above or below W_k would lead to an increase in the total disposal cost. First, suppose that the level of waste emission is increased from W_k to W_i. As shown in Figure 10.3, the total damage cost for this incremental emission, W_k to W_i, is indicated by the area W_kSMW_i, the area under the damage cost curve. However, as a result of the emission of this additional amount of untreated waste, there will be a reduction in pollution control cost. This incremental cost saving is shown by area W_kSNW_i, the area under the marginal control cost curve. The net result of increasing the level of waste emission from W_k to W_i is an increase in the total disposal cost by area SMN. A similar argument can be made to show that lowering the level of the waste emission from W_k to W_j would result in an increase in the total disposal cost by area SLR. Thus, the pollution level at W_k is Pareto optimal. In other words, the optimal level of pollution emission is attained when the *marginal* damage cost is equal to the *marginal* control cost, and hence the *total* disposal cost is minimized when this condition is met.

To illustrate the above concepts using a numerical example, let us assume that the marginal damage and control costs are represented by linear lines as shown in Figures 10.4a and 10.b. According to Figure 10.4a, the optimal level of pollution will be 150 tons. This means, given that a total of 250 tons of waste needs to be disposed of, to attain the optimal level of pollution, 100 tons (250 – 150) of waste must be cleaned up using some kind of pollution control technology.

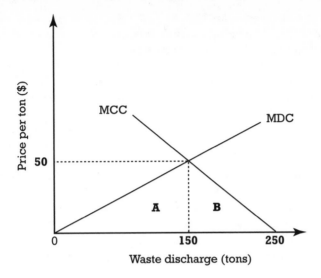

Figure 10.4a **Optimal level of pollution: a numerical illustration**

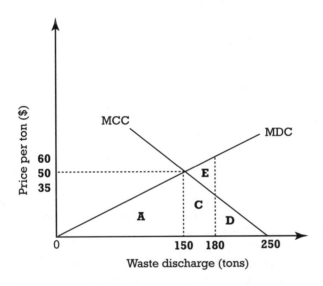

Figure 10.4b **What happens when optimality is not attained?**

In Figure 10.4a the total cost for controlling or cleaning up the 100 tons is represented by the area of triangle B (the relevant area under the marginal control cost curve). This will be $2,500 [½ (100 × 50)].

The damage cost associated with the 150 tons of untreated waste (the optimal level of pollution) discharged into the environment is represented by area of triangle A. Its monetary value will be $3,750 [½ (150 × 50)].

Thus, the total cost is $6,250 ($2,500 + $3,750) – that is, the sum of the total control and damage costs. Since this is the optimal level of pollution, it suggests that the total cost is the *minimum* at this level. To verify this, let us now look at Figure 10.4b. Suppose the amount of the untreated waste discharged into the environment is increased from 150 tons (the optimal pollution) to 180 tons. This entails a reduction in the amount of waste that needs to be treated from 100 to 70 tons (250 – 180). As a result, the *total pollution control (cleanup) cost* will decrease from $2,500 (the area of triangle B in Figure 10.4a) to $1,225 (the area of triangle D in Figure 10.4b).

However, because of the increase in the pollution level from 150 to 180 tons, the *total damage cost* will escalate from $3,750 (the area of triangle A in Figure 10.4a) to $5,400 (the area of the triangle that is composed of (A + C + E) in Figure 10.4b). Thus, when the level of pollution is raised to 180 tons, the total waste disposal cost equals $6,625 ($1,225 + $5,400). This total cost is $375 ($6,625 – $6,250) more than the cost at the optimal level of pollution, 150 tons. As can be easily verified, the $375 is the area of triangle E in Figure 10.4b.

10.4 CHANGES IN PREFERENCE AND TECHNOLOGY AND THEIR EFFECTS ON THE OPTIMAL LEVEL OF POLLUTION

Let us start by examining how changes in preference for environmental quality and technology may affect the socially optimal level of pollution by using Figures 10.5a, 10.5b and 10.5c. In Figure 10.5a, let us assume that MDC_0 and MCC_0 represent the initial marginal damage and control cost curves. Given this, the optimal level of pollution would be W_k. Suppose, now, because of a new environmental awareness campaign, people's demand for higher environmental quality has increased. The effect of this would be to shift the marginal damage cost curve to the left since, as discussed earlier, the marginal damage cost curve shows what people are willing to pay to avoid damage. In Figure 10.5a this is shown by the shift of the marginal damage cost curve from MDC_0 to MDC_1. Other factors being held constant, this change in the marginal damage cost will alter the position of optimal level of pollution from W_k to W_j. Hence, we can conclude from this observation that, other factors being equal, *a preference for a higher level of environmental quality would lead to a lower tolerance for pollution or a higher level of environmental quality* – which makes a good deal of sense. However, it is important to note that the higher environmental quality was realized at some cost; the total disposal cost is higher at the new equilibrium (area $0VW^{\star}$ instead of $0RW^{\star}$).

A similar approach could be used to analyze the effect of technology on the level of pollution that society is willing to tolerate at a point in time. To show this, suppose that there is a technological breakthrough in the control or treatment of a specific type of waste. Since this implies a cost saving in waste treatment, the marginal control cost curve will shift downward to the left. This is shown in Figure 10.5b by a shift in the marginal control cost

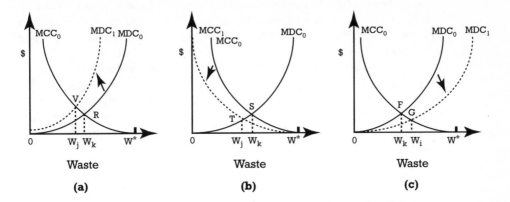

Figure 10.5 Effect of technological and preference changes on the optimal level of pollution

curve from MCC_0 to MCC_1. Assuming no changes in other factors, this shift will have the effect of reducing the level of pollution from its initial level W_k to W_j. Here again the conclusion we reach is that *improvement in waste treatment technology would allow society to reduce its level of pollution or improve its environmental quality.* Moreover, the improvement would be accomplished without an additional increase in the total disposal cost. As seen in Figure 10.5b, when the level of pollution is W_k, the total waste disposal cost is shown by area $0SW^\star$. However, with the new level of pollution, W_j, the total waste disposal cost is reduced to $0TW^\star$. In this particular case, therefore, *there is not only a decline in pollution, but also a reduction in waste disposal costs.* This is more like "you can have the cake and eat it too." Indeed, a good example of the miracle of technology!

Technology may also affect the level of pollution that society would like to have in some other ways. To see this, let us assume that there is a technological breakthrough in the treatment of a cancer caused by exposure to a certain pollutant. Other factors being equal, the obvious effect of this is to shift the marginal damage cost downward and to the right. In Figure 10.5c, this is shown by a shift in the marginal damage cost curve from MDC_0 to MDC_1. As a result, the new optimal level of pollution, W_i, will exceed the level of pollution present before the change in technology occurred, W_k. *Here is a case, then, where improvement in technology would lead to an increase, rather than, a decrease, in the level of pollution or a deterioration of environmental quality.* However, even under this condition, improvement in technology would lead to a reduction in total waste disposal costs. This can easily be verified using Figure 10.5c. The total disposal cost was area $0FW^\star$ before the technological breakthrough in cancer treatment occurred, but this cost is now reduced to area $0GW^\star$.

Clearly, as the above two cases illustrate, a technological improvement that causes a shift in either the MCC or the MDC leads to a reduction in total disposal cost. A *saving in disposal cost is, then, the unambiguous result of improved technology*. However, the effect of technological improvement on the level of pollution or environmental quality is not as straightforward. If the MCC were to shift to the left due to technological advances in waste treatment, other factors being equal this would lead to a decline in pollution, hence improved environmental quality. On the other hand, if the effect of the change in technology were to shift the MDC to the right, then if other factors remained constant, the outcome would be an increase in the level of pollution; hence, a further deterioration in environmental quality. These are important observations to keep in mind since they provide us with a clear warning that *technology does not provide an unequivocal resolution to environmental problems*.

10.5 AN ALTERNATIVE LOOK AT MARKET FAILURE

This section revisits market failure – a subject that was extensively explored in Chapter 5. The main intent is to demonstrate how the phenomenon of market failure can be explained using the model developed in this chapter. This is done using Figure 10.6. According to this figure, the optimal level of pollution is W_k, where the equality of marginal damage and marginal control costs is satisfied. The question is, could this level of pollution be attained through the free operation of the market? The answer is rather straight-forward once we recognize one important difference between damage and control costs. That is, as discussed earlier, *damage costs are externalities, while control costs are not*. Given this, what is cheapest for private firms would not be cheapest for society as a whole. In other words, with respect to the damage costs there will be a divergence between private and social costs. In general, the tendency is for private firms to totally ignore the damage costs. This point is illustrated using Figure 10.6. At the socially optimal level of pollution,

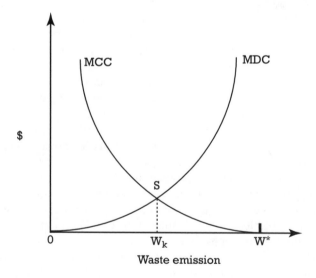

Figure 10.6 **Optimal level of pollution**

W_k, the *total* waste disposal cost is represented by area 0SW*. This total cost is composed of the *total* damage costs, area 0SW$_k$, and the *total* control costs, area W_kSW*. However, if this were done through the market, it would be in the best interest of private firms to minimize control costs and ignore damage costs altogether (since damage costs are externalities). This would move the market solution closer to W*. Thus, the optimal solution, W_k, could not be attained unless a measure were taken to make private firms internalize the externality. Hence, this is a clear case of market failure.

10.6 THE OPTIMAL LEVEL OF POLLUTION: AN ECOLOGICAL APPRAISAL

This section addresses whether or not basic ecological realities are consistent with the concept of an economically optimum level of pollution. Let us start by looking at an extreme case where no pollution is permitted, such as DDT in the United States. While the ecological justification for this is easy to see, how can this ban be addressed using the economic model discussed in this chapter? If a zero level of pollution is deemed socially optimal, then as shown in Figure 10.7, at every level of pollution the MDC is greater than the MCC, and the ban on any substance generating such waste is economically justified. In such an instance, no inconsistency exists between the economic and ecological resolutions of pollution.

Yet that is an extreme case. In most instances, the economic optimum is associated with a positive level of pollution emission. This is to be expected, and it is not necessarily inconsistent with ecological reality (refer to Section 5.2 in Chapter 5). However, there are several reasons why the economic optimum may not be ecologically desirable. This issue is illustrated using

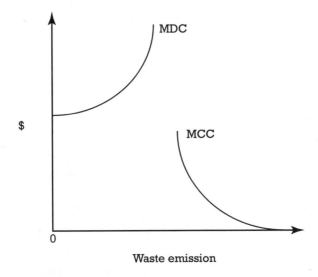

Figure 10.7 **A case where a zero level of waste emission is considered optimal**

three specific cases. The first case suggests that basing the "optimum" solely on human preference (willingness to pay) is not appropriate, especially when it is applied to the environment. The second case implies that the standard economic approach to pollution control may put more emphasis on pollution cleanup than pollution prevention. The third uses the results of three specific empirical studies to illustrate situations, in this case global warming, where the "optimum" pollution does not adequately safeguard the interests of future generations and the ecosystem as a whole.

1 As the discussion so far reveals, in estimating the damage function, only human preferences are considered. What is troubling is the extent to which a purely anthropocentrically based preference ordering adequately accounts for future human life (i.e., intergenerational equity) and the integrity of the natural ecosystems (Funtowicz and Ravetz 1994). Without such assurance, a divergence between economically and ecologically optimum pollution may be inevitable. In this respect, the bias is expected to be toward more pollution since the economic estimate of the damage function is likely to understate the welfare of the future generations and the diversity and resilience of the natural ecosystem (more on this in Chapter 13).

2 As is evident from our discussion throughout this chapter, the economic criterion for an optimal level of pollution is developed with the implicit assumption of a predetermined level of waste emission – a *benchmark*. For example, in each of the cases where the determination of optimal pollution level has been demonstrated, $W^\star$ was identified as the benchmark – the maximum level of a particular waste under consideration for cleanup. In searching for the optimum level of cleanup, no economic considerations are made concerning the absolute size of the benchmark itself. The focus is simply on the cheapest way of disposing a *predetermined* level of waste. Thus, optimum pollution is calculated without any consideration of what it would be worth to society if a reduction of the benchmark pollution, $W^\star$, were to take place. Given this, *the standard economic approach to pollution control is most likely to stress pollution cleanup, rather than pollution prevention*. A strategy of pollution prevention emphasizes *waste reduction at source* or reducing the amount of waste before it enters any waste system. To the extent that this is ignored or de-emphasized, the economic approach to pollution control may yield a suboptimal ecological outcome. The discussion in Exhibit 10.1 presents some of the difficulties as well as the opportunities involved in applying pollution prevention to manage environmental problems.

3 In determining the optimal level of pollution, we assume that we have all the relevant information needed to obtain a good estimate of both the pollution control and pollution damage costs. As discussed earlier, while estimates of pollution control cost may be relatively easy to obtain, it is extremely difficult to evaluate *all* aspects of the damage costs. This is especially true when the pollution under consideration involves *irreversible* ecological change and the risk of major adverse surprise over a long time

horizon. This is illustrated in the results of two studies by Nordhaus and one by Cline, as summarized in the remainder of this section. All three are motivated by a desire to find the best possible strategies to slow global warming over the coming century.

EXHIBIT 10.1 AN OUNCE OF POLLUTION PREVENTION?

It is Benjamin Franklin who is usually credited with the maxim *an ounce of prevention is worth a pound of cure*, although Franklin himself conceded that the sayings in *Poor Richard's Almanack* were derived from the wisdom of many ages and nations. Poor Richard also said: "*'Tis easier to prevent bad habits than to break them.*" Was he troubled by the vision thing and trying to tell us something? *Forewarn'd forearm'd*? The trouble with pollution prevention is that it wears many faces and is not always easily recognized. (What's more – bite thy tongue – it's not always feasible. How, for example, should we apply it to the problem of radon?) Designing an automobile engine to burn gasoline more completely, and thereby emit less carbon monoxide, is pollution prevention; hanging a catalytic converter on the tailpipe is not. Similarly, EPA's "green" programs, which conserve electricity, prevent pollution (electricity generation accounts for 35 percent of all US emissions of carbon dioxide); planting trees does not.

The Pollution Prevention Act of 1990 sets up a hierarchy of preferred approaches to protecting the environment. First and foremost, pollution should be prevented at the source whenever feasible. Pollution that cannot be prevented should be, in order of preference, recycled, treated or, as a last resort, disposed of in an environmentally safe manner. Operationally speaking, then, pollution prevention is source reduction, which is further defined in the Act as any practice that reduces the amount of any pollutant entering any waste stream. This applies to all activities in our society, including those carried out in the energy, agriculture, consumer and industrial sectors. Restricting development to protect sensitive ecosystems like wetlands is pollution prevention, as is cultivating crops that have a natural resistance to pests. Wrapping a blanket around your water heater is pollution prevention, and so is using energy-efficient lightbulbs.

Sounds easy. Pollution prevention is not one of the many tools that can be applied to manage environmental problems (see the May/June 1992 issue of *EPA Journal*); rather, it is the ideal result that all management programs should try to achieve. The trouble is we've had so little experience pursuing pollution prevention that when we get down to making real choices it sometimes eludes us. We may have to compare products over their entire life cycle – mining, manufacturing, use, reuse, disposal. Now that they are both recyclable, which should we use, paper or plastic grocery bags? Paper biodegrades, but not in most landfills, and it is both bulkier and heavier to handle. Plastic manufacture has an image as a pollution-intensive industry, but papermaking is too. In fact, when pollution prevention has been the result, it has sometimes been inadvertent: It is the rising cost of landfilling, for example, that has persuaded many companies to reduce the solid waste they generate. *As Poor Richard advised: Would you persuade, speak of Interest, not of Reason.*

Source: *EPA Journal* Vol. 19, No. 3, 1993, p. 8. Reprinted by permission.

First, it may be instructive to offer a very brief background on global warming and its expected consequences. According to the second report (1995) of the United Nations-sponsored Intergovernmental Panel on Climate Change, human activities have already caused global mean temperatures to rise by one half of a degree celsius since 1860 – about the beginning of the industrial period. The same report projects an increase in the range of 1 to 3.5°C in average temperatures over the next century if concentrations of greenhouse gases (GHGs) – carbon dioxide, methane, chlorofluorocarbons (CFCs) and nitrous oxides – continue to rise at current rates. If present trends continue, global warming is expected to trigger many changes in the natural environment, such as damage to world agriculture and forestry, and a rise in sea level, and to affect the adjustment capacities of many species (for more on the causes and consequences of global warming refer to Chapter 13, Section 13.4). In the three economic studies of global warming that follow, the emission of greenhouse gases is viewed as a *global externality*.

The first study (Nordhaus 1991) was based on an analytical framework identical to that presented in this chapter. Thus, the primary aim of the study was to find an "efficient" strategy for coping with greenhouse warming. In this study, the greenhouse damage function is defined as the cost to society due to climate change (such as effects on crop yields, land lost to oceans, human displacement, etc.). The control cost function reflects the added expenditures to the economy for the purpose of reducing GHG emissions in order to slow the greenhouse effect. These costs include, but are not limited to, the changes required to switch from fossil to nonfossil fuels, the search for substitutes for CFCs, and the protection of coastal properties and structures.

Additionally, this study assessed the impact of climate change assuming a *doubling* of preindustrial (before 1860) carbon dioxide concentration. This benchmark level of CO_2 concentration is projected to increase the global mean temperatures by 3°C. If nothing is done, the full impact of this climate change will start to be realized by 2050.

The results of this study depended on several factors, particularly the estimation of the damage function. Thus, three different levels of the damage costs were considered, and on the basis of the medium damage function, the optimal reduction (where MDC = MCC) was shown to be 11 percent of total GHG emissions. If this materialized, damage from the climate change would be roughly 1 percent of the world's gross national product, and for this reason a *modest* program of international abatement is warranted.

The study by Cline (1992) considered the above assessment to be too modest. This study also used a cost–benefit framework for determining the efficient control of GHG emissions. However, the Cline study estimates the damage function differently.

Cline argued that Nordhaus's study underestimated the damage cost from the greenhouse effect because it was based on a relatively short-term time horizon. That is, Nordhaus suggested that if policies to reduce GHGs emission were undertaken now, the global warming trend would stabilize by the year 2050 or so. However, this may not be the case because "global warming is cumulative and irreversible on a time scale of centuries" (Cline 1992: 4). Thus, a much longer time should be considered, perhaps as much as three hundred years. When this is done, "global warming potential in the very long term is far higher than the 2°C to 3°C range usually considered – simply because the process does not stop at the conventional benchmark of a doubling of carbon dioxide" (ibid.). The estimate of the damage cost should account for this dynamic effect of global warming.

In addition, Cline was quite deliberate in considering the *uncertainty* associated with the damage cost. He considered society to be risk averse and computed his final result after accounting for this risk factor. As a whole, the Cline study was based on a framework consistent with the precautionary principle discussed in both Chapters 8 and 9. As would be expected, the Cline study recommends an aggressive program of global reduction in GHG emissions. This is how the summary of the study reads:

> In sum, for several reasons, but especially because of the inclusion of more dramatic effects associated with nonlinear damage and very long-term warming, the policy conclusion in this study differs from that found in the Nordhaus steady-state analysis. The results here indicate that a program holding global carbon emissions to 4 [gigatons of carbon] per year – which would amount to a 71 percent reduction from baseline by 2050, an 82 percent reduction by 2100 and a 90 percent reduction by 2200 – is warranted under risk aversion.
>
> (Cline 1992: 309)

The third study (Nordhaus 1992) was based on what is known as the dynamic integrated climate–economy (DICE) model of global warming. One of the advantages of this model is it allows a comparative analysis of the impact of alternative policy measures designed to slow climate change. Nordhaus investigated five alternative policies, one of which was called the *ecological*, or *climate stablisation*, *policy*. This policy option attempts "to slow climate change to a pace that will prevent major ecological impacts. One proposal is to slow the rate of temperature increase to 0.1°C per decade from 1950" (p. 1317). Thus, the goal is to achieve this ecological end without any regard to cost.

As it turned out, the "ecological policy" favors a much higher emissions control rate than the policy based on economic efficiency – the optimal path. This is how Nordhaus described the result:

> Emissions control rates differ greatly among the alternative policies. In the optimal path, the rate of emissions reduction is approximately 10% of GHG emissions in the near future, rising to 15% late in the next century, whereas climate stabilization requires virtually complete elimination of GHG emissions.
>
> (Nordhaus 1992: 1318)

10.7 CHAPTER SUMMARY

- The primary objective of this chapter was to derive the condition for an "optimal" level of pollution. This was done by closely examining the trade-offs between two categories of costs associated with pollution: pollution control and damage costs.

- "Pollution control costs" refers to all the direct or explicit monetary expenditures by society to reduce current levels of pollution; for example, expenditure on sewage treatment facilities.

- Pollution damage costs denote the total monetary value of the damage from discharges of untreated waste into the environment. Pollution damage costs are difficult to assess since they entail assigning monetary values to damage to plants and animals and their habitats; aesthetic impairments; rapid deterioration to physical infrastructure and assets; and various harmful effects on human health and mortality.

- Furthermore, it was noted that pollution damage costs are externalities.

- A trade-off exists between pollution control and damage costs. The more spent on pollution control, the lower will be the damage costs, and vice versa.

- In view of these trade-offs, it would be beneficial to spend an additional dollar on pollution control only if the incremental benefit arising from the damage avoided by the additional cleanup (waste control) exceeded one dollar. It can then be generalized from this that it would pay to increase expenditure on pollution control provided at the margin the control cost is less than the damage cost; that is, MCC < MDC.

- It follows, then, that the *optimal* level of pollution (waste disposal) is attained when at the margin there is no difference between control and damage costs; that is, MCC = MDC. When this condition is met, the total waste disposal cost (the sum of the total control and damage costs) is minimized.

- Further analysis of the nature of the two categories of costs of pollution revealed the following:

  1 The marginal pollution control cost increases with an increase in pollution cleanup activities. This is because, incrementally, a higher level of environmental quality requires investments in technologies that are increasingly costly.

  2 The marginal pollution damage cost is an increasing function of pollution emission. This could be explained by the ecological principle that pollution reduces the capacity of a natural ecosystem to withstand further pollution.

  3 The marginal damage cost can be interpreted as depicting society's willingness to pay for pollution cleanup, and hence, the *demand* for environmental quality.

- Changes in preference for environmental quality and/or pollution control technology are exogenous factors that affect the optimal level of pollution. A clear understanding of this issue offers insights relevant to pollution control policies.

- Another important issue addressed in this chapter is the possible divergence between economic and ecological optima. Three specific cases were examined to illustrate the significance of this issue:

1 It was observed that since the economic problem is stated as finding the cheapest way to dispose of a predetermined level of waste, in searching for the economic optimum the emphasis has been on pollution cleanup rather than pollution prevention.

2 Inconsistency between the economic and the ecological optimum may arise when the pollution under consideration is likely to impose environmental damage that is irreversible in the long term.

3 Because damage costs are anthropocentrically determined, there is no assurance that the economic optimum level of pollution will adequately protect the well-being of other forms of life and the ecosystem as a whole.

---

review and discussion questions

1 Briefly identify the following concepts: pollution control cost, pollution damage cost, persistent pollutants, eutrophication, pollution prevention.

2 State *True*, *False* or *Uncertain* and explain why. Answer these questions using a graph of marginal damage and control cost curves.

   (a) Improvement in pollution control technology reduces pollution while at the same time allowing society to realize savings in its expenditure for waste control. A "win–win" situation, indeed!

   (b) An increase in the living standard of a nation (as measured by an increase in per capita income) invariably leads to an increased demand for environmental quality and consequently to a reduction in environmental deterioration.

   (c) The real pollution problem is a consequence of population.

3 Fundamentally, the economics of pollution control deals with the proper accounting of the trade-off between control and damage costs. Explain the general nature of the trade-off. Be specific.

4 Examine the following two statements. Are they equivalent?

   (a) Pollution damage costs are externalities.

   (b) Not all aspects of pollution damage costs can be evaluated in monetary terms.

5 Evaluate the relative merit of each of the following environmental management strategies. Identify a real-world case(s) under which one of these strategies is more appropriate than the others.

   (a) Pollution should be "prevented" at the source whenever feasible.

   (b) Pollution should be "controlled" up to a point where the total social cost for disposing it is minimized.

   (c) Pollution should be controlled to prevent major long-term and irreversible ecological impacts.

REFERENCES AND FURTHER READING

Cline, W. R. (1992) *The Economics of Global Warming*, Washington, D.C.: Institute for International Economics.

Field, B. C. (1994) *Environmental Economics: An Introduction*, New York: McGraw-Hill.

Funtowicz, S. O. and Ravetz, J. R. (1994) "The Worth of a Songbird: Ecological Economics as a Post-Normal Science," *Ecological Economics* 10: 197–207.

Intergovernmental Panel on Climate Change (1995) *Climate Change 1994: Radiative Forcing of Climate Change*, Cambridge: Cambridge University Press.

Miller, T. G., Jr., (1993) *Environmental Science*, 4th edn., Belmont, Calif.: Wadsworth.

Nordhaus, W. D. (1991) "To Slow or Not to Slow: The Economics of the Greenhouse Effect," *Economic Journal* 101: 920–48.

—— (1992) "An Optimal Transition Path for Controlling Greenhouse Gases," *Science* 258: 1315–19.

Tietenberg, T. H. (1988) *Environmental and Natural Resource Economics*, 2nd edn., Glenview, Ill.: Scott, Foresman.

chapter
eleven

THE ECONOMICS OF ENVIRONMENTAL REGULATIONS:
Regulating the Environment through Judicial Procedures

learning objectives

After reading this chapter you will be familiar with the following:

- the economic rationale for environmental regulations;
- general criteria used for evaluating a specific environmental policy instrument;
- deterring environmental abuse through liability laws;
- the Coasian theorem and its implications for environmental regulations;
- emission standards as a policy tool for regulating environment pollution;
- the United States Environmental Protection Agency (EPA) and its legal mandates in setting emission standards.

The tragedy of the commons as a food basket is averted by private property, or something formally like it. But the air and waters surrounding us cannot readily be fenced, and so the tragedy of the commons as a cesspool must be prevented by different means, by coercive laws or taxing devices that make it cheaper for the polluter to treat his pollutants than to discharge them untreated.

(Hardin 1968: 1245)

11.1 INTRODUCTION

In Chapter 10 the focus was on developing a theoretical framework that would direct us to the conditions under which a socially optimal level of environmental quality could be attained. One of the major revelations in that chapter (see Section 10.5) was that environmental resources are externality-ridden. For this reason, the socially optimal level of environmental quality cannot be achieved through the unbridled operation of private markets. What this suggests is, as discussed earlier, a clear case of market failure and, consequently, a justification for public intervention.

However, as will be evident throughout the next two chapters, public intervention is *not* both a necessary and sufficient condition for attaining the optimal allocation of environmental resources. Sufficiency requires that we attain the optimal environmental quality through means (policy instruments) that are *cost-effective* – that involve the least cost. Hence, on practical grounds, resolving environmental problems requires more than a mere recognition of market failure or the necessity of public intervention to correct an externality. With this important caveat in mind, in this chapter we evaluate three legal approaches for regulating the environment, namely liability laws, property rights or Coasian methods, and emission standards. The unifying theme of these three approaches is their focus on the *legal system* to deter abuse of the environment. In the case of liability laws, the court would set monetary fines on the basis of the perceived damage to the environment. The Coasian method uses the legal system to assign and enforce property rights. Emission standards are set and enforced through legally mandated laws. Each of these policy instruments is evaluated on the basis of the following specific criteria: efficiency, compliance (transaction) cost, fairness, ecological effects, and moral and ethical considerations.

11.2 ENVIRONMENTAL REGULATION THROUGH LIABILITY LAWS

In many countries, including the United States, liability laws are used as a way of resolving conflicts arising from environmental damage. The main idea behind this type of statutory enactment is to make polluters liable for the damage they cause (Starrett and Zeckhauser 1992). More specifically, polluters are the defendants and those who are affected by pollution, the pollutees, are the plaintiffs. Thus, since polluters are subject to lawsuits and monetary payments if they are found guilty (see Exhibit 11.1), it is in their best interest to pay special attention to the way they use the ambient environment as a medium for waste disposal. In this sense, liability laws can be used as a means of internalizing environmental externalities. The question then is how effective is the use of liability laws in internalizing environmental externalities?

We can address this question using as a hypothetical example the environmental dispute between two firms, a paper mill and a fish hatchery. As discussed in Chapter 5, the problem is a river that is used jointly by these two firms. The paper mill uses the river to discharge the by-products of its

---

EXHIBIT 11.1 ORE-IDA FOODS TO PAY $1 MILLION FOR POLLUTING SNAKE RIVER

After pleading guilty to five criminal violations of the Clean Water Act, Ore-Ida Foods Incorporated was fined $1 million and placed on three years' probation in the US District Court in Portland, Oregon. The violations included discharging potato and other vegetable wastes into the Snake River from the wastewater-treatment plant at Ore-Ida's facility in Ontario, Oregon, in violation of the company's permit issued under the National Pollutant Discharge Elimination System (NPDES). EPA's [EPA is the US Environmental Protection Agency] Criminal Investigation Division initiated the complaint after being tipped off by an employee about data manipulation, illegal discharges, and tampering with monitoring devices at the treatment plant. Ore-Ida will pay $250,000 of the fine immediately; it has until the end of the probation period to pay the rest or spend it on wastewater-recycling equipment at the treatment plant. The company has already spent $12 million on upgrading the plant. Ore-Ida Foods is headquartered in Boise, Idaho; it is a wholly owned subsidiary of H. J. Heinz Corporation.

Source: *EPA Journal* Vol. 20, 1994, p. 5. Reprinted by permission.

---

manufacturing process, and the fish hatchery relies on the same river to raise juvenile fish. By virtue of its upstream location, the production activity of the paper mill will have a negative impact on the operation of the hatchery. However, since neither of these firms can claim sole ownership of the river, there is no mechanism to make the paper mill pay for the damage it is imposing on the operation of the hatchery. As we have seen in Chapter 5, if this third party effect of the paper mill's production activity is not corrected, it will inevitably cause a misallocation of societal resources. In particular, there will be an overproduction of paper (hence, a higher level of waste discharge into the river) and an underproduction of fish, relative to what is considered socially optimal. How can a situation like this be rectified using liability laws?

As stated above, liability laws hold polluters accountable for the damage they cause to third parties (pollutees). This means that polluters are required to pay financial compensation in direct proportion to the damage they inflict on those third parties. For our two firms, this suggests that the paper mill, through a specific statutory mandate, will be ordered to compensate the owner of the fish hatchery. In general, for problems related to the environment the court sets the level of compensation on the basis of the damage cost function. Let us assume that the court has free access to detailed and accurate information about the damage cost relevant to our two firms. We can then draw the marginal damage cost curve (MDC), shown in Figure 11.1, using this information.

If the river is considered a free good, amount $W^\star$ of waste will be discharged by the paper mill. This corresponds to the situation in which the

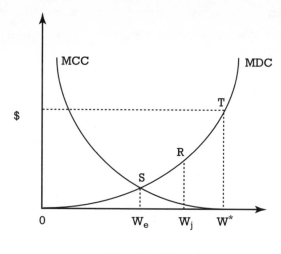

Figure 11.1 **Marginal damage and control costs of the paper mill**

river is treated as a "common" property resource; hence, the paper mill has free access to its use. However, at this level of waste emission the paper company is causing damage to the fish hatchery with a monetary value equal to the area $0TW^*$ – the area under the marginal damage cost curve when amount W^* of waste is emitted. Thus, under a strict liability law the court will use this monetary value as a benchmark for the compensation to be awarded to the fish hatchery. Suppose the paper mill is actually ordered to pay this amount of compensation to the owner of the fish hatchery. This order then will force the owner of the paper mill to reevaluate the mill's decision concerning waste disposal for reasons stated below.

Since compensation is awarded in direct proportion to the damage, the owner of the paper mill knows that the mill can always reduce its penalty by decreasing the amount of waste it is discharging into the river. For example, if the amount of waste emitted into the river is reduced from W^* to W_j, as shown in Figure 11.1, the monetary value of the penalty that the paper mill has to pay will be area $0RW_j$ – which is less than area $0TW^*$. However, this will not be accomplished without a cost since the paper mill now has to use an alternative mechanism(s) for disposing of its waste. Suppose, in Figure 11.1, the marginal control cost (MCC) curve represents the marginal cost of waste cleanup using the best alternative technology available to this firm. Given this, it would be in the best interest of the paper mill to reduce its waste discharge from W^* all the way to W_e. This is because, for any level of waste greater than W_e, the MDC (the legally sanctioned compensation the paper mill has to pay to the hatchery) is greater than the MCC – the amount the paper mill has to pay for using waste treatment technology. Thus, under this scenario the maximum waste that the paper mill will emit into the river will be W_e. Interestingly, this result is identical to the condition for an optimal level of pollution that was obtained in Chapter 10 – that is, MDC = MCC. The implication of this is that, in an ideal setting (where the regulators have full and accurate information about damage cost), environmental regulation through liability laws could force polluters to pay for an environmental service that would be consistent with its scarcity (social) value.

The above result clearly suggests that, at least conceptually, if environmental regulations are carefully designed and strictly enforced through liability laws, an optimal level of pollution will be secured. Furthermore, this optimal level of pollution is not determined by a government decree; rather, it is reached by a decision-making process of private concerns reacting only to a financial disincentive imposed on them by a fully enforced liability law. How effective are liability laws as an instrument for regulating the use of environmental resources? On the positive side, at least theoretically, liability laws are capable of causing private decision-makers to gravitate toward the socially optimal level of pollution. Furthermore, this can be accomplished without the need for prior identification of the optimal level of pollution, provided the court has detailed and accurate information on damage cost. In this sense, then, liability laws basically operate on the premise of *economic incentives*. In addition, liability laws tend to have *moral* appeal since they are based on the premise of punishing the perpetrator of the damage. In other words, the "polluter-pays principle" is strictly applicable.

However, using the courts to enforce victims' rights in relation to pollution damage has several disadvantages. First, legal remedies are generally slow and costly. Second, relying on dispute resolution by means of lawsuits may be *unfair* if the damaged individual does not have the resources to bring a suit. Third, when the number of affected parties (polluters and pollutees) is large, it may be difficult to determine who harmed whom, and to what exact degree. For instance, lawsuits would face almost insurmountable difficulties in solving problems concerning fouled air in crowded industrial areas. This approach seems to work best where the number of polluters is small and their victims are few and easily identified.

At this stage, it is important to note that these disadvantages of legal solutions to problems caused by pollution are in some way related to what is broadly identified as *transaction cost*. As defined earlier, transaction cost includes the monetary outlays for specifying, defining and enforcing property rights. In this sense, then, we can generalize by saying that the major drawback of using a system based on liability laws is its high *transaction cost*, especially when the parties involved in the dispute are numerous. If this is indeed regarded as a relevant concern, reliance on the legal system to solve environmental problems may leave society saddled with excessive waste – a waste level over and above what is considered to be socially optimal. This is not difficult to understand once we recognize that transaction cost is an opportunity cost to society, and thus should be included as part of the pollution control (cleanup) cost. Essentially, then, the effect of high transaction cost is to cause a rightward shift in the MCC. As can easily be demonstrated using Figure 11.1, the effect of this would be to justify emissions of pollution greater than W_e – the socially optimal waste emission level when transaction cost is assumed to be zero. How far we are able to depart from W_e depends on the size of the transaction cost or the shift in the MCC.

In most nations, liability laws were probably one of the earliest forms of public policy tools used to internalize environmental externalities. The use of this approach was perhaps justifiable at this early stage of environmental litigation because the problems tended to be local and, generally, the parties involved in the dispute fewer. Furthermore, at that time, courts tended to deal with cases that were considered more as environmental nuisance (such as littering) rather than environmental damage with considerable risk to human health and ecological stability.

Thus, as environmental concerns started to become complex, fresh approaches to solving these problems were sought. An approach that generated a considerable excitement in the economics profession in the 1960s was the property rights or Coasian approach, named after economist Ronald Coase. The initial impetus for this approach was lower transaction cost. Let us now turn to the discussion and evaluation of this approach.

11.3 THE PROPERTY RIGHTS OR COASIAN APPROACH

As discussed in Chapter 5, environmental resources are externality-ridden because they lack a clearly defined property right. Once this is acknowledged, any effort to internalize (remedy) environmental externalities requires an effective scheme of assigning property rights. This indeed captures the essence of the property rights approach. More specifically, this approach requires that property rights should be assigned to one of the parties involved in an environmental dispute. Furthermore, according to Coase (1960), the assignment of property rights could be completely *arbitrary* and this would have no effect on the final outcome of the environmental problem under consideration. For example, in the case of environmental pollution, the Coasian approach suggests that the optimal level of pollution can be achieved by an arbitrary assignment of property rights to either the polluter(s) or the pollutee(s). This proposition that the assignment of property rights to a specific party has no effect on the optimal level of pollution is the core concept of what is widely known as the *Coase theorem*. To demonstrate the essence of this theorem in a rather simple manner, we will again use the two familiar firms: the paper mill and the fish hatchery.

As discussed earlier, the problem between these two firms arises because their economic activities involve the *joint use* of a river. To demonstrate how this problem can be remedied using a property rights approach, let us start by assuming that the legal rights to the use of the river belong to the hatchery. Given this, the hatchery, if it wishes, could completely deny the paper mill access to the river. That is, the paper mill would not be permitted to use the river to discharge its waste. In Figure 11.2, this situation is represented by the origin, where the amount of waste emitted into the river from the paper mill is zero. This means that the paper mill has to find an alternative way of

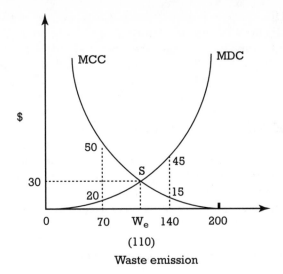

Figure 11.2 **Graphical illustration of the Coase theorem**

disposing the waste from its current operation – a total of 200 units. The key question is, then, will this be a stable situation? Given the MDC and MCC curves presented in Figure 11.2, the answer to this question would be a *no* for the following reason.

When the waste discharged by the paper mill is less than W_e, we observe that MCC (the incremental cost of cleanup for the paper mill using other means than the river) is greater than the MDC – the incremental damage cost to the hatchery. For example, as shown in Figure 11.2, for the seventieth unit of the waste that is emitted into the river, the marginal damage cost to the hatchery is $20. However, to achieve this same result, the cost to the paper mill is $50. Note that this $50 is the marginal control cost of treating (cleaning) the one hundred and thirtieth unit of waste (200 – 70). Thus, given this situation, the paper mill will clearly have an incentive to offer a financial bribe to the fish hatchery for the right to use the river for discharging its industrial waste. For example, as shown in Figure 11.2, to discharge the seventieth unit of waste the paper mill will be willing to pay the hatchery a fee of between $20 and $50. This should be acceptable to both parties. For the hatchery, a payment exceeding $20 more than compensates for the damage caused to its fish operation from the dumping of the seventieth unit of waste into the river. Similarly, this situation should also be advantageous to the paper mill because the cost of using an alternative technology to dispose of the seventieth unit (i.e., to clean up the one hundred and thirtieth unit) of waste to this firm is at least $50. In general, then, these two firms will be in a position to engage in a mutually beneficial transaction provided that, at the point where the negotiation is taking place, MCC > MDC. Furthermore, the negotiation between these two parties ceases when, for the last unit of waste discharged by the paper mill,

MCC = MDC. This is indeed the condition for the optimal level of pollution. In Figure 11.2, this is attained at W_e, or 110 units of emission.

As discussed earlier, the Coase theorem goes beyond the mere recognition of optimality. It also states that this optimal outcome is completely independent of the two parties who have rights to the river. To demonstrate this, let us now consider the case where the paper mill has exclusive legal rights to the use of the river. Under these circumstances the paper mill, if it wishes, can dispose of all its waste into the river. If this strategy is followed, then as shown in Figure 11.2, the paper mill will discharge a total of 200 units of waste into the river. However, this company is not limited to this option only. As shown in Figure 11.2, for each unit of waste discharged between 110 and 200 units, the MDC is greater than the MCC. This situation will allow the fish hatchery and the paper mill to engage in a mutually beneficial transaction. To see this, let us focus on what happens when the emission is at 140 units. When this unit of waste is discharged, the MDC to the fish hatchery is $45, but the cost to the paper mill of treating this same unit is $15. Note that the $15 is the marginal cost to the paper mill for controlling the sixtieth unit of emission (200 − 140). Thus, when the emission level is at 140 units the MDC is greater than the MCC. Given this, the hatchery will have an incentive to offer a financial bribe to the paper mill of anywhere between $15 and $45 to withhold this unit of waste. It is easy to see that the paper mill will most likely take this offer seriously since the cost of controlling the sixtieth unit of waste (200 − 140) is only $15. Thus, to the extent that the offer of the hatchery exceeds $15, the paper mill will abide by the wishes of the hatchery. A similar situation prevails for all the units where the MDC exceeds the MCC – that is, between 200 and 110 units. Thus, the optimal level of pollution is again reached at W_e or 110 units, where MDC = MCC. This result verifies the validity of the Coase theorem.

In the 1960s, for most economists the Coase theorem was an exciting and appealing revelation. The profound implication of this theorem has been that pollution problems can be resolved by an arbitrary assignment of property rights. What is appealing about this is that *it reduces the role of public regulators to a mere assignment of enforceable ownership rights*. Once this is done, as discussed above, the optimal level of pollution is attained through voluntary negotiation of private parties – which is consistent with the spirit of the private market.

Despite its appeal, however, the Coasian approach has several weaknesses. First, in our example above, the source of the pollution as well as the parties involved in the dispute are easily identifiable. However, in many real-world situations, the sources of the pollution are likely to be multifaceted and their impacts quite diffuse. In addition, environmental disputes normally involve several parties. In a typical real-world situation, then, the cost of negotiation and enforcement – the transaction cost – could be quite high. As discussed earlier, a high transaction cost could distort the final outcome of an environmental dispute in a rather significant manner. In such a situation, a resolution reached using the property rights approach might be far removed from what is considered to be socially optimal.

Second, a property rights approach, especially its Coasian variation, seems to support the ethos that "the end justifies the means." As is evident from the above discussion, in this approach the focus is singularly placed on attaining an optimal outcome. Whether the optimal outcome is attained by assigning property rights to the polluters or assigning them to the pollutees is considered entirely irrelevant. Clearly, this seems to counter what appears to be the conventional wisdom – the "polluter-pays principle."

Third, according to the Coase theorem, the optimal level of pollution can be achieved irrespective of which party was given the initial property rights: – the polluters or pollutees. However, what the theorem does not address is the impact the initial assignment of property rights has on *income distribution*. In general, the income position of the party empowered with property rights is positively impacted. To see this, let us refer back to Figure 11.2. Furthermore, let us assume that the hatchery has exclusive rights to the use of the river. Given this scenario, we have already demonstrated that W_e will be the optimal level of effluent. Let us suppose that this outcome was reached on terms stipulating that the paper mill would pay a uniform compensation of $30 dollars per unit of pollution discharged into the river. Note that the paper mill would be willing to pay $30 for each unit of untreated waste it discharged into the river until the emission level reached W_e or 110 units. This is because along this relevant range of waste emission, $30 < MCC – what the paper mill would have paid to control its waste using alternative means. Under this arrangement the hatchery will receive a total payment equal to $3,300 ($30 × 110). However, by letting the paper mill discharge 110 units of waste into the river, the hatchery incurs a damage cost represented by the area $0SW_e$ (the area under the MDC curve). The dollar value of this damage will be approximately $1,650 [½ (110 × 30)]. This represents a net gain of approximately $1,650 to the hatchery – a gain realized at the expense of the paper mill. Therefore, in terms of total societal income, the gain of the hatchery was offset by the loss of the paper mill. The reverse would be the case if the initial assignment of property right were switched from the hatchery to the paper mill.

Fourth, in the above analysis it is assumed that shifting the property rights from one party to another would not cause either party to cease to function. What if this is not the case? What if giving the property rights to the hatchery makes the paper mill go out of business or vice versa? Under this situation, as Starrett and Zeckhauser (1992) have demonstrated, the Coasian approach will not yield a unique optimal solution.

Fifth, when pollution problems (such as acid rain, global warming, ozone depletion – subjects to be discussed in Chapter 13) transcend national boundaries, involve irreversible changes and considerable uncertainty, and call for a coordinated and multifaceted response by a large number of nations, then the Coasian approach may be totally ineffective on the basis of either economic, political or ecological considerations.

So far we have examined two possible mechanisms by which a society could attempt to control pollution, namely liability laws and property rights regimes. In both of these types of pollution control schemes, the regulatory roles of public authorities were viewed as something to be minimized. In the case of liability laws, the principal role of the court is reduced to simply setting the fine (compensation) polluters have to pay to the damaged parties. Under the property rights approach the sole responsibility of the public authorities is to assign property rights to one of the parties involved in an environmental dispute. Once these are done, at least theoretically it is presumed that the interaction of the relevant parties involved in the dispute will lead to an efficient outcome. In this sense, then, it would be fair to say that the proponents of both liability laws and property rights are advocates for a *decentralized* approach to pollution control.

While this may be appealing in some professional circles, especially among economists, the fact remains that the above two approaches are of limited use in a real-world situation. This is because modern environmental problems are generally widespread in their scope and involve a large number of people with varying socioeconomic circumstances. For this reason, as public awareness of environmental problems has increased, at least until recently one of the most popular and appealing methods for reducing environmental damages has been *direct regulation* – a centralized form of pollution control. Let us now discuss and evaluate pollution control instruments that fall into the categories most often labeled the "command-and-control" approach.

11.4 EMISSION STANDARDS

An emission standard is a maximum rate of effluent discharge that is legally permitted. Since the standard mandated is supposed to reflect the public interest at large, any violators are subjected to legal prosecutions. Moreover, if found guilty, violators are punished by a monetary fine and/or imprisonment. In this sense, then, emission standards are environmental policies that are based on "command-and-control" approaches.

In the United States, the Environmental Protection Agency (EPA) is responsible for implementing environmental laws enacted by Congress. Table 11.1 provides a list of some of these laws. In implementing them, the EPA, which is a federal agency, works in partnership with state, county and local municipality governments to use a range of tools designed to protect the environment. State and local standards may exceed federal standards, but cannot be less stringent. All states have environmental agencies; some are separate agencies and others are part of state health departments. Although the EPA sets the minimum standards, these state agencies are responsible for implementing and monitoring many of the major environmental statutes, such as the Clean Air Acts provisions. Enforcement of the standards is usually a state or local responsibility, but many enforcement actions require the resources of both federal and state authorities.

Emission standards can take a variety of forms. The form that is intuitively most obvious is, of course, a standard expressed in terms of *quantity* of waste material released into the ambient environment per unit time. For example, it might be the case that in any given week, no more than 100 tons of

Table 11.1 **Some of the major environmental laws enacted by the United States Congress, 1938–90**

1938	Federal Food, Drug, and Cosmetic Act (last amended 1988)
1947	Federal Insecticide, Fungicide, and Rodenticide Act (last amended 1988)
1948	Federal Water Pollution Control Act (or the Clean Water Act; last amended 1988)
1955	Clean Air Act (last amended 1990)
1965	Shoreline Erosion Protection Act
1965	Solid Waste Disposal Act (last amended 1988)
1970	National Environmental Policy Act (last amended 1975)
1970	Resource Recovery Act
1970	Pollution Prevention Packaging Act (last amended 1983)
1971	Lead-Based Paint Poisoning Prevention Act (last amended 1988)
1972	Coastal Zone Management Act (last amended 1985)
1972	Marine Protection, Research, and Sanctuaries Act (last amended 1988)
1972	Ocean Dumping Act
1973	Endangered Species Act
1974	State Drinking Water Act (last amended 1994)
1974	Shoreline Erosion Control Demonstration Act
1975	Hazardous Materials Transportation Act
1976	Resource Conversation and Recovery Act
1976	Toxic Substances Control Act (last amended 1988)
1977	Surface Mining Control and Reclamation Act
1978	Uranium Mill-Tailing, Radiation Control Act (last amended 1988)
1980	Asbestos School Hazard Detection and Control Act
1980	Comprehensive Environmental Response, Compensation, and Liability Act
1982	Nuclear Water Policy Act
1984	Asbestos School Hazard Abatement Act
1986	Asbestos Hazard Emergency Response Act
1986	Emergency Planning and Community Right to Know Act
1988	Indoor Radon Abatement Act
1988	Lead Contamination Control Act
1988	Medical Waste tracking Act
1988	Ocean Dumping Ban Act
1988	Shore Protection Act
1990	National Environmental Education Act

Source: *EPA Journal* Vol. 21, No. 1, 1995, p. 48. Reprinted by permission.

untreated sewage waste is allowed to be released into a given river stream. In some cases, in setting emission standards the focus is on maintaining the overall quality of a more diffuse environmental medium. This is normally done by setting an *ambient standard* on the basis of an allowable concentration of pollution. For example, the ambient standard for dissolved oxygen in a particular river might specify that the level must not be allowed to drop below 3 parts per million (ppm). One other commonly used regulatory practice is *technology standards*. In this case, regulators specify the technologies that potential polluters must adopt (see Exhibit 11.2).

EXHIBIT 11.2 EMISSION STANDARDS PROPOSED FOR MARINE ENGINES

Working in cooperation with the marine industry, EPA [the US Environmental Protection Agency] has proposed the nation's first emissions standards for marine engines. The standards proposed would apply to all new outboard, inboard, sterndrive and personal watercraft engines (such as Jet Skis and Wave Runners). Manufacturers would begin phasing in the new standards over a nine-year period, beginning with the 1998 model year. The technology developed will create a new generation of low-emission, high-performance engines. Older models would be unaffected by the new standards.

The 12 million marine engines now in the United States give off about 700,000 tons per year of hydrocarbon (HC) and nitrogen oxide (NO_x) emissions; the new generation of marine engines is expected to reduce NO_x emissions to 37 percent and HC emissions by more than 75 percent. HC and NO_x emissions create ground-level ozone, which can irritate the respiratory tract, causing chest pain and lung inflammation. Ozone can also aggravate existing respiratory conditions such as asthma.

Of all "no-road" engines, only lawn and garden engines emit higher levels of HC, a 1991 EPA study found; only farm and construction equipment emit higher levels of NO_x. New standards for lawn and garden engines were proposed in May. Standards for land-based, nonroad diesel engines such as those in farm and construction equipment were finalized in June.

It is expected that the design changes necessary to reduce emissions will also improve performance and fuel economy, making starting easier and acceleration faster, and produce less noise, odor and smoke.

Source: EPA Journal Vol. 20, 1994, p. 3. Reprinted by permission.

Given this general description of emission standards, their advantages should be readily apparent. First, in principle, emission standards are *simple* and *direct* – to the extent that they aim at the attainment of clearly defined numerical or technological objectives. Second, they can be effectively used to keep extremely harmful pollution, such as DDT and industrial toxic wastes, below dangerous levels. In other words, when a given pollutant has well-known and long-lasting adverse ecological and human health effects, command-and-control approaches may be the most cost-effective. Last but not least, they tend to be politically popular because they have a certain moral appeal. Pollution is regarded as a "public bad," therefore the activities of polluters should be subject to considerable public scrutiny.

The basic economics of emission standards can be briefly discussed using the familiar graph presented in Figure 11.3. Let us suppose that the amount of waste that would have been emitted in the absence of regulation is 300 units. If we assume that the public authorities have full information about the damage and control cost functions, then they will be in a position to recognize that the socially optimal level of pollution is 150 units, which is

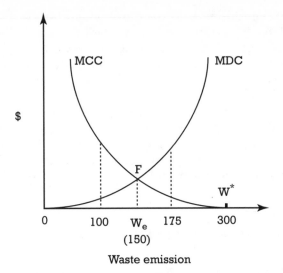

Figure 11.3 Emission standards as a policy tool to control pollution

less than 300. To attain the socially optimal level of pollution, public authorities would now set the emission standard at 150, and strictly enforce it. The ultimate effects of this are as follows: First, if the standard is successfully implemented, the socially optimal level of pollution is preserved. Second, polluters will be forced to internalize the cost of controlling pollution emissions up to the socially optimal level. As shown in Figure 11.3, polluters will be forced to reduce their waste from 300 to 150 units, and given their MCC curve, the total cost of doing this will be area W_eFW^*. Note that if it were not for the emission standard, polluters would have been in a position to entirely avoid this cost.

In our discussion we have explicitly assumed that the public authorities somehow have perfect information concerning the damage and control costs. That is a very strong assumption, given what we know about the nature of these two cost functions, especially the difficulty associated with estimating marginal damage cost. Is this assumption absolutely necessary? The short answer to this question is no. However, without the assumed perfect information there is no guarantee that the outcome will be socially optimal. Nevertheless, in the absence of full information on damage and control costs, the public authorities may set the initial emission standard on the basis of what appears to be the best available information about these costs at the point in time the decision is made. For example, in Figure 11.3, suppose that the emission standard is initially set at 100 – a standard stricter than the socially optimal level, W_e or 150 units. Clearly, this policy is likely to anger the polluters and cause a request for reevaluation of the emission standard. If, after a careful reevaluation of the damage and control costs, the outcome of the initial standard-setting is judged to be too stringent, then the public authorities will revise their standard in such a way that more pollution will be permitted. Similarly, if the authorities set emission standards that are below what is considered to be socially optimal, such as 175 units, this mandate will be vehemently challenged by advocates of the environment. The news account in Exhibit 11.3 illustrates typical public reactions to proposed changes in emission standards. In this case the specific issue involves public reactions to a stricter air quality standard proposed by the EPA.

The broader implication of the above analysis is that through trial and error and the competing voices of various special interest groups, the public authorities gravitate toward setting a standard that will, in the long run, lead to the attainment of the optimal level of pollution. In this respect, then, at least in principle, emission standards appear to provide room for flexibility.

EXHIBIT 11.3 EPA PROPOSES STRICT NEW AIR QUALITY STANDARDS

Washington – To the consternation of many state and business leaders, the Environmental Protection Agency proposed stringent new air quality standards Wednesday that would cost more than $6.5 billion a year to meet. The new rules would tighten pollution limits that many cities already fail to meet and regulate more of the tiny particles from smokestacks.

After reviewing more than 200 studies – its most extensive scientific peer review ever – the agency concluded that current standards do not adequately protect public health, especially for children. "Today, EPA takes an important step for protecting public health and our environment from the harmful effect of air pollution," said EPA Administrator Carol Browner.

But opponents criticized the agency for failing to consider the high cost of the proposals and said it lacked data to support some assumptions. "The US EPA is putting a huge mandate on the state, on local governments and on consumers without having fully evaluated the cost, the relative health benefits and the technical feasibility of meeting the standards," said Donald Schregardus, director of the Ohio Environmental Protection Agency.

But Browner said the EPA's mandate called for it to ensure that health standards meet current science regardless of cost. She estimated that meeting the new standards would cost between $6.5 billion and $8.5 billion annually. However, she claimed that would be offset by up to $120 billion in health benefits, such as fewer hospital stays or missed work. The decision was a setback for industry, which mounted a massive lobbying campaign against the proposal.

A coalition of industry and business groups predicted that states and cities would have to impose drastic pollution controls, including travel restrictions, mandatory car pooling and restrictions on pleasure boats, lawn mowers and outdoor barbecues. Owen Drew of the National Association of Manufacturers predicted that the restrictions would have "a chilling effect on economic growth."

But the EPA called that a scare tactic, and said most areas could meet the standards using smog-reduction programs already on the books. Also, in those areas needing changes, most will come in factories and refineries, not in changed driving or other habits, the agency said.

The new standards would require communities to cut ozone levels by one third to 0.08 parts per million cubic feet of air from 0.12 ppm, the current standard. The readings, however, will be taken over an average of eight hours, rather than during a single one-hour period, making it somewhat easier to meet the new standard.

The EPA also wants to regulate tiny particles of dust down to 2.5 microns in diameter. Currently standards apply only to particles of 10 microns or larger. It would take about 8 microns to equal the width of a human hair. Health experts argue that the minuscule particles – many of which come from industrial or utility smokestacks – cause the most harm because they lodge deep in the lungs.

Source: Kalamazoo Gazette/The Associated Press, November 28, 1996. Copyright © 1996 The Associated Press. Reprinted by permission.

However, despite their simplicity, flexibility and political appeal, emission standards as a policy instrument for environmental regulation have several flaws. Moreover, some of these flaws are considered to have serious adverse economic and social implications. First, standards are set solely by government fiat. To this extent they are highly interventionist and signify a major departure from the cherished spirit of the "free market." Second, pollution control practices applied through administrative laws, such as emission standards, generally require the creation of a large bureaucracy to administer the program. In this situation, the administrative and enforcement costs (i.e., the transaction costs) of emission standards can be considerable. Since these are opportunity costs to society, they should be included as part of the pollution control costs. Assuming no change in the damage cost, this means that the socially optimal level of pollution will now be somewhere to the right of W_e – implying a lenient emission standard. This leniency in emission standards is prompted by the inherent weakness of the policy tool under consideration: excessive administrative and enforcement costs. It represents government failure.

Third, in setting standards, a strong tendency may exist for the regulators and the established firms to cooperate. The end result of this may be a "regulatory capture" where regulators are influenced to set standards in ways that are likely to benefit the existing firms. Thus, standards have the potential to be used as barriers to entry.

Fourth, while the administrative and enforcement costs of pollution control laws are real and in some instances considerable, the regulatory agency is not designed to generate its own revenue, except for the occasional collection of fines from violators of the law.

A fifth problem with emission standards is that the administrative process that is used to set the standard may neglect consideration of economic efficiency. Economic efficiency requires that in the setting of a standard, both damage and control costs should be taken into account. Public regulators, in their desire to please a particular special interest group, may be inclined to set standards on the basis of either damage or control cost, but not both. For example, administrators wishing to please their environmentally conscious constituents would be inclined to set emission standards on the basis of damage cost only. This action might overly sensitize regulators to the risk of environmental damage (pollution) – which could ultimately result in a recommendation of excessively stringent emission standards.

Another related issue concerning standard-setting involves the fact that emission standards are generally applied uniformly across emission sources. In situations where there are multiple emission sources, should the standard be applied uniformly? For example, ambient air quality standards in the United States are essentially national. Would it not make sense to set different ambient air quality standards for each state, and within a given state for urban and rural areas? That is, emission standards should be sensitive to geographical variations, meteorological conditions, population density and seasonal variations. As discussed in Chapter 10, these are some of the factors that affect the relationships between damage and control costs. In other words, these are factors that could shift either the damage or the control cost or both. To this extent, then, economic efficiency considerations alone would warrant setting standards that are likely to vary from one source to another.

The question then is, why are emission standards, in practice, generally set uniformly across the emission sources? Two practical reasons explain this. First, the administrative and enforcement costs of designing and implementing standards that vary with the different circumstances of each source could be quite costly. Second, from a purely administrative viewpoint, it is much easier to administer standards that are uniform across emission sources.

When there are several emitters with a wide range of technological capabilities, however, pollution control policy based on a uniform emission standard would not be cost-effective. The reason for this is rather straightforward, as is demonstrated using Figure 11.4. In this example, for the sake of simplicity we are considering the activities of only two firms or sources. As is evident from the curvatures of their respective marginal control cost curves, these firms employ different emission control technologies. Furthermore, let us assume that the emission standard is set so that a *total* of 200 units of waste will be controlled by these two firms. In addition, the government authorities have decided to accomplish this through a uniform emission standard that splits the responsibilities of cleanup equally between the two parties. In Figure 11.4, this suggests that each firm would be responsible for cleaning up 100 units of waste. Under this mandate, the *total* waste control cost for these two firms would be represented by area K + L + M + N. This total is composed of the waste control costs of Firms 1 and 2, which are represented by areas M and K + L + N respectively. It is important to note that although the two firms are cleaning an equal amount of waste, their share of the waste control cost could vary considerably. For our hypothetical situation, the pollution control cost of Firm 2 is considerably higher than that of Firm 1. We should not be startled by this result since, as

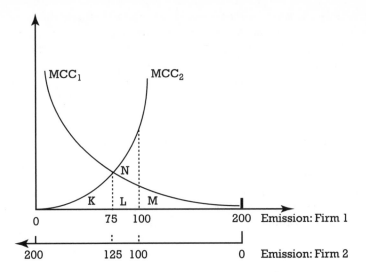

Figure 11.4 **The cost-effectiveness of emission standards**

indicated by the curvatures of the marginal control costs of these two firms, Firm 1 appears to be using a relatively more efficient waste processing technology than Firm 2.

However, the issue of paramount interest here concerns knowledge of the cost-effectiveness of a public policy that is based on a uniform emission standard. In other words, when several polluters are involved, is a policy based on a uniform emission standard cost-effective? The answer to this question is clearly no, as can easily be demonstrated using Figure 11.4. Suppose the government authorities order Firm 2 to clean up only 75 units of the total waste, and Firm 1 is charged to clean up the rest, which will be 125 units (200 – 75). Under this scenario, the total waste control cost (the combined cost of both firms) is measured by area K + L + M. Note that this cost is smaller than the cost the two firms incurred when a uniform emission standard was applied – area K + L + M + N. Furthermore, careful observation indicates that with the new allocation, the marginal control costs of the two firms are equal – that is, $MCC_1 = MCC_2$. This condition is significant because it suggests that area K + L + M is the minimum cost for cleaning up the desired level of total waste emissions, 200 units. This is the case because, at this level of emission, the marginal control costs for the two firms are equal, and hence there is no opportunity left to further reduce costs by reallocating resources from one firm to the other. Thus, we can conclude the following: *the total cost of controlling (cleaning up) a given amount of waste is minimized when the marginal control costs are equalized for all emitters*. This is an important lesson to note for policy-makers dealing with environmental pollution control. Awareness of this condition clearly reveals that unless the firms under consideration operate using identical waste processing technology, pollution control policy based on a uniform emission control will not be cost-effective.

Last but not least, a glaring weakness of emission standards as a policy tool is that they may fail to provide adequate *incentives* to reduce pollution once a standard is met. In fact, in some ways the unintended effect of setting a standard may be to *discourage investment* in new and improved pollution control technology. Figure 11.5 can be used to illustrate the essence of the above two points. In this figure, let MCC_0 and MDC_0 represent the initial marginal control and damage cost curves, respectively. To be more specific, let us assume these are costs associated with waste emissions from one of our most familiar firms: the paper mill. Given this information, the efficient level of pollution will be W_e. Let us further assume that, using an economic efficiency criterion as a policy guide, the current emission standard is set at W_e. That is, by law, W_e is the maximum amount of waste that the paper mill is allowed to emit into the river. Under this condition the total expenditure to the firm for complying with this law is represented by area $A + B$: the area under curve MCC_0 corresponding to emission level W_e. Note that if the firm were not regulated at all, it would have emitted amount W^* of waste into the river and its cleanup cost would have been zero.

At this point, the paper mill knows that it cannot do much to change the law. However, it is still at liberty to find a way of reducing its cleanup cost by some technological means. What economic conditions need to be met in order for this firm to have an incentive to invest in a new waste controlling technology? The simple answer is that the paper mill will insist that the cost savings from the use of the new technology be sufficiently large to recoup a fair rate of return from its initial investment expenditure. To see this logic clearly, suppose we assume that the paper mill is contemplating the introduction of a new waste processing technology. If this were implemented, as shown in Figure 11.5 the impact of the new technology would be to shift the

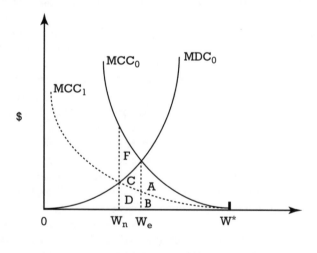

Figure 11.5 **Emission standards and the incentive to improve pollution control technology**

marginal control cost curve from MCC_0 to MCC_1. Given the current level of emission standards, W_e, with the new technology the pollution control cost to the paper mill would be measured by area B – the area under MCC_1 given that the emission standard is set at W_e. When compared with the old technology, this represents a cost saving indicated by area A. It should be noted, however, that this amount of saving can be realized if, and only if, the emission standard is kept at the current level, W_e. There is no guarantee that the regulatory authorities will not revise their decision when the firm's technological condition becomes fully apparent to them. That is, when policy-makers become aware of the new waste processing technology available to the firm, they may decide to change the emission standard to reflect this change. In Figure 11.5 the new standard would be W_n. Under this tighter emission standard, the total waste control cost to this firm would be represented by area B + D – the area under curve MCC_1 when the emission standard is set at W_n. This result implies an *increase* in the pollution control cost for this firm by area D. Hence, as a result of this further tightening of the emission standards, the net savings from implementing the new technology would now be reduced from what would have been area A to the difference in the areas of A and D. The implication here is that emission standards could have the potential to undermine firms' incentive to invest in new pollution control equipment. Furthermore, given the above scenario, with emission standards firms would have an incentive to hide technological changes from the regulatory authorities.

11.5 CHAPTER SUMMARY

This chapter discussed three alternative policy approaches used to internalize environmental externalities: liability laws, Coasian methods and emission standards. The unifying feature of these approaches is their direct dependence on the legal system to resolve environmental litigation.

- Liability law is one of the earliest methods used to deter abuses of the environment. This approach uses statutory enactment that is specifically intended to make polluters liable for the damage they cause. If found liable, polluters are ordered to pay to the plaintiff (in this case the pollutees) financial compensation in direct proportion to the damage they have inflicted.

- The principal advantages of liability laws are the following:
  1 They are effective in deterring environmental nuisance (such as littering).
  2 They have moral appeal since they are based on the polluter-pays principle.

- The main disadvantages of liability laws are:
  1 There is a high transaction cost when the number of parties involved is large.

2 They are "unfair" if the individual damaged does not have the resources to bring a lawsuit.

- The property rights or Coasian approach is conceptualized on the fundamental premise that the root cause of environmental externalities is the lack of clearly defined ownership rights. The legal system is then used to assign enforceable ownership rights.
- Furthermore, the Coase theorem affirms that the final outcome of an environmental dispute (in terms of pollution reduction) is independent of the decision made regarding the assignment of the property rights to a specific party: the polluter or pollutee.
- The principal advantages of the property rights approach are:

    1 It minimizes the role of regulators to a mere assignment of enforceable property rights.
    2 It encourages the resolution of environmental disputes through private negotiations. In other words, it advocates a decentralized approach to pollution control.

- The primary disadvantages of the property rights approach are:

    1 The transaction costs are high when the parties involved in the negotiation process are large in number.
    2 It appears to be indifferent to the polluter-pays principle.
    3 It has the potential to affect the income distribution of the parties involved in the negotiation. In this respect, the final outcome may be judged to be "unfair."

- Emission standards represent a form of command-and-control environmental regulations. The basic idea involves restricting polluters to a certain predetermined amount of effluent discharge. Exceeding this limit subjects polluters to legal prosecution resulting in monetary fines and/or imprisonment.
- The main advantages of emission standards are:

    1 Generally, less information is needed to introduce regulations. As a standard represents a government fiat, it is simple and direct to apply.
    2 They are effective in curbing or controlling harmful pollution, such as DDT.
    3 They are morally appealing and politically popular since the act of polluting is declared a "public bad."
    4 They appeal to "rent-seeking" behavior of existing firms.
    5 They are favored by environmental groups because standards are generally aimed at achieving a predetermined policy target.

- The primary disadvantages of emission standards are:

    1 They are highly interventionist.
    2 They do not generate revenue.
    3 They may require the establishment of a large bureaucracy to administer programs.

4 They are generally not cost-effective.
5 They do not provide firms with sufficient incentive to invest in new pollution control technology.
6 There is a strong tendency for regulatory capture: cooperation between the regulators and polluters in ways that provide unfair advantages to established firms.

---

review and discussion questions

1 Briefly explain the following concepts: liability laws, the polluter-pays principle, the Coase theorem, transaction cost, cost-effective.

2 State *True*, *False* or *Uncertain* and explain why.

  (a) Whether one likes it or not, the abuse of the environment cannot be effectively deterred without some degree of regulation of the free market. Thus, public intervention is both a necessary and a sufficient condition for internalizing environmental externalities.

  (b) The air pollution problem can be solved by simply specifying or assigning exclusive rights to air.

  (c) Environmental advocacy groups generally favor command-and-control approaches because these unambiguously convey the notion that pollution is bad and as such ought to be declared illegal.

3 Despite the appealing logic of the Coase theorem, private actors on their own often fail to resolve an externality problem because of transaction costs. Comment on this statement using two specific examples.

4 The core problem of a command-and-control approach to environmental policy is its inherent bias or tendency to standard-setting practice that is uniformly applicable to all situations. For example, the ambient-air quality standards in the United States are basically national. This may have serious efficiency and ecological implications because regional differences in terms of the factors affecting damage and control cost relationships are not effectively captured. Evaluate. Would considerations of transaction costs have a bearing to your response to this question? Why, or why not?

REFERENCES AND FURTHER READING

Coase, R. (1960) "The Problem of Social Cost," *Journal of Law and Economics* 3: 1–44.
Field, B. C. (1994) *Environmental Economics: An Introduction*, New York: McGraw-Hill.
Hardin, G. (1968) "The Tragedy of the Commons," *Science* 162: 1243–8.
Kneese, A. and Bower, B. (1968) *Managing Water Quality: Economics, Technology, Institutions*, Baltimore: Johns Hopkins University Press.

Schmalensee, R., Joskow, P. L., Ellerman, A. D., Montero, J. P. and Baily, E. M. (1998) "An Interim Evaluation of Sulfur Dioxide Emissions Trading," *Journal of Economic Perspectives* 2, 12: 53–68.

Starrett, D. and Zeckhauser, R. (1992) "Treating External Diseconomies – Market or Taxes," in A. Markandya and J. Richardson (eds.) *Environmental Economics: A Reader*, New York: St. Martin's Press.

Stavins, R. N. (1998) "What Can We Learn from the Grand Policy Experiment? Lessons from SO$_2$ Allowance Trading," *Journal of Economic Perspectives* 2, 12: 69–88.

Turner, D., Pearce, D. and Bateman, I. (1993) *Environmental Economics: An Elementary Introduction*, Baltimore: Johns Hopkins University Press.

United States Environmental Protection Agency (1994) *EPA Journal*, Fall issue.

—— (1995) *EPA Journal*, Winter issue.

chapter twelve

THE ECONOMICS OF ENVIRONMENTAL REGULATIONS:
Pollution Tax and Markets for Pollution Permits

---

learning objectives

After reading this chapter you will be familiar with the following:

- salient features of effluent charges;
- the advantages and disadvantages of using effluent charges as a policy tool for environmental regulations;
- transferable emission permits as a concept and environmental policy instrument;
- strengths and weakness of transferable emission permits;
- how emissions trading, banking, offset and bubble policies are designed to work;
- emissions trading in practice: the case of the United States acid rain reduction program.

Thrust a price theorist into a world with externalities and he will pray for second best – many firms producing and many firms and/or consumers consuming each externality, with full convexity everywhere. No problem for the price theorist. He will just establish a set of *artificial markets* for externalities, commodities for which property rights were not previously defined. Decision units, being small relative to the market, will take price as given. The resulting allocation will be competitive outcome of the classical type. *If artificial markets do not appeal, an equally efficient taxing procedure is available.*

(Starrett and Zeckhauser 1992: 253)

12.1 INTRODUCTION

The subject of this chapter is environmental regulations. In this respect, it is an extension of the previous chapter – Chapter 11. However, in this chapter we look at cases where the legal system is used only *indirectly*, and primarily to correct price distortions. This is done by imposing a financial penalty or tax pollution or by creating artificial market conditions that would allow pollution trading. Two approaches are used to address these issues: effluent charges and transferable emission permits. Effluent charges and transferable emission permits are alike in one important way. They represent a decentralized and cost-effective approach to pollution control.

12.2 EFFLUENT CHARGES

An effluent charge is a tax or a financial penalty imposed on polluters by government authorities. The charge is specified on the basis of dollars or cents per unit of effluent emitted into an ambient environment. For example, a firm may be required to pay an effluent charge of $0.30 per unit of waste material it is discharging into a lake. Note that structurally, effluent charge is just a variation of Pigouvian taxes, which were discussed in Chapter 5. For that matter, the only difference between these two policy tools is that a Pigouvian tax is assessed on a unit of goods or services whereas an effluent tax is charged on a unit of waste emitted.

As public policy instruments, effluent charges have a long history and have been used to resolve a wide variety of environmental problems. For example, in recent years, to address the concern of global warming, several prominent scholars have been proposing a global carbon tax (Pearce 1991). As will be evident from the discussions to follow, the major appeals of an effluent charge are: (a) It is less interventionist than emission standards and operates purely on the premise of financial incentive or disincentive, not on a command-and-control principle. (b) It can be relatively easy to administer. (c) It provides firms with incentives to reduce their pollution through improved technological means.

How does the effluent charge approach work? This question is addressed using Figure 12.1, which portrays a situation where a firm is discharging waste into a particular environmental medium (air, water or land). This firm is required to pay an effluent tax in the amount of t_k, or $20 per unit of waste discharged. We are also provided with the MCC curve of this firm. Given this information, it is fairly easy to draw the conclusion that a private firm interested in minimizing its cost would discharge 150 units of waste. Note that this means that the firm will control 250 units of waste (400 − 150) using its facility to clean the waste. This is cost-minimizing because at 150 units, the usual equimarginal condition is attained. More specifically, the marginal control cost is equal to the predetermined effluent tax; $MCC = t_k = \$20$. When this condition is met, the firm has no incentive to reduce its waste discharge to less than 150 units. To see this, suppose the firm decided to reduce its emission to 100 units. At this level of emission, as shown in Figure

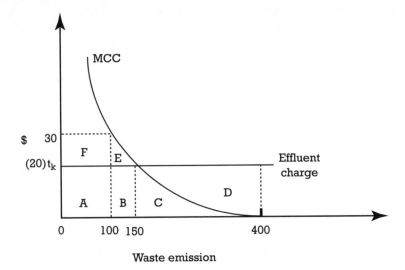

Figure 12.1 **Pollution control through effluent charges**

12.1, the MCC = \$30 > t_k = \$20. Thus, paying the tax to discharge the waste would be cheaper to the firm than using its facility to clean the waste. A similar argument can be presented if the firm decides to increase its waste discharge to a level exceeding 150 units. However, in this case it would be cheaper for the firm to clean the waste using its waste-processing facilities than pay the tax; that is, MCC < t_k. Simply stated, when a profit-maximizing firm is confronted with an effluent charge, it would be in its best interests to treat its waste whenever the cost of treating an additional unit of waste was less than the effluent tax (i.e., t_k > MCC). The firm would cease its effort to control waste when no gain could be realized from any additional activity of this nature (i.e., t_k = MCC).

At this stage, it is important to note the following two points. First, without the effluent charge, this firm would have had no incentive to employ its own resources for the purpose of cleaning up waste. In other words, in Figure 12.1, since the service of the environment is considered a free good, this firm would have emitted a total of 400 units of effluent into the environ-ment. This implies that an effluent charge reduces pollution because it makes the firm recognize that pollution costs the firm money – in this specific case, \$20 per unit of effluent. This shows how an externality is internalized by means of an effluent charge. Second, as shown in Figure 12.1, when the effluent charge is set at t_k, the total expenditure by the firm to control pollution using its own waste-processing technology is represented by area C – the area under the MCC curve when the emission level is 150 units or the firm chooses to control 250 units of its waste (400 – 150). In addition, the firm has to pay a tax (\$20 per unit) on the amount (150 units) of untreated waste it decided to emit into the environment, which is indicated by area A + B. In this specific case this will be \$3,000. Thus, the total cost for this firm to dispose its 400 units of waste will be the tax plus the *total* control cost, i.e., area A + B + C. Note that under an effluent charge regime, the public authorities will not only make the firm clean up its waste to some desired level, but also enable it to generate *tax revenue* that could be used to further clean up the environment or for other social objectives. This is an important advantage that an effluent charge has over emission standards.

It is important to note that the firm has the option not to engage in any waste cleanup activity. However, if the firm decides to exercise this option, it will end up paying an effluent tax in an amount represented by area A + B + C + D, which will be $8,000 ($20 × 400). Clearly, this will not be desirable, since it entails a net loss equivalent to area D when compared to the effluent charge scheme.

So far we have discussed effluent charge on a purely conceptual level and considering only a single firm. We have yet to inquire how the "optimal" level of effluent discharge is determined. Ideally, what we would like the effluent charge to represent is the *social* cost, on a per unit basis, of environmental service when it is used as a medium for emitting waste. For this to happen, the effluent charge needs to be determined by taking both the damage and control costs into consideration at an aggregate level. In Figure 12.2, the MCC curve represents the aggregate (sum) of the marginal control costs for all the relevant firms (or polluting sources). Given this, the *optimal* effluent charge, t_e, is attained at the point where MCC = MDC. In other words, t_e is the uniform tax per unit of waste discharged that we need to impose on all the firms under consideration so that collectively they will emit no more than W_e amount of waste – the optimal level of waste. This level of waste is achieved after a full consideration of all the damage and control costs and from the perspective of society at large.

However, obtaining all the information that is necessary to impute the ideal effluent charge would be quite costly (Baumol and Oates 1992). Thus,

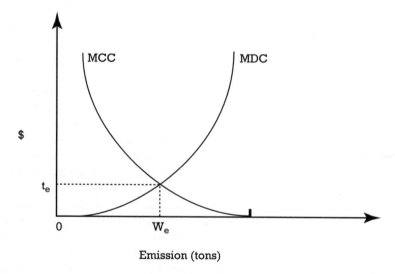

Emission (tons)

Figure 12.2 **Optimal level of effluent charge**

in practice, policy-makers can only view this ideal as a target to be achieved in the long run. In the short run, government authorities determine effluent charge using a trial-and-error process. Initially, they will start the motion by setting an "arbitrary" charge rate. This rate may not be totally arbitrary, to the extent that it is based on the best possible information about damage and control costs available at that point in time. Moreover, this initial rate will be adjusted continually after observing the reaction of the polluters and as new and refined information on damage and control costs became available. The ultimate objective of the government authorities in charge of setting the tax rate is to realize the optimal rate as expeditiously as possible. This, more than anything else, requires the use of a carefully crafted trial-and-error process and flexible administrative programs and procedures.

However, Roberts and Spence (1992) basically rejected the idea that the regulatory authorities, simply by means of an iterative process, could arrive at the optimum solution when they are uncertain about the actual costs of pollution control. They showed that, in the presence of uncertainty, government authorities base their decision on what they *expect* to be the MCC of the firm. When control costs turn out to be greater than expected, environmental policy based on effluent taxes would allow waste discharges in excess of what is considered to be socially optimal, and the opposite result (excessive cleanup) will occur if control costs turn out to be less than expected. In either case, optimality is not attained.

One of the most heralded advantages of an effluent charge is that it is *cost-effective*. A public policy instrument, such as an effluent charge, is cost-effective when the implementation of this instrument guides private concerns to allocate their resources in such a way that they are minimizing their pollution control costs. In Chapter 11 we developed the economic criterion for cost-effectiveness. To restate this criterion, *the total cost of cleaning up a given amount of waste is minimized when the marginal control costs are the same for all the private concerns engaged in pollution control activities* (refer to Figure 11.5). In that chapter, using this criterion, we saw that emission standards are *not* cost-effective.

Why is effluent charge cost-effective? Under the effluent charge regime, each firm (polluting source) is charged a uniform tax per unit of waste discharged, such as t_k in Figure 12.1. As discussed earlier, each firm independently would determine its emission rate by equating its marginal control cost with the predetermined emission tax, t_k. Suppose we have ten firms; since they all are facing the same effluent charge, then, at equilibrium, $MCC_1 = MCC_2 = MCC_3 = \ldots = MCC_9 = MCC_{10} = t_k$. This, as shown earlier, is precisely the condition for a cost-effective allocation of resources, and it results in the effluent charge that *automatically* minimizes the cost of pollution control. This is indeed a startling and desirable result. Nonetheless, *it is important to note that a cost-effective allocation of resources does not necessarily imply a socially optimal allocation of resources*. This is because a cost-effective allocation of pollution control requires only that all the parties involved in pollution cleanup activities face the *same* effluent charge; and nothing more. On the other hand, a socially optimal allocation of pollution cleanup presupposes a single and uniquely determined effluent charge. As shown in Figure 12.2, this unique rate, t_e, is attained when the condition MCC = MDC is met. *It is important to note, however, that t_e is not necessarily equal to t_k.*

At the outset of this section, a claim was made that an effluent charge provides firms with an incentive to improve their waste control technology. How? Using Figure 12.3, suppose we have a single firm (polluter) that is subjected to an effluent charge of t_k per unit of emission. The shift of this firm's marginal control cost curve from MCC_0 to MCC_1 is caused by an introduction of a new and improved method of pollution control. Of course, since the innovation and implementation of the new technology costs money, the firm will undertake this project if, and only if, the expected cost savings from the project under consideration are substantial. In general, other factors being equal, the higher the expected cost savings from a given project, the stronger the firm's incentive to adopt the new and improved pollution control technology. Having stated this, using the information in Figure 12.3 we can vividly illustrate the following two points: (a) the potential cost savings of our hypothetical firm resulting from new pollution control technology; and (b) the fact that, when compared to emission standards, a policy based on effluent charge will provide greater financial incentives (cost savings) to investors in pollution control technology.

Given that t_k represents the effluent charge per unit of emission, before the introduction of the new technology the firm is discharging 1,000 units of its waste. This means that the firm is controlling or cleaning up 500 units (1,500 − 1,000) of its waste. For discharging 1,000 units, the regulatory agency would be able to collect effluent tax (revenue) of $5,000, which is

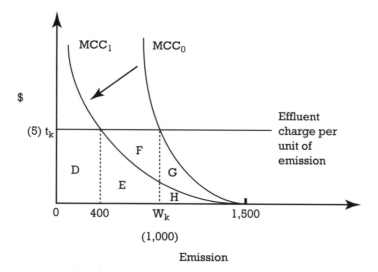

Figure 12.3 Effluent charge and a firm's incentive to invest in a new pollution control technology

represented by area D + E + F. In addition, this firm incurs a further expenditure for cleaning up or processing 500 units of its waste. The expenditure for controlling this amount of waste is measured by area G + H. Thus, area D + E + F + G + H represents the combined expenditure of effluent tax and waste processing for this firm.

By applying logic similar to that above, it can be shown that if the new waste processing technology is adopted, area D + E + H represents the total (effluent charge plus waste processing) expenditure of this firm. Note that the relevant MCC curve is MCC_1. Thus, area F + G represents the cost saving directly attributable to the adoption of the new technology. Is this cost saving large enough to warrant the adoption of the new technology? Unfortunately, the answer to this question cannot be addressed here. However, what we will be able to demonstrate at this stage is that this cost saving from the new technology would have been smaller if the firm's activity had been regulated using an emission standard instead of an effluent charge. In other words, an effluent charge provides stronger financial incentives to the firm to adopt new technology than does an emission standard.

To see this clearly, suppose the emission standard is set at 1,000 – that is, at the level of the firm's operation prior to introducing the new technology. To process the required waste, 500 units, the firm's total expenditure for controlling its waste is represented by area G + H. However, provided the emission standards remain unchanged, this cost can be reduced to area H if the firm decides to adopt the new technology. Thus, the area G represents the cost saving to this firm as a result of adopting the new waste processing plant. Clearly, the magnitude of this saving is smaller than the cost saving that was gained under the effluent charge system – area F + G. Thus, under the effluent tax regime the saving is greater by area F.

Of course, there is no great mystery about this result. Under the effluent charge regime, the firm's cost saving is limited not only to the efficiency gains in its waste processing plants, but also by what the firm is obliged to pay to the government authorities in the form of effluent tax. To see this, first note that, with the new technology, the firm is able to reduce its waste from 1,000 to 400 units – a reduction of 600 units. In doing this, the firm is able to reduce its tax by $3,000 (5 × 600). This tax saving corresponds to area E + F. However, the firm's expenditure to clean up the 600 units using the new technology is only area E. Thus, the net saving to the firm is area F. Note that under emission standards, there is no saving from tax.

The discussion so far clearly indicates that, as a public policy instrument, an effluent charge has a good many attractive features. However, no policy tool can be free of weaknesses, and effluent charge is no exception. The following are some of the major weaknesses of an effluent charge.

First, the waste monitoring and enforcement costs of a pollution control policy based on an effluent charge could be high, especially when a large number of polluters are scattered over a wide geographical area. That is, when compared to an emission standard setting, an effluent charge requires the gathering and monitoring of more refined and detailed information from each pollution source, since the effluent charge requires the processing of both financial and technological information. Unlike emission standards, it is not based on a purely physical consideration.

Second, an effluent charge can, and rightly so, be viewed as an emission tax. The question is then, who actually ends up paying this tax? This is a relevant issue because firms could pass this tax to the consumers by charging a higher price to the consumers of their products. Furthermore, how does the tax impact consumers in a variety of socioeconomic conditions: for example, the poor versus the rich, and the black versus the white? What this warns us is that we need to be aware of the income distribution effect of effluent charge.

It is important to note, however, that an effluent charge generates *revenue*. If government adopts a policy that is fiscally neutral, the revenue raised by taxes on pollution can be used to correct the income distribution or any other negative effects caused by the tax. Some argue that it is important to be mindful about the *double dividend* feature of pollution tax. That is, pollution tax can be used to correct market distortion (i.e., externalities arising from excessive use of environmental services) and raise revenues which could be used to finance worthwhile social projects, such as helping the poor, providing an incentive to firms to undertake environmentally friendly projects, etc. (Pearce 1991).

Third, we have already seen that an effluent charge automatically leads to the minimization of pollution control costs. However, while an effluent charge is cost-effective in this specific way, this result in itself does not imply optimality. Whether an effluent charge produces an optimal outcome or not depends entirely on the choice of the "appropriate" effluent tax. The determination of this tax requires not just pollution control, but the simultaneous consideration of both control and damage costs.

Fourth, because of the amount of detailed information needed to estimate the appropriate charge, in practice an effluent charge is set on a trial-and-error basis. If nothing else, this definitely increases the uncertainty of private business ventures concerning pollution control technology. Furthermore, in some situations (e.g., where significant regional differences in ecological conditions exist), optimality may require imposing a nonuniform effluent charge policy. For example, the correct level of carbon tax imposed to control greenhouse-gas emissions may vary in different countries of the European Union. Situations of this nature clearly add to the problems of imposing the appropriate absolute level of charges in relation to the level and nature of emissions caused by each source.

Fifth, effluent charge is a financial disincentive given to polluters. This system of charge does not say that it is morally wrong to knowingly engage in the pollution of the environment. It simply states that it is okay to pollute provided one pays the assessed penalty for such an activity. Of course, the justification for this is that damage to the environment can be restored using the money generated by penalizing polluters. To some people, this conveys a perverse logic. There is a big difference between *protecting* the natural environment from harm and *repairing* it after it has been damaged.

The fact that effluent charge is set on a trial-and-error basis has been a source of considerable concern to economists. The upshot of this concern has been the development of an alternative policy instrument to control pollution, namely *transferable emission permits*. This policy tool, the subject of the following section, has all the advantages of effluent charges, and it is not set on a trial-and-error basis.

12.3 TRANSFERABLE EMISSION PERMITS

Essentially, the main idea behind transferable emission permits is to create a market for *pollution rights*. A pollution right simply signifies a permit which consists of a unit (pound, ton, etc.) of a specific pollutant. Under the transferable emission permit approach, government authorities basically have two functions. They determine the total allowable permits and decide the mechanism to be used to distribute the *initial* pollution permits among polluters.

How do government authorities determine the total number of permits or units of pollutants? Ideally, the total should be set by considering both the damage and the control costs from the perspective of society at large. Accordingly, W_e in Figure 12.2 would satisfy such a condition. In practice, however, accurate estimates of damage and control costs may not be readily available because they may involve astronomically high transaction costs. Thus, generally, the total number of permits is determined by government agencies using the best information available about both damage and control costs at a point in time. It is important to note that, as a policy instrument designed to curb the abuse of the natural environment, the success of a transferable permit scheme very much depends on the *total* size of pollution permits. Thus, this is not a decision that should be taken lightly, although government authorities can always readjust the number of pollution permits issued to a polluter at any point in time.

Once the total emission permits are determined, the next step requires finding a mechanism by which the total permits are initially distributed among polluters. No single magic formula exists that can be used to distribute the initial rights among polluters, especially if "fairness" (equity) is an important consideration. Despite this concern for equity, provided pollution permits are freely *transferable*, the initial distribution of rights will have no effect on how the total permits are eventually allocated through the market mechanism. In other words, as we will see soon, the efficient allocation of the total permits will be independent of the initial distribution of pollution rights provided permits are freely transferable. Is this the Coase theorem in disguise?

From the discussion so far, it is important to observe that a system of transferable permits operates on the basis of the following basic postulates:

1 It is possible to obtain a legally sanctioned right to pollute.
2 These rights (permits) are clearly defined.
3 The total number of permits and the initial distribution of the total

permits among the various polluters are assigned by government agencies. In addition, polluters emitting in excess of their allowances are subject to a stiff monetary penalty.

4   Pollution permits are freely transferable. That is, they can be freely traded in the marketplace.

These four attributes of a system of transferable permits are clearly evident in Exhibit 12.1. This exhibit describes the actual procedures that the United States Environmental Protection Agency (EPA) was proposing to use to limit sulfur dioxide emissions from the major electric power plants in the eastern and Midwestern states by means of a program of market-based trading of allowances.

EXHIBIT 12.1   ACID RAIN EMISSION LIMITS PROPOSED FOR OVER 900 POWER PLANTS

Proposed plant-by-plant reductions in acid rain emissions have been listed by EPA for most of the electric-power generating plants in the United States. One hundred and ten of the largest plants, mostly coal-burning utilities in twenty-one eastern and Midwestern states, will have to make reductions beginning in 1995; at the turn of the century, over 800 smaller plants must also cut back on their emission, and the larger plants must make further reductions. Electric power plants account for 70 percent of sulfur dioxide (SO_2) emissions in the United States; SO_2 is the chief contributor to acid rain.

Under the 1990 Clean Air Act, each power plant is to be issued emissions allowances. Each allowance equals one ton of SO_2 emissions per year. The number of allowances a plant gets is determined by formula and is based in large part on the plant's past consumption of fuel. As the program gets under way in 1995, each plant must hold enough allowances to cover its annual emissions. It can meet its requirement either by reducing emissions or by purchasing allowances from other utilities. For every ton of SO_2 a plant emits in excess of its allowances, it will pay a penalty of $2,000 and will forfeit on allowance. This program of market-based trading in allowances, combined with tough monitoring and enforcement, is believed to have significant advantages over traditional "command-and-control" regulations. By allowing utilities that can reduce emission cheaply to sell excess allowance to those whose control costs are high, total reductions can be achieved most cost-effectively. As a safeguard, no utility – no matter how many allowances it holds – will be allowed to emit SO_2 in amounts that exceed federal health standards.

Source: *EPA Journal* Vol. 18, no. 3, 1992, pp. 4–5. Reprinted by permission.

To illustrate how a resource allocation system that is based on transferable permits is supposed to work, let us consider the following simple examples. Suppose that after careful consideration of all the relevant information, government agencies of some hypothetical place issue a total of 300 permits for a period of one year. Each permit entitles the holder to

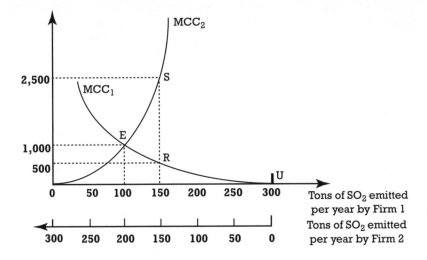

Figure 12.4 **How transferable emission permits work**

emit a ton of sulfur dioxide. There are only two firms (Firm 1 and Firm 2) emitting sulfur dioxide. Using a criterion that is considered to be "fair," government authorities issue an equal number of permits to both firms. That is, the *maximum* that each firm can emit into the air is 150 tons of sulfur dioxide per year. Finally, let us suppose that in the absence of government regulation each firm would have emitted 300 tons of sulfur dioxide. Thus, by issuing a total of 300 permits, the ultimate objective of the government policy is to reduce the current level of total sulfur emission in the region by half (300 tons). Figure 12.4 incorporates the hypothetical data presented so far. Furthermore, in this figure the marginal control costs for these two firms are assumed to be different. Specifically, it is assumed that Firm 1 uses a more efficient waste processing technology than Firm 2.

Given the conditions described above, these two firms can engage in some form of mutually beneficial negotiations. To begin, let us look at the situation that Firm 1 is facing. Given that it can discharge a maximum of 150 units of its sulfur emission, Firm 1 is operating at point R of its MCC. At this point it is controlling 150 units of its sulfur emission. For this firm, the marginal control cost for the last unit of the SO_2 is $500. On the other hand, Firm 2 is operating at point S of its MCC, and it is controlling 150 units of its waste and releasing the other 150 units into the environment. At this level of operation, point S, the marginal control cost of Firm 2, is $2,500. What is evident here is that at their current level of operations, the marginal control costs of these two firms are different. More specifically, to treat the last unit of emission, it costs Firm 2 five times as much as Firm 1 ($500 versus $2,500). Since permits to pollute are freely tradable commodities, it would be in the best interest of Firm 2 to buy a permit from Firm 1 provided its price is less than $2,500. Similarly, Firm 1 will be willing to sell a permit provided its price is greater than $500. This kind of mutually beneficial exchange of permits will continue to persist as long as, at each stage of the negotiation between the two parties, $MCC_2 > MCC_1$. That is, as long as the marginal control cost of Firm 2 exceeds that of Firm 1, Firm 1 will be in a position to supply pollution permits to Firm 2. This relationship will cease to occur when the marginal control cost of the two firms attain equality – that is, $MCC_2 = MCC_1$. In Figure 12.4, this equilibrium condition is reached at point E. At this equilibrium point, Firm 1 is emitting 100 tons of sulfur (or controlling 200 tons of sulfur). This means that Firm 1 is emitting 50 tons of sulfur less than its maximum allowable permits. On the other hand, at the equilibrium point, Firm 2 is emitting 200 tons of sulfur, 50 tons more than its maximum allowable pollution permits. However, Firm 2 is able to fill this deficit by purchasing 50 tons worth of pollution permits from Firm 1. Note also that at equilibrium the total amount of sulfur emitted by these two firms is 300 tons, which is exactly equal to the total pollution permits issued by government authorities.

What exactly is the difference between the initial situation of these two firms (points R and S) and the new equilibrium condition established through a system of transferable pollution permits, point E? In both instances, the total units of sulfur emission are the same: 300 tons of sulfur. However, what is desirable about the new equilibrium position (point E) is that it is *cost-effective*. First, note that it satisfies the usual condition for cost-effective allocation of resources – that is, the marginal control costs of the firms under consideration are equal. Using Figure 12.4, it is also possible to show that both firms are better off at the new position. At the initial level of operation (points R and S), the total pollution control cost for these two firms is represented by area 0ESRU. The total pollution control cost at the new equilibrium position (point E) is measured by area 0EU. Therefore, by moving to the new equilibrium, the total control cost is reduced by area ERS. This clearly constitutes a Pareto improvement since – by moving from the old to the new position – no one is made worse off. This is because the movement is done through a voluntary and mutually beneficial exchange between the two firms.

Furthermore, like an effluent charge system, the use of transferable permits would provide strong incentives to encourage investment in new pollution control technologies. For those who are curious, this can be easily demonstrated using an approach similar to that used in the previous section, Figure 12.3.

As a public policy instrument, perhaps the most remarkable feature of transferable permits is that, once the size of the total permits is determined, the allocation of these permits among competing users is based entirely on the market system. This was demonstrated above using a rather simple case of only two firms. However, *the remarkable feature of the transferable pollution permits system is that it works even better when the number of parties involved in the exchange of permits increases.* The only thing that this system requires, as discussed earlier, is the creation of clearly defined new property rights: pollution permits. Once this is accomplished, as in the case for the markets for goods and services (see Chapter 2), individual firms will be guided, via an "invisible hand," to use environmental resources in a manner that is considered "socially" optimal. Furthermore, this system of allocation creates an actual market price for the environmental commodities under consideration. For example, in Figure 12.4 the market equilibrium price is $1,000 per permit.

Given these features of transferable pollution permits, it is not difficult to see why such a system should command the enthusiastic support of economists. Since the early 1980s, economists have been strongly lobbying the EPA to adopt transferable pollution permits as the primary policy tool for regulating the environment. As a result of this effort, in recent years there have been increasing applications of transferable permits in a wide variety of situations. In some sense, the growing application of transferable permits is creating what amounts to a revolutionary reform not only of the way the EPA has been conducting its regulatory affairs, but of how the general public is reacting to environmental concerns. The reading in Case Study 12.1 is a good illustration of this.

CASE STUDY 12.1 PURCHASING POLLUTION

Meg Sommerfeld

What can $20,500 buy?

More than 1,800 reams of photocopier paper, 6,833 pints of Ben and Jerry's ice cream, or a new car, among other things.

How about 290 tons of sulfur dioxide? At least that's what students at Glens Falls (N.Y.) Middle School want to buy with money they have raised.

The students have raised $20,500 to buy so-called pollution allowances at the US Environmental Protection Agency's annual auction at the Chicago Board of Trade this week.

Each credit allows the purchaser to emit a ton of sulfur dioxide, a colorless, suffocating gas. The students would retire the allowances they buy, thereby reducing the amount of sulfur dioxide that is released into the air. The EPA will auction about 22,000 credits this year.

The school in upstate New York raised about $13,640 from a community auction, more than $4,000 from a letter-writing campaign, and $3,860 through 25-cent "gum allowances" and 50-cent bubble-blowing permits.

While gum is usually verboten, a Glens Falls teacher had permission to sell gum for one day. The teacher sold 1,000 pieces of gum before 8:30 a.m.

Leading the charge was sixth-grade teacher Rod Johnson.

"We study the problem, and buying the pollution allowances gives us a solution," he said.

Glens Falls and fifteen other elementary, middle and secondary schools participating in the pollution auction got involved with the help of the National Healthy Air License Exchange, a Cleveland-based nonprofit environmental group. Most of the other schools have raised a few hundred dollars.

Is such an enthusiastic endorsement of the EPA and the economic profession justifiable? It would be fine provided the enthusiasm were tempered with proper qualifications. For one thing, it should be recognized that transferable pollution permits are not panaceas. Like many other systems of resource allocation, in some instances they can have high administrative and transaction costs. Furthermore, it is extremely important to note that what a system of transferable pollution permits guarantees us is a cost-effective allocation of the total permits that are issued by the government authorities. *Whether such a system leads to an optimal use of environmental resources depends largely on how government authorities determine the total permits to be issued.* As stated earlier, this requires the compiling of detailed and accurate information about damage costs – a very difficult and costly task to accomplish. Without such information, we can never be sure that the market price for permits accurately reflects the "true" scarcity value of the environmental resource under consideration.

In fact, Roberts and Spence (1992) demonstrated that, in the presence of *uncertainty*, a regulatory scheme based on transferable pollution permits would yield results that differ from the socially optimal outcome. When control costs turn out to be higher than expected, a policy based on transferable permits will tend to yield an outcome that suggests a cleanup costing more than the socially optimal level and vice versa. Note that this result is the opposite of what is stated with regard to effluent charges. For this reason, Roberts and Spence (1992) argued for using a combination of effluent charges and transferable pollution permits when uncertainty is prevalent.

In addition, as mentioned earlier, we need to be aware that the mechanism by which government agencies eventually decide to distribute the total permits among potential users can have significant *equity* implications. Should permits be distributed *equally* among the potential users? Should they be distributed in proportion to the size of the firms under consideration? Should they be distributed by means of a lottery? Should permits be publicly auctioned? Since each one of these allocation systems has varying impacts among the various users of the permits, it will be impossible to completely avoid the issue of fairness or equity. For example, in the United States, permits are allocated on the *grandfathering principle* (where permits are allocated relative to the size of a firm's historical level of emissions), which favors the existing major polluters. Evidence of this is the permit allocation formula the EPA used in Exhibit 12.1, which is based on the utility companies' past consumption of fuel (coal) – the primary source of sulfur dioxide pollution.

Pollution permits can be subject to the abuses of special-interest groups. What if an environmental group decides to buy a number of permits for a certain pollutant and retires them? Of course, this action may serve conservation-minded souls very well, but will this be true for society at large? Furthermore, what this entails is that any group with a considerable amount of money can influence the market price and hence the quantity traded of pollution permits. For example, established firms can deter new entrants by hoarding permits. Ultimately, unless suitable mechanisms are used to deal with abuses of the above nature, the notion of protecting the environment through marketable pollution permits may be far less satisfactory than theory suggests. Note also that any effort to curb market abuses entails transaction costs – which is problematic if they are too high.

Finally, to some individuals the very idea of pollution rights or permits to pollute conveys reprehensible moral and ethical values. As discussed above, a system of allocation based on transferable permit supports the notion that the environment is just another commodity to be traded piecemeal using the market. Here the fear is that since several aspects of environmental amenities are not subject to market valuation, such a system of allocation would eventually lead to the abuse of the natural environment.

12.4 AN EVALUATION OF THE EMISSION TRADING PROGRAMS IN THE UNITED STATES

Emissions trading programs began to be implemented by the EPA in the mid 1970s. Until the mid-1980s, the experiments with this market-based environmental policy measure were limited in their scope and were primarily designed for controlling local air pollutants (Tietenberg 1998). In general, market-based environmental policy instruments are favored because they promise to be flexible and as such cost-effective, especially when compared with the traditional command-and-control type of environmental regulation.

12.4.1 Programs to phase out leaded gasoline and ozone-depleting chlorofluorocarbons (CFCs)

In the mid-1980s the EPA used emissions trading programs to phase out leaded gasoline from the market (Stavins 1998). In adopting this method, the EPA's primary aim was to provide greater flexibility to refiners in how the deadlines were met without increasing the amount of lead used. Under this program, over the transition period a fixed amount of lead was allocated to the various refiners. Refiners were then permitted to trade (buy and sell), provided that the total amount of lead emitted did not exceed the authorized lead permits issued by the EPA. However, the fact that these permits were freely transferable allowed some refiners to comply with the deadlines with greater ease and without having to fight the deadlines in court. In this respect, the lead permits program was quite successful in facilitating the orderly adoption of more stringent regulations on lead in gasoline in the United States. Furthermore, the program ended as scheduled on December 31, 1987.

Another area where transferable permits programs were used in the United States was in phasing out ozone-depleting chlorofluorocarbons (CFSs). The United States initially adopted such a program to comply with the ozone international agreement at the Montreal Protocol in September 1988 (more on this in Chapter 13). The Montreal Protocol required the signatory nations to restrict their production and consumption of the chief ozone-depleting gases to 50 percent of 1986 levels by June 30, 1998 (more on this in Chapter 13). In response to this, on August 12, 1988, the EPA officially instituted a tradable permit system to meet its obligations. To achieve the targeted reductions, all major producers and consumers of ozone-depleting substances in the United States were rationed to baseline production or consumption permits (allowances) using 1986 levels as the basis. These permits were transferable within producer and consumer categories. In general, the EPA's efforts to achieve the reductions of ozone-depleting substances have been quite successful both in terms of cost-effectiveness and in meeting the deadlines. However, what may not be clear at this stage is how much of this success can be attributed to the EPA's use of a tradable permits program.

12.4.2 The acid rain control program

The first large-scale use of tradable pollution permits in the United States was introduced with the passage of the 1990 Clean Air Act Amendments. More specifically, Title IV of this Act was responsible in initiating a nation-wide use of market-based approaches primarily designed to reduce sulfur dioxide (SO_2) emissions from power plants by about half the amount of the 1980 levels by the turn of the century. Why was sulfur dioxide emission a major concern?

In the 1980s, acid rain was a hotly debated worldwide environmental concern. In the United States, emissions of sulfur dioxide (SO_2) from power plants were the chief precursor of acid rain. Sulfur dioxide emissions were steadily increasing during the 1970s and the 1980s. By the late 1980s, in the United States alone the total SO_2 emission was approaching 25 million tons per year. Accumulated over time, acid rain depositions on lakes, streams, forests, buildings, and people are believed to cause substantial damage to aquatic organisms and trees, erode and disfigure stone buildings and historical monuments, and impair the lungs of people (for more on this see Chapter 13).

Confronted with the prospect of growing acid rain-related problems, the United States government started Phase I of its ambitious sulfur emissions reduction program in 1995. The goal of the program has been to cut the annual sulfur dioxide emissions from power plants by 10 million tons from

1980 levels by the year 2000 (see Exhibit 12.1). The acid rain reduction programs in Phase I involved 110 mostly coal-burning plants. Phase II is expected to start in the year 2000, immediately following the end of Phase I. In Phase II, the goal will be to further reduce sulfur dioxide emissions by another 10 million tons per year by 2010. This will be achieved by increasing the number of power plants participating in the acid rain reduction programs and by further tightening emissions standards – sulfur dioxide emitted per million British thermal units. The projection is that by 2010, total sulfur dioxide emissions in the United States will dwindle to 8.95 million tons per year.

However, when Congress passed the 1990 Clean Air Act Amendments, the cost of the acid rain control programs was a major concern. The cost estimates for Phase I alone were running as high as $10 billion a year, which is equivalent to $1,000 per ton of sulfur dioxide controlled (Kerr 1998). This cost estimate was based on the assumption that sulfur dioxide emissions will continue to be regulated through "command-and-control" approaches. Given this, considerable attention was given to searching for cost-effective ways of operationalizing the acid rain control programs. One outcome of this was the adaption of a flexible system of emissions trading.

Under the system of emissions trading, the EPA still retains the power to set the upper limits on the annual levels of sulfur dioxide emissions for the nation. Furthermore, to achieve the total annual emissions goal, the EPA limits individual power plants under the acid rain programs by issuing a fixed number of tradable permits (allowances) on the basis of historical emissions and fuel use (see Exhibit 12.1). Each allowance is worth one ton of sulfur dioxide released from the smokestack, and to obtain reductions in emissions, the number of allowances declines yearly. A small number of additional allowances (less than 2 percent of the total allowances) are auctioned annually by the EPA (Tietenberg 1998). At the end of each year, utilities that have emitted more than their pollution permits allow them will be subjected to a stiff penalty, $2,000 per ton. In addition, all power plants under the acid rain program are required to install continuous emission monitoring systems (CEMS), machines that keep track of how much sulfur dioxide the plant is emitting.

However, although each participant in the acid rain reduction program is given a fixed number of allowances, power plant operators are given *complete freedom* on how to cut their emissions. On the basis of cost considerations alone, a plant operator might install scrubbers (desulfurization facilities that reduce the amount of SO_2 exiting from the stack), switch to a coal with a lower sulfur content, buy or sell allowances, or save allowances for future use. As we will see shortly, these are the unique features that greatly contributed to the overall flexibility and cost-effectiveness of the United States acid rain reduction programs. Note that the overall flexibility of the acid rain reduction programs is not limited to a consideration of allowance trading. The options provided to plant operators with regard to the types of scrubber and the different qualities of coal that they can purchase are significant contributors to the overall flexibility and cost-effectiveness of the acid rain reduction programs.

Allowance trading can be effected using the *offset*, the *bubble* or the *banking* policies. The offset policy is designed to permit allowance trading in a geographic region known as a *nonattainment area* – a region in which the level of a given air pollutant (sulfur dioxide, in the case of the acid rain reduction program) exceeds the level permitted by the federal standards. Under this policy, an increase in sulfur dioxide emissions from a given smokestack can be *offset* by a reduction (of a somewhat greater amount) of the same pollutant from any other smokestack owned by the purchase of allowances equal to the offset amount from other companies in the non-attainment area. Hence, trading offset among companies is permitted, provided the permit requirements are met and the nonattainment area keeps moving toward attainment. This is feasible because companies are required to more than offset (by an extra 20 percent) any pollution they will add to the nonattainment area through new sources (Tietenberg 1998). Under the offset policy, the new sources could be new firms entering into the nonattainment area – hence allowing economic growth.

By contrast, the *bubble* policy allows emissions trading opportunities among multiple emission sources (collectively recognized as forming a bubble) to be controlled by existing emitters. Provided the total pollutants leaving the bubble are within the federal standards, polluters are free to pursue a cost-effective strategy for controlling pollution. In other words, not all sources are held to a uniform emission standard; thus, within a given bubble, emitters are allowed to control some pollution sources less stringently than others, provided a sufficient amount of emission reduction is realized from the other sources within the same bubble.

The emissions *banking* policy simply allows polluters to save their emission allowances for use in some future year. These saved allowances can be used in offset, bubble or for sale to other firms. This is an important feature of the United States sulfur dioxide reduction program as it allows firms an opportunity for intertemporal trading and optimization (Schmalensee *et al.* 1998).

As stated earlier, Phase I of the United States acid rain reduction program has been in effect since 1995. Early indications are that the use of tradable allowances has been quite successful. According to a recent study by Schmalensee *et al.* (1998), for the first two years the reduction in sulfur emissions from participating power plants was, on average, about 35 percent below the legal limit – total allowances issued or auctioned for each of these two years. Furthermore, this was done at a cost of less than $1 billion per year (Kerr 1998). Note that this cost figure is far below the initial cost estimate of the acid rain control program, which, as pointed out earlier, was expected to run as high as $10 billion per year. Thus, the preliminary empirical evidence indicates that, so far, the sulfur dioxide allowance trading programs have been remarkably economical. Furthermore, the costs for Phase II, although likely to be higher than the costs for Phase I, are also expected to be much lower than initial estimates.

To what factor(s) can the successes of the acid rain reduction programs, so far, be attributed? It is important to note that not all the cost savings can be attributed to the allowance trading program. According to some estimates, 30 percent of the overall cost savings from the acid rain reduction programs can be attributed to allowance trading, which is by no means insignificant (Kerr 1998). However, the contribution of allowance trading would have been higher than 30 percent if it had not been for the low volume of allowance trading during the first two years of Phase I. This situation is expected to improve in future years as the market conditions for allowance trading further develop.

At this point, therefore, the bulk of the cost savings stem from the *overall flexibility* of the acid rain reduction programs. This means that other external factors, such as the unexpected decline in prices for scrubbers and substantial fall in coal transportation costs due to railroad deregulation, were important contributing factors to the overall cost savings realized by the United States acid rain program during its first two years of operation.

The early success of the acid rain reduction experiment is raising hope that allowance trading could be similarly applied to several major environmental programs, including carbon dioxide reduction programs intended to slow down the trend in global warming. For example, during the 1997 Kyoto Protocol on global warming, the United States insisted on the use of tradable permits to limit global carbon dioxide emissions (more on this in Chapter 13). This was also a hotly contested issue in the Buenos Aires conference held exactly a year after the Kyoto conference. However, so far the United States push for international carbon trading has been greeted with a great deal of skepticism and resistance for the following two reasons. First, in general, tradable permits work best when transaction costs are low, which may not be the case for the proposed carbon dioxide reduction programs because the compliance (monitoring and enforcement) costs are likely to be high for any environmental program that relies heavily on international accords involving countries from diverse cultural, political and economic orientations. Second, as Stavins (1998: 83) rightly pointed out,

> the number and diversity of sources of carbon dioxide emissions due to fossil fuel combustion are vastly greater than in the case of sulfur dioxide emissions as a precursor of acid rain, where the focus can be placed on a few hundred electric utility plants.

Thus, the success in the sulfur dioxide emission reduction program in the United States does not provide a blanket endorsement for the use of allowance trading programs for cutting carbon dioxide emissions designed to reduce the risk of global climate change.

12.5 CHAPTER SUMMARY

This chapter discussed two alternative policy approaches that can be used to correct environmental externalities: effluent charges and transferable emission permits. The common feature of these two policy instruments is that they both deploy market incentives to influence the behavior of polluters. Effluent charges and transferable emission permits are alternative forms of market-based environmental policy instruments.

- Effluent charges represent a tax per unit of waste emitted. Ideally, a tax of this nature reflects the imputed value (on a per unit basis) of the services of an environment as repository for untreated waste. Thus, the idea of the tax is to account for external costs; effluent charge is used to correct price distortion.
- The principal advantages of the effluent charges are:

  1 They are relatively easy to administer.
  2 They are generally cost-effective.
  3 They generate revenues while correcting price distortions – the double-dividend feature of effluent charges.
  4 They provide firms with incentives to invest in pollution control technology.

- The main disadvantages of the effluent charges are:

  1 Monitoring and enforcement costs are high.
  2 They could have a disproportionate effect on income distribution.
  3 They do not condemn the act of polluting on purely moral grounds. It is okay to pollute, provided one pays for it.
  4 Firms are philosophically against taxes of any form, especially when they are perceived to cause increased prices and an uncertain business environment.
  5 Environmental organizations generally oppose effluent charges for both practical and philosophical reasons. Pollution taxes are "licenses to pollute." Taxes are generally difficult to tighten once implemented.

- The transferable emission permits approach to pollution control requires, first and foremost, the creation of artificial markets for pollution rights. A pollution right represents a permit that consists of a unit of a specific pollutant. The role of the regulator is limited to setting the total number of permits and the mechanism(s) by which these permits are distributed among polluters. Once they receive their initial allocation, polluters are allowed to freely exchange permits on the basis of market-established prices.
- Primary advantages of transferable emission permits are:

  1 They are least interventionist.
  2 They are cost-effective, especially when the number of parties involved in the exchange of permits is large.
  3 They provide observable market prices for environmental services.
  4 They can be applied to a wide range of environmental problems.

- The principal disadvantages of transferable emission permits are:

  1 The mechanisms used to distribute permits among potential users could have significant equity implications.

2 The idea of permits to pollute conveys, to some, a reprehensible moral and ethical value.

3 Their applicability is questionable for pollution problems with an international scope.

4 They are ineffective when there are not enough participants to make the market function.

5 Permits can be accumulated by firms for the purpose of deterring entrants or by environmental groups for the purpose of attaining the groups' environmental objectives.

- Preliminary empirical evidence indicates that the United States sulfur dioxide emissions trading program has performed successfully. Targeted emissions reduction have been achieved and exceeded, and at costs significantly less than what they would have been in the absence of the trading provisions.

- This success would not necessarily apply in cases of international pollution. For example, could an emissions trading program be effective in cutting carbon dioxide emissions intended to reduce the risk of global warming? It will most likely be less effective than the United States' experiment in sulfur dioxide emissions reduction programs because of high enforcement and monitoring costs of a pollution problem with a global dimension.

---

review and discussion questions

1 Briefly describe the following concepts: effluent charges, transferable pollution permits, the grandfathering principle, the Clean Air Act amendment of 1990, the bubbles, offsets and emissions banking policies.

2 State *True*, *False* or *Uncertain* and explain why.

(a) To say that an effluent charge is *cost-effective* does not necessarily mean that it is optimal. This is because cost-effectiveness does not account for damage costs.

(b) The remarkable feature of tradable permits is that they work best when the parties involved in the trade are large in numbers.

(c) Pollution taxes and tradable permits are "licenses to pollute."

(d) Effluent charges and permits provide unfair competitive advantages to existing firms.

3 Some economists argue that a policy instrument to control pollution (such as effluent charges and transferable pollution permits) should not be dismissed on the basis of "fairness" alone. The issue of fairness can always be addressed separately through income redistribution. For example, the tax revenue from effluent charges can be used to compensate the losses of the damaged parties. Critically evaluate.

4 As you have read in this chapter, since the mid-1980s the Environmental Protection Agency (EPA) in the United States has seemingly come to rely increasingly on transferable emission permits.

   (a) In general, do you support this fundamental change in policy from the traditional "command-and-control" regulations to market-based trading of pollution allowances? Why, or why not?

   (b) Why do you think the rest of the world is rather slow or not enthusiastic in adopting this type of pollution control policy? Speculate.

5 Environmental organizations have opposed market-based pollution control policies out of a fear that permit level and tax rates, once implemented, would be more difficult to tighten over time than command-and-control standards. Is this fear justifiable? Why, or why not?

6 Which of the environmental policy options discussed in this and previous chapters would you recommend if a hypothetical society were facing the following environmental problems? In each case, briefly explain the justification(s) for your choice.

   (a) a widespread problem with campground littering;
   (b) pollution of an estuary from irrigation runoffs;
   (c) air pollution of a major metropolitan area;
   (d) the emission of a toxic waste;
   (e) damage of lakes, streams, forests and soil resulting from acid rain;
   (f) a threat to human health due to stratospheric ozone depletion;
   (g) the gradual extinction of endangered species.

REFERENCES AND FURTHER READING

Baumol, W. J. and Oates, W. E. (1992) "The Use of Standards and Prices for Protection of the Environment," in A. Markandya and J. Richardson (eds.) *Environmental Economics: A Reader*, New York: St. Martin's Press.

Field, B. C. (1994) *Environmental Economics: An Introduction*, New York: McGraw-Hill.

Kerr, R. A. (1998), "Acid Rain Control: Success on the Cheap," *Science* 282: 1024–7.

Kneese, A. and Bower, B. (1968) *Managing Water Quality: Economics, Technology, Institutions*, Baltimore: Johns Hopkins University Press.

Pearce, W. D. (1991) "The Role of Carbon Taxes in Adjusting to Global Warming," *Economic Journal* 101: 938–48.

Roberts, M. J. and Spence, M. (1992) "Effluent Charges and Licenses under Uncertainty," in A. Markandya and J. Richardson (eds.) *Environmental Economics: A Reader*, New York: St. Martin's Press.

Schmalensee, R., Joskow, P. L., Ellerman, A. D., Montero, J. P. and Baily, E. M. (1998) "An Interim Evaluation of Sulfur Dioxide Emissions Trading," *Journal of Economic Perspectives* 2, 12: 53–68.

Starrett, D. and Zeckhauser, R. (1992) "Treating External Diseconomies – Market or Taxes," in A. Markandya and J. Richardson (eds.) *Environmental Economics: A Reader*, New York: St. Martin's Press.

Stavins, R. N. (1998) "What Can We Learn from the Grand Policy Experiment?

Lessons from SO$_2$ Allowance Trading," *Journal of Economic Perspectives* 2, 12: 69–88.

Tietenberg, T. (1992) *Environmental and Natural Resource Economics*, 3rd edn., New York: HarperCollins.

—— (1998) "Ethical Influences on the Evolution of the US Tradable Permit Approach to Air Pollution Control," *Ecological Economics* 24: 241–57.

chapter thirteen

GLOBAL ENVIRONMENTAL POLLUTION:
Acid Rain, Ozone Depletion and Global Warming

(Contributed by Marvin S. Soroos)

---

learning objectives

After reading this chapter you will be familiar with the following:

- three major environmental problems with international or even global dimensions;
- the causes and consequences of acid rain;
- the causes and consequences of depletion of the ozone layer;
- the causes and consequences of global warming;
- international efforts to address the problem of acid rain, ozone depletion and climate change;
- the economics of atmospheric pollution.

Most of the world's climate scientists say global warming is a real and serious threat. Market forces won't solve the problems, because markets treat pollution as a costless byproduct and underprice it. "Free-Market" advocates are promoting a complex scheme of tradable (transferable) emission rights. But this "market" does not exist in nature; it must first be constructed – by government diplomats and regulators. And these emissaries must resolve complex policy questions: how much overall pollution to allow; how to allocate the initial stock of tradable permits; whether to have waivers or subsidies for poor countries; and whom to empower to police the system. Here, globalization demands more statecraft, not more market.

(*Business Week*, November 11, 1977)

13.1 INTRODUCTION

Chapter 4 explained that the atmosphere is one of the four components of the ecosystem, along with the hydrosphere, lithosphere and biosphere. The atmosphere is a mixture of gases, primarily nitrogen and oxygen, that circulates around the Earth at an altitude which is equal to only about 1 percent of the radius of the planet. The atmosphere moderates the flow of energy coming from the sun, including intense ultraviolet radiation that is harmful to plant and animal species. Gases in the atmosphere also capture some of the heat radiated from the Earth toward space, and in doing so maintain a climate that has been hospitable to a multitude of species.

Human beings pollute the atmosphere when they use it as a medium for disposing of a vast array of waste substances in the form of gases or tiny liquid or solid particles. Pollutants contribute to two types of environmental problems that may take on international or even global dimensions. First, certain types of pollutants are transported by air currents over hundreds, if not thousands, of miles before they are washed out of the atmosphere by rain or snow or fall to the earth in a dry form. In the process, some of these pollutants pass over international boundaries. Such is the case with sulfur dioxide and nitrogen oxides, which form acids when they combine with water vapor in the atmosphere or with moisture on the Earth's surface after being deposited in a dry form. Other pollutants pose a problem when they alter the chemical composition of the atmosphere in ways that modify the flow of energy to and from the earth. Scientists have linked chloro-fluorocarbons (CFCs) and several other synthetic chemicals to a thinning of the stratospheric ozone layer that intercepts ultraviolet radiation from the sun. Human additions to naturally occurring concentrations of greenhouse gases such as carbon dioxide and methane are believed to be raising the average temperature of the planet, which is triggering other climatic and environmental changes.

13.2 CAUSES AND CONSEQUENCES OF ACID RAIN

Acid rain is a term commonly used to refer to several processes through which human-generated pollutants increase levels of acidity in the environment. The problem arises when pollutants such as sulfur dioxide and nitrogen oxides are released into the atmosphere, primarily from power plants, metal smelters, factories and motorized vehicles. Some of these pollutants, which are known as precursors of acid deposition, quickly precipitate to the earth in a dry form near their source, where they combine with surface moisture to form acidic solutions. Under certain circumstances, however, these pollutants remain in the atmosphere for periods of up to several days, during which they may be carried by wind sources over considerable distances. While in the atmosphere, the pollutants may undergo a complex series of chemical reactions in the presence of sunlight and other gases, such as ammonia and low-level ozone, which are also generated by human activities. The resulting chemicals may be absorbed by water vapor to form tiny droplets of sulfuric and nitric acids that are washed out of the atmosphere in the form of rain, snow, mist or fog (Park, 1987: 40–8).

Acid rain was largely a localized problem near the source of the pollutants until well into the twentieth century. The problem became increasingly regional as governments began mandating taller smokestacks to disperse pollutants more widely as a strategy for relieving local air pollution problems. Originally, it was thought the pollutants would become so diluted as they were dispersed that they would pose no further problems. By the 1960s, however, it had become apparent that an increasingly serious condition of acidification in southern Sweden and Norway was caused by air pollutants from the industrial centers of Great Britain and mainland Europe. Subsequent studies soon revealed that large amounts of air pollution were flowing across national frontiers throughout the European region, and between the United States and Canada as well. More recently, much of the pollution responsible for Japan's acid rain has been traced to China and Korea (Cowling 1982).

Acid rain has several harmful effects. The most visible of its consequences is corrosion of the stone surfaces of buildings and monuments, as well as of metals in structures such as bridges and railroad tracks. In Scandinavia and eastern North America, the heightened acidity of rivers and lakes has been linked to the disappearance of fish and other forms of aquatic life. The severity of the impact of acid rain on freshwater environments varies considerably depending on the extent to which the rocks and soils of the region neutralize the acids. Acid rain also appears to have been a cause of the widespread damage to trees that was observed in the forests of Central Europe by the early 1980s, a phenomenon known by the German word *Waldsterben*, which means "forest death." A similar pattern of forest decline has been observed in eastern North America, especially at the higher levels of the Appalachian Mountains. Scientists have had difficulty, however, isolating the natural processes through which pollution causes widespread damage to trees (Schütt and Cowling, 1985).

13.3 CAUSES AND CONSEQUENCES OF DEPLETION OF THE OZONE LAYER

Low-level ozone resulting from human pollutants is undesirable because not only is it one of the principal components of the health-threatening photochemical smog that plagues many large cities, it is also an oxidant that contributes to the production of acid rain. Thus, it is ironic that ozone resulting from natural processes, which resides in the stratosphere at altitudes of 10–40 km in concentrations of only a few parts per million (ppm), is critical to the survival of most life forms that have inhabited the planet. Ozone is the only chemical in the atmosphere which absorbs certain frequencies of intense ultraviolet (UV) radiation that are damaging to plants and animals. Microscopic organisms at the bottom of the food chain, such as phytoplankton and zooplankton, are especially vulnerable to increased doses of UV radiation.

In 1974 scientists Mario Molina and F. Sherwood Rowland called attention to the possibility that chlorofluorocarbons (CFCs) posed a threat to the stratospheric ozone layer. CFCs are a family of chemical compounds that were used widely in refrigeration, aerosol sprays, foam insulation and the computer industry. These chemicals had proved to be useful for numerous applications because they do not react with other chemicals under normal conditions and thus are noncorrosive, nontoxic and nonflammable. Noting that CFCs apparently were not precipitating out of the atmosphere, Molina and Rowland hypothesized that the highly stable CFC molecules would rise slowly through the atmosphere until they reached the stratosphere, where they would encounter intense solar radiation that would finally break them apart. In the process, highly unstable chlorine molecules would be released, which would break ozone molecules apart in a catalytic reaction that would leave the chlorine molecule available to attack other ozone molecules. Thus, a single CFC molecule reaching the stratosphere might lead to the destruction of hundreds of thousands of ozone molecules (Molina and Rowland 1974).

The first evidence of a significant decline in stratospheric ozone came from a team of British scientists, who in 1985 reported that concentrations of ozone over Antarctica during several preceding spring seasons were down 40 percent from what they had been two decades earlier (Farman *et al.* 1985). By 1988, further research had conclusively attributed the Antarctic "ozone hole" to human-generated substances, including CFCs. By then, other commercially used chemicals, including halons, carbon tetrachloride and methyl chloroform, were also believed to threaten the ozone layer. Moreover, evidence was mounting that stratospheric ozone concentrations were declining at other latitudes, although not nearly to the degree seen over Antarctica, where each year the ozone hole showed signs of expanding and deepening (Watson *et al.* 1988).

Scientists have had greater difficulty determining the extent to which declining ozone concentrations have resulted in an increase in the amount of UV radiation passing through the atmosphere and reaching the surface of the planet. Likewise, evidence of damage to plant and animal species has been slow to accumulate, although it appears that a worldwide decline in populations of amphibians, such as frogs, toads and salamanders, may be attributable to the effects of increased doses of UV radiation on the eggs of these species (Blaustein *et al.* 1994).

13.4 CAUSES AND CONSEQUENCES OF GLOBAL WARMING

Nearly half of the solar energy that approaches the planet Earth is reflected or absorbed by gases and aerosols in the atmosphere, with the greatest amount, approximately 22 percent, being intercepted by the white tops of clouds. The remaining solar radiation, most of which is in the form of infrared or visible light waves, passes through the atmosphere to the surface of the planet. There it is either reflected off light surfaces such as snow and ice or absorbed by land, water or vegetation. Much of this energy that is absorbed by the Earth is reradiated out from the planet toward outer space in the form of longer-wave infrared rays. A portion of this escaping energy is absorbed by certain gases found in the atmosphere, in particular carbon dioxide, methane and nitrous oxide. In the process, heat is released that warms the lower atmosphere (Anthes 1992: 50–4). These substances that are so critical to the Earth's climate account for only about 0.03 percent of atmospheric gases. Water vapor, which occurs in concentrations of from 0 to 4 percent of the atmosphere, also intercepts outgoing infrared radiation. This process has become known as the "greenhouse effect," because as with the glass roof of a greenhouse, the atmosphere allows solar energy to pass inwards while blocking its escape, thus keeping the space beneath it warm compared to outside conditions. Thus, it is the so-called greenhouse gases (GHGs) – carbon dioxide, methane and nitrous oxide – along with water vapor, which account for the Earth's moderate climate. Much larger amounts of carbon dioxide in the atmosphere of Venus explain its intensely hot climate, while the frigid conditions on Mars are attributable to lesser concentrations of GHGs (Fisher 1990: 18–20).

Human activities are adding significantly to the concentrations of the principal GHGs in the Earth's atmosphere. The burning of fossil fuels, in particular coal and petroleum, releases carbon dioxide which can remain in the atmosphere for a century or longer. The clearing of forests not only releases the carbon stored in the trees, but also removes an important sink for carbon dioxide, as trees absorb carbon dioxide from the air through the process of photosynthesis. Concentrations of carbon dioxide in the atmosphere have risen from approximately 280 ppm prior to the industrial age to 365 ppm today. Levels of methane, a gas that is shorter-lived in the atmosphere, have also been rising even more sharply due to a variety of human activities, such as wet rice cultivation, livestock raising, and the production and transport of natural gas. Atmospheric scientists are concerned that human-generated pollutants are responsible for an "enhanced greenhouse effect" that will be reflected in a significant rise in global mean temperatures (Intergovernmental Panel on Climate Change 1995: 12–13).

Long ice cores extracted from deep in the glaciers of Greenland and Antarctica provide a record of the composition of the Earth's atmosphere and climate over the past two hundred thousand years. By analyzing the chemical composition of gases trapped in air pockets in the ancient ice, scientists have been able to determine that there is now substantially more carbon dioxide in the atmosphere than at any other time during the era covered by the ice cores. Their research also reveals that over this extended period there is a striking relationship between major shifts in climate and fluctuations in concentrations of carbon dioxide (Barnola *et al.* 1987).

How much global warming can be expected as a result of human additions to GHGs in the atmosphere? The United Nations-sponsored Inter-governmental Panel on Climate Change concluded in its second report, which was released in 1995, that human activities have already caused global mean temperatures to rise by one half a degree Celsius since 1860. The same report projects an increase in the range of 1 to 3.5°C in average temperatures over the next century if concentrations of greenhouse gases continue to rise at current rates (Houghton *et al.*, 1996: 6). To put this amount of change in perspective, global mean temperatures were about 1°C lower during the Little Ice Age from approximately 1400 to 1850 and about 5°C colder during the most recent major glacial era, which ended about ten thousand years ago (Oeschger and Mintzer 1992: 63).

A significant warming of the atmosphere is likely to trigger substantial climatic changes. These impacts are expected to vary considerably by region. Some areas will experience warmer and drier climates, while others may become cooler and moister. Substantial changes in temperatures and rainfall patterns would have significant implications for agriculture. Reductions in stream flows might trigger water shortages, jeopardize irrigation and limit the production of hydroelectric power. Unusually dry conditions in some areas might set the stage for immense, uncontrollable forest and range fires, which would generate large amounts of smoke and release additional carbon into the atmosphere. As ocean waters warm, potentially destructive tropical storms, such as hurricanes, cyclones and typhoons, may become more frequent and intense.

Global warming is likely to trigger many other changes in the natural environment. If present trends continue, sea levels are projected to rise by between 10 and 95 cm over the next century due to both thermal expansion of the ocean waters and the melting of polar and mountain glaciers. Rising sea levels pose a threat to low-lying coastal zones, where many of the world's major cities are located. Small island states, many of which are located in the Caribbean Sea and western Pacific Ocean, are especially vulnerable to sea level rises as well as to tropical storms and associated storm surges (Warrick and Rahman 1992: 100). Shifts in climate zones may exceed the adjustment capacity of many species, while other, more adaptable species, including agricultural pests and disease vectors, may be able to spread more widely. Forests are specially vulnerable to climatic changes because trees migrate very slowly and are susceptible to infestations.

The greatest amount of warming is expected to take place in the polar regions. With the shrinking of glaciers and ice packs, less solar energy will be reflected while more is absorbed, thus contributing to further warming. Warmer conditions may also accelerate the melting of permafrost, which would release large amounts of the GHG methane into the atmosphere. A lessening of the temperature gradients between the equator and the poles could strongly influence the prevailing weather patterns in the temperate mid-latitude regions. It could also weaken major ocean currents that distribute heat around the planet. If the warm, northward-flowing Gulf Stream were to weaken considerably, the climate of northern Europe might cool significantly (Leggett 1992).

While there is a general convergence of opinion among scientists that human additions to atmospheric concentrations of GHGs are likely to trigger significant climatic and environmental changes, considerable uncertainties remain about how much change will take place and how these changes will play out in specific regions. Questions remain on key factors such as the amount of atmospheric carbon dioxide that will ultimately be absorbed by the oceans and the impacts that clouds will have on future climates. Furthermore, it is difficult for scientists to isolate the causes of recent weather and environmental anomalies that appear to bear out the global warming scenario, such as the spate of unusually warm years since 1980. Are they a consequence of a human-enhanced greenhouse effect? Or simply naturally occurring fluctuations in the climate of the planet?

13.5 INTERNATIONAL RESPONSES TO ACID RAIN, OZONE DEPLETION AND CLIMATE CHANGE

International responses are needed to effectively address environmental problems that transcend the boundaries of individual nations. There is no world government with the authority to impose and enforce solutions to such problems. Nations claim the sovereign right to regulate what takes place within their borders without interference from outside. Thus, it is up to the community of nations, which currently number about 190, to enter voluntarily into agreements with one another to limit the flow of pollutants that contribute to environmental problems of international and global scope. Such agreements normally take the form of treaties, or what are commonly called conventions, which are negotiated among interested countries, usually under the auspices of an international institution such as the United Nations. Only those countries which formally become parties to a treaty, in accordance with their constitutionally specified ratification procedures, are legally obliged to comply with its provisions.

International responses to environmental problems typically take the form of a series of treaties. The initial agreement is a vaguely worded *framework convention* which acknowledges the emergence of a potentially important problem that warrants international attention while encouraging the parties to cooperate on additional scientific research that will further illuminate the nature of the problem and its possible consequences. Most framework agreements call upon the parties to take voluntary steps to control or limit activities within their jurisdictions that are contributing to the problem. Finally, such a treaty establishes procedures for the parties to meet periodically to consider adopting additional measures to address the problem. These supplemental agreements commonly take the form of *protocols* which set target dates for limiting the emission of certain air pollutants, or even reducing them by specified amounts. As with other treaties, protocols are binding only on the countries that formally ratify them. This multiple-stage process involving framework conventions and a succession of protocols has proven to be a flexible format for negotiating progressively stronger agreements as scientific evidence mounts on the severity of the threat and political support mounts for adopting more stringent international regulations.

Sweden and Norway made the case for international rules that would stem the flow of acid-forming air pollutants across international boundaries as early as the United Nations Conference on the Human Environment, which was held in Stockholm in 1972. The first treaty on the subject was adopted in 1979 at a meeting convened in Geneva by the United Nations Economic Commission for Europe (ECE). At the time, few countries shared the sense of urgency that the Scandinavian nations had about the problem of acidification. Thus, there was little support for the adoption of a schedule for mandatory reductions of emissions of sulfur dioxide and other acid-forming pollutants. The outcome of the conference was a weakly worded framework agreement known as the Convention on Long-Range Transboundary Air Pollution (LRTAP). The LRTAP Convention contains the vague expectation that states will ensure that activities taking place within their boundaries do not cause damage in other countries. It goes on to suggest that the parties should "endeavor to limit and, as far as possible, to gradually reduce and prevent air pollution, using "the best available technology that is currently available" (see Jackson 1990).

The alarming spread of the *Waldsterben* syndrome through the forests of central Europe prompted West Germany and several neighboring countries to abruptly shift from being staunch opponents to becoming strong advocates of international regulations on air pollution. A 1985 meeting of the parties to the LRTAP Convention adopted a protocol that required ratifying states to reduce their emissions of sulfur dioxide by 30 percent from 1980 levels by 1993. Each country would decide on the measures it would adopt to accomplish this reduction. Several of the parties to the original LRTAP Convention refused to become parties to the Sulfur Protocol, most notably the United Kingdom, the United States, Poland and Spain. Eleven countries, however, felt that the Sulfur Protocol did not go far enough and made individual commitments to reduce their emissions of sulfur dioxide by more than 50 percent by dates ranging from 1990 to 1995. Sweden, followed by Norway and Finland, set out to achieve 80 percent reductions by 1995 (Soroos 1997: 127–30).

The parties to the LRTAP Convention went on to negotiate several additional protocols. In 1988 they concluded a protocol that would limit emissions of nitrogen oxides to 1987 levels after 1994. Disappointed that the protocol failed to mandate any reductions in nitrogen emissions, twelve countries signed a separate declaration setting out a goal of cutting their emissions by 30 percent by 1998, using any year between 1980 and 1986 as a base. The next in the series of protocols, which was concluded in 1991, targeted volatile organic chemicals (VOCs), a broad category of substances that is responsible for ground-level ozone and photochemical smog. The parties to the protocol are expected to cut their VOC emissions by 30 percent by 1998. The recommended base year was 1988, although the parties had the option of selecting any year between 1984 and 1990. The parties also have the option of achieving the reduction for their country as a whole, or only in certain designated regions within the country which contribute significantly to ozone problems in other countries (Soroos 1997: 130–2).

The parties to the LRTAP Convention adopted a Revised Sulfur Protocol in 1994. This agreement is based on the concept of "critical load," which is the amount of acidic deposition that a geographical region can absorb without significant environmental damage. As the negotiations got under way, each country was given its own target percentage for reducing its sulfur emissions. These targets were derived from a computer model which took into account how much each emission of each country contributed to acidic deposition in excess of the critical loads in other countries, as well as the costs that would be entailed in reducing the emissions. The initial objective of the negotiations was to secure commitments that would reduce excess acidic deposition in the European region by 60 percent by 2000. Austria, Denmark, Germany, Sweden and Finland agreed to reductions of 80 percent or more from 1990 levels by 2000. Other countries were not willing to commit themselves to the full sulfur reduction goals that were assigned them or pushed the target date back to 2005 or 2010. Thus, only a 50 percent reduction in excess acidic deposition is projected if all countries follow through on their commitments. Recent negotiations have been directed toward concluding a revised protocol for nitrogen oxides and VOCs that will also be based on the critical loads for acid deposition (Soroos 1997: 132–6).

International efforts to address the problem of depletion of the ozone layer took a similar track in the early stages, although in this case the nego-tiations were global in the sense of being open to all countries. A strong public reaction to the initial warnings of Molina and Rowland about the threat that CFCs may pose to the ozone layer prompted the United States in 1978 to ban nonessential uses of the chemical, such as in aerosol sprays. Several other countries followed suit – most notably Canada, Norway and Sweden. However, other nations, including major users and producers of CFCs, were not persuaded that such action was necessary, given the state of knowledge about the threat to the ozone layer. The first international treaty on the subject, the Vienna Convention on the Ozone Layer of 1985, was a typical framework agreement. It called upon the parties to control, limit, reduce or prevent activities that may be found to diminish the ozone layer, but, as with the LRTAP Convention, did not set a timetable for mandatory limits or reductions in the production or use of substances linked to ozone depletion (Benedick 1991: 77–97).

The announcement of the Antarctic ozone hole in 1985 lent greater urgency to efforts to preserve the ozone layer. Even before scientists had definitively linked the ozone hole to human causes, agreement was reached in 1987 on the landmark Montreal Protocol on Substances that Deplete the Ozone Layer. The protocol requires the parties to reduce their production and use of CFCs by 20 percent by 1993 and by 50 percent by 1998, with 1986 being the base year. Production and consumption of halons, a family of chemicals used widely in fire extinguishers, were not to exceed 1986 levels after 1993 (Litfin 1994: 78–119).

When it was adopted, the Montreal Protocol was viewed as a major breakthrough toward preservation of the ozone layer. Its adequacy quickly came under question, however, as scientific evidence mounted that ozone loss was taking place more rapidly than had been anticipated, not only over Antarctica, but also at other latitudes. Accordingly, the parties to the Montreal Protocol met in London in 1990 and adopted amendments to the document that would require a complete phasing out of CFCs and halons by the year 2000. Carbon tetrachloride and methyl chloroform, two other chemicals that had been linked to ozone loss, would be banned by 2000 and 2010 respectively. Even more ominous reports on the ozone layer prompted the adoption of another set of amendments at a meeting of the parties to the Montreal Protocol in Copenhagen in 1992. The date for discontinuing halons was advanced to 1994, while production of CFCs, carbon tetra-chloride and methyl chloroform would end by 1996. Use of HCFCs, a substitute for CFCs that poses less of a threat to the ozone layer, would be gradually phased out by 2030 (Litfin 1994: 119–76).

The Montreal Protocol of 1987 and the amendments adopted in 1990 and 1992 have drastically cut back the flow of CFCs and other ozone-destroying chemicals into the atmosphere. Concentrations of stratospheric ozone are expected to bottom out by the year 2000 and gradually return to previous natural levels toward the middle of the twenty-first century. However, there are two reasons for caution about whether the ozone layer will begin recovering so soon. The first is a disturbing level of illicit trade in the banned substances, in particular CFCs. Second, methyl bromide, another significant contributor to ozone depletion, remains to be controlled due to the resistance of agricultural interests who depend upon the chemical to fumigate their fields (Dowie 1996).

The success in concluding the Montreal Protocol and the London amendments offers reason for hope that decisive action can also be taken to limit human-induced climate change, the other major global atmospheric problem confronting humanity. The threat of significant global warming was first taken up at high-level international conferences in the late 1980s, following a series of years with unusually warm global average temperatures. Negotiations begun in 1991 led to the signing of the Framework Convention on Climate Change at the Earth Summit in Rio de Janeiro the next year. At the time, many of the industrial countries and a coalition of nearly forty small island nations strongly favored inclusion of a schedule for mandatory limits, if not actual reductions, in emissions of GHGs such as carbon dioxide. No such provision was included in the convention, however, due largely to the refusal of the United States to commit itself to limits that might be costly to implement, while in its view significant scientific uncertainties remained on the need for such measures.

Though similar to the framework agreements that address the problems of transboundary pollution and depletion of the ozone layer, the Climate Change Convention is a stronger document in certain respects. It establishes an ambitious goal of stabilizing concentrations of GHGs in the atmosphere at a level that would prevent dangerous anthropogenic interference with the climate system. The developed countries are called upon, but not required, to limit their GHG emissions to 1990 levels by the year 2000. They may accomplish this goal either individually or collectively with other countries. Finally, developed countries are expected to submit periodic reports on the steps they are taking to reduce GHG emissions or, alternatively, to enhance carbon sinks, such as through forestry projects (see Bodansky 1993).

In recent years the parties to the Climate Change Convention have been giving further consideration to mandatory limits on GHG emissions. At a meeting in Berlin in 1995 the parties adopted a declaration which recognized that the original treaty did not go far enough and committed them to negotiate a schedule for binding reductions that would be ready for adoption when they gathered in Kyoto in 1997. As the decade wore on, GHG emissions in most developed countries continued to increase. Thus, there was little prospect that they would accomplish the goal set out in the Framework Convention of reducing emissions to 1990 levels by the year 2000. On the eve of the Kyoto meetings, the prospects appeared dim for a compromise on a significant agreement. The European Union proposed that developed countries reduce their greenhouse emissions by 15 percent by 2010, while the Alliance of Small Island Nations repeated its call for a 20 percent cutback by 2005. To the disappointment of these nations, the United States simply proposed returning GHG emissions to 1990 levels during the period 2008–2012, after a decade of encouraging voluntary measures to conserve energy and develop alternative energy sources (Lanchbery 1997).

To the surprise of many, agreement was reached at Kyoto on a protocol that committed the developed countries to collectively achieve at least a 5 percent reduction in GHG emissions by 2008 to 2012. Most of the European countries, and the European Union as a whole, agreed to reduce GHG emissions by 8 percent, while the United States and Japan committed themselves to 7 percent and 6 percent cutbacks, respectively. Several countries, including Norway and Australia, simply promised a return of GHGs emissions to 1990 levels by the designated time. Under the terms of the agreement, enhancements of carbon sinks may substitute for reductions of GHG emissions. Thus, the Kyoto Protocol provides for significant cutbacks in GHG emissions by the developed countries, which may be costly for them to achieve. It does not, however, require developing countries to restrain their emissions of GHGs, which are on course to exceed those of the developed countries by about 2025 ("Kyoto Protocol . . ." 1997). Moreover, the protocol is only a first step toward the 60–80 percent reductions of GHGs emissions that will be needed to stabilize concentrations of these gases in the atmosphere, which already far exceed naturally occurring concentrations.

The Framework Convention on Climate Change and the Kyoto Protocol are unique among international environmental agreements for offering the option of "joint implementation." This concept presumes that a reduction in GHG emissions by a certain amount has the same result in terms of mitigating the problem, regardless of the country in which it takes place. The joint implementation option would allow a developed country to fulfill its obligations to limit GHG emissions by investing in emission-reducing projects in other countries where the cost of achieving such reductions may be much lower.

Prior to the Kyoto meetings, the United States offered a proposal that would allocate tradable emission permits, which would also promote economically efficient strategies for cutting back GHG emissions by making it possible to concentrate reductions where they can be achieved at lowest cost. While such schemes have been successfully implemented within countries, they have yet to be adopted internationally. As the epigraph to this chapter suggested, agreement may be difficult to reach among nations on a mutually acceptable distribution of emissions permits.

13.6 THE ECONOMICS OF ATMOSPHERIC POLLUTION

Nations negotiate international treaties and other agreements to achieve preferred outcomes that would be more costly, if not impossible, to achieve on their own. Treaties are contracts in which each party to the agreement accepts certain obligations in return for commitments from others to limit or curb activities that are damaging to its interests. Thus, the terms of the agreement determine how the cost of producing certain benefits will be divided among the parties. In the give-and-take of the negotiating process, countries normally pursue their national interests by seeking to incur as few obligations as possible, especially those that would be costly to fulfill, while obtaining the greatest possible concessions from other states.

The task of negotiating international agreements on transboundary acid-forming pollution would have been less complicated if the pollutants circulated equally in all directions. In most cases, however, prevailing winds carry much more pollution in some directions than in others. Thus, upwind countries are net "exporters" of pollution to other countries, while downwind states are net "importers" of acid pollutants from other states. Canada, for example, receives approximately four times the volume of acid-forming air pollutants from the United States as flows in the opposite direction from Canada to the United States (Cowling 1982: 118). Likewise, in the European region, the United Kingdom contributes far more to the problem of acidification in Scandinavia and mainland Europe than they do in the reverse direction.

The predominantly upwind countries such as the United States and United Kingdom have little incentive to become parties to international agreements that obligate them to reduce emissions of acid-forming pollutants. They would incur the substantial cost of preventing air pollution, such as smokestack scrubbers, while the principal benefactors of these expenditures would be their downwind neighbors. Alternatively, whatever downwind countries agreed to do to limit their emissions would do very little to diminish any problems the upwind country had with acidification. Thus, it is not surprising that the United States and United Kingdom were unwilling to become parties to the 1985 Sulfur Protocol, which would have required them to reduce their sulfur dioxide emissions by 30 percent by 1993.

Numerous countries in Europe, such as Germany, Switzerland and Austria, are both major exporters and major importers of air pollution. Much of the acidic deposition within their territories originates in other countries, while a large proportion of their emissions is deposited outside their borders. For these countries the costs of complying with international limits are offset by the benefits of less acidic deposition within their boundaries. Thus, these centrally located countries have been willing to join the Scandinavian countries and Canada in advocating international controls on emissions of acid-forming air pollutants.

Who should bear the cost of reducing the transnational flow of air pollutants? Should it be the polluting countries? Or should it be paid by the countries that are victimized by acidic deposition originating beyond their borders? The predominant principle in international law is that the polluter should pay the costs of reducing its emissions or, alternatively, for the damage that its pollution causes beyond its borders. The *polluter-pays* principle was affirmed in the landmark Trail Smelter case in which the United States brought a complaint against Canada for pollution from a large smelter operation in Trail, British Columbia, which was alleged to have damaged orchards across the border in the State of Washington. In deciding the case in 1941 an international tribunal sided with the United States. Canada was not only required to take steps to reduce the pollution in the future, but also instructed to compensate the United States for past damages (see Wirth 1996).

The polluter-pays doctrine was reaffirmed by the declaration adopted at the Stockholm Conference in 1972. The frequently cited article 21 of the declaration provides that states "have the sovereign right to exploit their resources in accordance with their environmental policies." The article also suggests, however, that states have an obligation to "insure that activities within their own jurisdiction or control do not cause damage to the environment of other states or areas beyond the limits of national jurisdiction" ("Declaration on the Human Environment . . ." 1972). The series of protocols that limit emissions of sulfur dioxide, nitrogen oxides and VOCs also place the burden of complying with these limits on the countries where the pollutants originate.

The alternative is for the victim of pollution to pay for its reduction. The *victim-pays* doctrine presumes that nations have a right to engage in activities that generate reasonable amounts of pollution, some of which may be deposited beyond their borders. Accordingly, if the benefits from stemming this flow of pollution are substantial enough to the countries that receive the pollutants, it should be up to them to absorb the costs entailed in reducing them. Thus, a downwind country might compensate its upwind neighbors for the expenses they incur in curbing their emissions. The victim-pays principle has not been widely applied in international law. One notable example, however, is the payments that the Netherlands and Germany made to the French government to invest in measures to reduce chloride pollution entering the river Rhine from France's upstream potash mines (see Bernauer 1996).

The circumstances are somewhat different in the cases of ozone depletion and climate change. Here the problem is one not of pollutants simply being transported by air currents from one country to another, but of pollution altering the chemistry of the atmosphere in ways that modify the flow of energy to and from the planet. No country or region of the world will fully escape the impacts of these atmospheric changes. Thus, whatever steps are taken to limit the amount of these changes go toward the creation of global public goods in the form of a protected ozone layer and the maintenance of desirable climates. The challenge for negotiators is to induce nations to invest in the creation of global public goods that they can enjoy even if they do not shoulder their fair share of the cost of producing them. The temptation for nations is to be "free riders," taking advantage of the sacrifices of others while shirking their own responsibility to contribute to the creation of a public good.

The willingness of states to enter into international agreements to mitigate global atmospheric problems depends in part on the stakes that are involved for them. Some countries are likely to be more heavily impacted than are others. The amount of observed ozone loss, and consequently increased exposure to damaging UV radiation, varies considerably by latitude, with the far northern and far southern regions being the most affected. Likewise, the amount and type of climate change will differ considerably by region, with the largest amount of warming being expected in the higher latitudes. Other areas, however, may see greater changes in the frequency and intensity of storms and rainfall patterns. Countries with low-lying coastal areas are especially vulnerable to sea-level rises caused by warmer climates.

How should the cost of producing these global public goods be divided? The polluter-pays doctrine would place most of the responsibility on the advanced industrial countries, which are the source of the lion's share of the pollutants that are causing stratospheric ozone depletion and climate change. Over time, however, the proportion from the developing countries has been increasing. Most of the industrial countries have indicated their willingness to shoulder this responsibility by advocating international rules that would require developed countries to reduce emissions of the pollutants responsible for these problems. There have been notable exceptions, however. The United States and several other industrial countries have been slow to accept binding reductions on their emissions of GHGs out of concern for the economic cost of conserving energy or of shifting away from fossil fuels to other sources of energy.

Developing countries have been reluctant to agree to limits on their release of the pollutants responsible for global atmospheric changes. For them, economic development and reducing poverty are more immediate priorities than limiting ozone depletion and global warming. There is also the issue of fairness. If the developed countries are largely responsible for the most of the human-generated pollutants that have accumulated in the atmosphere thus far, then presumably they should take the first major steps to address the problems that arise. By cutting back sharply on their emissions of pollutants such as CFCs and carbon dioxide, the industrial countries would make it possible for the developing countries to increase their relatively low level of emissions to further their economic development, without seriously aggravating the atmospheric problems they trigger. Furthermore, if the cooperation of the developing countries in limiting pollutants is desired, then the richer countries should be willing to compensate them for the costs that they incur in controlling pollution.

While the industrial countries have been largely responsible for past emissions of the pollutants responsible for depletion of ozone layer and climate change, the share of the developing countries has grown rapidly in recent decades. Thus, the future success of the international responses to these problems will depend on the willingness of the developing countries to limit their emissions of these pollutants to levels that are considerably lower than they have been in the highly developed countries. To encourage their participation in the 1987 Montreal Protocol and its subsequent amendments, the developing countries were allowed ten-year grace periods for complying with schedules for reducing and phasing out of the chemicals linked to ozone loss. The London amendments of 1990 provided for a special multilateral fund of $160–$240 million to assist developing countries to reduce their use of CFCs and other ozone-depleting substances. Technologies related to the production and use of suitable substitutes were to be provided to developing countries "under fair and most favorable conditions."

The 1992 Framework Convention on Climate Change explicitly acknowledges that emissions of GHGs of the developing countries are low, but can be expected to increase as these countries meet the social and developmental needs of their people. The agreement placed the primary responsibility for limiting GHG emissions and preserving carbon sinks on the developed countries, which were asked, but not required, to reduce their net emissions to 1990 levels by the year 2000. While the Kyoto Protocol of 1997 obligates developed countries to reduce their GHG emissions by more than 5 percent over the next decade, there are no provisions requiring the developing countries to limit their emissions. The absence of limits on the GHG emissions of the developing countries, which it is feared may offer them a competitive advantage in international trade, has been seized upon by opponents of the Kyoto Protocol in the United States who seek to block its ratification by the Senate.

There are limits to how hard a bargain the developing countries should try to drive with the industrial countries over dividing up the costs that would be entailed in limiting global atmospheric changes. If negotiations fail, developing countries are likely to be the most seriously impacted. For example, many of them have large coastal cities and low-lying agricultural regions that are especially susceptible to rising sea levels and tropical storms. Some of them are highly vulnerable to changing rainfall patterns that could lead to the expansion of deserts. Numerous developing countries are located in tropical regions where heat stress would become more prevalent and disease vectors flourish. Furthermore, developing countries have significantly fewer resources with which to adapt to whatever environmental changes take place, such as to rebuild after being struck by tropical storms. Reducing these environmental threats may not yet be a high priority for developing countries, but to ignore them could prove to be very costly over the long run.

13.7 CHAPTER SUMMARY

- This chapter discusses three atmospheric pollution problems that have international or even global consequences: acid rain, depletion of the stratospheric ozone and climate change.
- Acid rain has become a serious problem affecting forests and freshwater aquatic life in Europe, North America and, increasingly, in developing regions. The problem takes on international dimensions when pollutants such as sulfur dioxide and nitrogen oxides are emitted in one country and then are transported by air currents over national boundaries before being deposited in other countries.
- The two other atmospheric pollution problems, depletion of the stratospheric ozone layer and climate change, are global in scope. They arise because human-generated pollutants have the effect of altering the chemical composition of the atmosphere in ways that alter the flow of energy either to or from the planet Earth. The thinning of the ozone layer allows greater amounts of damaging ultraviolet radiation to reach the surface of the Earth. Human additions to atmospheric concentrations of GHGs keep more of the heat radiated from the Earth from escaping into outer space, thus warming the world's climate.
- Each of the three atmospheric problems discussed in this chapter is the subject of a series of international agreements, beginning with a general framework convention that was followed by one or more protocols which specify target dates for mandatory reductions of emissions of pollutants.
- The transboundary flow of acid-forming pollutants in Europe has been partially stemmed by a series of protocols that target emissions of sulfur dioxide, nitrogen oxides and volatile organic compounds.
- Agreements on transboundary air pollutants causing acid rain have been difficult to conclude because upwind countries, such as the United Kingdom and the United States, have been reluctant to bear the costs of reducing emissions largely for the benefit of downwind states. Their resistance to regulations on these pollutants runs counter to the principle of "polluter pays" which was established in international law with the Trail Smelter case of 1941.
- The production and consumption of CFCs and other principal ozone-destroying chemicals have been *sharply* diminished by the 1987 Montreal

Protocol as amended in 1990, 1992 and 1995. Much of the success is attributable to the availability of substitutes for the banned chemicals.

- Under the terms of the Montreal Protocol and its amendments, developing countries were given ten additional years to phase out ozone-depleting substances and promised economic and technical assistance to facilitate their use of substitutes for the banned chemicals.
- The threat of climate change has been addressed by the 1997 Kyoto Protocol, which provides for reductions in GHG emissions by developed countries and acknowledges the historical responsibility of the industrial countries for the enhanced greenhouse effect. Some industrial countries, however, have been reluctant to make a commitment because the protocol asks them to limit their GHG emissions, while imposing no similar expectations on the developing countries.

---

review and discussion questions

1 Briefly identify the following concepts: chloroflurocarbons (CFC), acid rain, ozone hole, greenhouse gases (GHGs), climate change, global warming, long-range transboundary air pollution, framework convention, protocols, and the victim-pays doctrine.

2 State *True*, *False* or *Uncertain* and explain why.

(a) The acid rain problem is a clear indication that in coping with environmental problems, what we have accomplished in the past three decades has been to transfer local air pollution concerns into transboundary air pollution problems.

(b) Science played a positive role in calling attention to the problems of acid rain, depletion of the ozone layer and climate change. On the other hand, scientific controversy about the causes and consequences of these problems has acted as an obstacle to achieving regional and international cooperation in effectively addressing such complex environmental problems.

(c) The resolution of long-range transnational air pollution problems "demands more statecraft, not more market."

3 The conventional wisdom is that international solutions to environmental problems are possible only after there is compelling evidence of serious harmful effects. Was this the case for the three atmospheric pollution problems discussed in this chapter? Alternatively, is there evidence that the international community is capable of an "anticipatory response" in the face of scientific warnings of future undesirable consequences?

4 All three of the atmospheric pollution problems discussed in this chapter have been addressed through a series of agreements including a framework convention followed by protocols. What are the differences between these types of agreements? Why is it not possible to address each of these problems through a single, comprehensive agreement?

5 Some economists have argued for a carbon tax – a tax set on the basis of the carbon content of fossil fuels – as a way of addressing the global warming problem. What do you think would be the advantages and disadvantages of such policy? Be specific.

REFERENCES AND FURTHER READING

Anthes, R. A. (1992) *Meteorology*, 6th edn., New York: Macmillan.

Barnola, J. M., Raynaud, D., Korotkevich, Y. S. and Lorius, C. (1987) "Vostok Ice Core Provides 160,000-Year Record of Atmospheric CO_2," *Nature* 329: 408–14.

Benedick, R. E. (1991) *Ozone Diplomacy: New Directions in Safeguarding the Planet*, Cambridge, Mass.: Harvard University Press.

Bernauer, T. (1996) "Protecting the Rhine River against Chloride Pollution," in R. O. Keohane and M. L. Levy (eds.) *Institutions for Environmental Aid: Pitfalls and Promise*, Cambridge: Cambridge University Press.

Blaustein, A. P. *et al.* (1994) "UV Repair and Resistance to Solar UV-B in Amphibian Eggs: A Link to Population Decline," *Proceedings of the National Academy of Sciences* 91: 1791–5.

Bodansky, D. (1993) "The United Nations Framework Convention on Climate Change: A Commentary," *Yale Journal of International Law* 18: 451–558.

Cowling, E. B. (1982) "Acid Precipitation in Historical Context," *Environmental Science and Technology* 16, 2: 110–22.

"Declaration on the Human Environment of the United Nations Conference on the Human Environment" (1972) *International Legal Materials* 11: 1462.

Dowie, M. (1996) "A Sky Full of Holes: Why the Ozone Layer is Torn Worse than Ever," *Nation*, July 8: 11–16.

Farman, J. C., Gardiner, B. G. and Shanklin, J. D. (1985) "Large Losses of Total Ozone in Antarctica Reveal Seasonal ClO_x/NO_x Interaction," *Nature* 315: 207–10.

Fisher, D. (1990) *Fire and Ice: The Greenhouse Effect, Ozone Depletion, and Nuclear Winter*, New York: Harper & Row.

Houghton, J. T., Harris, N. B., Filho, L. G., Maskell, K., Callander, B. A. and Kattenburg, A. (1996) *Climate Change 1995*. Cambridge: Cambridge University Press.

Intergovernmental Panel on Climate Change (1995) *Climate Change 1994: Radiative Forcing of Climate Change*, Cambridge: Cambridge University Press.

Jackson, C. I. (1990) "A Tenth Anniversary Review of the ECE Convention on Long-Range Transboundary Air Pollution," *International Environmental Affairs* 2: 217–26.

"Kyoto Protocol to the United Nations Framework Convention on Climate Change," (1997) UNDOC. FCCC/CP/L.7/Add.1.

Lanchbery, J. (1997) "What to Expect from Kyoto," *Environment* 39, 9: 4–11.

Leggett, J. (1992) "Global Warming: The Worst Case," *Bulletin of the Atomic Scientists* 48: 28–33.

Litfin, K. T. (1994) *Ozone Discourses: Science and Politics in Global Environmental Cooperation*, New York: Columbia University Press.

Molina, M. J. and Rowland, F. S. (1974) "Stratospheric Sink for Chloro-fluoromethanes: Chlorine Atom-Catalyzed Destruction of Ozone," *Nature* 249: 810–12.

Oeschger, H. and Mintzer, I. M. (1992) "Lessons from the Ice Cores: Rapid Climate Changes during the Last 160,000 Years," in I. M. Mintzer (ed.) *Confronting Climate Change: Risks, Implications and Responses*, Cambridge: Cambridge University Press.

Park, C. C. (1987) *Acid Rain: Rhetoric and Reality*, New York: Routledge.

Schütt, P. and Cowling, E. B. (1985) "Waldsterben, A General Decline of Forests in Central Europe: Symptoms, Development, and Possible Causes," *Plant Disease* 69: 548–58.

Soroos, M. S. (1997) *The Endangered Atmosphere: Preserving a Global Commons*, Columbia, S.C.: University of South Carolina Press.

Warrick, R. A. and Rahman, A. A. (1992) "Future Sea Level Rise: Environmental and Socio-political Considerations," in I. M. Mintzer (ed.) *Confronting Climate Change: Risks, Implications and Responses*, Cambridge: Cambridge University Press.

Watson, R. T., Rowland, F. S. and Gille, J. (1988) "Ozone Trends Panel Executive Summary," Washington, D.C.: NASA.

Wirth, J. D. (1996) "The Trail Smelter Dispute: Canadians and Americans Confront Transboundary Pollution, 1927–41," *Environmental History* 1, 2: 34–51.

chapter fourteen

THE ECONOMIC THEORY AND MEASUREMENT OF ENVIRONMENTAL DAMAGE (BENEFIT):
Valuing the Environment

---

learning objectives

After reading this chapter you will be familiar with the following:

- the marginal damage cost curve as representing the demand for environmental quality;
- the methodological issues of measuring benefit for social projects;
- the practical problems of eliciting willingness to pay for an environmental good or environmental bad;
- implicit measures of willingness to pay for environmental quality:

  (a) the replacement cost approach;
  (b) hedonic price approaches;
  (c) the household production function approach;
  (d) the contingent valuation method;

- environmental valuation methods and their applications in some empirical studies;
- a critical appraisal of the standard economic approaches to environmental valuation.

We want the maximum good per person; but what is good? To one person it is wilderness, to another it is ski lodges for thousands. To one it is estuaries to nourish ducks for hunters to shoot; to another it is a factory land. Comparing one good with another is, we usually say, impossible because goods are incommensurable. Incommensurables cannot be compared. . . . Theoretically this may be true; but in real life incommensurables are commensurable. Only a criterion of judgment and a system of weighting are needed. . . . The problem for years ahead is to work out an acceptable theory of weighting. Synergistic effects, non-linear variation, and difficulties in discounting the future make the intellectual problem difficult, but not (in principle) insoluble.

(Hardin 1968: 1244)

14.1 INTRODUCTION

In Chapters 10–12, the concepts of marginal control (cleanup) and marginal damage costs were extensively used for the purpose of deriving the economic condition for an optimal level of waste emission and for setting environmental policy goals. However, so far the use of these two cost concepts has been kept at a purely conceptual level, and no attempt has been made to actually *measure* or quantify these costs. This is a crucial and unavoidable issue that needs to be confronted, if these concepts are going to be used as a guide for setting environmental policy objectives that are considered to be socially optimal. Thus, the primary objective of this chapter is to investigate the various methods by which economists attempt to measure the damage costs of environmental pollution. This is a very important field of study in environmental economics.

Before starting the discussion of the arduous process involved in measuring environmental damage costs, however, it would be instructive to have a clear idea of what exactly are being measured and for what purposes. Figure 14.1 shows the usual marginal damage and control costs except that the x-axis is labeled differently. In this particular case the x-axis measures the amount of waste cleaned up rather than emitted. Thus, as we move along the x-axis from the origin to the right, a higher level of environmental quality is observed. Note that Q* denotes the quality of the environment when an unrestricted amount of waste is emitted into the environment (which corresponds to W* in Chapter 10).

This new setup, as discussed in Chapter 10, provides a different interpretation to marginal damage and control costs. The marginal damage cost depicts the amount society is *willing to pay* to avoid damage or improve the quality of the environment at the margin. Given this, consistent with our discussion in Chapter 2, the marginal damage cost represents the *demand curve* for environmental quality. The fact that it is negatively sloped is explained by a decline in society's willingness to pay as higher levels of environmental quality are sought – the law of demand.

On the other hand, the marginal control cost represents the monetary value of all the resources (labor, capital and conventional natural resources)

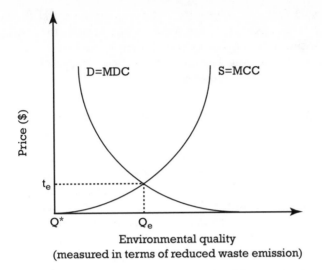

Figure 14.1 **Demand and supply curves for environmental goods and services**

used by private and public concerns to control environmental damage or improve environmental quality. Clearly, this is analogous to the discussion of the supply curve for a product in Chapter 2. Thus, the marginal control cost should represent the *supply* curve for environmental goods. It is positively sloped, indicating that pollution control (cleanup) cost increases as higher levels of environmental quality are attained (produced).

Thus, in Figure 14.1, Q_e and t_e represent the *optimal* (since MDC = MCC) level of environmental quality and price, respectively. Furthermore, under this ideal condition, t_e represents the *true* scarcity value of the environmental service (e.g., clean air) in question. However, since damage costs are *externalities*, the *true* scarcity value of environmental resources (such as clean air) cannot be readily and directly generated through the free play of the market (see Chapters 5 and 10). This suggests that discovering the demand function (or the marginal damage function) is the key to success in any effort directed to imputing the price for environmental goods and services.

Unfortunately, discovering the demand (damage) function for environmental goods is not an easy matter. The difficulty of this task can be illustrated using once more our simple example of the fish hatchery and the paper mill (Section 11.2). In this case, the damage to the river by effluent discharges from the paper mill can be assessed by the additional cleanup cost this action imposes on the hatchery. However, it may also require assessing the monetary values of aesthetic losses and the harmful effects that the waste discharge may have on certain animal species and plant life. The problem is that the values of aesthetic appreciation of nature and the sheer existence value of certain biological species are often *intangible* and as such difficult to measure in monetary terms. How economists actually attempt to measure such intangible benefits and costs is the central theme of this chapter. In the next section the methodological basis for measuring the benefits arising from improved environmental quality is examined. The focus is on understanding the exact context in which economists attempt to measure the value of the environment.

14.2 VALUATION OF BENEFITS: THE METHODOLOGICAL ISSUE

As discussed in Chapter 2, *willingness to pay* is the standard measuring stick of benefit in economics. For products where a market exists, individuals exercise choice by comparing their willingness to pay with the price of the product under consideration. They purchase the good or service when their willingness to pay equals or exceeds the price, and not otherwise. Thus, viewed this way, decision-making based on willingness to pay must reflect individuals' *preferences* for the good in question. What do all these mean to our task at hand, the measurement of social benefits from an environmental project? (A project here refers to any intentional actions undertaken for the purpose of changing the quality of the natural environment.)

To answer the above question more clearly, let us assume that the specific project under consideration is a government mandate to control sulfur emission from electric power plants located in certain regions of a nation. In this case, benefit is a direct result of improved air quality or the environmental damage avoided as a result of reduced sulfur emissions. Benefits of this nature are measured by using a demand curve (marginal damage cost curve) as shown in Figure 14.2.

Suppose point A on the demand curve represents the situation that prevailed before the project was initiated. Note that the project here is the

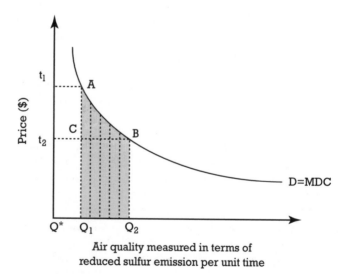

Figure 14.2 **Demand for improved air quality**

legislative mandate to control sulfur emissions. Thus, before the legislative mandate, individuals were willing to pay the price t_1 to avoid the last unit of sulfur emission, Q_1. Now, suppose that due to the new government initiative, sulfur emission is reduced from Q_1 all the way to Q_2. That is, with the stricter sulfur pollution control, society is allowed to move from point A to B along its demand curve for environmental quality. At the new position, point B, individuals are willing to pay the price t_2 in order to avoid the last unit of emission; that is, Q_2. Given this, what is the total social benefit of this project? This total benefit is represented by the shaded area under the demand curve – area Q_1ABQ_2, which represents the sum of society's willingness to pay for moving from its initial position, point A, to the new position, point B. A total benefit derived in this fashion is subject to several interesting interpretations. One interpretation is to view it as a measure of the *maximum sum of money* members of a given society are willing to pay to reduce sulfur emission from Q_1 to Q_2. Hence, viewed this way, it is a measure of willingness to pay (WTP). Alternatively, it could be interpreted as the *minimum monetary compensation* that members of a given society need in order to voluntarily accept that the proposed project (reduction in sulfur emission from Q_1 to Q_2) is not undertaken. This is a measure of willingness to accept (WTA). As will be evident later, under certain circumstances these two measures (WTP and WTA) may result in different estimates of benefits. (For a detailed discussion on this subject matter see Hanemann (1991).)

Furthermore, it is important to note that since economic valuation of benefit is based on the concept of willingness to pay, the shaded area measures people's "preferences" for changes in the state of their environment (Pearce 1993). What this suggests is that when economists attempt to measure the benefits from improved environmental quality, they are measuring not the *value of the environment* but the *preferences* of people for an environmental good or environmental bad. To further clarify this, consider this: one effect of a higher air quality standard may be improvement in human health, which causes a decrease in the average mortality rate. Thus, in this particular case, benefit is synonymous with increased quality of life or increased "life" expectancy. Despite this, the economic measure of benefit makes no pretension of valuing "life" as such. Instead, the measure is of people's preferences for a healthier and longer life. Essentially, then, economists do not and cannot measure the value of life or the environment as such. Instead, what they attempt to measure is the preferences of people for a healthier life or for a preservation of environmental amenities. This, indeed, represents one of the key methodological foundations of the economic valuation of environmental quality.

At this stage it is very important to note the following three points regarding the above approach to the estimation of benefits arising from environmental damage avoidance. First, valuation of the environment is based on *human preferences* alone, and it is assumed that *all* aspects of environmental damage can be valued in *monetary terms*. This means that a dollar value should be assigned to species and ecosystems that are considered to be irreplaceable. The alternative is, of course, to assume that nothing in life is irreplaceable (or has substitutes). Second, as shown in Figure 14.2, the estimation of benefit is not time specific. This approach either assumes perfect foresight or simply neglects to address the uncertainty involved in environmental damage. This is an important point to keep in mind since many relevant environmental concerns (such as acid rain, ozone depletion, climate change, species preservation, etc.) involve a considerable degree of uncertainty (Krutilla 1967). Third, it is assumed that the *changes* in the environmental quality (such as the move from A to B in Figure 14.2), are reasonably small. Thus, losses from environmental damage are either unmeasurable or infinitely small (Johansson 1990).

Thus far the discussion has focused on the methodological basis for measuring environmental benefits (damage). In this regard, it is established that economic benefits should be measured on the basis of individuals' "willingness to pay." However, to say that benefit is measured on this basis will not be sufficient, since the actual measurement of "willingness to pay" requires information on the prices (demand) which – in the case of environmental assets – are, if not impossible, difficult to obtain directly through the usual market mechanism. Therefore, economists have no choice but to look for various alternative techniques of directly and indirectly eliciting willingness to pay for environmental assets. In recent years considerable advances have been made in this area, and a fairly wide range of techniques are now available for eliciting willingness to pay for various aspects of environmental assets – which is the subject of the next section.

14.3 PRACTICAL METHODS FOR MEASURING THE BENEFITS OF ENVIRONMENTAL IMPROVEMENT

In the previous section we explored the methodological issues pertaining to the measurement of benefits from environmental improvement. The consensus within the economic profession appears to be that such benefits or avoided damage costs should be measured by eliciting individuals' willingness to pay for incremental changes in environmental quality. Once the issue of interest is identified this way, then the challenge becomes a matter of discovering methods of eliciting this information under the condition where market failure is the rule rather than the exception. This section deals with discussions of the techniques most commonly used by economists for the purpose of eliciting people's willingness to pay for changes in the quality of environmental services or assets.

The choice of the specific technique used for the purpose of eliciting willingness to pay depends on the specific nature of the types of environmental damage that are being avoided in order to achieve the desired environmental quality. Among others, the avoided damage may include impairment to human health – a higher risk of mortality and morbidity; loss of economic outputs, such as fish harvest and extraction of certain minerals; increased exposure to environmental nuisance, such as noise, odor and debris; amenity and aesthetic losses; simplification of natural habitats;

and irreversible damage to an ecosystem. While several techniques may be used to elicit a willingness to pay from which the demand for avoiding a particular type of environmental damage (for example, noise) can be derived, economists have yet to develop a *single* technique that could be used effectively in all circumstances. Also, in a specific situation some techniques tend to be better than others. Thus, in many cases the choice of technique could be an important issue in itself. For this reason, the rest of this section is devoted to highlighting the salient features of the most widely used techniques for the purpose of eliciting a willingness to pay for improvement in environmental assets.

14.3.1 The market pricing approach

The market pricing approach is used when the environmental improvement under consideration causes an increase or decrease in real outputs and/or inputs. Examples may include a decrease in timber harvest and/or extraction of minerals from a legislative enactment that effectively expands the acreage set aside as a wilderness area; the expected increase in fish harvest due to the implementation of a new water pollution control technology; or an increase in crop yield arising from a legislative mandate of a higher air quality standard.

In the above examples, benefits from environmental improvement are identified in terms of changes in outputs or inputs; more specifically, timber, minerals, fish and crops. These outputs or inputs are expected to have market prices that accurately reflect their scarcity values or, where this is not the case, shadow prices (i.e., values of similar goods in private markets) can be easily imputed. Thus, where environmental improvement is directly associated with changes in the quantity or price of marketed outputs or

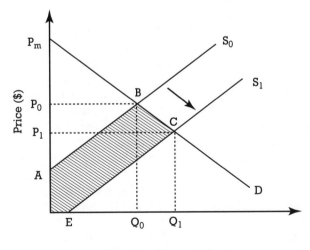

Figure 14.3 **Change in consumers' surplus as a measure of social benefit**

inputs, the benefit directly attributable to the environmental improvement in question can be measured by changes in the consumers' and producers' surpluses. To illustrate this point, consider the effect of a higher air quality standard on crop yield. As shown in Figure 14.3, the actual effect of the higher air pollution standard is a shift in the supply curve from S_0 to S_1, indicating an improvement in crop yield. As a result, the market price for the agricultural commodity will fall from P_0 to P_1. As stated above, the benefit from improved air quality is measured by difference in consumers' and producers' surpluses before and after the mandated change in air quality standard – area ABCE (the difference in the net social benefits between the original – triangle ABP_m, and the new position – area ECP_m). For an excellent case study that uses this approach see Dixon and Hufschmidt (1986: 102–20). These authors attempted to place a value on the loss of the fishery resource caused by the coastal development of Tokyo Bay using the market value of lost marine products (shrimp and crab, seaweed and fish) production.

14.3.2 The replacement cost approach

This approach is used as a measure of benefit when the damage that has been avoided as a result of improved environmental conditions can be approximated by the market value of what it cost to restore or replace the damage in question. For example, acid rain, among its other effects, is known to accelerate the deterioration of a nation's infrastructure, such as highways, bridges and historic monuments. Suppose a given nation passed a bill that reduces the emissions of acid rain precursors (sulfur and nitrates) by 50 percent. For the sake of simplicity, assume that all the sources of these pollutants emanate from within the boundary of the nation. One obvious outcome of a legislative mandate of this nature is to slow down the deterioration of the nation's physical infrastructure. If the replacement cost approach is used to measure this benefit, it will be assessed on the basis of the savings realized from reduced expenditures on repairing, restoring and replacing the nation's infrastructure. In what way does the replacement cost approach measure people's willingness to pay? It can elicit people's willingness to pay to the extent that the reduction in replacement and restoration costs (due to improved environmental conditions) closely reflects people's willingness to pay to avoid environmental damage (Pearce 1993). In some cases, environmental damage may not be capable of being completely repaired or replicated. Even if it could be, the replicas would probably be of little worth compared to the original. For this reason, this approach should be used with some care. Despite this apparent weakness, the replacement cost approach is quite appealing because it is generally easy to find estimates of replacement costs.

As an example, in one case study (Dixon and Hufschmidt 1986: 63–82) this approach was used to estimate the cost of recovering and replacing eroded soil from an agricultural project in Korea. In this case study the productive asset that had been damaged was the soil in the upland areas.

The costs of *physically* replacing lost soil and nutrients was used as a benchmark by which to measure the replacement costs. These replacement costs were then viewed as measures of the *minimum* benefits to be realized from preventive steps (new soil management techniques) that could be undertaken to restore and maintain the original productivity of the damaged soil.

14.3.3 Hedonic price approaches

Environmental features can increase land and house values if they are viewed as attractive or desirable, or they can reduce values if they are viewed as nuisances or dangerous, and therefore undesirable. For example, because of the associated odor, noise, debris and health risk, people in search of housing sites would tend to equate a landfill site's proximity with diminished environmental quality. Given a choice between two houses offered for the same price and identical in every other respect, except that one is closer to a landfill site, home buyers will choose the house that is further away. Only when the closer house is offered for less money will families consider it a suitable alternative. At some lower market price of the closer house, home buyers will become indifferent in choosing between that site and a higher-priced one further away from the landfill site. In this way, then, people are *implicitly* revealing their *willingness to pay* for avoiding the nuisances associated with a landfill by paying higher prices for houses located further away from such a site. This is the typical case of a *hedonic price* where the value or price of an environmental feature (neighborhood amenities, clean air, clean water, serenity, etc.) is assessed by looking at actual markets in which the attributes are traded. Other examples where hedonic prices can be effectively used include noise pollution by a point source (an airport, say), which can reduce the nearby residential property values; the effect of the construction of a nuclear plant on the property values of nearby residential areas; and urban residential development and its effect on nearby agricultural land value.

For example, Nelson *et al.* (1992) conducted an empirical study to estimate the price effects of landfill sites on house values. Using a sample of 708 single-family homes in the Ramsey, Minnesota, area that were located within close proximity of a landfill site, they found that the site adversely affected home values. More specifically, according to the empirical results of this study, "house value rises by nearly $5,000 for each mile it is located away from the landfill. On a percentage basis, house value rises by about 6.2 percent per mile from the landfill" (p. 362). This report also showed the effect on house values of a landfill site to vary with distance. The adverse effect on home values was 12 percent for homes located at the landfill boundary and 6 percent at about one mile. The adverse effect on home values was negligible for homes that were located beyond two miles from the landfill site.

The above discussion limits the application of a hedonic price approach to cases where environmental attributes can be, in some way, inferred by looking at the market prices for housing and/or land or, in general, property values. In cases where such data are easily available, a hedonic price approach of this nature can be of great utility because it is based on people's actual behavior. However, its major drawback also stems from the fact that the approach is completely dependent on property values and as such has a limited application. For example, it will not be applicable to measuring benefits relating to national parks, endangered species, ozone depletion, and so on.

Another area where the hedonic price method can be used is the economic valuation of changes in human health conditions, such as *mortality* and *morbidity*. In these cases, as we will observe shortly, willingness to pay is inferred from available data on medical expenditures and income or wages.

Pollution is often perceived as an environmental factor that exposes humans to some degree of health risk. For example, groundwater contamination that is caused by toxic waste disposal on a landfill site that is not properly sealed may be a serious human health hazard. This health hazard, over time, may result in a significantly higher than average incidence of disease and premature death among the population in the nearby community. How can we measure, in monetary terms, an environmental effect that increases the mortality and morbidity rates of a community? Are we not here implicitly measuring such things as human "life," pain and suffering? After all, is not life priceless?

These are all legitimate questions to raise. However, as stated in the previous section, if the objective is to measure benefits from avoiding environmental damage by means of individuals' willingness to pay, what is being measured is not values of "life" or "pain" but people's preferences for health risk – how much damage they are willing to avoid. We all take risks of this nature on a daily basis. What else can explain people's behavior when they drive a car, especially on congested highways such as Los Angeles freeways? Accordingly, then, the "life" that is measured is a "statistical life." With this caveat, how do we measure morbidity and mortality using the hedonic price approach?

As stated earlier, in the hedonic price approach the value or price of the environmental feature is assessed by looking at actual markets in which those attributes are traded. Using this method, the economic value of morbidity is approximated by society's loss of labor productivity (real income) as a result of an individual's premature death caused by specific pollution-related ailments. An empirical study conduced by Peterson (1977) may help to clarify how this method actually works.

This study dealt with estimating the social cost of Reserve Mining Corporation discharges of nonmagnetic rock or tailings into Lake Superior. The tailings contaminated the lake's water with asbestos-form fibers – a known carcinogen. This incidence exposed the North Shore citizens to serious health risks since these communities draw their public water from the lake. It was estimated that contamination of the lake water would increase the average annual number of deaths in the North Shore region by

274 over the 25 years of remaining operation of the plant. It was also determined that the mean age at death of the North Shore victims would be 54 years of age, or 12.8 years less than the average life expectancy of a US male, which was 66.8 years.

In addition, the *social cost* caused by each individual premature death was computed by estimating the annual present value of the lost productivity society suffers from each victim. This was estimated to be $38,849 (at 1975 prices) per victim. Then, given the projected death of 274 per year, the total social cost imposed by Reserve's pollution to the North Shore community was estimated to be $10,644,626.

At this point, it is important to note that the estimate of $38,849 does not represent the value of the 12.8 extra years of living (life) to an individual. Can you imagine anyone willing to sacrifice 12.8 years of her or his life for as little as the above sum of money, or even ten or more times that figure? To an individual, life, however short, is perhaps priceless. Therefore, what the above estimate measures is the economic value of 12.8 years of *statistical life* and nothing else (Mishan 1971). Hence, from the perspective of society at large, an individual, in terms of her or his economic contribution, is nothing more than a statistical entity.

Similarly, in using the hedonic price approach, *morbidity* risks are assumed to be factored into wages paid by different occupations. That is, jobs which are associated with a higher than average health risk, such as mining, tend to pay risk premiums in the form of higher wages. Such wage–risk differentials can be used for measuring changes in morbidity resulting from environmental pollution. For example, let us assume that the average wage rate of coal miners is fifteen dollars an hour, whereas the average wage of blue-collar workers in the manufacturing sector is only ten dollars an hour. The five-dollar wage premium offered in the mining industry can be used as a measure of the relatively higher health risk associated with this industry.

Measuring the economic value of changes in morbidity and mortality is much more involved, however. Prior to even starting the economic valuation process, it is necessary to establish a clear understanding of the various ways in which the specific pollutant(s) in question impair human health. Formally, this is done by using a technique known as the *dose–response approach*. In general, the steps required to carry out an effective dose–response analysis include measuring emissions and determining the resulting ambient quality, estimating human exposure and measuring impacts on human health. These are biological and ecological relationships that need to be established before estimating the economic value of changes in mortality and morbidity arising from environmental pollution. In several situations, dose–response could be, although necessary, an expensive procedure to undertake. Thus, economic valuation of mortality and morbidity using the hedonic price approach could be an expensive proposal.

14.3.4 The household production function approach

In the household production function approach benefits from improvement in environmental quality are measured by looking at households' expenditures on goods and/or services. Examples of such types of household expenditures include installing soundproof walling to reduce noise; purchasing radon-monitoring equipment to protect oneself from radon gas exposure; purchasing water filters to reduce the risk of drinking contaminated water; frequent hospital visits to reduce the chance of serious ailments from prolonged exposure to air pollution; and frequent painting of residential dwellings due to smoke emissions from a nearby factory. In each of these cases, we observe that households are willing to pay a certain amount of money (price) to avert specific environmental damage(s). Therefore, these expenditures, commonly known as *aversive expenditures*, can be used as a measure of households' willingness to pay (benefit) for a certain level (standard) of environmental quality (quietness, clean water, clean air). Note that in many cases, in order to attain a given change in environmental quality, several types of aversive expenditures may be undertaken simultaneously. In this situation, total benefit is measured by summing the various expenditures needed to attain the desired level of environmental attribute(s).

Another variation of the household production function approach involves the valuation of environmental services from *recreational sites*, such as national parks. A special technique that is used to estimate the benefit from changes in the environmental amenities of recreational sites is known as the *travel cost method*. This method measures the benefit (willingness to pay) stemming from a recreational experience, by looking at households' expenditures on the cost of travel to a desired recreational site. The basic idea behind this approach is this. The services of a recreation site, for example a camping ground, cannot be adequately measured by the gate price, which is usually very low. However, users of this campsite come from various locations. Therefore, instead of the gate price, the price or the willingness to pay of each user can be approximated by her or his travel cost. This method originated in the 1950s, and ever since then it has been used widely and with considerable success to empirically estimate the demand (hence willingness to pay) for recreational sites.

For example, in one study (Dixon and Hufschmidt 1986), the recreational value of Lumpinee Park in Bangkok was estimated using the travel-cost approach. Lumpinee is a public park located in the middle of Bangkok, the capital of Thailand. As the population and the economic activities around this city continued to grow, the opportunity cost (the commercial value of the park for other activities) of maintaining this park had been increasing steadily. What this prompted was a doubt in the minds of the public about the economic viability of the park. How would the recreational and amenity value of the park compare with the commercial value for other activities?

If the value of the park were to be assessed on the basis of the entrance fee (which was zero or nominal), its value would be virtually nothing. The alternative was to use the travel-cost approach, and this was done to get a more accurate measure of consumers' surplus for the park. The use of this approach basically entails the construction of an empirical demand function for the public park. As discussed above, this was done by hypothesizing that the costs in money and time spent traveling to a free or nominally priced recreational site could be used to approximate consumers' *willingness to pay* for the site. For people living close to the recreational site the travel cost was low, and the expectation was that they would tend to visit the site more often. The opposite would be the case for those visitors traveling to the site from more distant places. Thus, other things remaining constant, the general expectation would be that an inverse relationship between the travel cost and the number of visits to the given recreational site would be observed. In essence, this would represent the demand for a recreational site.

This kind of demand was estimated for Lumpinee Park using survey data. The survey was conducted through interviews of 187 randomly selected visitors arriving from 17 different administrative districts. The actual interviews took place at the park on two separate occasions, one in August and the other in November 1980. During the interview, among other questions each visitor was asked the amount she or he would be willing to pay to maintain the park. Afterwards, on the basis of this survey data and using a statistical demand analysis, the demand for Lumpinee Park was estimated. Given this demand estimate, the consumers' surplus enjoyed by the visitors of the park was estimated to be 13,204,588 baht annually. This was equivalent to $660,230 at the 1980 exchange rate of US$1 = 20 baht annually. At 10 percent the capitalized value of park would be $6.6 million. Thus, even though visitors did not pay an admission fee, the large consumers' surplus realized by its users clearly indicated that Lumpinee Park was a very valuable environmental asset.

However, the travel cost method has the following two glaring drawbacks: First, the application of the method is limited to the valuation of recreational sites. Second, the valuation itself is incomplete, since this method does not account for a recreational site's *existence* value. People may still value a recreational area even if they themselves have never been in the area. A simple example would be people who value the Grand Canyon even though they have never been there and have no plans to visit this site in the near future. In this case the primary motivation to protect it may be for future use by themselves or their offspring. It could also be derived from the strong ethical and moral commitment that some people have to preserve nature. As important as this issue is in environmental and resource economics, the travel cost method does not capture existence value. For example, for Lumpinee Park, when an explicit effort was made to account for the existence value of the park, the capitalized value was increased from $6.6 million to $58 million. The particular method used to capture the nonuse value of an environmental asset such as Lumpinee Park is the subject of the next subsection.

14.3.5 The contingent valuation method

The four approaches considered so far share two common features. First, willingness to pay is measured by using market prices either *explicitly* (in the case of the market pricing approach) or *implicitly*, such as prices of substitutes and complementary goods and services traded through the ordinary market. Second, in these approaches the stress has been exclusively on estimating *use values*. These are benefits or satisfactions received by individuals who are directly utilizing the services (amenities) provided by the natural environment. For example, as discussed above, the travel cost method measures the value of wilderness only from a very narrow perspective of its use: the recreational value to humans.

However, there are several attributes of the natural environment from which individuals obtain satisfaction, and hence benefits. For example, the value of wilderness cannot be measured only by its recreational values to current users; it has *nonuse values* to the extent that there are people who are willing to pay to preserve wilderness for future uses. Such nonuse value may not be captured by approaches that are anthropocentric in their focus and confined to measuring the willingness to pay of resource users at a point in time. This could be a serious problem when the resources under consideration involve *long time horizons*, considerable *uncertainty* and/or *irreversibility* (Krutilla 1967; Arrow and Fisher 1974). Unfortunately, these are characteristics common to many environmental assets. Thus, any effective method designed to measure benefits arising from changes in the condition of environmental assets cannot afford to simply dismiss the need to account for nonuse values. As much as possible, a serious effort should be made to measure both the use and the nonuse values. *Contingent valuation* represents the general techniques or procedures used to elicit *willingness to pay* in this broad and inclusive sense. Before we discuss the specific procedures associated with contingent valuation, it will be instructive to have a clear understanding of the principal components of nonuse values associated with environmental assets. In the environmental and resource economics literature, nonuse values are hypothesized as having three separable components, namely option, bequest and existence values or demands.

Option value refers to a sort of insurance premium individuals may be willing to pay to retain the option of possible future use. For example, people will be willing to pay some amount of money for the preservation of wilderness or the protection of a unique site – such as the Grand Canyon or Yosemite – not because they are currently using them, but because they want to reserve an option that would guarantee their future access to these resources. Note here that people behave this way because of their *uncertainty* regarding the future demand for or supply of these natural resources (Krutilla 1967; Johansson 1990). In this sense, consideration of option value is important when uncertainty is prevalent (Johansson 1990).

Bequest value refers to the satisfaction that people gain from the knowledge that a natural resource endowment is being preserved for future generations.

Strictly speaking, bequest value is an intergenerational component of the option value. Bequest value would have considerable relevance in a situation where the natural resources under consideration are unique and irreversible, and there exists uncertainty regarding future generations' demand for and/or the supply of these resources. Examples are national parks, wilderness, tropical forests, aquifers, blue whales, coastal wetlands, coral reefs, and so on. Basically, bequest demand exists to the extent that the present generation is *willing to pay* for preserving natural resources for the use of future generations.

Existence value refers to the satisfaction that some people derive from the preservation of natural resources so that there remains a habitat for fish, plants, wildlife and so on. In other words, it refers to what people are *willing to pay* (demand) for preserving the ecological integrity of the natural environment – stewardship. Recent *debt-for-nature* swaps by several internationally renowned conservation organizations for the purpose of protecting the tropical forest are examples of such an activity.

The general conceptual model that captures the essence of the above discussion can be presented by the following identities:

(a) Total value = Use value + Nonuse value

and

(b) Nonuse value = Option value + Bequest value + Existence value

Thus, the *total value* of an environmental asset is composed of not one, but several willingnesses to pay. This is because in many instances environmental assets are characterized by economic factors, but also by special attributes such as uniqueness, irreversibility and uncertainty as to future demand and supply. When any one of the above attributes is relevant, the economic value of a natural resource should include both the use and nonuse values (see Case Study 14.1). To ignore this fact and exclusively

CASE STUDY 14.1 ECONOMICS AND THE ENDANGERED SPECIES ACT

Jason F. Shogren

Economic benefits of species protection

Economists have suggested that economic value has two parts, *use* and *nonuse* values. Some use values of species are straightforward; for example, the economic value of current commercial, consumptive and recreational use. Commercial and recreational harvesting of species are perhaps the most straightforward benefits to estimate, given a visible market price. For example, commercial and recreational salmon fishing in the Pacific Northwest helps support 60,000 jobs and adds over $1 billion in personal income in the regional economy (Irvin 1995). Commercial recreation can also be nonconsumptive, as with the $200 million California whale-watching industry.

The value of other commercial uses can be more difficult to measure and involves the issues of substitution and adaptation. Economic value depends on the number of available substitutes, and one's ability to *adapt* around scarce goods.

An example of these concepts is in the potential use of new species in pharmaceutical research. If one species substitutes for another in potential market success, the value of extensive genetic exploration declines as the odds increase that a firm will find a profitable substitute quickly. . . .

Estimating *nonuse* values is more problematic and controversial. Most people are unfamiliar with many services provided by endangered species. This lack of realization of the services provided by species makes estimating nonuse values especially problematic. How do we assign economic value to goods that most people will never directly use and may not even recognize exist, and are the tools we use to estimate these benefits accurate?

Critics complain that nonuse value acts as a surrogate measure of environmental preferences, rather than for the particular species in question. One study, for example, showed the average perceived benefits from preventing 2,000 birds from dying in oil-filled ponds was no different than the value from preventing 20,000 or 200,000 birds from dying (Desvousges *et al.* 1992).

In other studies, a bimodal distribution of values has been observed. The distribution of hypothetical willingness to pay for nonmarket goods such as species conservation is split between those who see no reason to pay anything (due to either low value or their willingness to "free ride" on other people's bids) and those who want to pay their fair share – typically about $40. . . .

The contingent valuation survey (CV) has been used to measure benefits of a nonmarket good such as an endangered species. The results suggest that the average person's lump sum willingness to pay ranges from $12.99 to $254 for sea turtle or bald eagle preservation. The average individual's annual willingness to pay ranges from $6 to avoid the loss of the striped shiner to over $95 to avoid the loss of the northern spotted owl.

A piecemeal species-by-species approach, however, overestimates total ESA economic benefits because it does not address potential substitution and adaptation possibilities. Adding the average person's benefits elicited in eighteen CV surveys suggests that he or she would be willing to pay about $953 to protect eighteen different species (Loomis and White 1996). Multiplying this payment by the number of US households (about 75 million) gives a total benefit estimate of $71 billion. This estimate is roughly 1 percent of the 1995 US gross national product, for less than 2 percent of all threatened and endangered species. Clearly this estimate is inflated, and shows that a better understanding of the relationship between the values of species and their substitution/adaptation possibilities is necessary before any national estimate of nonuse values will be useful in the ESA debate.

focus on use value could lead to severe underestimation of benefits and, as a result of this, unwarranted exploitation of valuable natural resources. For example, if the decision to preserve wilderness is to be based solely on benefit derived from recreational use (use value), the result could lead to the allocation of an insufficient amount of public land to wilderness protection. The real challenge, then, is to find ways of eliciting a willingness to pay for option, bequest and existence values so that nonuse value will be adequately considered. How can this be done, when the environmental attributes under consideration (such as aesthetic properties, survival of species, varieties of ecosystems) have no substitutes or complements traded through the ordinary market? This question suggests that it is impossible to assess nonuse values by using *implicit* prices. Therefore, a technique designed to estimate nonuse values cannot use *real* market information. The best it can do is to create *hypothetical* or *artificial market* conditions that elicit willingness to pay for the purpose of estimating nonuse values. This is, in fact, how the estimation of nonuse values is addressed in *contingent valuation methods*.

In the contingent valuation approach, willingness to pay is elicited by conducting a *survey*. A carefully selected sample from the relevant population is asked to respond to a series of meticulously worded questions about their willingness to pay, contingent on changes in the availability and/or quality of an environmental amenity, such as the preservation of coastal wetlands or wilderness. The survey is designed in such a way that individuals are faced with a hypothetical market-like choice and are then asked about their willingness to pay for a specific end. For example, an individual might be asked the following question: "How much money are you willing to pay to preserve wilderness so that you will be assured of its availability for use to your children's children?" A question, perhaps, intended to get a measure of bequest values. In the contingent valuation method, the design of the questionnaire is extremely crucial. It requires an in-depth knowledge of statistical survey methods, economics, ecology and, most importantly, a good deal of creativity and imagination.

The major advantage of the contingent valuation approach is its potential to emerge as a general procedure for assessing the *total* economic value (use values plus nonuse values) of any type of environmental asset. A mere three decades has passed since the concept of nonuse value started to receive serious attention in the discipline of environmental and resource economics. Applications of contingent valuation are even more recent. So far, some empirical work has been done using this method, with mixed, but encouraging, results (e.g., Schulze *et al.* 1981; Walsh *et al.* 1983, 1984). Furthermore, what is even more promising from the growing use of the contingent valuation method in the field of natural resources is that it is promoting an enduring awareness – within the economic discipline – that the economic value of the natural environment goes beyond what can be captured by direct and/or indirect observations of market information. In other words, natural resources have *intrinsic values* that cannot possibly be captured through market or extramarket information – which, as discussed in Chapter 1, has never been the natural inclination of mainstream economists. It still remains the case, however, that even the most sophisticated design of contingent valuation instruments cannot fully capture the total value of environmental assets for several reasons (more on this in the next section).

On technical grounds alone, several potential biases may arise that could undermine the validity of the preference information gathered by using the contingent valuation method. Among others, these include the following:

1 *Strategic bias*: the fact that respondents may refuse to respond to survey question(s) or would not reveal their "true" willingness to pay for strategic reasons. They may do this if they think there is a "free rider" situation. However, there appears to be limited evidence of strategic bias (Bohm 1979).

2 *Information bias*: the survey result is not independent of the information provided to respondents. Thus, what people are willing to pay for environmental assets depends on the quantity and quality of the information provided to them, including the way questions are constructed. For example, many empirical studies reveal a marked divergence between willingness to pay (WTP) and willingness to accept (WTA). That is, it matters a great deal whether respondents are asked how much they are willing to pay to preserve a wilderness in its pristine condition, or how much they are willing to accept in compensation for its loss.

3 *Hypothetical bias*: refers to the fact that respondents are not making "real" transactions. In this situation respondents tend to be sensitive to the instruments used for payment (such as entrance fee, sales tax, payroll tax, income tax and so on.)

At this stage, it may be helpful to demonstrate the use of the contingent valuation approach in a real-world situation. Walsh *et al*. (1984) sought to estimate the preservation value of increments in wilderness designations in Colorado. For this case study, a mail survey was conducted during the summer of 1980, covering a sample of 218 Colorado households. These participants were shown four maps of the State of Colorado, and on each map a different acreage was designated as wilderness. One of the maps showed the 1.2 million acres of land currently (1980) designated as wilderness in Colorado. This represented 2 percent of the state land. The other three maps showed hypothetical wilderness designation, and their sizes were respectively 2.6, 5 and 10 million acres. As far as possible, every effort and precaution were taken to provide the respondents of the survey with realistic and credible information about the contingent market. This information was intended to offer a solid background on the scientific, historical and economic significance of wilderness areas for the current and future citizens of Colorado.

With the above information in hand, each respondent was asked to write down the maximum amount of money they would be willing to pay annually for the preservation of four increments in wilderness depicted on four maps. This was followed by asking the respondents to allocate their reported willingness to pay among the four categories of value: recreational use, option, existence and bequest demands. Note that option, existence and bequest values are measures of *nonuse*; hence, of the preservation value of wilderness. Viewed this way, *total* preservation value is the *residual* after recreational use benefits have been subtracted from the total willingness to pay for wilderness.

Once all the necessary survey data had been gathered and processed, a statistical demand analysis was employed to estimate preservation values. This involved estimating a separate demand for each component of the preservation value, namely option, existence and bequest value. It would be beyond the scope of this text to go into the details of the procedures used to estimate these demand functions. The final result of the study is presented in Table 14.1.

The last row of Table 14.1 shows the estimate of the *total values* for each of the four wilderness designations. For example, for the existing (1980) level of wilderness areas of 1.2 million acres, the total value was estimated to be $28.5 million. The total values of each designation group are split into two major groups, namely *use value* (which represents the recreational use of the wilderness) and *nonuse value* (which corresponds to the preservation value of the wilderness). For example, again focusing on the existing wilderness designation areas of 1.2 million acres, the total value ($28.5 million) was obtained by summing recreational use value ($13.2 million) and the preservation or nonuse value ($15.3 million). The preservation value was further broken down into its three major components, namely the option, existence and bequest values. For the existing wilderness area, these values were reported to be 4.4, 5.4 and 5.5 million dollars, respectively. All categories of the preservation value are reported in both per household and total basis.

Several inferences can be drawn from the above results. For example, increasing the number of acres for wilderness designation from 1.2 to 2.6 (which amounted to slightly more than a doubling of the existing wilderness designation areas) was shown to increase the total value by 46 percent (from $28.5 to $41.6 million). Thus, doubling the areas of the wilderness designation does not double the total value. As interesting as this observation may seem to be, however, for our purpose here what is important to notice is this: for all the four wilderness designation categories, the *nonuse* or *preservation* values represented a significant portion of the total value. Even at the lower end (which was associated with the wilderness areas of 10 million acres), nonuse value was 37 percent of the total value. What this shows is, at least in principle, the significance of valuation techniques (such as the contingent valuation approach) that deliberately attempt to incorporate the estimation of *nonuse values* (benefits) to the analysis. Obviously, failure to account for such benefits may lead society to take decisions that could cause irreversible damage to wilderness areas and other environmental resources of similar nature.

This concludes the discussion of the various techniques modern economists are currently using to assess benefits arising from an improvement in

Table 14.1 Total annual consumer surplus (US$) from recreation use and preservation value to Colorado households from increments in wilderness designation, Colorado, 1980

Value categories	Existing and potential wilderness designation			
	Wilderness areas, 1980 (1.2 million acres)	Wilderness areas, 1981, (2.6 million acres)	Double 1981 wilderness areas (5 million acres)	All potential wilderness areas (10 million acres)
Recreation use value				
Per visitor day	14.00	14.00	14.00	14.00
Total, million	13.2	21.0	33.1	58.2
Preservation value to Colorado residents				
Per household	13.92	18.75	25.30	31.83
Total, million	15.3	20.6	27.8	35.0
Option value				
Per household	4.04	5.44	7.34	9.23
Total, million	4.4	6.0	8.1	10.2
Existence value				
Per household	4.87	6.56	8.86	11.14
Total, million	5.4	7.2	9.7	12.3
Bequest value				
Per household	5.01	6.75	9.10	11.46
Total, million	5.5	7.4	10.0	12.5
Total annual recreation use value and preservation value to Colorado households, million	28.5	41.6	60.9	93.2

Source: R. B. Walsh, J. B. Lommis and R. H. Gillman, *Land Economics* Vol. 60, No. 1, February 1984. © 1984. Reprinted by permission of the University of Wisconsin Press.

the condition of the natural environment (clean air, water, etc.). However, it will be a worthwhile exercise to reflect on some of the major controversial issues that are specifically related to the economic approaches to measuring environmental benefit (or damage).

14.4 SOME GENERAL PROBLEMS ASSOCIATED WITH THE ECONOMIC APPROACH TO ENVIRONMENTAL VALUATION

In the previous section a concerted effort was made to point out some of the major drawbacks associated with each of the techniques that economists use to assess the benefits of environmental projects. However, this was done without questioning the fundamental premises of the neoclassical economic valuation methodology. In this section, an attempt will be made to highlight four of the most serious criticisms of the neoclassical approaches to valuing the environment. These are as follows: First, environmental values should not be reducible to a single one-dimensional standard that is ultimately expressed only in monetary terms. Second, high levels of uncertainty make the measurement and the very concept of total value meaningless. Third, survey techniques used to elicit willingness to pay confuse preferences with beliefs. Fourth, important ecological connections may be missed when valuing components of a system separately.

1 The conventional approaches to valuations assume that a monetary value can be assigned to all aspects of environmental amenities. Furthermore, as Funtowicz and Ravetz (1994: 199) put it:

> the issue is not whether it is only the marketplace that can determine value, for economists have long debated other means of valuation; our concern is with the assumption that in any dialogue, all valuations or "numeraires" should be reducible to a single one dimensional standard.

They described this whole effort as a "commodification of environmental goods."

It is argued that this principle should not be accepted because it blatantly denies the existence of certain *intangible* values of the natural environment that are beyond the economic. They are unmeasurable and can be described only in qualitative terms that are noneconomic in nature. Improved quality of life, the protection of endangered species and ecosystems, the preservation of scenic or historic sites (such as Grand Canyon), and the aesthetic and symbolic properties of wilderness are examples of this nature. The main message here is that it would be wrong and misleading to ignore intangibles in an effort to obtain a single dollar-value estimate for benefits. There are irreplaceable and *priceless* environmental assets whose values cannot be captured either through the market or by survey methods designed to elicit people's willingness to pay. However, it is important to note that to describe an environmental asset as *priceless* cannot mean that such a resource has an *infinite* value. This would imply that it would be worth devoting the whole of a nation's GNP (and beyond) to the preservation of its environmental assets.

2 The conventional measure of environmental damage stems from the difficulties associated with the uncertainty inherent in certain uses of environmental resources. Uncertainties of this nature are particularly

important when the resources in question are difficult or impossible to replace and for which no close substitute is available (Krutilla 1967). Under these circumstances the potential costs of current activities could be, although uncertain, very high. This is particularly significant where the outcomes are expected to be irreversible. Contemporary examples are global warming, biodiversity loss, ozone destruction, and so forth.

There are important implications from uncertainties of the above nature. Among them are the following: (a) Uncertainty compounds the difficulty of evaluating environmental damage. (b) Where irreversibility is a serious concern, the damage may be unmeasurable or infinitely high (Johansson 1990). In such a case, the very notion of total value may be meaningless. (c) As Krutilla (1967) effectively argued, the maximum willingness to pay could be less than the minimum amount that would be necessary to compensate for the loss of the natural phenomenon in question. This is because the more difficult it is to replace a loss of environmental goods with other goods, the higher the compensation needed in order for people to accept the loss. Under this condition, attempts to determine individuals' willingness to pay for nonuse values (i.e., existence, option and bequest values) using the contingent valuation method could have misleading outcomes. (d) When the potential for catastrophic outcomes in the future is a major concern, proper management of the underlying uncertainty requires explicit consideration of the interest of the future generations – intergenerational equity. According to Perrings (1991), this can be done using the *precautionary principle* as a guide for decision-making. This approach assigns a worst-case value to the uncertain outcome of current activities. The "optimal" policy is then the one that minimizes the worst imaginable outcome. Under this approach it makes perfect sense to opt for preservation of the natural environment if costs are potentially large and very long-term.

3 Sagoff (1988b) wrote a stinging criticism of the whole approach of evaluating environmental damage on the basis of survey data that purport to reflect the respondents' willingness to pay. His main objection is based on what is or is not conveyed by people's preferences, which are used as a means of eliciting willingness to pay. More specifically, he argued that the conventional wisdom in economics is to treat judgments (or belief) expressed about the environment as if they are preferences (or desires). According to Sagoff, judgments (ethical or otherwise) involve:

> not desires or wants but opinions or views. They state what a person believes is right or best for the community or group as a whole. These opinions may be true or false, and we may meaningfully ask that person for the reasons that he or she holds them. But an analyst who asks how much citizens would pay to satisfy opinions that they advocate through political association commits a category mistake. The analyst asks of beliefs about objective facts a question that is appropriate only to subjective interests and desires.
>
> (Sagoff 1988b: 94)

This consideration is especially significant when property rights are not clearly delineated (such as in the case of the environment). The main reason for this is that people's preferences for these kinds of resources include aspects of their *feelings* that are not purely economic. These feelings may be based on aesthetic, cultural, ethical, moral and political considerations. Therefore, under this condition, it is quite possible that some people may prefer not to sell publicly owned resources at any price. This perhaps explains why some respondents in contingent valuation surveys refuse to indicate the price at which they are willing to buy or sell environmental resources; not, as often claimed, for strategic reasons.

The implication is that environmental policy should be based not only on market information (prices) but also on a decision-making process that includes open dialogues on the basis of democratic principles (see Sagoff 1988a). In this way, the various dimensions of environmental policy (aesthetic, cultural, moral and ethical) are adequately incorporated.

4 Another drawback, particularly relevant to the contingent valuation method, results from a potential failure to account for certain *ecological* factors. More specifically, to the extent that total value (use values plus nonuse values) is based on economic values, it may fail to account for *primary values* – "system characteristics upon which all ecological functions are contingent" (Pearce 1993). In this sense, total value may not really be total after all! As discussed in Chapter 4, one of the lessons of ecology is that all matters in a natural ecosystem are mutually interrelated. Therefore, strictly from an ecological viewpoint, the *value* of a particular entity in the natural environment (an animal species, a valley, a river, humans, etc.) should be assessed on the basis of its overall contribution to the sustainability (health) of the ecosystem as a whole. Essentially, assessing the total value of a natural environment (such as wilderness) as the sum of the values of the parts or individual attributes does not account for the whole. However, this is the underlying premise of the contingent valuation approach (see Exhibit 14.1).

EXHIBIT 14.1 TOWARD ECOLOGICAL PRICING

Alan Thein Durning

Ecological pricing is [a] . . . necessary condition of a sustainable forest economy. Virgin timber is currently priced far below its full costs. For instance, the price of teak does not reflect the costs of flooding that rapacious teak logging has caused in Myanmar; nor does the price of old-growth fir from the US Pacific Northwest include losses suffered by the fishing industry because logging destroys salmon habitat. Those losses are estimated at $2,150 per wild Chinook salmon in the Columbia River, when future benefits to sports and commercial fishers are counted.

Few attempts have been made to calculate the full ecological prices of forest products but they would undoubtedly be astronomical for some goods. A mature forest tree in India, for example, is worth $50,000, estimates the Center for Science and Environment in New Delhi. The full value of a hamburger produced on pasture cleared from rain forest is about $200, according to an exploratory study conducted at New York University's School of Business. These figures, of course, are speculative. Calculating them requires making assumptions about how many dollars, for instance, a species is worth – perhaps an imponderable question. But the alternative to trying – failing to reflect the loss of ecological functions at all in the price of wood and other forest product – ensures that the economy will continue to destroy forests.

The full economic value of a forest ecosystem is clearly huge. Forests provide a source of medicines worth billions of dollars. Their flood prevention, watershed stabilization and fisheries protection functions are each worth billions more. Their scenic and recreational benefits also have billion-dollar values for both the world's growing nature tourism industry and local residents.

The full value of forests includes each of these components, from sources of medicines to pest controls. But, again, market prices count only the direct costs of extracting goods, not the full ecological costs. In accounting terms, the money economy is depleting its natural capital without recording that depreciation on its balance sheet. Consequently, annual losses come out looking like profits, and cash flow looks artificially healthy. For a business to do this – liquidate its plant and equipment and call the resulting revenue income – would be both self-destructive and, in many countries, illegal. For the money economy overall, however, self-destruction generally goes unquestioned.

How can we move toward ecological pricing? By changing government policies. A primary responsibility of governments is to correct the failures of the money economy, and global deforestation is surely a glaring one. Yet forest policies in most nations do the opposite: They accelerate forest loss. The first order of business for government, therefore, is to stop subsidizing deforestation. The second is to use taxes, user fees and tariffs to make ecological costs apparent in the money economy. Until the money economy is corrected in these ways, forest conservation will remain an uphill battle.

Source: Worldwatch Institute, *States of the World 1993*, Copyright © 1993. Reprinted by permission.

14.5 CHAPTER SUMMARY

- This chapter dealt with the economic approaches to the evaluation of benefits arising from changes in environmental quality.
- Following the standard practice in economics, the benefit (or avoided damage cost) from a project to improve environmental quality is captured by individuals' willingness to pay at the margin. Total benefit is then measured by the sum of society's willingess to pay – the area under the relevant range of the demand curve for an environmental good or, more specifically, the marginal damage cost curve.
- When environmental benefit is measured in this manner, two important issues require particular notice:

  1 The benefit from improved environmental quality is not intended to measure the "value" of the environment as such. Instead, what is

measured is people's preferences or willingness to pay for an environmental good or to avoid an environmental bad (damage).

2 The estimation of the total benefit includes consumers' surplus. In other words, total benefit is not computed by simply multiplying equilibrium market price and quantity.

- Because measuring the area under the marginal damage cost curve entails assessment of benefits (in monetary terms) of entities normally not traded through ordinary markets, a system must be developed to implicitly measure willingness to pay – that is, when environmental goods and services have no directly observable market prices. This is done by using prices of substitutes and complementary goods and services which are traded through the ordinary market.

- In this chapter, we examined the three most common approaches to measuring implicit willingness to pay, namely the replacement cost approach, the hedonic price approach and the household production approach – which incorporates, among other things, the travel cost method.

- These approaches have one common feature: they measure benefits on the basis of *use* values. These are benefits or satisfactions received by individuals who are directly utilizing the services or amenities provided by the natural environment. But some environmental assets, such as wilderness, have *nonuse values*; for example, the value of preserving wilderness so that it will be available for the use of future generations.

- Three distinctively different features of future uses were discussed in this chapter, namely option, bequest and existence values.

- The *economic value* of the natural environment goes beyond what can be captured by direct and/or indirect observations of market information or use value. Thus, the total benefit of environmental assets (such as wilderness) should reflect *total value* – the sum of use and nonuse values.

- However, techniques designed to estimate nonuse values cannot use real market information, which means that willingness to pay for nonuse values must be estimated by means of a hypothetical market condition. This is done using the *contingent valuation method*.

- This method elicits willingness to pay by conducting an extensive survey.

- In general, the economic approaches to environmental valuation have been criticized for a number of reasons. Chief among them are:

1 The "commodification" of environmental goods – the idea that environmental values are reducible to a single one-dimensional standard that is ultimately expressed only in monetary terms – is objectionable to some.

2 Survey techniques used to elicit willingness to pay confuse preferences with belief.

3 Where uncertainty and irreversibility are serious concerns, the damage may be unmeasurable or infinitely high. In this case, the very notion of total value may be meaningless.

4 Important ecological connections may be missed when valuing components of a system separately. In this case, the total value may not be total after all!

review and discussion questions

1 Briefly explain the following concepts: statistical life, dose–response techniques, aversive expenditure, use values, intangibles, incommensurable, option values, bequest values, existence values, total value, the precautionary principle, commodification of environmental goods, debt-for-nature swaps.

2 State *True*, *False* or *Uncertain* and explain why.

 (a) To describe an environmental asset as "priceless" does not mean that it has an infinite value.

 (b) Economists do not attempt to measure the *value* of the environment. What they attempt to measure is the preferences of people for an environmental good or environmental bad.

 (c) The estimation of benefits from environmental assets would be unaffected by whether the method used to measure benefit was based on willingness to pay (WTP) or willingness to accept (WTA).

3 According to a study conducted in 1977, excessive tailings discharge into a lake is expected to reduce the average life expectancy of those in a nearby community by approximately 12 years (from 66 to 54 years). The monetary value to the community of this premature death was estimated to be $40,000 per victim annually. Let us suppose that because of a general price increase over the past twenty years, $40,000 in 1977 is worth $120,000 currently. Does this mean the value of 12 years of life for an individual in this community (at current prices) is $1,440,000? If your answer to this question is no, then what does this figure represent? If your answer is yes, would you be willing to trade 12 years of your life for $1,440,000? Explain.

4 In this chapter, we discussed five commonly used techniques for measuring the monetary values of environmental damages (benefits), namely market pricing, replacement cost, hedonic price, household production function (which includes the travel cost method) and contingent valuation. Below, you are given a hypothetical situation where environmental damage of some nature has occurred. For each of these cases choose the best technique(s) to estimate the cost of the damage in question, and provide a brief justification for your choice of the particular technique(s).

 (a) excessive soil erosion due to deforestation;
 (b) decline in property values due to groundwater contamination;
 (c) loss of habitats due to development project of ecologically sensitive wetlands;
 (d) excessive noise from a nearby industrial enterprise;
 (e) loss of scenic value of a lake shore due to eutrophication.

5 A colleague said to me, "I have my own personal doubts about contingent valuation when respondents are ethically committed to environmental preservation. If they are asked a willingness-to-accept question, then they may respond with an infinite or very large price. In essence, they see the resource as priceless or incommensurable with respect to monetary values. If they are asked a willingness-to-pay question, they may object on grounds that they are being forced to pay for something that has ethical standing and on moral grounds should not be damaged or destroyed; or they might simply offer what they can afford in order to meet what they see as their moral obligation to save the environment. The point is that contingent valuation analysis, while interesting, could be conceptually problematic." Do you agree or disagree with my colleague? Why, or why not?

REFERENCES AND FURTHER READING

Arrow, K. and Fisher, A. C. (1974) "Environmental Preservation, Uncertainty, and Irreversibility," *Quarterly Journal of Economics* 88: 312–19.

Baumol, W. J. (1968) "On the Social Rate of Discount," *American Economic Review* 58: 788–802.

Bohm, P. (1979) "Estimating Willingness to Pay: Why and How?" *Scandinavian Journal of Economics* 84: 142–53.

Carson, R. and Mitchell, R. (1991) *Using Surveys to Value Public Goods: The Contingent Valuation Method*, Baltimore: Resources for the Future.

Desvousges, W., Johnson, F. R., Dunford, R., Boyle, K., Hudson, S. and Wilson, K. (1992) *Measuring Natural Resource Damages with Contingent Valuation: Tests of Validity and Reliability*, Research Triangle Park, N.C.: Research Triangle Institute.

Dixon, J. A. and Hufschmidt, M. M. (eds.) (1986) *Economic Valuation Techniques for the Environment: A Case Study Workbook*, Baltimore: Johns Hopkins University Press.

Freeman, A. M. (1979) *The Benefits of Environmental Improvement*, Baltimore: Johns Hopkins University Press.

Funtowicz, S. O. and Ravetz, J. R. (1994) "The Worth of a Songbird: Ecological Economics as a Post-Normal Science," *Ecological Economics* 10: 197–207.

Hanemann, W. M. (1991) "Willingness-to-Pay and Willingness-to-Accept: How Much Do They Differ?" *American Economic Review* 81: 635–47.

Hardin, G. (1968) "The Tragedy of the Commons," *Science* 162: 1243–8.

Irvin, W. R. (1995) Statement to the Subcommittee on Drinking Water, Fisheries, and Wildlife of the Senate Environment and Public Works Committee.

Johansson, P.-O. (1990) "Valuing Environmental Damage," *Oxford Review of Economic Policy* 6, 1: 34–50.

Kneese, A. (1984) *Measuring the Benefits of Clean Air and Water*, Washington, D.C.: Resources for the Future.

Krutilla, J. V. (1967) "Conservation Reconsidered," *American Economic Review* 57: 787–96.

Loomis, J. and White, D. (1996) *Economic Benefits of Rare and Endangered Species: Summary and Meta-analysis*, Colorado State University, Col.: Fort Collins.

Mishan, E. J. (1971) "Evaluation of Life and Limb: A Theoretical Approach," *Journal of Political Economy* 79: 687–705.

Nelson, A. C., Genereux, J. and Genereux, M. (1992) "Price Effects of Landfills on House Values," *Land Economics* 68, 4: 359–65.

Pearce, D. W. (1993) *Economic Values and the Natural World*, Cambridge, Mass.: MIT Press.

Perrings, C. (1991) "Reserved Rationality and the Precautionary Principle: Technological Change, Time, and Uncertainty in Environmental Decision Making," in R. Costanza (ed.) *Ecological Economics: The Science and Management of Sustainability*, New York: Columbia University Press.

Peterson, J. M. (1977) "Estimating an Effluent Charge: The Reserve Mining Case," *Land Economics* 53, 3: 328–40.

Sagoff, M. (1988a) "Some Problems with Environmental Economics," *Environmental Ethics* 10, 1: 55–74.

—— (1988b) *The Economy of the Earth*, Cambridge Mass.: Cambridge University Press.

Schulze, W. D., d'Arge, R. C. and Brookshire, D. S. (1981) "Valuing Environmental Commodities: Some Recent Experiments," *Land Economics* 57: 11–72.

Shogren, J. F. (1997) "Economics and the Endangered Species Act," *Endangered Species Update*, School of Natural Resources and Environment, University of Michigan.

Walsh, R. G., Miller, N. P. and Gilliam, L. O. (1983) "Congestion and Willingness to Pay for Expansion of Skiing Capacity," *Land Economics* 59, 2: 195–210.

Walsh, R. G., Lommis, J. B. and Gillman, R. A. (1984) "Valuing Option, Existence, and Bequest Demands for Wilderness," *Land Economics* 60, 1: 14–29.

chapter fifteen

A FRAMEWORK FOR ASSESSING THE WORTHINESS OF AN ENVIRONMENTAL PROJECT:
Cost–Benefit Analysis

---

learning objectives

After reading this chapter you will be familiar with the following:

- cost–benefit analysis as a widely used technique for environmental or, in general, social project appraisal;
- the methodological basis of cost–benefit analysis;
- the net present value criterion;
- the methodological link between the net present value criterion and the standard cost–benefit analysis approach;
- the difference between private and social appraisal of projects;
- social project appraisal and the problem of double counting of benefits and/or costs;
- the choice of the discount rate: private versus social discount rate;
- discounting and intergenerational equity;
- the social costs and benefits of the Endangered Species Act.

[Cost–benefit analysis is] about the choices of investment projects. But why bother with cost–benefit analysis at all? What is wrong with deciding whether or not to undertake any specific investment, or to choose among a number of specific investment opportunities, guided simply by proper accounting practices and, therefore, guided ultimately by reference to profitability? The answer is provided by the familiar thesis that what counts as a benefit or a loss to one part of the economy – to one or more persons or groups – does not necessarily count as a benefit or loss to the economy as a whole. And in cost–benefit analysis we are concerned with the economy as a whole, with the welfare of a defined society, and not any smaller part of it.

(Mishan 1982: xix)

15.1 INTRODUCTION

In Section 14.3 we discussed the various techniques that economists employ to assess the benefits of implementing an environmental project. A project in this case is defined as a concrete action taken to alter the state of the natural environment – generally, against its deterioration. A case in point is an intentional plan taken by a given society to control sulfur dioxide emissions from an electric power plant. As shown in Figure 15.1 (which is a replica of Figure 14.2), undertaking this project allows society to move from the status quo, point A, to a new position, point B. Furthermore, in this particular case, the total benefit resulting from the implementation of the project is identified by the shaded area under the society's demand curve for environmental quality.

However, if a society wants to evaluate the worthiness of this project, information about a project's benefit alone will not be sufficient. Undertaking a project requires the use of scarce societal resources. Thus, in order to determine a project's worthiness, the benefit of the project has to be weighed against its cost. The basic technique economists use for project

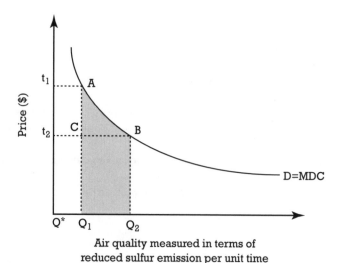

Figure 15.1 **Demand for improved air quality**

appraisal is popularly known as *cost–benefit analysis* (CBA). Cost–benefit analysis is commonly used to appraise a wider range of *public* projects. Highways, bridges, airports, dams, recycling centers, emission control technology, and a legislative mandate to conserve or preserve resources are just a few examples of projects that can be evaluated using cost–benefit analysis (see Mishan 1982).

From the beginning, it is important to know that cost–benefit analysis involves making a *value judgment*. This is because, in assessing the relative worthiness of a project, it is necessary to declare that a given state of nature is either "better" or "worse" than another. For example, in Figure 15.1 we moved from state A (the status quo) to state B – a position attained after the sulfur emission control technology has been implemented. In cost–benefit analysis, what we want to develop is a "norm" by which we can judge that state A is "better" or "worse" than state B. Thus, cost–benefit analysis falls directly into the province of what is known as normative (welfare) economics.

15.2 THE WELFARE FOUNDATION OF COST–BENEFIT ANALYSIS

Welfare economics deals with economic methodologies and principles indispensable to policy-makers engaged in the design and implementation of collective decisions. The following two principles of welfare economics are specially important since they form the foundation by which economists base their judgment on the relative desirability of varying economic states of nature.

Principle I: "actual" Pareto improvement states that if by undertaking a project no members of a society become worse off and at least one becomes better off, the project should be accepted.

Principle II: "potential" Pareto improvement states that a project should be considered if, by undertaking it, the gainers from the project can compensate the losers and still remain better off in their economic conditions than they were before.

Let us examine the implications of these two principles by using Figure 15.2. The hypothetical production possibility frontier describes the choices that a given nation is facing between conservation (setting aside more land for wilderness) and development (using land to produce consumption goods and services or to increase the production capacity of the economy). Suppose point M on the production possibility frontier represents the status quo. Recently, the government of this hypothetical nation has passed legislation that mandates the expansion of the public land holding that is specifically designated for wilderness. The expected effect of this legislative mandate on the economic state of this nation is shown by a movement along the production possibility frontier from point M to N.

According to the criterion outlined by Principle I, the move from point M to N should be *accepted* if, and only if, not a single member of this hypothetical nation becomes worse off and at least one becomes better off

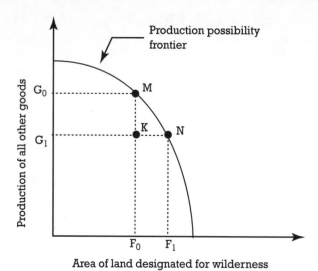

Figure 15.2 **The choice between conservation and economic development**

as a result of such a move. However, it is highly unlikely that a situation of this nature could occur in the real world. In the case of our hypothetical nation, some individuals, who are pro-development, are likely to be made worse off by the move from M to N. This is because such a move could be attained only at the sacrifice of goods and services (the move from G_0 to G_1) that are appealing to these particular members of this nation. "Actual" Pareto improvement would be possible if, and only if, our hypothetical nation has been operating *inefficiently* to begin with, such as at point K. In this case, it is possible to move from K to N without violating Principle I.

On the other hand, according to Principle II, the move from M to N should be *acceptable* if, and only if, the gain by the pro-conservation individuals (the monetary value of $F_1 - F_0$) is greater than the loss by the pro-development individuals (the monetary value of $G_0 - G_1$). Thus, at least conceptually, the gainers could be able to compensate the losers and still remain ahead. It should be noted, however that, Principle II does not require that compensation actually has to occur. What is stressed is merely that the "potential" for compensation exists. Essentially, then, Principle II simply states that the move from M to N would be considered economically "efficient" provided that the aggregate benefit from such a move exceeded the aggregate cost. That is, the *net* benefit of the project is *positive*. In other words, if we let the letters B and C represent aggregate benefit and cost, respectively, then, according to Principle II, the move from M to N would be economically efficient provided B – C > 0. In short, real income is higher at point N than at M. However, it is important to note that this criterion does not even pretend to address the *income distribution* effect of a project. That is, who gains or loses from undertaking a project is considered irrelevant, provided that the net benefit from the project in question is positive.

15.3 THE NET PRESENT VALUE CRITERION

The fundamental normative (welfare) criterion of cost–benefit analysis is actually based on "potential" Pareto improvement. To understand this, let us see how a project appraisal ordinarily is performed using a cost–benefit analysis approach. First, this approach requires information on the *flow of expected benefits and costs* of the project in question. Let B_t and C_t represent the streams of benefits and costs in year t, where $t = 0, 1, 2, 3, \ldots, n-1, n$; and n is the expected lifetime of the project. Second, knowledge of the *discount rate*, the rate at which future benefits and costs are discounted, is needed. A more systematic and detailed discussion of discount rate will follow later. For now, let the variable r represent the discount factor, and assume $r > 0$. Finally, given this information, a typical cost–benefit analysis weighs the benefit and cost streams of a project using the following decision rule:

(1) Compute the net present value (NPV) using the formula

$$\text{NPV} = \Sigma \qquad (B_t - C_t)[1/(1 + r)^t]$$

(2) A project should be accepted if its NPV is greater than 0.

The expression $1/(1 + r)^t$ represents the present value of a dollar of *net* benefit coming at the end of t years. The concept of present value will be more fully explained soon. For now, however, from the above relationships it is apparent that provided $r > 0$, the expression $1/(1 + r)^t$ suggests that a dollar of net benefit is valued less, the further it appears in the future. For example, if $r = 0.05$ or 5 percent and $t = 5$, the present value of \$1 of net benefit coming five years from now would be $1/(1.05)^5$, or roughly 78 cents. It can be also shown, with the same discount rate, that the present value of a \$1 net benefit coming ten years from now would be 61 cents, which is less than 78 cents. What economic rationales can be given to people's behavior of discounting future benefits?

According to conventional wisdom, this behavior depicts a simple fact that people generally have a *positive time preference* – that is, other things remaining equal, people prefer their benefit now rather than later. Two explanations are given for this behavior: (a) people tend to discount the future because they are myopic or impatient (Mishan 1988), and (b) people are uncertain about the future (Mishan 1988; Pearce and Nash 1981). Discounting is an important issue in cost–benefit analysis, and it will be further discussed in Section 15.5.

As discussed above, according to the net present value criterion a project is declared acceptable if the *sum* of the *net discounted benefit* over the lifetime of the project is positive. This result is, in fact, consistent with potential Pareto improvement, according to which a project is worthy of consideration provided the net benefit from the project is positive – that is, $B - C > 0$. It is in this sense, then, that potential Pareto improvement serves as the theoretical foundation for cost–benefit analysis that is based on the net present value criterion. However, this also means that a cost–benefit analysis that is based on the net present value criterion has the same pitfalls as the potential Pareto improvement. First, when a net present value criterion is used for a project appraisal, the acceptability of the project is based purely on *economic efficiency*. In other words, a positive net present value means nothing more than an improvement in real income. Second, the net present value criterion does not address the issue of *income distribution*. It focuses exclusively on the project's contribution to aggregate real income of a society. In other words, the impact that the project may have on income distribution is simply ignored.

As is evident from the above discussion, the use of NPV for project appraisal requires three concrete pieces of information, namely estimates of the stream of *benefits* and *costs* and the *discount rate*. Since the net present value criterion is used to assess public projects, these three variables need to be assessed from the perspective of society at large. To fully understand what this actually entails, it would be a worthwhile exercise to compare and contrast how benefits, costs and discount rates are treated in project appraisals in the private and public sectors.

15.4 PRIVATE VERSUS PUBLIC PROJECT APPRAISAL

As noted above, cost–benefit analysis is primarily used for project appraisal in the public sector. An analogous approach used in the private sector is called *financial appraisal* or *capital budgeting*. When the net present value is used, both cost–benefit analysis and financial appraisals follow the same criterion for accepting or rejecting a project. That is, a project is accepted if NPV > 0. However, the two approaches differ significantly in the methods used to estimate the costs and benefits of a project and the choice of the discount rate.

In the private sector, benefit is identified as revenue or cash flow, and it is obtained by simply multiplying market price and quantity. As we have already seen on several occasions, for public projects benefit is measured by the sum of individuals' willingness to pay along the relevant range of the demand curve for a product under consideration. These two approaches to measuring benefit could result in markedly different outcomes. To see this, let us revisit our earlier example of a project designed to control sulfur dioxide emissions from electric power plants located in a certain region. As shown in Figure 15.1, for society at large in any given year, the total benefit from this project is represented by the shaded area. (The value of this shaded area is obtained by summing the willingness to pay along the relevant range $(Q_1$ to $Q_2)$ of the demand curve for environmental quality.) However, if the project's benefit is to be evaluated using willingness to pay, or price at Q_2, the incremental benefit of increasing the environmental quality from Q_1 to Q_2 would be $t_2 (Q_2 - Q_1)$ or the area of the rectangle $Q_1 CBQ_2$. This would have been the case if the project had been viewed as a private concern. Accordingly, in this particular case the benefit estimate by the public sector would be greater than for the private concern by the area of the triangle ABC – the consumers' surplus realized by this particular society as a result of improving its environmental quality from Q_1 to Q_2. In summary, the estimate of benefit from a public project includes the cash flows plus consumers' and producers' surpluses, whereas in the private sector the estimate of benefit from a project includes only cash flows received by private concerns. Thus, unless the size of the project is very small, the difference in the estimates of benefits using these two approaches could be quite significant.

In addition, the approaches used to assess the costs of a project are materially different between these two sectors as well. In the private sectors, the cost estimate of a project is obtained in such a way that it reflects all of the direct costs associated with the implementation and operation of the project in question. In other words, in the private sector, cost estimates include all the monetary expenditures by private firms on acquiring resources to make the project operational. These costs are considered relevant to the extent that they directly affect the interests of the private firms under consideration. Furthermore, these costs are "financial" to the extent that their estimate is based on market prices; therefore, they may or may not reflect opportunity costs. On the other hand, in the public sector, costs are measured in terms of *forgone opportunities* (see Case Study 15.1). Moreover, both the *internal* and the *external* costs of the project should be included. In short, an estimate of a cost for a public project should reflect *social* costs – which include both the internal and the external costs of a project evaluated in terms of opportunity costs.

However, one has to be extremely cautious in evaluating the *social cost* of a project. In an attempt to include all of the relevant internal and external costs, it is quite easy to count some costs more than once. *Double counting* is, therefore, a very serious problem in cost–benefit analysis. To illustrate this let us go back once more to the example dealing with a legislative mandate enacted for the purpose of conserving wilderness. As shown in Figure 15.2, the effect of this project or legislative mandate has been to move this society from its initial position, M, to a new position, N. The new position is associated with less consumption of goods and services and more wilderness. More specifically, the *opportunity cost* of expanding the acreage allotted to wilderness from F_0 to F_1 is measured by a decrease in the production of conventional economic goods and services from G_0 to G_1. To illustrate the problem of double counting, let us suppose that lumber is one of the

CASE STUDY 15.1 ECONOMICS AND THE ENDANGERED SPECIES ACT: COSTS OF SPECIES PROTECTION

Jason F. Shogren

When Congress passed the Endangered Species Act (ESA) of 1973, it was explicit in stating that economic criteria should play no role in species listings or in the designation of critical habitat. It was not until the amendments to the ESA in 1978 that economics first entered into the ESA.

Today it does not take an economist to see that economic issues are critical to the ESA debate. With a large fraction of endangered or threatened species inhabiting private land (75 percent according to a 1993 estimate by The Nature Conservancy), a significant portion of the ESA costs are borne by private property owners, while the ESA benefits accrue to the entire nation. Assessing costs and benefits in endangered species protection, however, is not simple. This exhibit illustrates the difficulties associated with assessing the costs of species preservation. These costs include the transaction costs of species protection, opportunity costs to property owners of restricted property rights, and opportunity costs of public funds used in species recovery.

The best measure of economic loss is *opportunity cost*. Opportunity costs include the reduced economic profit from restricted or altered development projects including agriculture production, timber harvesting, minerals extraction and recreation activities; wages lost by displaced workers who remain unemployed or who are reemployed at lower pay; lower consumer surplus due to higher prices; and lower county property and severance tax revenue.

Opportunity costs have been estimated for a few high-profile, regional ESA conflicts such as the northern spotted owl. One study estimated that an owl recovery plan . . . would decrease economic welfare by between $33 and $46 billion (Montgomery *et al.* 1994). Another study estimated the short-run and long-run opportunity costs of owl protection to Washington and Oregon at $1.2 billion and $450 million (Rubin *et al.* 1991).

Opportunity costs also exist with public programs, because resources devoted to species conservation could have been spent on something else viewed as potentially more valuable to the general public. The US Department of the Interior estimated that the potential direct costs from the recovery plans of all listed species were about $4.6 billion (US Fish and Wildlife Service 1990).

The General Accounting Office (1995) compiled estimates of the predicted direct outlays needed to recover selected species, including the costs of implementing the most important, "high-priority" recovery actions. The total for the 34 plans with complete cost estimates was approximately $700 million.

Of the money actually expended on endangered species recovery by federal and state agencies between 1989 and 1991 (1989 was the first year data were published), over 50 percent was spent on the top ten species including the bald eagle, northern spotted owl, and Florida scrub (Metrick and Weitzman 1996).

In addition to direct public spending, private expenditures add to the cost of ESA implementation. These expenditures include the time and money spent on applications for permits and licenses, redesign of plans, and legal fees. National estimates for these expenditures do not exist for the ESA. As a possible benchmark, private firms fighting over Superfund spent an estimated $4 billion through 1991 (Dixon 1995).

conventional goods that is affected negatively. That is, one effect of the new conservation initiative is a decline in lumber production. How should we measure this as part of the social cost to the conservation initiative? One way to do this would be to impute the market value of the decline in lumber that is directly attributable to this particular conservation initiative. To more clearly show how this can be done, let the variables L_0 and L_1 represent the output of lumber (in cubic feet) before and after the conservation project is implemented. Since we have already postulated that $L_0 > L_1$, $(L_0 - L_1)$ represents the amount in cubic feet by which lumber output is reduced. Then, let P_0 and P_1 represent the real prices of lumber (in cubic feet) before and after the conservation initiative. Other things being equal, we expect that $P_1 > P_0$. Given this information on the changes of the prices and outputs for lumber, we can impute the market value of the decline in lumber that is directly attributable to the wilderness conservation project to be $P_1(L_0 - L_1)$.

However, the decline in lumber from L_0 to L_1 may have additional economy-wide effects. For example, a shortage of lumber may cause an increase in the prices for new housing constructions, and household and office furniture. Should cost increases of this nature be imputed as part of the overall costs for the decline in lumber output? In other words, the social cost of the wilderness conservation project should include not only the market value of the decline in lumber, namely $P_1(L_0 - L_1)$, but also the increases in the costs of new houses and household and office furniture. Although at first glance this idea may seem to make sense, a closer look would suggest that only the market value of the decline in *real* output of lumber should be counted. The *inflationary* impact of lumber shortages on the construction of new houses and office furniture should not be counted as part of the costs of the new conservation initiative. Otherwise, it would amount to counting cost twice: once by the increase in the price of lumber (from P_0 to P_1), and then again by the inflationary or *secondary* effects of this same price increase throughout the economy. It is important not to confuse secondary effects of the above nature with externalities or external effects. Unlike externalities (see Chapter 5), secondary effects are not associated with changes in *real* output. For instance, in the example above, no indication is given that the increase in price for lumber is causing a decline in new housing starts and/or the output of the furniture industry.

On the other hand, if the decrease in lumber production has caused an actual decline in new housing construction and/or the output of the furniture industry, then the market value of these real output effects should be a part of the overall cost attributable to the wilderness conservation project. To sum up, in imputing the costs of a project, all *real output* effects should be included. However, in cost–benefit analysis, special care should be taken not to include inflationary or secondary effects of price changes as part of the cost of a project. Otherwise, for reasons already stated above, we will be double-counting costs.

A third and final difference between public and private project appraisal is the choice of the *discount rate*. Both the private and public sectors use positive discount rates; that is, $r > 0$. The difference is that, in general, the public or *social* discount rate, r_s, is lower than the *private* discount rate, r_p. There are two major reasons for this difference. First, individuals (or private concern) will not view the future in the same way as society, which represents the collective concern of individuals. In general, individuals are seen as being selfish and shortsighted (Mishan 1988). They seem to be mostly concerned with their own welfare in the present or in the very near future. Hence they do not assign much importance to benefits that might be forthcoming in the future. On the other hand, the public sector, which represents society as a whole, is believed to have a longer-term perspective. Thus, the discount rate used in the public project should be lower than that used in the private sector. Of course, as we will see, the effect of this will be to shift investments from the private to the public sector. The second argument is based on the assumption that individuals are more *uncertain* about the future than society at large. After all, for all practical purposes society can be viewed as having an eternal life. What this means is that private projects are exposed to more risk while public projects are virtually immune. Under this circumstance, efficient allocation of societal resources would dictate that a relatively higher discount rate should be applied to private investment projects (Pearce and Nash 1981).

A pertinent question, then, is how big is the difference between social and private discount rates? From past empirical work, both in the United States and elsewhere, the difference between these two discount rates can range between 3 and 5 percentage points. For social projects, although no consensus view exists, a discount rate of 4 percent (net of inflation) is generally recommended. On the other hand, the private discount rate (net of inflation) could be as high as 10 percent. If this is the case, would a difference of 3 to 5 percentage points matter much? From the viewpoint of resource allocation over time, the answer to this question depends on the *time horizon* of the project under consideration. For project appraisals with short time duration – with a life of no more than twenty years or so – a small variation in the discount rate could have a significant effect on the decision to either accept or reject a given project(s) using the NPV criterion. *On the other hand, if the time duration of the projects under consideration is long, say over fifty years or more, what matters will not be the discount rate, but the very fact that discounting is done at some positive rate, $r > 0$.* To see exactly how project appraisal is sensitive to small changes in the discount rate, depending on the time horizon of the projects under consideration, we need to closely examine the NPV formula:

$$\text{NPV} = \Sigma \qquad (B_t - C_t)[1/(1 + r)^t]$$

where, as discussed earlier, the expression $B_t - C_t$ is the net benefit per year, $(1 + r)^t$ is the discount factor for any given year, and $1/(1 + r)^t$ is the present value of a dollar of net benefit coming at the end of t years.

First, the denominator of the above formula, $(1 + r)^t$ – which is known as the *discount factor* – measures the factor by which a dollar's worth of net benefit at the end of a specific point in time is discounted. For example, if the value of the discount factor is 2 when $t = 10$, a dollar's worth of net benefit expected to accrue at the end of the tenth year of a project life is discounted by a factor of 2. The inverse of the discount factor, $1/(1 + r)^t$, measures the *present value* – how much a dollar's worth of net benefit at the end of a specific point in time is worth today. Thus, a discount factor of 2 suggests a present value of 50 cents. The discount factor, as shown in the above NPV formula, depends on two variables, namely t and r. The higher the discount rate, r, and the longer the time horizon, t, the larger the value of the discount factor. In other words, the discount factor increases as r and/or t increases. This is illustrated using Figures 15.3a and 15.3b. In both figures, it is clearly evident that for a given discount rate, the discount factor increases with an increase in time, t. For example, in Figure 15.3a, where the discount rate is held constant at 5 percent, the value of the discount factor increases from 1 to 80.7 over a period of ninety years. Similarly, as shown in Figure 15.3b, when the interest rate is 10 percent, over the same time interval – 90 years – the value of the discount factor increases from 1 to 5,313.

These results on their own are neither surprising nor particularly interesting. *What will be more intriguing will be to observe the rate at which the discount factor increases over time for a given discount rate.* When the discount rate is 5 percent – Figure 15.3a – in the first fifteen years the interest factor grows from 1 to 2.07 – slightly more than double. In the second fifteen years (year 15 to 30) the discount factor increases from 2.07 to 4.32 – again slightly more than doubled. Thus, when the interest rate is 5 percent, it takes the same number of years, fifteen years to be exact, to double the discount factor from 1 to 2 as it does to raise it from 2 to 4. It follows, then, that every fifteen years the discount factor is growing geometrically, as for 2, 4, 8, 16,

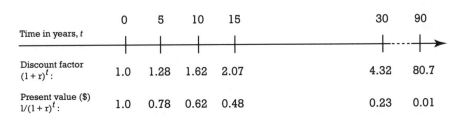

Figure 15.3a **The discount factor when $r = 0.05$**

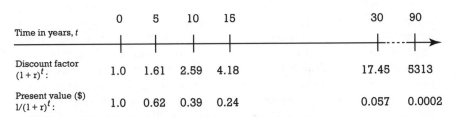

Figure 15.3b **The discount factor when $r = 0.10$**

etc. That is, the discount factor is growing *exponentially* over time. Similarly, when the interest rate is 10 percent (Figure 15.3b), in the first fifteen years the interest factor grows from 1 to 4.18 – slightly more than quadruple. In the second fifteen years (years 15 to 30), the discount factor increases from 4.18 to 17.45 – again slightly more than quadruple. Thus, when the interest rate is 10 percent, it takes about fifteen years to quadruple the discount factor from 1 to 4, as it does from 4 to 16. It follows, then, that approximately every fifteen years the discount factor is growing geometrically, as for 4, 16, 64, 256, and so on. In other words, the discount factor is growing *exponentially* over time.

Thus, from the above discussion it is clear that regardless of what the interest rate is, the discount factor increases exponentially over time. This is very significant because it clearly demonstrates the pervasive nature of discounting. To see this, note that in Figures 15.3a and 15.3b the discount factor is inversely related to the present value of a dollar, $1/(1 + r)^t$. If, as we have observed above, the discount factor increases over time exponentially, then *the present value of a dollar tends to converge to its lower limit of zero within a finite time, t*. For example, as shown in Figures 15.3a and 15.3b the present value of a dollar is reduced virtually to zero ($0.01 and $0.0002) within 90 years – less than one potential human lifetime. This is an extremely important result since it suggests that *when the time duration of a project under consideration is fairly long, the difference between private and social discount rates that are normally within the range of 3 to 5 percent is irrelevant*. This is because discounting reduces benefits coming in the far distant future to virtually zero within a finite time, as long as the discount rate is positive. As will be discussed in the next section, this has far-reaching economic and ethical implications.

On the other hand, for projects with a relatively shorter life span, a difference of 3 to 5 percentage points in the discount rate used to evaluate the projects would matter a great deal. In general, other things being equal, the greater the difference between the private and social discount rates, the more favorable this would be for projects with a shorter life span; that is, private projects.

15.5 DISCOUNTING AND INTERGENERATIONAL EQUITY

In our discussions in the previous section, we noted that projects dealing with the conservation of environmental assets (such as coastal wetlands, wilderness, national parks, estuaries, etc.) are highly sensitive to discounting. Moreover, while the decision about project appraisal is done on the basis of the preferences of the current generation, a particular feature of environmental costs and benefits is that they often accrue to people in generations yet to come. Under these circumstances, since discounting implies that gains and losses to society are valued less the more distant they are in the future, can the use of a positive discount rate be ethically justifiable? What restraints, if any, should the current generation voluntarily accept for the benefit of the future? As would be expected, even within the economics profession the responses to this question vary widely depending on one's point of view about humankind's future predicament.

For many economists, the use of a positive discount rate *per se* is not an issue of significance. It simply reflects that people have positive time preference; that is considered as given. For most economists, what is important in appraising any project is the appropriate discount rate to be used. More specifically, in the case of public projects, which includes most projects of an environmental nature, the *social* discount rate should be used. For reasons that have been discussed already, in most instances the social discount rate tends to be smaller than its private counterpart. In this sense, then, the preference of social to private discount rates alone constitutes an intentional allowance to the issue of distributional fairness among generations. However, will this be adequate? In other words, since discounting, however small, implies *unequal* weighting of costs and benefits over time, can there be distributional fairness when the discount rate is not reduced to zero? Those professionals who uphold the position that intergenerational fairness need not demand a zero discount rate use the following line of reasoning to support their position.

First, generations do overlap. The current population includes three generations: grandparents, parents and children. Parents care for their children and grandchildren. Current children care for their children and grandchildren, etc. Thus, this chain of generational caring clearly indicates that the *preference function* of the current generation takes the interest of the future generation into account. Second, to argue for a zero social discount rate when market conditions indicate otherwise would lead to an inefficient allocation of resources; the current generation would be operating inside its production possibility frontier. Concern for intergenerational fairness can be addressed through public policy measures that have no effect on prices, such as some sort of lump-sum tax. In other words, addressing the concern for intergenerational equity need not impoverish the current generation *unnecessarily*. Last but not least, historically the average wealth (income) of the current generation has been higher than that of its immediate predecessor. Given this historical trend of upward mobility in standard of living, why should the current generation voluntarily accept such a condition (such as zero discount rate), thinking that it might benefit the future? This sentiment is eloquently expressed by Baumol (1968: 800), a prominent economist: "in our economy if past trends and current developments are any guide, a redistribution to provide more for the future may be described as a Robin Hood activity stood on its head – it takes from the poor to give to the rich. Average real per capita income a century hence is likely to be a sizable multiple of its present value. Why should I give up part of my income to help support someone else with an income several times my own?"

On the other hand, there are a few economists (Mishan 1988; Sen 1982) who oppose the use of positive discount rates when appraising public projects (especially projects designed to conserve the amenities of the natural environment). The reasoning behind this position is that, as shown by Figures 15.3a and 15.3b, for projects with long time horizons discounting effectively reduces future benefits and costs to zero after a finite number of years. This has the effect of favoring projects associated with either short-term benefits (such as development projects instead of projects designed to conserve environmental amenities) or long-term costs (such as nuclear plant). In either case, the well-being of the future generation is put at risk. Given this, some economists argue that intergenerational fairness justifies no discounting at all. The emphasis should instead be on what rights are passed between generations. This consideration will bring *equity* back into neoclassical analysis in such a way that the focus will be on resolving the contradiction between efficiency and the concern for the future (Norgaard and Howarth 1992).

15.6 CHAPTER SUMMARY

- The assessment of the benefits arising from environmental projects was addressed in the previous chapter. In this chapter, the various relevant concepts of costs were discussed in detail. Cost–benefit analysis is one of the most widely used techniques for appraising environmental projects in the public domain.
- Both costs and benefits have to be estimated in certain ways, and evaluated from the perspective of society as a whole.
- In considering the costs of an environmental project, social cost is the relevant factor. Both the internal and the external costs of the project should be carefully considered using the opportunity cost concept to assess them.
- In an attempt to include all of the relevant internal and external costs, it is quite easy to count some costs more than once, and this *double counting* is a serious problem in assessing the costs of environmental projects, forcing one to be cautious in estimating social costs.
- Once both the social benefits and costs of a project are evaluated, the next step in project appraisal is to develop a criterion (a norm) for weighing the benefits of a project against its costs: cost–benefit analysis.
- For an appraisal of public projects, the fundamental normative (welfare) criterion of benefit–cost analysis is based on *potential Pareto improvement*. That is, the sum of the net discounted benefits over the lifetime of the project (or net present value) must be positive.
- This criterion leads to the economically efficient outcome, but positive net present value focuses only on the project's contribution to aggregate real income. No explicit consideration is made of the effect that the project may have on income distribution.
- The choice of the *discount rate* is critical when the net present value method is used as a norm for project appraisal. For public projects (which include most environmental projects) the standard procedure is to use the *social* discount rate, which is lower than the "private" discount rate because, in general, compared to individuals, society is more certain and less myopic about environmental projects that extend over a long time horizon.

- However, when the time horizon of a project under consideration is fairly long, as is the case for many environmental projects, the difference between private and social discount rates that are within the range 3 to 5 percent is *irrelevant*. This is because discounting reduces benefits coming in the far distant future to virtually zero within a finite time, *as long as the discounting rate is positive*. What matters is the very fact that a positive discount rate is used.

- Since discounting implies that gains and losses to society are valued less the more distant they are in the future, can the use of a positive discount rate be ethically justified?

- This question points to the unsettling issue of *intergenerational equity*. Furthermore, since the choice of discount rate is made entirely by the current generation, the responsibility to bring a resolution to this ethical dilemma cannot be shifted to future generations. What is significant is the one-sided nature of this intergenerational dependency.

- What is unsettling here is that, in principle, the current generation could take actions that have the potential to adversely affect the well-being of future generations without any fear of retaliation. Should we care (on moral and ethical grounds) about the well-being of future generations? The answer to this question is clearly beyond the realm of economics unless, of course, the current generation wishes to identify itself with posterity to such an extent that its preference function is markedly influenced. If this is to happen then, as Boulding (1993: 306) put it, "posterity has a voice, even if it does not have a vote; and in this sense, if it can influence votes, it has votes too."

---

review and discussion questions

1 Briefly identify the following concepts: "actual" Pareto improvement, "potential" Pareto improvement, capital budgeting, double counting, net discount benefit, private discount rates, social discount rates, the discount factor, positive time preference.

2 State *True*, *False* or *Uncertain* and explain why.

 (a) Double counting is a potentially serious problem often encountered in assessing both social and private projects.

 (b) Addressing the concern for intergenerational fairness need not impoverish the current generation.

3 Carefully explain the differences and/or similarities between the following pairs of concepts:

 (a) capital budgeting and cost–benefit analysis;

 (b) net present value criterion and potential Pareto improvement;

 (c) private and social discount rates.

4   The State of Michigan has a surplus of $200 million in its budget for the fiscal year just ended. Several proposals have been examined for the use of this money, two of which are emerging as leading candidates for serious consideration. One of the favored projects is to use the entire surplus money for statewide road repairs. This project is assumed to have an expected life of ten years. The alternative is a proposal to invest the entire $200 million in a long-overdue environmental cleanup. The table shows estimates of the flow of the net benefits for these two projects:

Project 1: road repair		Project 2: environmental cleanup	
Years	Benefit/year	Years	Benefit/year
1–5	$40 million	1–5	$5 million
6–10	$15 million	6–10	$15 million
		11–20	$25 million

(a) Using the net present value (NPV) approach, evaluate the two projects using a 5 percent and 10 percent discount rate.

(b) Would it make any difference which discount rate is used in the final selection between these two projects? Why, or why not?

(c) If the discount rate is reduced to zero, Project 2 will be automatically chosen. Why? Does this represent evidence that environmental projects are sensitive to discount rate? Explain.

REFERENCES AND FURTHER READING

Baumol, W. J. (1968) "On the Social Rate of Discount," *American Economic Review* 58: 788–802.

Boulding, K. E. (1993) "The Economics of the Coming Spaceship Earth," in H. E. Daly and K. N. Townsend (eds.) *Valuing the Earth: Economics, Ecology, Ethics*, Cambridge, Mass.: MIT Press.

Dixon, L. (1995) "The Transaction Costs Generated by Superfund's Liability Approach," in R. Revesz and R. Stewart (eds.), *Analyzing Superfund: Economic, Science, and Law*, Washington, D.C.: Resources for the Future.

General Accounting Office (1995) Correspondence to Representative Don Young on estimated recovery costs of endangered species, Washington, D.C., B-270461.

Metrick, A. and Weitzman, M. (1996) "Patterns of behavior in endangered species preservation," *Land Economics* 72: 1–16.

Mishan, E. J. (1982) *Cost–Benefit Analysis*, 3rd edn., London: George Allen & Unwin.

—— (1988) *Cost–Benefit Analysis*, 4th edn., London: George Allen & Unwin.

Montgomery, C., Brown, G., Jr. and Darius, M. (1994) "The Marginal Cost of Species Preservation: The Northern Spotted Owl," *Journal of Environmental Economics and Management* 26: 111–28.

Nature Conservancy (1993) *Perspective on Species Imperilment: A Report from the Natural Heritage Data Center Network*, Arlington, Va.: The Nature Conservancy.

Norgaard, R. B. and Howarth, R. B. (1992) "Economics, Ethics, and the Environment," in J. M. Hollander (ed.) *The Energy–Environment Connection*, Washington, D.C.: Island Press.

Pearce, D. W. and Nash, C. A. (1981) *The Social Appraisal of Projects: A Text in Cost–Benefit Analysis*, New York: John Wiley.

Rubin, J. Helfand, G. and Loomis, J. (1991), "A Benefit–Cost Analysis of the Northern Spotted Owl," *Journal of Forestry*, 89: 25–30.

Sen, A. K. (1982) "Approaches to the Choice of Discount Rates for Social Benefit–Cost Analysis," in R. Lind, K. J. Arrow, G. Corey *et al.* (eds.) *Discounting for Time and Risk in Energy Policy*, Washington, D.C.: Resources for the Future.

Shogren, J. F. (1997) "Economics and the Endangered Species Act," *Endangered Species Update*, School of Natural Resources and Environment, University of Michigan.

US Fish and Wildlife Service (1990) *Report to Congress: Endangered and Threatened Species Recovery Program*, Washington, D.C.: US Government Printing Office.

part seven

BASIC ELEMENTS OF THE ECONOMIC THEORIES OF RENEWABLE AND NONRENEWABLE RESOURCES

In addition to its function as a repository for waste (discussed in Part Six), the natural environment is also a source of food and other extractive materials essential for the human economy. Part Seven examines the economics of natural resources that are either biological or geological by their nature and origin.

Chapter 16 examines economic theories and management strategies applicable to biological resources such as fish, forests, and other plant and animal varieties. Biological resources have one distinctive feature that is important for consideration here. That is, while these resources are capable of self-regeneration, they can be irreparably damaged if they are exploited beyond a certain critical threshold. Hence, their use is limited to a certain critical zone. In Chapter 16 only the basic elements of the economics of renewable resources are discussed, and with a primary focus on fishery.

Chapter 17 concerns the economics of nonrenewable resources – resources that either exist in fixed supply or are renewable only on a geological timescale and therefore for all practical purposes are assumed to have zero regenerative capacity. Examples of these resources include metallic minerals like iron, aluminum, copper and uranium; and nonmetallic minerals like fossil fuels, clay, sand, salt and phosphates.

As evident from these examples, nonrenewable resources can be classified into two broad categories. The first group includes those resources that are recyclable, such as metallic minerals. The second group consists of nonrecyclable resources, such as fossil fuels.

Chapter 17 offers only a brief introduction to the economics of non-renewable resources. An expanded treatment of this subject requires the use of mathematical models and concepts that are beyond the scope of this book. Hence, the objective is to provide the essential elements of economic theory of nonrenewable resources in a clear and concise manner with an emphasis on understanding the public policy recommendations that are often advocated by economists regarding the management (use) of nonrenewable resources.

chapter sixteen

FUNDAMENTAL PRINCIPLES OF THE ECONOMICS OF RENEWABLE RESOURCES:
The Case of Fishery

---

learning objectives

After reading this chapter you will be familiar with the following:

- basic features of renewable resources;
- a general framework for understanding the basic factors affecting the natural growth rate of the population or the biomass of biological resources such as fish and wildlife;
- general characteristics of the natural growth function of a fishery population;
- the concept of natural or ecological equilibrium biomass or population size;
- derivation of the production function of fishery;
- understanding why renewable resources, such as fishery, may be potentially destructible;
- the economics of fishery management;
- regulation of fishery:

  - the rationale for regulating the fishery;
  - tax on fishing effort;
  - tax on fish catch;

- some important limitations of the steady-state bioeconomic model of fishery.

The natural processes that produce resource renewal do not operate automatically. They are subject to human interference and disruption as well as to the vagaries of nature. This fact becomes even more salient when effective property rights governing access to the resource do not exist or are not enforced. Resources that are not governed by well-defined access rules are called common-property resources. Because no private or public sector agent controls the disposition of the stock, users of the resource must pay only the cost of harvesting it. Because the price is lower than it would be if the asset value of the stock were taken into account, the resource will be over-exploited, and there will be inadequate incentives for resource conservation.

(Working Group on Population Growth and Economic
Development 1986: 18–19)

16.1 INTRODUCTION

In Chapters 10–13 we covered topics relating to the economics of the natural environment with specific reference to the use of the environment for the disposal of waste products from human activities. This is a relevant economic issue because the environment has a limited but not necessarily fixed capacity to assimilate waste – which is subject to the natural biological processes of decomposition. Moreover, the natural environment cannot degrade all wastes with the same efficiency. Thus, because of these naturally imposed limitations, exceeding the assimilative capacity of the environment involves economic costs (these include ecological damage) to society that should be carefully considered.

In this chapter and the next (Chapter 17), attempts will be made to examine two other uses of the natural environment. More specifically, the focus will be on understanding the extent to which the natural environment can be used as a source of *renewable* and *nonrenewable* resources. This requires, as will be evident shortly, careful considerations of ecological, biological, geological, socioeconomic and technological factors. Furthermore, the management of renewable resources and exploitation of nonrenewable resources present a dynamic problem that is dependent on time.

This chapter examines the basic economic theories of renewable resources – resources that are capable of regenerating themselves within a relatively short period of time, provided the natural environment in which they are residing is not unduly disturbed. Examples include various *biological* resources such as plants, fish, wildlife populations and forests. Renewable resources also include *flow* resources such as solar radiation, wind, water streams and tides, which are not at all considered in this chapter. Furthermore, this chapter deals only with the economics of renewable resources as it applies to fishery. Even the discussion of fishery is kept at a rudimentary level, using only a simple model so that fundamental points common to all fisheries can be analyzed. The objective of the chapter is to use a simple fishery model that provides certain fundamental principles common not only to all fisheries but also to the management of biological resources in general.

16.2 THE NATURAL GROWTH FUNCTION OF BIOLOGICAL RESOURCES

Biological resources such as fish and wildlife populations are renewable because they are living creatures that reproduce, grow and die. As discussed in Chapter 4, the reproduction, growth and death of these resources are largely governed by natural processes involving complex interactions and interrelationships between living and nonliving matters, including humans.

To speak of the "management" of biological resources suggests the use (harvesting) of these resources for human ends on a sustainable basis. This requires, first and foremost, information on the nature of the reproduction and growth capacity of the biological resources in question. However, obtaining this kind of information is very difficult, given that there are so many unknowns in the biology and ecology of the resource populations under consideration. Despite this, however, in recent years advances have been made in developing models useful for assessing and projecting the growth of the population of biological resources relevant for harvesting strategy. In most of these models the following factors are considered to be critical for assessing the allowable population for harvest: the initial population size, the age and sex mix, the spatial and temporal distribution of the resource under consideration, and the natural mortality rate. Models with a specification of this nature have been vital in the empirical working and management practices of fishery and wildlife, in general.

In what follows, S_t is the population (number) or the biomass (aggregate weight) of a biological resource measured in some standard unit at a point in time t, Δt is the time interval, generally a short period of time measured in months or years, and $S_{(t+\Delta t)}$ is the population or biomass after a time interval Δt has elapsed. Note that S_t is a *stock* concept as it represents the population measured at a point in time. This stock is composed of a population of a biological species composed of different sex, ages, sizes and weight. $S_{(t+\Delta t)}$, on the other hand, is a *flow* concept since it indicates the change in the stock over a specified interval time Δt. The change in the stock could result from a combination of biological and ecological and socioeconomic factors: natural reproduction through birth, growth of the biomass of the existing population, natural death, and predator–prey relationships, where the predators include humans.

Then, given the general features of biological resources (i.e., new stocks are created by the process of self-regeneration), the following simple relationship may be postulated:

$$S_{(t+\Delta t)} = S_t + g(S_t, \theta)\Delta t \tag{16.1}$$

where $g(S_t, \theta)$ is a function representing the natural growth of the population biomass per unit of time. Note that this natural growth function is assumed to depend on the size of the initial population size, S_t, and the variable θ, which represents factors like the age distributions, sex compositions, other unique biological traits of the resources under consideration, and the environmental factors vitally important in determining the rate of growth of

338 ECONOMIC THEORIES OF RESOURCES

the population biomass, especially natural mortality rate. Note also that the expression $g(S_t, \theta)\Delta t$, on the right-hand side of equation (16.1), indicates the *total* increase in biomass during the time interval $[t, (t + \Delta t)]$.

If we assume θ to be an exogenously determined variable and, as such, capable of being treated as a constant parameter (i.e., under normal conditions, in the long run, the factors accounted by this variable on the average tend to even out or self-stabilize), then the increment in the biomass of the initial population, S_t, during the time interval $[t, (t + \Delta t)]$, can be expressed as:

$$[S_{(t + \Delta t)} - S_t] = \Delta S_t = g(S_t)\Delta t \qquad (16.2)$$

Or, if we divide both sides of equation (16.2) by Δt, the growth of the stock or biomass *per unit time* would be given by

$$\Delta S_t/\Delta t = g(S_t) \qquad (16.3)$$

Equation (16.3) simply states that under normal conditions (i.e., if the variable θ is held constant), the *growth* of the biological resource per unit time depends solely on the size of the initial population. Note that this growth in biomass or population is *net* of natural mortality, since this factor is already accounted by the variable θ. Thus, the growth function $g(S_t)$ represents a *net* addition to the natural size of the underlying population or biomass per unit time. In other words, it represents the natural growth function of the biological resource in question. It is important to note that the fact the stock, S, grows over time suggests that the size of the stock is a function of time. If this *dynamic* feature of biological resources is to be captured, then the growth function needs to be respecified as $g[S(t)]$. To the extent this is not done, therefore, equation (16.3) is a static model that denotes merely the growth of stock per unit time without accounting for the dynamic change in the stock over time. Even under this simplifying assumed condition, it would not be an exaggeration to say that a good understanding of the nature and characteristics of this growth function is one of the key factors needed for a "proper" management of biological resources.

To ensure that the above notations and equation (16.3) are clearly understood, let us use the following simple and purely hypothetical example. Suppose that a given county claims that it has a deer population of 3 million head. On the basis of past experience, the department in charge of wildlife management for this county claims that, on average, the population growth (net of natural predators) of the deer population (in terms of head count) has been about 100,000 biannually (every other year). Given these estimates of the initial population size and the rate of the biannual recruitment, what is the annual growth of the deer population for this county?

From the above data we know that S_0, the estimate of the initial (that is, when $t = 0$) deer population, is 3,000,000; Δt is 2 years; and $S_{(0 + 2)} = S_2 = 3,100,000$ deer – the deer population two years after the initial period. Note that this is after accounting for natural mortality. Given this, the annual growth of the deer population for this county can be calculated using equation (16.3). That is,

$$g(S_t) = \Delta S/\Delta t = [S_{(0+2)} - S_0]/\Delta t = 100,000/2 = 50,000 \text{ deer}$$

What could be the practical value of this estimate? Specifically, the county could use it to decide on the number of deer-hunting licenses to issue annually. For instance, if the county wished to maintain the present population of deer, which is 3,000,000, it would limit the number of licenses to 50,000 deer – the annual natural growth of the deer population. Of course, this is a very simple example and it does not address the complicated issues that wildlife game managers actually face. For example, an increase in head count is not the same as an increase in biomass. The biomass depends on the size distribution of the population (i.e., more head of a certain size of deer may actually yield a smaller biomass less capable of reproducing itself). Furthermore, if the age and sex mix of the deer population is to be maintained, the license should account for these factors. In other words, game managers would not allow a random killing of 50,000 deer.

For the rest of this chapter, fish are going to be the biological resource of interest. In the analysis that follows, no attempt will be made to differentiate between different types of fish or marine animals. Instead, for simplicity, fish is assumed to represent all marine animals, such as salmon, cod, tuna, lobster, oysters and whales. The objective here is not to develop a natural growth model specific to a single species of fish or marine animals. It is to develop a growth model that is broadly representative of marine animal life in general. This type of biological growth model for fish and other marine animals will then be interfaced with economic models to generate a hybrid model commonly referred to as a *bioeconomic* model. It is the systematic derivation of this type of model that will occupy a good part of the rest of this chapter. Let us start by first developing a model that attempts to capture the general characteristics of fishery populations.

16.3 GENERAL CHARACTERISTICS OF THE NATURAL GROWTH FUNCTION OF FISHERY POPULATIONS

Theoretical and empirical works involving fishery, and in some cases forestry and wildlife, often postulate that the natural growth function can be closely approximated by what is known as the *logistic function*. This function assumes that instantaneous growth rate of the biomass or population of a biological resource such as fish follows a distribution shown by a parabola as in Figure 16.1. Consistent with the discussion in the previous section, this figure depicts the relationships between the growth in biomass or population per unit time, $g(S_t)$, and the size of the biomass, S_t, if all other factors, θ, affecting the growth of the biomass are held constant. It is also important to note again that the growth in biomass is considered to be net of natural mortality.

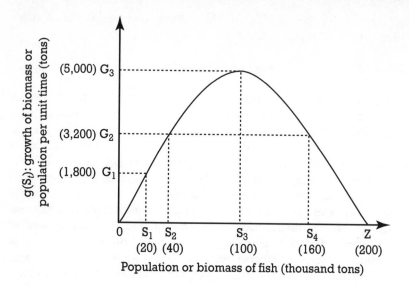

Figure 16.1 **Natural growth curve for fishery population**

The basic characteristic of the logistic model is that, as shown in Figure 16.1, the population biomass will tend to increase until it has reached the limit of the *carrying capacity* of the environment. This carrying capacity is attained when the level of population reaches Z. *The general implication of this observation is that in a stable (i.e., constant θ) and unmanaged ecosystem, over time the biomass of the fish population in question tends to gravitate toward a definite maximum size, Z.* As will be explained shortly, Z represents a biological *equilibrium* biomass or population.

Further observation of this logistic model reveals the following relationships between population size and the growth of biomass per unit time: First, the growth of the biomass per unit time is zero when the population size is zero or when the population size reaches its natural equilibrium at Z. That is, $g(0) = 0$, and $g(Z) = 0$. However, it is important to note that although the general model (or Figure 16.1) does not show this, in many instances the extinction of biological species (including fish populations) may occur before the population actually plummets to zero. Accordingly, it is natural for $g(S_m)$ to equal 0, where $S_m > 0$ and S_m represents the extinction threshold or critical zone. In other words, for a biomass or population of less than S_m, the net growth would be negative – leading toward the inevitable extinction of the species under consideration. The important implication of this is that for biological species such as fish, a small population could be quite susceptible to a sudden and unexpected demographic accident or ecological perturbation. In essence this affirms the stochastic nature of fish populations in general.

Second, for population sizes between 0 and Z, the increase in biomass per unit time will be positive – that is, $g(S_t) > 0$. When the population size is small, the biomass is growing at a progressively higher level since food and space, among other factors, and other environmental considerations are not constraining factors at this stage. In Figure 16.1, this will be the case for the population size between 0 and S_3. For example, when the total population biomass is S_1 (20,000 tons), the biomass is expected to grow at a rate of G_1, or 1,800 tons per unit time (let us say a year). The rate of growth per unit time increases to 3,200 tons when the underlying population size is allowed to increase to 40,000 tons, S_2. This trend of increasing growth will continue until the population size S_3 (100,000 tons) is reached.

At S_3, the growth per unit of time of the population biomass will attain its maximum, which is assumed to be 5,000 tons. Beyond this point, however, as the population biomass increases, space and food on a per capita basis will be reduced. Thus, although the total population biomass will continue to grow, i.e. show a positive increment, the rate of growth of the biomass per unit time will continue to decrease. For example, when the population biomass increases from S_3 (100,000 tons) to S_4 (160,000 tons), the rate of growth of the total biomass per unit time declines from G_3 (5,000 tons) to G_2 (3,200 tons). Eventually, the rate of growth of the biomass declines to zero, and this will occur when the population size reaches its biological limit or carrying capacity, Z. Assuming all the exogenous factors affecting the natural growth curve (i.e. θ) are held constant, the population size cannot extend beyond Z (or 200,000 tons). If this were to occur, the natural mortality rate would tend to exceed the rate of natural growth because of space and food shortages. Hence at this point the net rate of growth of the biomass or the population would become negative. This process will continue until the population size was restored back to level Z. It is for this reason that a population such as Z is referred to as the *natural* or *biological equilibrium* population size; and, in the absence of harvesting by humans, this will constitute the population size that will tend to persist in the long run. Note also that the natural equilibrium is a *stable* equilibrium, since it is only at this point that *growth is equal to natural mortality; hence, there is no net growth in biomass.* Any tendency to deviate from this point in either direction will be offset by either a net positive or a net negative growth in biomass that will restore the population size to the level of its natural equilibrium.

Despite its simplicity, from the viewpoint of biological resource management the logistic model discussed above has the following implications: First, because of their self-regenerative capacity, within certain limits *it is possible to harvest biological resources (such as fish, wildlife and forestry) while maintaining the size of the underlying population.* Hence, the natural growth curve can tell us, for each population size, the maximum amount that can be harvested without depleting the underlying stock of the resource under consideration. For example, in Figure 16.1, if the population size is S_2 (40,000 tons), a harvest of G_2 or 3,200 tons of biomass can be sustained on a regular basis and the population size will remain at S_2 indefinitely. This implies a harvest rate of 8 percent (3,200/40,000) per unit time (say a year) on a sustained basis. On the other hand, if the underlying population size is S_3 (100,000 tons), G_3 or 5,000 tons of biomass can be harvested on a sustained basis – a harvest rate of 5 percent on a regular basis.

Second, since there are an infinite number of population sizes, each capable of being harvested on a sustained basis, along a given natural growth curve the feasible set of alternative choices in managing biological resources are practically *infinite*.

So far, in developing the concept of the natural growth curve I have purposely avoided the effects that socioeconomic factors may have on population equilibrium. In this sense, the natural growth curve is a purely biological concept. However, unless the resource is considered totally useless, humans' interest concerning this resource cannot be ignored. When humans choose to intervene, they then become another predator with the potential of disturbing the natural population equilibrium. Hence, the primary objective of the management of biological resources is to find the proper balance between the natural growth rate of the biomass of a given species and the mortality rate of the same species due to exploitation by humans. In other words, the relevant growth model has to incorporate both the biological and the economic factors relevant to the resource in question. This is the essence of a *bioeconomic model*, which is the subject of the next section.

16.4 THE PRODUCTION FUNCTION OF FISHERY: A STEADY-STATE BIOECONOMIC EQUILIBRIUM MODEL

As stated earlier, the natural growth curve – as seen in Figure 16.1 – shows us, for each population size, the maximum amount that can be harvested on a sustained basis without affecting the underlying population size. Thus, during any given period of time (say one year), if humans remove an amount equal to the natural annual increase, then the population size will remain unchanged. This pattern of harvest could, therefore, be repeated each year indefinitely, and may be termed the *sustainable* harvest or catch. However, note that there are *infinite* numbers of sustainable harvests along the natural growth curve, each corresponding to a different population size. The question is, then, which one of this infinite number of choices is most desirable?

If one addresses the above question from a purely biophysical viewpoint, the most desirable choice would be the one that maximizes the biomass that can be harvested on a sustainable basis. In other words, the management strategy involves maintaining the population size consistent with the *maximum* level of sustainable harvest or, as it is more popularly called, maximum sustainable yield (MSY). For example, in Figure 16.1 the maximum level of sustainable harvest is G_3 or 5,000 tons; and it is attained when the population size is S_3 (100,000 tons).

Can MSY be used as a guide for fisheries management? Before I answer this question, first and foremost it is important to note that MSY is a purely physical concept. It informs us of the maximum amount of a renewable resource that can be harvested on a sustainable basis after full consideration of the relevant biophysical factors affecting the natural growth function of the resource in question. What is important to note is that this decision is reached without any consideration of the cost (in terms of labor, capital and other materials) and benefit of the harvest in question. For example, in Figure 16.1 the maximum sustainable harvest is 5,000 tons, as we have seen. In reaching this conclusion, no considerations are made about either the *cost* of harvesting this amount of fish biomass or the total social *benefit* (as measured by the market value) to be derived from this level of harvest. What if the total cost of harvesting the 5,000 tons exceeds its market value? In that case, a strict cost–benefit consideration will render the MSY uneconomical. However, this may be an unlikely situation. Let us, then, consider a different and more viable scenario. Is it possible that society can harvest less than 5,000 tons (the maximum sustainable yield) and obtain a *net* benefit (total benefit − total cost) that is greater than at the maximum sustainable yield harvest level? If this is at all viable, then the maximum sustainable yield (MSY) may not always represent an economic optimum (where net benefit is the maximum). More on this later. In fact, there is only one situation in which a maximum sustainable resource management will certainly be expected to yield a result consistent with an economic optimum. This occurs if, and only if, the cost of labor, capital and other materials used for harvest is assumed to be zero – a rather unrealistic situation.

Hence, an alternative approach, the bioeconomic perspective, suggests that the choice of the most desirable sustainable harvest should depend on the interactions of three key variables: the nature of the underlying natural growth function; the specific size of the fish population; and the amount of economic resources used for harvesting. In fishery economics, the phrase *fishing effort* is used to describe a composite economic factor (such as labor, capital, energy and other raw material) used in fish harvesting activities. Clearly, "effort" encompasses a wide-ranging and heterogeneous group of factors of production, such as trawlers of different sizes, various kinds of fishing nets and fishers' time with varying fishing skills. As such, it is an *index* of factor inputs with significant measurement difficulties.

In general, we would expect that for a given population size, the higher the level of effort, the larger will be the harvest or catch; and given the level of effort, the larger the population size, the larger will be the catch. To show these relationships among the levels of catch, effort and population size more systematically, let us define the production function of a fishery as follows:

$$H = f(S, E) \tag{16.4a}$$

where H is the fish catch or harvest due to human exploitation, E is the level of fishing effort, and S is the stock or population size.

This production relationship simply states that the catch or harvest at any point in time depends on the level of effort applied, E, and the stock or population size, S. To keep our analysis simple, let us now assume that for a given level of effort, the amount of catch is directly proportional to the population size. This being the case, the production function can be expressed simply as

$$H = \alpha S \qquad\qquad\qquad (16.4b)$$

where α is some parameter. Then, as shown in Figure 16.2, catch can be plotted as a function of population, holding effort, E, constant at some predetermined level. From Figure 16.2 we observe that, given the level of effort E_1, when the population biomass is 100,000 tons, the harvest or catch per unit time will be 2,500 tons. This would suggest an α value of 25 since, by equation (16.4b) the value of α is equal to the size of the harvest, or H, divided by the size of the population biomass, S. Given this, when the effort level is set to E_1, the production function is explicitly stated as $H = 25S$. Thus, the specific value of the parameter α measures the increase in the harvest rate per unit time resulting from a unit increase in the underlying population biomass. In this specific case where the effort level is set to E_1, when the population biomass is allowed to increase by a unit (a thousand tons), the harvest will increase by 25 tons. Hence, in general, *given the level of effort, an increase in population will increase catch*. For example, if the population biomass is increased from 100,000 to 120,000 tons, as shown in Figure 16.2, the harvest per unit time will increase from 2,500 to 3,000 tons. This should be intuitively understandable given that a fisher using a particular type of fishing gear or technique would harvest more fish in an area where the fish population was large. Figure 16.2 also shows what effect a change in the level of effort would have on harvest given the population size. For example, when the level of effort is increased from E_1 to E_2 for a given population biomass, say 100,000 tons, the harvest per unit time will be increased from 2,500 to 4,500 tons. In other words, from a given level of fish biomass a fisher would harvest more fish by applying a higher

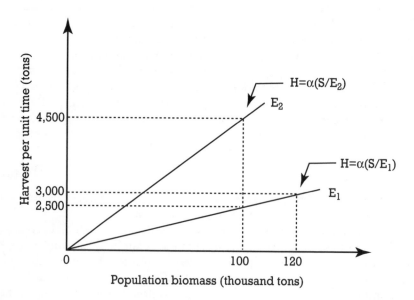

Figure 16.2 **The relationships between harvest, population size and effort**

level of fishing technology. In this particular example, this change in fishing technology is manifested by a change in the value of the parameter α. More specifically, the change in the effort level from E_1 to E_2 is accompanied by a corresponding change in the value of the parameter α from 25 to 45.

However, the above interrelationships among the levels of harvest, effort and population size do not address the issue of whether the harvest under any given condition is *sustainable* or not. To do this we need to superimpose the natural growth curve (Figure 16.1) on Figure 16.2, which results in Figure 16.3.

Let us suppose that the effort exerted by humans is represented by a straight-line curve from the origin, E_2, as shown in Figure 16.3. Given this, we observe that a level of harvest equal to H_2 or 3,200 tons can be harvested each year indefinitely because it is replaced by natural growth. That is, H_2 is the sustainable harvest associated with the level of effort E_2 and a *uniquely* determined population size, S_4 – a biomass of 160,000 tons. For later analysis, it is important to note that this information about harvest and population biomass suggests that the α value associated with E_2 is 20 (H_2/S_4 or 3,200/160).

How can S_4 be considered *unique* when S_2 is also associated with the same level of harvest or growth of biomass? Close observation would show that given the effort level E_2, S_2 will not be an equilibrium population size. In fact, when the effort level is E_2, for any population biomass between S_2 (40,000 tons) and S_4 (160,000 tons), the natural growth in population will exceed the harvest per unit time. This will allow the population biomass to grow over time until it gradually reaches S_4.

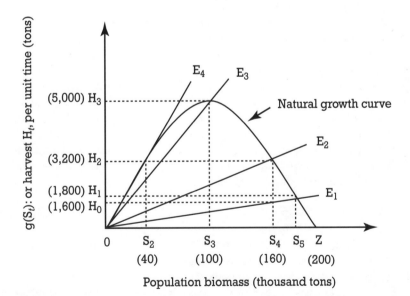

Figure 16.3 **A steady-state bioeconomic equilibrium model of fish harvest**

To see this, let us consider the population size at S_2 – a biomass of 40,000 tons. At this level of biomass, the natural growth is 3,200 tons. However, if the effort level E_2 is used to harvest fish from this size of biomass, the actual harvest per unit time will be 800 tons. This is because, as shown earlier, the α value associated with the effort level E_2 is 20. Thus, in this specific case the natural growth in biomass exceeds the actual harvest by 2,400 tons (3,200 – 800). As long as this situation prevails, the tendency is for the population biomass to grow. It is in this sense, therefore, that S_2 will not be an equilibrium population size when the effort level is held at E_2. This is also the case for all the population sizes between S_2 and S_4. To offer one more example, when the population biomass is S_3 or 100,000 tons, the natural growth rate will be 5,000 tons. However, with the effort level E_2, the harvest per unit time will be 2,000 tons. Again, the natural growth exceeds the actual harvest, and this will eventually push the population to grow beyond S_3. Thus, S_3 will not be an equilibrium population size when the effort level is held at E_2. In fact, given that the effort level is held at E_2, the population biomass will continue to grow until it reaches 160,000 tons, S_4. At this point, the natural growth *equals* the biomass that can be harvested on a sustainable basis, 3,200 tons. Therefore, S_4 is the equilibrium population size *uniquely* associated with the effort level E_2. Note also that this observation implies a one-to-one correspondence between effort and equilibrium population size. More specifically, the equilibrium population size is a function of effort.

To see this, suppose the effort level is changed to E_1 (which is less than E_2). If the population size remains at S_4 (the equilibrium size when the level of effort is E_2), the harvest will be H_0 or 1,600 tons. However, given the population size is S_4, the natural growth of the biomass of the population would have allowed a harvest at a rate of H_2 or 3,200 tons. Since H_0 (the actual harvest) is less than H_2 (the harvest equivalent to the natural growth rate), the population will tend naturally to grow over time until it reaches a new equilibrium, S_5, or 180,000 tons. Thus, S_5 becomes the *new* equilibrium population size associated with the effort level E_1. Similarly, it can also be demonstrated that if the effort level is E_3, the equilibrium population size associated with this level of effort will be S_3. *We may, then, generalize that for a given level of effort, a unique equilibrium population size will result, yielding a sustainable harvest.* This occurs because, as is evident from Figure 16.3, harvest is replaced by a natural growth rate. This is referred to as a *steady-state bioeconomic equilibrium*. Algebraically, this equilibrium condition is attained when the following condition is met:

$$\Delta S_t / \Delta t = g(S_t) - H_t = 0 \qquad\qquad\qquad (16.5)$$

where H_t is the harvest per unit time. According to equation (16.5), at any point in time, harvest is offset by natural growth, thus allowing the underlying population size to remain constant.

From economists' perspective, it is significant to formally relate the equilibrium harvest (yield) to effort. This, in fact, represents a familiar concept in economics, namely production function. A production function shows a relationship between output (in this case fish) and inputs (labor, capital and other resources used for catching fish). However, it becomes complicated in the case of fishery because the production function has to explicitly incorporate the biological growth function. Figure 16.4 shows a production function of this nature.

The production function in Figure 16.4 is derived from Figure 16.3 by tracing the locus of all the points representing *sustainable* harvest (yield) at each level of effort. In tracing these points, it is important to note that each level of effort is associated with an equilibrium population size that is *unique* to the effort in question. For example, in both Figures 16.3 and 16 4, the effort level E_1 is related not only to the sustainable harvest of H_1 but also to an equilibrium population size of S_5. This is the case for all the points along the graph of the production function in Figure 16.4, and in fishery economics this graph is called the *sustainable yield curve*.

As should be expected, a look at Figure 16.4 shows that the sustainable yield curve is exactly the same as the natural growth curves in Figure 16.3 and 16.1 in almost all respects, except that the unit of measurement on the horizontal axis is effort, rather than population biomass. In this sense, *the sustainable yield curve is nothing more than the natural growth curve expressed in terms of effort*. It is important to reemphasize that each point along the sustainable yield curve assumes an equilibrium population size that corresponds to a given level of effort. To show the significance of this statement, in Figure 16.4 an additional horizontal axis is drawn parallel to the main axis of effort. This axis shows the equilibrium population size that

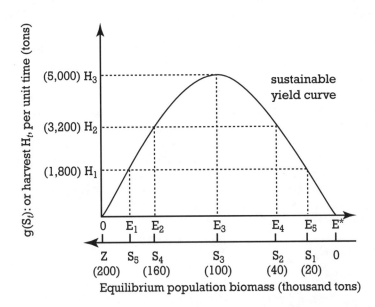

Figure 16.4 **Production function of fishery: the sustainable yield curve**

corresponds to each level of effort on the main axis. A closer look at these two axes reveals that the level of effort and the equilibrium population size are inversely related. That is, the larger the level of effort, the smaller the size of the equilibrium population and vice versa. This also suggests that excessive harvesting (or application of effort) of a renewable resource could lead to its irrevocable destruction or extinction. For example, if the effort level $E^\star$ is applied, the population biomass will dwindle to zero. Thus, in this sense, *renewable resources are potentially destructible.*

This transition from the natural growth curve to the sustainable yield curve is an extremely important step because the sustainable yield curve shows the quantity or biomass of a biological resource that can be harvested on a sustainable basis as a function of effort *only*. Since effort is under human control, the sustainable yield curve has the most direct application to resource management. In fact, the sustainable yield curve can be viewed simply as the *long-run production function* of the biological resource under consideration, since it relates effort (the amount of labor and capital used to harvest the resource) to the amount of harvest (output). This is a key concept that is needed to explain the economic approach to the management of renewable resources – the subject of the next section.

16.5 ECONOMICS OF FISHERIES MANAGEMENT

Once the sustainable yield curve is identified as the long-run production function in managing a fishery enterprise, the economic problem is reduced to finding the efficient allocation of effort (labor, capital and other material resources) under certain socioeconomic conditions. In this section this issue is examined under two alternative conditions. In the first case, fish is taken to be an open-access resource, and in the second case, a private property harvest is assumed. The analyses of these two cases will clearly demonstrate the effect property rights have on the economics of harvesting a given fish population.

Furthermore, so that we can conduct the analysis in the simplest possible manner, it is assumed that the fishery industry is perfectly competitive in both the inputs and output markets. Thus, the prices for both the output (fish) and inputs (labor and capital and other material resources used for fish harvesting) are determined by competitive market forces. That is, the producers (fishers) are *price-takers* in both the output and the input markets. Given these assumptions, the relationships between total revenue and effort and total cost and effort are shown in Figure 16.5a.

The total revenue is defined as:

$$TR = P_H \times H_E$$

where TR is total revenue, P_H is the equilibrium price of fish per unit catch, and H_E is the *sustainable harvest* for a given effort level. The total revenue curve will have the same shape as the sustainable yield curve. In fact, it is nothing more than the *monetized* version of the sustainable yield curve. For example, the value of the total revenue that corresponds to level of effort E_3 in Figure 16.5a is the market value of the 5,000 tons of fish biomass shown in Figure 16.4 corresponding to the same level of effort, E_3.

Since firms in the fishery are assumed to be price-takers, the cost curve is a line with a constant slope equal to the market price of effort, P_E. Thus, total cost is simply expressed as

$$TC = P_E \times E$$

where P_E is the unit cost (market price) of effort and E is the level of effort – an index of capital, labor and other materials used by the fishing industry.

16.5.1 The open-access equilibrium yield

In this subsection we will examine the condition for the equilibrium level of fishing effort by considering the case where there is complete open access to fishing. That is, no one has exclusive property rights to harvest fish from a particular fishing ground or location. As we have seen in Chapter 5, when a resource has no clearly defined ownership rights, economic pursuits on the basis of private self-interest tend to lead to overexploitation of the resource in question. A similar outcome can be shown to hold when a fishery is exploited under open-access harvest, and this is demonstrated using Figures 16.5a and 16.5b.

When fish is treated as an open-access resource, as shown in Figure 16.5a, the equilibrium level of effort will be E_4. At this point, total revenue is exactly equal to total costs (TC); thus, profit in the fishery industry is zero. To demonstrate that this is, in fact, the open-access equilibrium effort, we should note that each fisher pursues his or her own self-interest as an individual – seeking to maximize the difference between his or her revenue and costs and continuing to fish as long as any profit exists. Moreover, because there are no restrictions on the number of fishers who can enter the industry, any positive profit will attract additional fishers. For

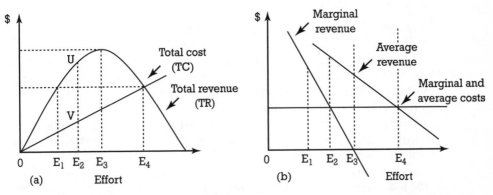

Figure 16.5a **Long-run total revenue, total cost and fishing effort for a fishery**
Figure 16.5b **Socially optimal level of fishing effort**

example, if the effort level is E_3, as shown in Figure 16.5a, total revenue for the fishery as a whole is greater than total cost; therefore, there will be an incentive for new fishers to enter into the industry and for the existing fishers to expand their operations. Consequently, as more and more effort is applied to the fishery, total cost will continue to rise, and at some point the industry's profit as a whole will be reduced to zero. In Figure 16.5a, this occurs where TR = TC, and the level of effort associated with this outcome is E_4.

What can be said about this equilibrium outcome? First, it is quite evident that the open-access equilibrium effort, E_4, does not represent bioeconomic efficiency because the same level of revenue would have been obtained by using less effort, E_1, as shown in Figure 16.5a. Or, in terms of biomass, as shown in Figure 16.4, the open-access equilibrium is associated with a stock level, S_2, that is less than the biomass associated with the maximum sustainable yield, S_3. Second, the open-access equilibrium effort is not economically efficient because, as shown in Figure 16.5b, at this level of effort, E_4, marginal revenue is less than marginal cost. As discussed in Chapter 2 and elsewhere, this suggests that more resources than necessary are being used to harvest fish (more on this in the next subsection).

Accordingly, this practice, if pursued, will have two undesirable and perhaps "tragic" consequences. First, excessive effort will result in a lower level of equilibrium fish population for harvest since, as noted earlier (see Figure 16.4), effort and the equilibrium level of the fish population are inversely related. In other words, open access to a fishery has a depleting effect on fish stock. It is this kind of effect that Hardin most aptly classified as the "tragedy of the commons." Second, on purely economic grounds, the open-access equilibrium is inefficient – that is, it allows excessive use of fishing efforts. The discussion in Case Study 16.1 clearly indicates that the primary cause of overfishing is the fact that, worldwide, many fisheries are still open access.

16.5.2 The socially optimal level of effort under private property rights

Suppose a fishery is owned by a society, and it is managed in such a way as to maximize the social surplus from the use of this enterprise. In this case, a fishery will be viewed as a project that requires scarce resources in its operation (harvest of fish). Then the allocation of these scarce resources into this industry cannot be free from social scrutiny. In other words, since the amount of effort (labor and capital) used in a fishery has alternative uses, it is necessary to fully account for the associated *opportunity costs*. When this consideration is explicitly recognized, as will be evident shortly, the result will suggest a socially optimal allocation of fishery resources.

To see this, we need first to note that when the issue involves determining the socially optimal level of equilibrium effort, it is necessary to consider the relationship between the marginal cost and marginal revenue of effort as seen in Figure 16.5b. Note that Figure 16.5b is derived from Figure 16.5a.

CASE STUDY 16.1 THE ROOTS OF OVERFISHING

Peter Weber

Despite warnings of slowdown in the marine catch in the 1970s and 1980s, the fishing industry geared up. Today it has something like twice the capacity needed to make the annual catch. Between 1970 and 1990, FAO recorded a doubling in the world fishing fleet, from 585,000 to 1.2 million large boats. According to FAO fisheries analyst Chris Newton, "We could go back to the 1970 fleet size and we would be no worse off – we'd catch the same amount of fish."

Almost invariably, when a country looks closely at its fishery, it finds overcapacity. Norway, for instance, estimates its fishing industry is 60 percent over the capacity necessary to make its annual catch. And European Union nations are estimated to have 40 percent overcapacity.

Individual fisheries have shown even greater overcrowding. In the late 1980s, the Nova Scotia dragger (trawler) industry was estimated to have four times the capacity needed to make the yearly quota for cod and other bottom-feeding fish (groundfish). In the United States, a simulation in 1990 indicated that as few as 13 boats would be sufficient for the East Coast surf clam fishery; at the time, there were 10 times that number.

How did this overcapacity develop? Many fisheries are open to all comers. In its simplest form, open access allows people to fish at will. If regulators want to limit the total catch, they must calculate the potential take of all boats and adjust the length of the open season accordingly. Fishers then race each other to get the biggest catch possible. As the number of fishers or their capacity increases, the season gets shorter. In the extreme case of the Alaska halibut fishery, the season is restricted to just two or three 24-hour periods a year.

Under open access, boats continue to enter the fishery well after fish yield and profits begin to fall. As stocks decline, fishers often buy bigger, faster boats with more advanced equipment and gear. The pressure to overfish, to underreport the catch, and even to poach can undermine management programs. If the cycle of overfishing and overcapacity continues, profits decline until people start to go out of business, fewer people take up fishing, and fishers have no incentive to increase their effort. At this point, the catch in the damaged fishery may stabilize – but at a level below its sustainable potential.

As more and more fishers slide to the brink of financial ruin, pressure on politicians can trigger subsidies that keep overextended individuals in business, maintaining overcapacity. . . . FAO estimates that countries provide on the order of $54 billion annually in subsidies to the fishing industry – encouraging its overexpansion in recent decades. . . .

An alternative approach would have been to support more traditional forms of fishing. With its fisheries declining, in 1984 the Kerala government appointed an expert committee to study the problem. The committee cited overcapacity as the culprit and advised emphasizing small-scale, traditional fishing to maximize employment and protect the livelihood of the poorest fishers. The committee recommended reducing the number of trawlers from 2,807 to 1,145, eliminating all 54 boats that used purse seine nuts, cutting back on motorized small boats from 6,934 to 2,690, and keeping all 20,000 of the non-motorized craft. If the government had followed this advice, Kerala's fisheries might be in better shape today.

Source: Worldwatch Institute, *State of the World 1995*, pp. 23–5. Copyright © 1995. Reprinted by permission.

The difference between the two figures is that one is expressed in terms of total cost and the other in terms of marginal and average costs. From Figure 16.5b, if we apply the usual equimarginal condition, the socially optimal level of effort is E_2, where the marginal revenue of effort exactly equals the marginal cost of effort.

To see why this level of effort is socially optimal, say that the fishery operates using a level of effort represented in Figure 16.5b by E_1. It is clear that at this level of effort, the marginal revenue is greater than the marginal cost; hence, profit can be increased by increasing the level of effort. This situation will, indeed, hold for any level of effort that is less than E_2. Similarly, consider the case where the level of effort is E_4 (note this is the level of equilibrium effort when the fishery is unregulated). Here, the marginal cost of effort is greater than the marginal revenue of effort (note that its value is in fact negative); hence, reduction in effort for any level greater than E_2 will increase profit. Thus, only when the level of effort equals E_2 is the marginal cost of effort exactly equal to the marginal revenue of effort, and the opportunity for further increase in profit is zero. In fact, when this marginal condition is met, the total profit (as indicated in Figure 16.5a by line UV) of the fishery industry is at its maximum.

Still, it is important to note that the significance of the social equilibrium condition is not that the annual profit to the fishery as a whole is maximized, but rather that *society's resources (labor, capital and other material resources) are used to exploit the fishery only when they cannot be used more advantageously elsewhere.* Furthermore, the fact that E_2 is the socially optimal level of effort clearly reaffirms that harvesting under open access would lead to excessive use of effort, E_4, and consequently to overfishing.

At this point it will be instructive to offer a different version of the economic rationale for why fishery management on the basis of maximum sustainable yield (MSY) would not be socially optimal. In both Figures 16.5a and 16.5b, the equilibrium effort which corresponds to the maximum sustainable yield is E_3. Clearly, this effort level is greater than the socially optimal level of effort E_2, and it is attained when MR = 0. Furthermore, what is being maximized is not the profit (rent) of the fishery, but rather the revenue – that is, fish harvesting is allowed until MR = 0. For these reasons, the socially optimal level of fishing effort will always be less than the one prescribed by adhering to the management philosophy of maximum sustainable yield.

Given the above results, what can be done to safeguard the over-exploitation of the fishery, or for that matter any biological resources which have traditionally been treated as open-access resources? Is regulation the answer to overfishing?

16.6 REGULATION OF FISHERY: AN OVERVIEW

From the above discussions, the economic rationale for regulating the fishery should be very clear. Furthermore, from a purely economic perspective, the desired policy objective would be to restrict access to the fishery in such a way that misallocation of societal resources is avoided. Traditionally, several policy instruments have been used to regulate fishery. Among them, the most commonly used methods of fishery regulations fall into the following categories: (a) fines, such as *taxes* on harvest or on effort; (b) *quotas* – limits on the total quantity of harvest within a given season; (c) *technological standards*, such as restrictions on the kinds of fishing nets, boats and fishing gear to be used; and (d) assignment of private property rights – most recently, a variation of this approach called individual transferable quotas (ITQs) has been gaining increasing popularity (see Case Study 16.2).

In theory, it is quite simple to show how taxes and quotas can be used to bring about the socially desirable equilibrium level of effort and harvest. For example, as shown in Figure 16.6, a unit tax, t, on fishing effort would have the effect of rotating the total cost from TC_0 (the cost with open-access harvest) to TC_1 [where $TC_1 = P_E E + tE = (P_E + t)E$], and the desired level of effort, E_2, is achieved when $TC_1 = TR$.

Similarly, as shown in Figure 16.7, the same result can be achieved by imposing a tax on each pound of fish caught. In this case, the total revenue will shift inward, from TR_0 (which is $P_H H$) to TR_1 [$(P_H - t)H$]. In so doing, the desired level of effort is attained when TC intersects TR_1. Although it will not be discussed here, it can also be shown that properly set and strictly enforced fishery management through quotas of various types could be used to achieve the socially optimal levels of effort and harvest.

Thus, in theory, the misallocation of fishery resources can be corrected through judicious application of publicly mandated policy measures which may take the form of taxes, quotas, technological standards, etc. However, in practice, the real problem is generally not in deciding which particular

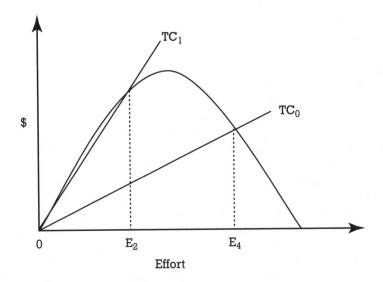

Figure 16.6 **Effect of a tax on fishing effort**

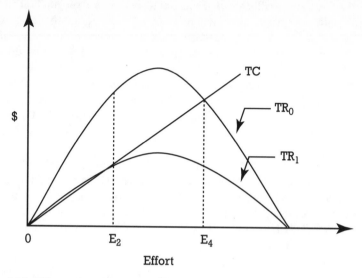

Figure 16.7 **Effect of a tax on fish catch**

public policy instrument(s) to use but rather the effective implementation of the policy under consideration. This happens because, by their very nature, most commercially valuable fisheries are located over extensive areas, sometimes crossing national and international boundaries. For this reason, implementation of public policy may require the untangling of sticky political issues involved in making international treaties. Furthermore, even in the absence of such a political problem, the *transaction costs* (in particular, the costs of policing violators) would be extremely high. Evidence of this is the difficulty many nations encounter in protecting the integrity of marine resources within the confines of internationally sanctioned boundaries 200 miles off coastal lines.

Thus, the challenges of fishery regulations are quite formidable, and they cannot be resolved by simply relegating the responsibilities of resource allocation to public authorities. Furthermore, on several occasions well-intentioned public policy measures have failed to adequately address the core problem(s) in question. This is clearly demonstrated in Case Study 16.2, where public policies (both market-based and "command-and-control" varieties) to deal with overcrowded fisheries are creating economic hardship for many coastal communities. Even so, public policy measures conceived and formulated on the basis of reliable biological information and sound economic analyses can further the progress toward effective management of not only fishery resources, but any biological resources which have traditionally been treated as open-access resources. These are in no way trivial resource concerns. They involve, among others, concerns such as the protection of endangered species, the overgrazing of federally owned grasslands, deforestation, and the excessive exploitation of some marine resources.

CASE STUDY 16.2 OVERREACTING TO OVERCAPACITY

Peter Weber

Despite the benefits of smaller-scale fishing, government after government is implementing consolidation programs that encourage bigger boats and smaller fleets to address the problems of overcapacity and overfishing. . . . Although consolidation is arguably necessary in many cases, poorly considered programs can eliminate badly needed sources of employment, concentrating the benefits of the fishery in the hands of privileged people. In the United States, a consolidation program started in 1990 for the East Coast surf clam fishery did not involve crew members or address employment issues. . . .

At the request of the surf clam boat owners, regional regulators had put in place a market-based system known as individual transferable quotas (ITQs). Under this, each boat owner received a share in the annual catch, and the quota holders could buy, sell or lease them like property. For boat owners, who did not have to pay for fishing rights that they could now sell, ITQs yielded a windfall profit, and small operators who were having hard economic times were able to sell out or lease their portion of the quota. For the unemployed crew members, the implications are obvious. The unexpected result were that a leaner and presumably more efficient fishery nevertheless did not lower the price of clams – nor did it raise income for most of the remaining crew, despite longer working hours.

Although the results can be questionable, as this example shows, ITQs are one of the most widely discussed management solutions for overcrowded fisheries. They have a certain appeal because, through transferable fishing rights, market forces can direct the allocation of resources, presumably increasing economic efficiency. ITQs have the benefit of allowing marginal shareholders to get out of the fishery with some money. The down side is that such systems allow a small number of individuals or companies to buy control over the fishery.

When New Zealand was in the process of instituting an ITQ system, highly capitalized fishing companies expanded their operations beyond the level of catch they could sell profitably so that they would control a higher percentage of the fishery at the time of the initial allocation of quotas. If regulators do not act to prevent such "capital stuffing," ITQs can reward the very fishers who overcapitalized the fishery in the first place, while squeezing out smaller operations.

Limitations on the transferability of ITQs, such as restricting the portion an individual or company may own, could help limit consolidation. Under an ITQ system for Alaska's halibut fishery, which is scheduled to begin in 1995, quotas for small boat owners would be allocated in blocks. In principle, these regulations will keep the small-boat portion of the quota in the hands of small operators.

But before going this route, policy-makers should recognize that management systems that promote consolidation also concentrate wealth and can be devastating for coastal communities, particularly if changes come rapidly and without support for developing new jobs. Small-scale fishers are too numerous – and too vital to coastal communities – to sacrifice in an effort to control overfishing.

Source: Worldwatch Institute, *State of the World 1995*, pp. 31–3. Copyright (c) 1995. Reprinted by permission.

16.7 SOME IMPORTANT LIMITATIONS OF THE STEADY-STATE BIOECONOMIC MODEL

By design, the focus of this chapter has been on presenting the basic economic principles of biological resources with a focus on fishery, and to do this in ways that will be understandable to students who have had no more than a semester of an introductory microeconomics course. For this reason, the economic analysis has been admittedly limited in scope. A number of important socioeconomic, technological, biological and ecological considerations have been intentionally overlooked. In this section, an attempt will be made to enumerate and briefly discuss some of the key considerations that have not been specifically addressed or have simply been omitted in our discussions thus far.

Time

In the analysis so far, the socially optimal level of effort was determined by looking at the difference between total revenue and total costs to the fishery at a given point in time; namely, the current period. According to this approach, the socially optimal level of effort is associated with the largest positive difference between the revenues and costs; for example, E_2 in Figure 16.5a. This approach is indeed *static*, because it considers the operation of fishery only at a single point in time. This is allowed because a steady-state population of fish stock is assumed. That is, the biological growth function that underlies the economic analysis does not recognize that the fish population is dependent on *time*.

However, when the fish population and harvest are assumed to be time dependent, the principle of optimization outlined above for a single time period needs to be modified. In this dynamic setting, the main concern is the *intertemporal allocation* of fishery resources. When viewed this way, the objective is to maximize the *present value* of the stream of net benefits – total revenues minus total costs, discounted at the "social" discount rate – that the enterprise in question will earn over time (see Chapter 15). Although it is not formally demonstrated here, the socially optimal allocation of fishery resources is attained when a state of indifference is reached, with regard to the usage of an additional effort, between each pair of times, and across the entire range of the period under consideration. When this condition is met, there will be no *net* gain by diverting resources from one period to another; hence, optimality is attained. As long as the discount rate is positive, it can be demonstrated that the static and dynamic private property equilibria will *not* coincide. *The most important thing to note here is the pivotal role the discount rate plays when the allocation of resources becomes time dependent* (for more on this see Chapter 15).

Changes in prices and technology

The economic analysis thus far has been done assuming constant input and output prices and no technological changes. However, prices do indeed vary in the short run, and change in the techniques of catching fish is a recurring phenomenon. The question is, then, how would considerations of this nature affect the economic analysis? In addition, from the viewpoint of fishery management, could considerations of price and technological changes significantly alter the basic findings of our economic analysis?

With other factors held constant, the immediate effect of a change in the price of output alone would be a shift in the total revenue curve, such as the one shown in Figure 16.5a. For example, an increase in the price of fish will shift the entire total revenue curve upward. If the input prices, hence the total cost, have not changed, *both the open access and the socially optimal level of efforts will be higher than before the price increase*. A similar result would be observed if the prices for inputs (fishing effort) declined while everything else remained constant. In this case, however, this result would occur because of a leftward rotation in the total cost function. If changes in the prices of output and/or inputs of this nature are not *temporary*, the effect would lead to overfishing. This is because an increase in output price and/or a decrease in input prices are associated with a higher level of equilibrium effort utilization.

A change in the technique of catching fish (or any other biological resources) can also cause a similar effect. Basically, change in technique implies an improvement in the tools and methods used to harvest a biological resource. For example, by employing a new technology, a fisher could catch more fish per unit time than previously possible. Unlike price changes, the effect of technological changes on the yield curve is direct. That is, technical improvements of this nature alter the relationship between the yield function and the level of effort; at each level of effort there will be more catch than before the technological innovation. Yet this cannot be sustained without negatively impacting the equilibrium population size associated with each level of effort. Thus, *other factors remaining constant, an improvement in the technique of harvesting would accelerate the reduction in the underlying population size of fish*.

The case of multiple species fishery

In our simple model, the fishery is assumed to involve harvesting of only a single species. However, problems arise when the method of harvest is aimed not at one particular species but rather at a group: multiple species. In such instances, complications are caused by additional economic and ecological constraints that need to be considered. From economic perspective, the cost of harvesting a particular species may be affected by the presence of the stock of another species. Analysis of joint production is common in economics, and multispecies models have been developed considerably in recent years.

From an ecological perspective, the problem arises when selective fishing is done on the basis of the commercial values of the species under consideration and with no regard to the ecological dynamics of the entire fishery. Under this condition, economic optimum (which assigns no value to species with no commercial value) may not account for the integrity of the fishery ecosystem as a whole. In the long run, such a practice may bring disaster.

The assumption of a stable steady-state equilibrium

The assumption in our simple bioeconomic model has been that natural systems tend toward states of equilibrium – that is, static steady-state equilibrium analysis. In fact, natural systems may be characterized by constant instability (i.e., stability is not the "natural" state). Changes in water temperature, new predators, disease, pollution, current and other environmental factors are continually affecting the fish stock population of a particular fishery. Furthermore, it is misleading to talk about reaching equilibrium for a particular fishery until we know how a given fishery relates to others within the ecosystem. What all these considerations suggest is that, at the minimum, the stock of fish population must be reevaluated continually; and optimal harvesting practices require careful monitoring of the stock before each fishing season.

The stochastic nature of fishery populations

As briefly discussed in Section 16.3, if fish population is reduced below a certain threshold (the critical zone), the net growth could be negative, leading toward inevitable extinction. In other words, a small population could be highly susceptible to demographic accidents and ecological disturbances. When this stochastic behavior of fish population is recognized, fisheries management inevitably involves greater uncertainty. In situations where the element of uncertainty is prevalent, sustainable fishing may dictate a precautionary approach to fisheries management:

> The precautionary principle holds that society should take action against certain practices when there is potential for irreversible consequences or for severe limits on the options for future generations – even when there is as yet no incontrovertible scientific proof that serious consequences will ensue.
>
> (McGinn 1998: 57)

Table 16.1 provides a summary of the policy implications for fisheries management regimes based on the precautionary principle. Evidently, this approach calls for caution in the use and introduction of new technologies; stricter monitoring of fish catches; establishment of a more secured form of fishing tenure or limited access; and protection for rare, threatened or endangered fisheries ecosystems and habitats. For these reasons, a precautionary approach is bound to be far more ecologically sound than

Table 16.1 **Examples of precautionary measures**

- Control access to the fishery early, before problems appear.
- Encourage responsible fishing through some form of fishing tenure or limited access.
- Place a cap on both fishing capacity and total fishing catch rate.
- Develop conservative catch limits and define upper range.
- If upper range is exceeded, implement recovery plans immediately to restore the stock.
- Reduce subsidies and encourage development of fisheries that are economically self-sufficient.
- Establish data collection and reporting systems.
- Avoid targeting fish that are too young or too small.
- Minimize bycatch through the use of more selective gear.
- Use area closure and marine protected areas to limit risks to the resource by providing refuges for stocks and restoring habitat.
- Develop management plans cooperatively with stakeholders and ensure ongoing participation and feedback.

Source: A. P. McGinn, *Worldwatch Paper No. 142*. Washington, D.C.: Worldwatch Institute. Copyright © 1998. Reprinted by permission.

a maximum sustainable yield approach, still commonly used as the standard for fisheries management in many parts of the world.

16.8 CHAPTER SUMMARY

- This chapter discussed basic economic principles that are important to the understanding of biological resource management, and focused on a fishery.
- Fundamental to any management strategy of biological resources is the understanding of the *natural growth function*. This function relates growth rate to population level of a given biological resource, holding all other relevant factors constant (such as the age distributions and sex compositions).
- For a fishery, it was postulated that the natural growth function could be specified using a *logistic* function. Given this, the following two general observations were made:

  1 Within certain limits, it is possible to exploit fishery resources while maintaining the size of the underlying population. That is, a fishery can be harvested on a sustainable basis.
  2 Since there are an infinite number of population sizes, each capable of being harvested on a sustained basis, the feasible set of alternatives is practically *infinite*.

- From an economic perspective, the issue of interest is to find which of these *feasible* choices is the "optimal" for society. Note that the term "feasible" implies sustainability; thus, the *harvest rate must be sustainable*.

- As usual, optimality requires weighing the costs and benefits of *all* alternative feasible choices (or sustainable harvests) of the fishery under consideration.
- The cost of fishery has two components: (a) the cost of production – the cost associated with level of *fishing effort* (labor, capital, energy and other material resources), and (b) the rental values of the fish stock. Furthermore, optimality requires that both of these be assessed in terms of their opportunity costs.
- The long-run production function of a fishery is derived by carefully tracing the correspondence between the level of fishing effort and sustainable fish catch or harvest per unit time. This production function is called the *sustainable yield function*, and is intimately associated with the natural growth function of the particular fishery.
- Once the sustainable yield function is identified, the economic problem is reduced to finding the *optimal* level of fishing effort and fish harvest.
- To complete this task, the fishery was assumed to operate under a *perfectly competitive market structure*; that is, fishers were assumed to be *price-takers* in both the input and output markets. Given these simplifying assumptions, the economics of fishery was analyzed under three alternative scenarios:

  1 *the open-access equilibrium effort regime*, where complete access to fishing is permitted. This case became relevant because traditionally, the fishery has been treated as an open-access resource. This regime will not yield a socially optimal outcome because the return from a fishery is evaluated without considering the opportunity cost of the rental value of the fishery – fish stock. Ownership of the fish stock is not clearly defined and, therefore, it is exploited as though it is a *free good* – the tragedy of the commons.
  2 *maximum sustainable yield regime*, where the largest fish catch is sought among the infinite number of catches that can be harvested on a sustainable basis. This regime would also fail to yield a socially optimal outcome because it ignores the opportunity cost of fishing effort. This is because the operation rule of this fishery management strategy is based on a purely physical consideration: fish stock and its rate of growth per unit time.
  3 *The socially optimal level of effort regime*, where the equilibrium level of fishing effort is determined after accounting for the opportunity costs of *all* the resources used for harvesting fish including the rental value of the fish stock. This regime is the least exploitative.

- Another concept briefly discussed was the *precautionary* approach to fishery management. Application of this regime could have a socially beneficial outcome when the fishery under consideration is susceptible to extreme uncertainty and irreversibility.
- Overfishing remains a major problem for many fisheries worldwide. As discussed briefly, various forms of taxes and individual transferable quotas could be used to discourage overfishing.

- From a public policy perspective, the long-term solution to fishery management definitely requires socially negotiated access rules. The difficulty arises from severe and long-standing political inadequacies (as may be the case in the developing countries) and/or from fundamental technical problems in restricting access to a resource, such as fisheries extending beyond a single political jurisdiction. Clearly, the management of fishery confronts us with seemingly insurmountable institutional and technical problems.

---

review and discussion questions

1 Identify the following concepts: nonrenewable resources, flow resources, biomass, bioeconomic, open access, carrying capacity, fishing effort, sustainable yield, steady-state bioeconomic equilibrium, individual transferable quotas (ITQs).
2 State *True*, *False* or *Uncertain* and explain why.

   (a) Renewable resources are potentially destructible.
   (b) Fisheries are likely to be managed more conservatively under the regime of a maximum economic yield (MEY) than a maximum sustainable yield (MSY).
   (c) The sustainable yield curve is nothing more than the natural growth curve expressed in terms of effort.

3 Why do you think maximum sustainable yield (MSY) is the standard for fishery management internationally? Do you think this is done for convenience or other sound economic and scientific reasons? Be specific.
4 Discuss the conditions under which the use of a precautionary approach to fishery management is justified. In general, how would you compare this management principle with a maximum sustainable yield (MSY) or a maximum economic yield (MEY) regime of fishery management?
5 In recent years, among economists the policy instrument of choice for regulating fisheries has been a market-based system known as individual transferable quotas (ITQs). How does this system of regulation work (see Case Study 16.2)? What apparent weaknesses do you see in the application of this policy instrument? Are you convinced that this system is better than a system of regulation based on taxes, technological standards or nontransferable quotas? Why, or why not?
6 As discussed in Chapter 9, proponents of the ecological economics advocate a "sustainability rule" that reads as follows: "The rate of exploitation of renewable resources should not exceed the regeneration rate." However, as observed in this chapter, there are an *infinite* number of sustainable yields associated with a renewable resource such as fish population. In fact, the natural growth curve shows that sustainability can be maintained while keeping a *very* small or a *very* large size of fish population. Given this, the above sustainability rule apparently

lacks specificity. Do you think that the rule should be modified? If your answer is yes, can you offer a suggestion as to how to modify it? If your answer is no, give your reasons.

REFERENCES AND FURTHER READING

Anderson, L. G. (1977) *The Economics of Fisheries Management*, Baltimore: John Hopkins University Press.

Beverton, R. J. H. and Holt, S. J. (1957) "On the Dynamics of Exploited Fish Populations," *Fishery Investigations*, series III, 19, London: Her Majesty's Stationery Office.

Christy, F. T., Jr. and Scott, A. (1965) *The Common Wealth of Ocean Fisheries*, Washington, D.C.: Resources for the Future, Johns Hopkins University Press.

Ciriacy-Wantrup, S. V. and Bishop, R. C. (1975) "Common Property as a Concept in Natural Resources Policy," *Natural Resources Journal* 15, 4: 713–29.

Clark, C. W. (1973) "The Economics of Over Exploitation," *Science* 181: 630–4.

—— (1990) *Mathematical Bioeconomics: The Optimal Management of Renewable Resources*, 2nd edn., New York: Wiley-Interscience.

Gordon, H. S. (1954) "The Economic Theory of a Common-Property Resource: The Fishery," *Journal of Political Economy* 62: 124–42.

Hardin, G. (1968) "The Tragedy of the Commons," *Science* 192: 1243–8.

Munro, G. R. (1982) "Fisheries, Extended Jurisdiction, and the Economics of Common Property Resources," *Canadian Journal of Economics* 15: 405–25.

Rees, J. (1985) *Natural Resources: Allocation, Economics and Policy*, London: Methuen Press.

Ricker, W. E. (1958) "Maximum Sustainable Yields from Fluctuating Environment and Mixed Stocks," *Journal of Fishery Resource Bd. of Canada* 15: 991–1006.

Schaefer, M. B. (1957) "Some Considerations of Population Dynamics and Economics in Relation to the Management of Marine Fisheries," *Journal of Fisheries Research Board of Canada* 14: 669–86.

Scott, A. D. and Neher, P. A. (1981) *The Public Regulation of Commercial Fisheries in Canada*, Ottawa: Economic Council of Canada.

Townsend, R. E. (1990) "Entry Restrictions in the Fishery: A Survey of the Evidence," *Land Economics* 66: 359–78.

Working Group on Population Growth and Economic Development of the Committee on Population (1986) *Population Growth and Economic Development: Policy Questions*. Washington, D.C.: National Academy Press.

chapter seventeen

FUNDAMENTAL PRINCIPLES OF THE ECONOMICS OF NONRENEWABLE RESOURCES

learning objectives

After reading this chapter you will be familiar with the following:

- basic features of nonrenewable resources;
- the problems of assessing the future availability of nonrenewable resource stocks;
- the hypothesis of smooth tonnage grade and its implications;
- the conditions for the optimal intertemporal allocation of nonrenewable resources;
- the user cost as intergenerational externality and the policy implications thereof;
- the time path of nonrenewable resource prices;
- the Hotelling rule;
- the optimal price path and resource exhaustion in a perfectly competitive market setting and with perfect foresight about future resource conditions;
- nonrenewable resource prices and extraction rates in the less than perfect world;
- the notion of backstop technology: its implications for resource exhaustion and economic growth.

When people question the adequacy of existing market arrangements for the intertemporal allocation of natural resources, they are basically raising questions of the appropriate definition and consideration of user costs.

(Howe 1979: 75)

If it is very easy to substitute other factors for natural resources, then there is in principle no problem. The world can, in effect, get along without natural resources, so exhaustion is just an event, not a catastrophe.

(Solow 1974: 11)

17.1 INTRODUCTION

Nonrenewable resources are geological resources of which only a fixed supply and/or nonincreasing stock exists on the planet. However, as will be discussed in Section 17.2, while these resources exist in fixed supply, the actual size of the stocks have not necessarily been completely discovered by humans. Examples of such resources include mineral fuels like oil, coal, natural gas and other fossil fuels; metallic minerals, such as iron, gold, aluminum, copper, lead; and nonmetallic mineral resources like natural phosphate and potash deposits. It should be noted that an important feature of these resources is that they require geological time spans to regenerate. So, for all practical purposes the rate of stock creation over time is *zero*.

Nonrenewable resources can be of two categories – nonrecyclable, such as fossil fuels, and recyclable, like metallic resources. The relationship of the stock of nonrenewable resources and the flow of services that these resources provide over time can be described as follows. Let S_0 be the fixed quantity or stock of a particular nonrenewable resource at the time of discovery; let S_t be the quantity or stock of the resource of interest at a point in time, t; let τ be time, where $\tau = 0, 1, 2, \ldots, t-1, t, \ldots, \infty$; and let R_t be the rate of extraction or flow of service at time t. Using these notations, we can state that in the absence of extraction and natural entropic degradation,

$$S_t = S_0 \tag{17.1}$$

That is, if left undisturbed (or unused), a nonrenewable stock resource is a fixed amount equal to the quantity at the time of discovery. In other words, *the rate of stock creation over time is zero*. This is, in fact, one of the most significant differences between a nonrenewable and renewable resource.

Assume the existence of a positive extraction rate per unit time. Then, the relationship between the *stock* and *service flow* of a nonrenewable resource can be identified by the following:

$$S_t = S_0 - \sum R_\tau \tag{17.2}$$

This equation simply verifies that, with each use, the stock of a non-renewable and nonrecyclable resource is *depleted* by the rate of the extraction, R_t. Therefore, at any given point in time, the deposit of a nonrenewable stock resource, S_t, is the difference between the quantity of the resource at the time of discovery, S_0, and the cumulative extraction of the resource up to that point in time. Furthermore, we would expect that

$$S_0 \geq \sum R_t \tag{17.3}$$

That is, the flow of services that can be realized from a nonrenewable stock resource cannot exceed the fixed quantity of the resource available at the time of discovery. Thus, in the limit, continuous use of nonrenewable stock resources would inevitably lead to *exhaustion* – that is, $S_0 = \sum R_t$. However, as discussed in the next section, this is a physical, not an economic, concept of exhaustion.

So far, recycling has not been considered. Would the basic relationships between the stock and the flow services of nonrenewable resources outlined so far be significantly altered if recycling were to be considered? It is true that consideration of recycling would alter the one-to-one relationship between physical stock and the flow of services that can be obtained from the use of a nonrenewable resource. This occurs because, during each period, the physical stock of the natural resource, S_t, is diminished by the rate of extraction, R_t, but it is also augmented by the rate of recycling, g_t. Thus, the *net* extraction rate per unit time would then be R_t minus g_t. Yet, by the second-law of thermodynamics, it is *impossible* to have a perfect recycling technology. Thus

$$R_t - g_t > 0 \tag{17.4}$$

The implication of this is that, even with recycling capability, nonrenewable resources are eventually *exhaustible*. What is different in this case is that with recycling potential, the use of a unit of the physical stock of nonrenewable resources, S_t, does not necessarily suggest *the total and permanent loss of future use* – a key feature of nonrenewable but recyclable resources.

As observed from the discussion in Chapters 6–9, concerns about the future availability of nonrenewable resources have been a recurring theme throughout human history. Of course, such concerns can be addressed prudently, if we are able to devise a fairly reliable method for assessing resource *adequacy* – that is, measuring current and future availability of resources. Devising such a method, however, is an extremely difficult task. The next section analyzes several attempts aimed at this objective.

17.2 ASSESSMENT OF NATURAL RESOURCE STOCKS

Assessment of resource adequacy requires not only the current and future projected rates of resource consumption or utilization, but also a fairly good quantitative estimate of the size (total deposit) of the resource under consideration. As will be evident soon, quantitative estimates of total deposits of nonrenewable resources can be made only through careful examination of the geological, economic and technological factors affecting their availability.

To be available for productive use, these resources have to be geologically, economically and technologically feasible. Although it is a point often ignored, one might also add that extraction or use of nonrenewable resources should be ecologically feasible. In other words, even if a resource is economically feasible, it may not be employed if its use seriously threatens humans or some other forms of life. Examples of such resources include cadmium, mercury and nuclear radioactive substances.

Geologic feasibility concerns the very existence and the spatial distribution of the mineral elements in our planet, whereas *economic feasibility* takes into account factors like the amount of capital and labor required for exploration, development and extraction, and the expected market price of the resource in question. Economic feasibility also includes considerations of environmental, social, legal and economic factors. *Technological feasibility* simply refers to the fact that the resource is accessible for extraction using the existing state of the art.

17.2.1 Reserves, resources and resource bases

Following the lead of the US Bureau of Mines standardized procedure, on the basis of geologic, economic and technological conditions mineral resources are grouped in the manner shown in Figure 17.1. Careful examination of this figure shows that the total resource (the entire box) is classified into *resource base*, *resources* and *reserves*, and in terms of two dimensions: geologic, economic and technological feasibility. A movement along the box from right to left (as indicated by the arrow at the bottom of the box) indicates increasing geologic certainty – increasing likelihood for the existence of mineral deposits. A vertical movement along the side of the box (as shown by

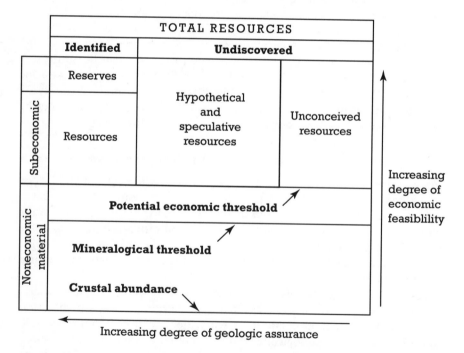

Figure 17.1 **The relation of resources to noneconomic materials**
Source: Reprinted by permission from V. K. Smith, *Scarcity and Growth Reconsidered*, copyright © Resources for the Future (Washington, D.C., 1979), p. 118.

the arrow on the right-hand side of the box) indicates increasing economic feasibility.

Thus, using the above scheme, the term *reserve* refers to a portion of the total resource base (the entire box) that is found in a known location. Furthermore, it is clearly identified and can be extracted at a profit using existing technology. As shown in Figure 17.1, reserves constitute a small part of any given resource. Note also that, even in the case of reserves, the measurement of the total quantity is subject to some degree of uncertainty. This is because the existence of some portion of the reserves is only inferred.

Additionally, it is important to note that reserve is a dynamic concept. It can be augmented both by new discoveries and by changes in economic conditions, such as higher natural resource prices and lower extraction costs. Thus, forces of this nature would tend to expand the "reserve" area towards the bottom right direction in Figure 17.1. *What this suggests is that the very concept of a socially relevant reserve depends largely on technological and economic circumstances.*

The discussion so far suggests that any attempt to estimate the *total deposit* of a stock resource is at best no more than an educated guess. As shown in Figure 17.1, total resources include not only the reserves, but also the *yet undiscovered hypothetical and speculative resources*. These portions of the total resources are extremely difficult to quantify since they are beyond the realm of economic and technological consideration. For this reasons, the accuracy of such estimates is very low, and therefore unreliable. In short, it amounts to nothing more than geologic extrapolation.

Given this situation, it is no wonder that there exists variation in the estimation of the total available deposits of nonrenewable resources. First, each analyst makes his or her projection of resource availability on the basis of specific assumptions about geologic, economic and technological conditions. For example, resource estimates based on only geological considerations are likely to present a more optimistic picture about future availability than those estimates that, in addition to geologic factors, explicitly take into account economic and technological considerations. Geologic considerations emphasize only the very existence of the resource; thus, in Figure 17.1, they include the entire box. In other words, what is being estimated here is the *total resource base*. Furthermore, there exist variations in resource estimates even among the studies that are done on the basis of geologic considerations alone because the estimation of un-discovered resources (the hypothetical and speculative portion of Figure 17.1) is subject to variations from one study to another. These may result from the particular techniques used for quantifying the estimates, as well as from the subjective assessment of the analysts.

Thus, to hear widely conflicting reports of estimates of nonrenewable resources should not be totally surprising. In this regard, it is crucial to know how the estimates are arrived at, who conducted the studies and for what purpose. For example, is the particular study conducted by a private or public concern? Does the group undertaking the project espouse a particular ideological view concerning natural resources and how they should be used and managed by humans? What kind of resource concept is central in conducting a particular resource estimate? That is, are we using resource base, resources or reserves (see Figure 17.1)? These are the kinds of question that need to be addressed in evaluating the significance, reliability and usefulness of estimates given of stock resources.

17.2.2 A measure of resource adequacy: reserve-to-use ratio

Reserve-to-use ratio is a concept that is commonly used as a first approximation regarding the amount of time it takes before the estimated reserve of a particular stock resource is exhausted. In its simplest form,

$$\gamma = S_t / R_t$$

where γ represent the number of years necessary to completely deplete the reserve, or depletion period; S_t is the most current estimate of the known reserve; and R_t is the rate of extraction or resource utilization at the present time.

From the above description, it is quite clear that the concept of reserve-to-use ratio is *static*, and for this reason alone it has very limited use. This would be true even if an adjustment were made to the rate of resource utilization, R_t, to account for future growth rate. This is because reserve is not a static concept, and is therefore subject to change for a number of reasons. Specifically, reserve estimates could change due to geological factors like discoveries of new deposits or economic and technological factors, such as a change in the demand for the resource under consideration, a change in the prices of substitutes or improvement in the technology of resource extraction. Despite its apparent limitations, reserve-to-use ratio remains the most commonly used measure of natural resource adequacy. If used with proper caution, the estimates of resource adequacy on the basis of reserve-to-use ratio can be helpful in formulating short- to intermediate-term resource policy measures.

In any serious discussion of resource adequacy, one has to consider not only the quantitative but also the qualitative aspects of resource deposits. For mineral resources, qualitative dimensions can be identified by examining the nature of the *ore grades* (as measured by the concentration of minerals) and the *spatial distribution* of ore deposits. These issues and their implications are briefly addressed in the next subsection.

17.2.3 The hypothesis of smooth tonnage grade

The total amount of useful element (tonnage of ore) to be extracted from a given mineral deposit cannot be adequately inferred from extrapolation based on the volume of mineral-containing rocks alone. This is because such a procedure will not fully account for the difference in abundance or quantity of the elements that are contained within the average rock.

Furthermore, the abundance of rock types is not distributed uniformly; it varies in different parts of the Earth's crust. Despite these problems, geologists have been able to offer several descriptive models that can be used to understand the general geochemical distribution of mineral elements. One model that is particularly applicable for describing the geochemical distribution of metals such as iron, aluminum and titanium is the hypothesis of smooth tonnage grade. *Smooth tonnage* refers to the assumption that there is no mixing of different ores in a given mineral-containing rock.

The hypothesis of smooth tonnage grade refers to the distribution of ore grade (ore content in grams per ton of rock materials) with respect to crustal abundance (tonnage of ore containing rock material). As shown in Figure 17.2, this distribution is bell-shaped. At the initial stage of mining, we expect to find a higher-grade material (rocks with high concentration of ore), but lower crustal abundance. However, as mining increases, although the grade (in terms of ore concentration) continues to diminish, the elements (the rock materials containing ore) will continue to increase. In other words, *as we deplete the materials with high ore content, we find lower-grade materials with greater abundance.*

If this hypothesis is valid, it has the following important implications. First, for a local deposit of minerals, the fact that the crustal abundance increases as extraction proceeds suggests that *exhaustion of mineral resources is primarily an economic event.* In other words, economic exhaustion precedes the geological thresholds for exhaustion of mineral resources. Second, in the absence of a breakthrough in extraction technology, an increase in extraction from a given mine would entail an increase in extraction costs. In other words, more labor, capital and energy resources are needed to continue extracting and

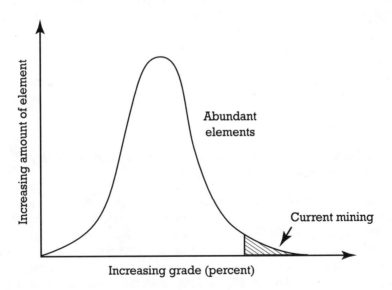

Figure 17.2 **Possible geochemical distribution of abundant and scarce elements**

processing a progressively poorer quality of element. However, this increase in extraction costs may be offset through continued technological advancement in the extraction and processing of mineral substances. In a situation like this, where we hypothesized the existence of abundant rock elements of homogeneous quality (in terms of ore concentration), with continued advances in the technology of resource extraction it is possible to envision a situation where a mineral resource can be nearly exhausted while the cost of extraction is still declining. Third, ultimately, *energy* is the limiting factor to further extraction and processing of ever-increasing poor-grade, but abundant, quantities of ore-containing substances.

Before we leave this subject, it is important to note that the hypothesis of smooth tonnage is applicable to the distribution of the most geochemically abundant metals such as iron, aluminum and titanium. In fact, for many scarce mineral elements, such as mercury, tin, nickel and diamond, their geochemical distribution tends to show sharp discontinuities. That is, "after the easily found high concentrations are exploited, the minerals may be found only in very diffused and molecularly different forms requiring 1,000 to 10,000 times as much energy to extract" (Brobst 1979). In these instances the technological effect on reducing extraction costs will be less pronounced, and energy will be a very potent limiting factor to the availability of these types of mineral resources.

So far, we have observed that nonrenewable resources exist as stocks in definite fixed quantities. Although it is difficult to measure current and future availability of nonrenewable resources, it is evident that, over time, these resources are diminished through extraction and entropic degradation, though in some cases the loss may be partially offset by recycling. Thus, the economics of nonrenewable resources basically concerns the study of the *intertemporal* allocation of these type of resources. This entails deciding how much of a nonrenewable resource should be used for present consumption and how much of it should be left for future use. This is the core of the economics of exhaustible resources – the subject of this chapter. In the next section, using a simple analytical framework, the Pareto optimal conditions for intertemporal allocation of nonrenewable resources are derived.

17.3 THE OPTIMAL INTERTEMPORAL ALLOCATION OF NONRENEWABLE RESOURCES

In this section I will attempt to derive the general condition for an optimal intertemporal allocation of nonrenewable resources. An economic problem of this nature can only be addressed with dynamic models – that is, models which allow for an explicit consideration of *time*. A rigorous treatment of this subject requires a mathematical background beyond the intended audience for this book. The basic analysis of intertemporal allocation of resources will be explained using a two-dimensional graphic approach – an analytic approach pioneered by James McInerney (1976).

17.3.1 Basic assumptions and preliminary analyses

When using a two-dimensional graphic approach, it is necessary to conduct the analyses by collapsing the entire time horizon into two distinct time periods: *present* and *future*. Both the present and future demands for the resource under consideration are assumed to be known with *certainty* and remain constant over time. Usually, the resource under consideration is exchanged under an institutional setting characterized by a perfectly competitive market system. Thus, resource owners are price-takers (see Chapter 2). Also, future benefits and costs are discounted using the social discount rate (see Chapter 15). To simplify the analysis, it is further assumed that the marginal cost of extraction does not change over time.

Let us begin the analysis with a simple case where the nonrenewable resource under consideration is assumed to exist in abundance. Given this condition, the decision as to how much of this resource to use now and in the future is demonstrated with Figure 17.3. In this figure, MSB_0 and MEC_0 represent the marginal social benefit (demand) and the marginal extraction costs of the present period. Similarly, MSB_1 and MEC_1 are the marginal social benefit (future demand) and the marginal social extraction costs of the future period. Note that both MSB_1 and MEC_1 are discounted using the social discount rate. Furthermore, since perfect competition is assumed, demand and marginal social benefits should be the same (see Chapter 2). One last point to consider is that, in Figure 17.3, the entire length of the horizontal line which extends from the origin to the broken vertical line (or the distance $0S_0$ on the *x*-axis) measures the total quantity of the nonrenewable stock resource available for both present and future use.

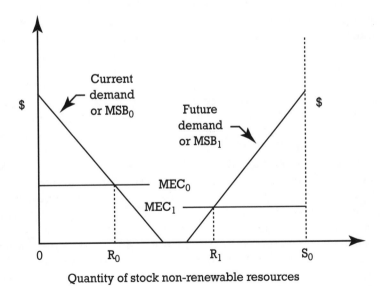

Figure 17.3 **Optimal intertemporal allocation of an abundant nonrenewable resource**

In this situation, with full consideration of the current and future demands and extraction costs, the optimal intertemporal allocation of the resource in question will be attained when amount $0R_0$ is extracted for present use and amount S_0R_1 for future use. *These results are obtained by equating the marginal social benefit with the marginal extraction cost for each period independently.* It is possible to do this because when amount $0R_0$ is used during the present period, what is left for future use, $0S_0 - 0R_0$, is greater than the amount that is actually needed of this resource for future use, S_0R_1. Thus, in a situation where the stock resource under consideration is *abundant* – that is, $(0S_0 - 0R_0) > S_0R_1$ – present use of the resource would not prevent use of the same resource in the future. In other words, *the cost of the present resource use in terms of forgone future use of the same resource is zero.* Therefore, under this condition, the optimal intertemporal use of a nonrenewable stock resource can be determined by equating the marginal social benefit and marginal extraction cost in each time period *independently.*

17.3.2 The general condition for optimal intertemporal allocation of nonrenewable and nonrecyclable resources

Thus far we have considered the optimal allocation of nonrenewable resources in a situation where present use will have no effect on the availability of the resource for future use; in other words, there is no conflict between present and future use of the resource. Undoubtedly this represents an unlikely situation. In reality, present consumption of nonrenewable resources would entail a cost in terms of forgone future use. In this subsection, an attempt will be made to derive the general condition for an optimal intertemporal allocation of a nonrenewable and nonrecyclable resource where the conflict between present and future use of this resource is vividly apparent. This is done using Figure 17.4.

Let us start the analysis by noting that if the present generation ignores future needs, then as discussed above, amount $0R_0$ of the resource will be used (where $MSB_0 = MEC_0$). This will leave amount R_0S_0 of the resource to future generations. However, given future demand and cost conditions for the resource (MSB_1 and MEC_1, respectively), later generations would have preferred to use amount R_1S_0 of the resource. This would be impossible, because the *sum* of the present and future uses of this resource would exceed the fixed supply of this resource – that is, $0R_0 + R_1S_0 > 0S_0$. Under this condition, beyond a certain level the use of this resource by the present generation will impose a cost on the future generation by denying availability of that resource for future use. In Figure 17.4, $0R_1$ would be the maximum amount of the resource that the present generation could use without denying the consumption opportunity of this resource to the future generation. Thus, the present use of this resource beyond $0R_1$ would automatically entail *opportunity cost.* What exactly is the nature of this opportunity cost? How is it determined or identified? As we will see soon,

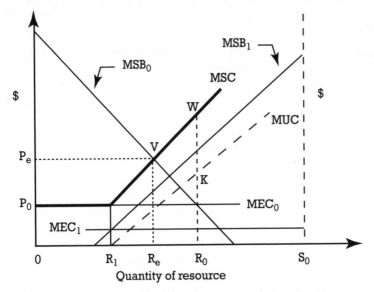

Figure 17.4 **Optimal intertemporal allocation of a nonrenewable and nonrecyclable resource**

this concept plays a pivotal role in determining the optimal intertemporal allocation of nonrenewable resources.

For resource use beyond $0R_1$, the opportunity cost can be measured by the present value of future sacrifice associated with the use of a particular *unit* of the natural resource at the present time. In the literature of environmental and resource economics, the term used to describe this concept of opportunity cost is often referred to as the *marginal user cost* (MUC). In Figure 17.4, for each unit of present consumption exceeding $0R_1$, the marginal user cost is measured by the difference between MSB_1 and MEC_1 – that is, the *net* discounted incremental benefits to the future generation. As shown in Figure 17.4, the marginal user cost, $MSB_1 - MEC_1$, increases with an increasing use of the resource in question by the present generation beyond $0R_1$. This will be the case provided the demand for the resource by the future generation, MSB_1, has a negative slope.

By definition, an "optimal" intertemporal allocation of a resource suggests that the decision on resource extraction by the present generation should explicitly account for all the costs and benefits, including, if any, the opportunity cost imposed on future generations – user costs. If this logic is strictly applied, in Figure 17.4, when current resource use exceeds $0R_1$, the marginal *social* cost (MSC) of using a unit of the resource in question by the present generation would be obtained by adding MEC_0 and MUC. Given this, the optimal resource use is attained when the following condition is met:

$$MSB_0 = MSC \qquad (17.5)$$

or

$$MSB_0 = MEC_0 + MUC \tag{17.6}$$

Equation (17.6) is, in fact, the general condition for optimal inter-temporal allocation of nonrenewable resources. Note how this condition differs from those that we discussed in the previous subsection, when the natural resource under consideration was not time dependent. For instance, see the case portrayed by Figure 17.3. Under this circumstance, the optimal condition did not include marginal user cost. Specifically, the present generation is able to use all it desires, $0R_0$, without affecting the resource needs of future generations, R_1S_0. Therefore, the marginal user cost is clearly zero. It is in this sense, then, that the condition shown by equation (17.6) above is general; it is applicable for all cases.

According to Figure 17.4, the optimal resource allocation between the present and future would be $0R_e$ and S_0R_e, respectively. This is because at $0R_e$, $MSB_0 = MSC$ (point V in Figure 17.4). Furthermore, the sum of the present and future uses of this resource exactly equals the fixed and nonaugmentable total endowment that is available for use between the two periods. That is, $0R_e + S_0R_e = 0S_0$. This result is socially optimal in the sense that it represents the *maximum*, *total*, *net* social benefit from the use of the entire resource, $0S_0$, after considering the preferences, benefits and costs of both the present and the future users of the resource under consideration. In other words, point V in Figure 17.4, where $MSB_0 = MSC$, is Pareto optimal.

To formally demonstrate that $0R_e$ is, in fact, Pareto optimal, let us suppose that the present generation is extracting amount $0R_0$ of this particular natural resource. As shown in Figure 17.4, when the present level of extraction is $0R_0$, $MSB_0 = MEC_0$. In other words, the present generation is using this natural resource without taking into account the cost they are inflicting upon the future generation. However, at $0R_0$, the MUC is *positive*, as indicated by the vertical distance of line R_0K (or the difference between MSB_1 and MEC_1 at level of extraction $0R_0$). When this cost is explicitly considered, the marginal social cost ($MSC = MEC_0 + MUC$) at level of resource use $0R_0$ will be greater than MSB_0. Clearly, then, this allocation is not optimal. Since MSC exceeds MSB_0, the use of the resource by the present generation is excessive, thereby suggesting a reduction in the use of the resource in question.

A similar argument could be presented if the current resource use was below $0R_e$. In this case, the condition would dictate that for each level of resource use by the present generation below $0R_e$, MSB_0 would be greater than MSC; therefore, society would be better off by increasing its current consumption level. This adjustment process will continue until MSB_0 equals MSC, which is attained at $0R_e$. This clearly verifies that $0R_e$ is Pareto optimal; society would be worse off from a move in either direction from this level of resource use.

There is one last observation that needs to be made before ending the discussion in this subsection. At the point where the socially optimal level of resource use is attained, $0R_e$, the marginal net benefit (MNB) received from the use of the particular resource under consideration is *equal* for both time periods – present and future. That is, at $0R_e$, $MSB_0 - MEC_0 = MSB_1 - MEC_1$. This can also be generalized by stating that *the optimal intertemporal allocation of nonrenewable resources requires the marginal net benefit from the last unit of a resource use to be the same for the whole of the relevant time period.* This makes sense because any deviation from this condition would entail the need for a reallocation of resources. For example, at a certain level of resource use, suppose that the marginal net benefit to the present generation (MNB_0) is greater than the marginal net benefit to the future generation (MNB_1). In this situation, if the objective is to maximize total *social* benefit, it makes perfect sense to increase the use of the natural resource during the current period. This in turn suggests a reduction in the amount that would be available for use by the future generation. The reverse would hold if MNB_0 were less than MNB_1. To recapitulate what has been discussed so far, an optimal intertemporal allocation of nonrenewable resources is attained when the following two interrelated conditions are met:

$$MSB_0 = MSC = MEC_0 + MUC \qquad (17.7)$$

and

$$MNB_0 = MNB_1 \qquad (17.8)$$

17.3.3 The optimal intertemporal allocation of nonrenewable but recyclable resources

The analysis in this subsection uses the same set of assumptions as above. Most importantly, we are still concerned with an intertemporal allocation of nonrenewable resources; this is done using a simple framework of analysis which involves only two time periods: present and future. However, in this subsection we consider the case where the nonrenewable resources are *recyclable*. The question of interest is then, how would consideration of recycling affect the conditions for intertemporal allocation of nonrenewable resources that were presented in the previous subsection – equations (17.7) and (17.8)?

As discussed earlier, for nonrenewable stock resources, each time a unit of these resources is used, it will be completely and irrevocably lost (destroyed). Fossil fuels are an example of this. In this situation, a unit of a nonrenewable resource use by present users completely prevents future use. However, for a nonrenewable resource that is recyclable, each time a unit of the resource is used, only *part* of it is completely destroyed. (Remember that 100 percent recycling is impossible.) The amount of useful resource materials that are recovered through recycling could vary widely, and generally depends on a number of geological, economic and technological factors. Yet the fact remains that under no circumstances can recycling, *per se*, achieve the complete recovery of all the useful substances embodied in already "manufactured" or processed materials. This partial loss of useful materials from repeated use of resources suggests that the marginal user cost is *positive* for nonrenewable, but recyclable, resources in fixed supply. That is, each time a unit of resource is used by present users, some portion of that resource will never be available for future use. In this sense, then, present use implies a sacrifice in terms of lost opportunity for future use. Nevertheless, we would expect the marginal user cost of a nonrenewable resource to be less if it is recyclable. As shown in Figure 17.5, the effect of recycling would be to *rotate* the marginal user cost curve downward from $MUC_{w/o}$ (marginal user cost without recycling) to MUC_w (marginal user cost with recycling). It is important to note that the magnitude of the rotation depends on a number of geological, economic and technological factors.

A final item necessary for consideration is the cost of extraction. In contrast to the use of "virgin" materials, materials recovered through recycling do not require extraction costs. For this reason, the relevant marginal user cost for recyclable, nonrenewable resources should explicitly take this factor into account. In Figure 17.5 this is shown by the marginal user cost curve labeled MUC_n. The points along this curve are obtained by subtracting the marginal extraction cost (MEC_1) from the marginal user cost with recycling (MUC_w) across all the relevant points. Thus, MUC_n actually represents the marginal user cost, net of extraction cost. Once this is accomplished, then as shown below, stating the condition for optimal intertemporal allocation of nonrenewable and recyclable resource is rather straightforward:

$$MSB_0 = MSC = MEC_0 + MUC_n \qquad\qquad (17.9)$$

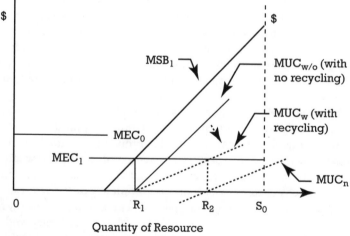

Figure 17.5 Effect of recycling on marginal user cost

The only difference between equation (17.7), the general condition for optimal intertemporal allocation of nonrenewable resources, and equation (17.9) is the way MUC is treated. Since we expect MUC_n to be less than MUC (the marginal user cost without recycling), the optimal resource use with recycling will permit a more liberal use of nonrenewable resources during the current period than would have been the case if recycling were not considered to be a viable option. *Hence, the ultimate effect of recycling is to free up more of a renewable resource for present use.*

17.3.4 Further reflections on the nature of the user cost and some public policy implications

So far we have been able to derive the equilibrium conditions for a Pareto optimal intertemporal allocation for both nonrecyclable and recyclable nonrenewable resources (equations (17.7)–(17.9)). In deriving these conditions, extraction cost was assumed to be constant over time, and the environmental damage of resource extraction was not taken into consideration. In this subsection an attempt will be made to reassess the above optimality conditions when these two factors are explicitly considered. This will be followed by a brief discussion of the policy implications of the intertemporal resource allocation of nonrenewable resources, in general.

In the simple model that we have focused on so far, the *user cost* became relevant because present extraction of a nonrenewable natural resource is expected to have the effect of reducing the availability (or stock) of a resource for future use. However, this progressive decline in the level of stock is assumed to have no effect on future marginal extraction cost. That is, the marginal extraction cost is assumed to be constant over time. Despite this, as discussed in Section 17.2, it has been found that as the level of stock declines, the marginal cost of extraction increases. The above simple model ignores a change in the extraction costs of this nature.

In addition to the above consideration, the extraction of nonrenewable resources for present use could cause environmental damage with far-reaching consequences for future generations. For instance, consider the ecological destruction (scarring of landmass) and disturbances that are caused when strip-coalmining is carried out indiscriminately.

Clearly, then, on the basis of the above discussions, a more inclusive and socially relevant concept of user cost should represent *the present value of all future sacrifices (including forgone use, higher extraction costs and increased environmental costs) associated with the use of a particular unit of a nonrenewable natural resource.*

Now that we have examined the user cost in this comprehensive manner, it will be quite instructive at this point to discuss some of the public policy implications of the general condition for optimal intertemporal allocation of nonrenewable resources developed so far. Clearly, the user cost plays a key role in addressing this issue. First, it should be noted that the user cost is an *externality* because of its third-party effect. That is, part of the user cost includes the unintended effect(s) that current use of natural resources has on the welfare of future generations (users). For example, as discussed earlier, present resource use may result in higher future extraction costs and/or negative environmental effects. If this is the case, then as discussed in Chapter 5, the market, if left alone, would *fail* to allocate nonrenewable resources efficiently. In particular, an allocation based on the free play of private markets is unlikely to take account of all of the relevant components of user cost (more on this later). Consequently, the market prices for nonrenewable resources will most likely be undervalued when an intertemporal allocation of this resource is guided by the free play of private markets because the market price fails to fully take into account user costs – which are externalities. If not corrected, this will ultimately lead to unwarranted environmental and ecological damage and a faster rate of resource depletion. The discussion in Case Study 17.1 vividly depicts the ecological and human price arising from the global community's failure to consider the full costs of mineral extraction and processing. So, what can be done to remedy this situation?

The simple answer to this question is to use similar types of public policy measures to those discussed in Chapters 11 and 12 for the purpose of remedying environmental externalities. These measures may include raising the market price for nonrenewable resources through some form of *fines*, so that the price users pay corresponds to the social value of the resource under consideration, P_e in Figure 17.4. Another way of achieving the same objective would be, as Herman Daly and others (see Chapters 8 and 9) have suggested, by setting *quotas*. Note, however, that as discussed in Chapter 5 at some length) it is not costless to actually implement public policy measures of this nature. They require the acquiring of information (on future demand conditions, changes in technology and changes in preferences) that is difficult and costly to obtain. Furthermore, once implemented, to be effective these policies need to be strictly enforced. Thus, in some instances the costs of information and enforcement (the transaction costs) may be so high that public policies of the above nature could be rendered ineffective.

Another issue of interest from a public policy perspective is the role that recycling could play in mitigating the limits on the future availability of

CASE STUDY 17.1 MINING THE EARTH

John E. Young

Human welfare and mineral supplies have been linked for so long that scholars demarcate the ages of human history by reference to minerals: Stone, Bronze and Iron. Cheap and abundant minerals provided the physical foundation for industrial civilizations.

Industrial nations' abiding preoccupation with minerals is thus not surprising. In the United States, for example, periodic waves of concern over future mineral supplies have led to the appointment of at least a half-dozen blue-ribbon panels on the subject since the 1920s. In 1978, a US congressional committee requested a study whose title expressed the central question of virtually all these inquiries: Are we running out?

Recent trends in price and availability of minerals suggest that the answer is "not yet." Regular improvements in exploitative technology have allowed the production of growing amounts at declining prices, despite the exhaustion of many of the world's richest ores. For many minerals, much of the world has yet to be thoroughly explored.

The question of scarcity, however, may never have been the most important one. Far more urgent is, can the world afford the human and ecological price of satisfying its voracious appetite for minerals? Today's low mineral prices reflect only the immediate economics of extraction: purchases of equipment and fuel, wages, transportation, financing, and so on. They fail to consider the full costs of devastated landscapes, dammed or polluted rivers, the squalor of mining camps, and the uprooting or decimation of indigenous peoples unlucky enough to live atop mineral deposits. . . .

Why are mineral prices so low? One reason is that many nations subsidize development of their domestic mineral resources. Since the 1920s, for example, the United States has offered mining companies generous tax exemptions called depletion allowances. Miners can deduct from 5 to 22 percent of their gross income, depending on the mineral. . . .The US mining industry receives another large but uncalculated subsidy through virtual giveaways of federal land under the General Mining Act of 1872. This legal relic of the frontier era allows those who find hard-rock minerals (such as gold, silver, lead, iron and copper) in public territory to buy the land for $12 per hectare or less.

Japan offers loans, subsidies and tax incentives for exploration and development of domestic mineral deposits. Similarly, the French government offers financial assistance for minerals exploration, and also makes direct investments in mineral projects through the Bureau de Recherches Géologiques et Minières (BRGM), a state-owned enterprise. Germany is considerably less generous, but does offer direct support for exploration.

Industrial nations have thus also tried to ensure continued access to cheap minerals supplies through their international trade and aid policies. . . .These nations have also often supported efforts by development institutions, including the World Bank, to finance mineral projects in developing countries – at times with the explicit intention of securing future mineral resources. . . .

The overall result of these developments was a dramatic transformation of the world mineral industry – from a relatively stable, lucrative oligopoly to an unpredictable, intensely competitive business. This change undermined overnight the development strategy followed by many Third World minerals producers. . . .

The other, often forgotten side of developing countries' involvement in mining is the effects on *local people* and their *environment*. The rush to produce more minerals and gain export revenue has had devastating consequences for those whose homelands are underlain by minerals.

Source: Worldwatch Institute, *State of the World 1992*. Copyright © 1992. Reprinted by permission.

nonrenewable resources. In this instance, as shown in Figure 17.5, the effect of *recycling* is to reduce user cost. How much the user cost will decline depends upon the amount of the original materials that can be recovered from a resource already in use. Some of the most important factors which affect the recycling potential of a natural resource include the recycling technology, the biochemical composition of the resource under consideration, and how the resource in question is combined with various other resources to form a final product.

From a public policy perspective, recycling should naturally be encouraged since it prolongs the life expectancy of a natural resource. In fact, one can view recycling as a resource conservation measure, and rightly so. The most traditional means of encouraging recycling is by providing financial incentives to improve the technology of materials recycling. However, technology should not be the only answer to improving the potential of recycling. Materials recycling, as pointed out in Chapter 8, can be significantly improved by producing products that are *replaceable* and by producing goods and services that are *durable*. These two criteria, replaceability and durability, require considerations that go beyond technology. Basically, they require changes in the preferences of the consumers (society) at large. These changes are difficult to accomplish, but can be done through a systematic, deliberate and prolonged campaign designed to promote public awareness of the value of recycling.

It should be noted, however, that recycling must not be viewed as a cure-all remedy to counter the limits imposed by nature on the future availability of nonrenewable resources. Recycling cannot overcome technological limits imposed by nature (the laws of thermodynamics rule out 100 percent recycling). That is, while recycling can be used to prolong the life cycle of natural resources, it cannot create new resources.

Finally, within the context of intertemporal allocation of nonrenewable resources, the user cost cannot be fully addressed by considering only technological and economic factors. As discussed in Chapters 8, 9 and 15 in some detail, the amount of natural resources that we are willing to pass along for use by future generations (consideration of intergenerational equity) *depends on the moral and ethical values that we collectively uphold as a society* (more on this later).

In this section we concentrated on formal analyses that allowed us to derive the general equilibrium condition for an optimal intertemporal allocation of nonrenewable resources. Clearly, these equilibrium conditions establish the general rule by which society should decide the amount of fixed and nonreproducible resources to use now and in the future. Furthermore, from the discussions so far, the spot (current) market equilibrium price, P_e in Figure 17.4, is determined at the point where the optimality condition is met – that is, $P_e = MSB_0 = MEC_0 + MUC$. However, *this condition provides no insight into the price and extraction paths of nonrenewable resources over time.* This is the subject of the next section.

17.4 THE OPTIMAL PRICE AND EXTRACTION PATHS OF NONRENEWABLE RESOURCES

The main objective of this section is to trace the "optimal" time paths or movements of the prices and extraction rates of nonrenewable resources through time. By its very nature, this kind of analysis is dynamic and, as such, requires an advanced level of mathematical knowledge. Despite this, an attempt will be made to address the essence of the above-stated objective by using a simple analytical approach. Admittedly, this cannot be done without having to resort to some heuristic techniques and intuitive arguments which are based on the following assumptions:

First, it is assumed that the nonrenewable resource of interest exists in a known location and finite amount. Furthermore, the ownership rights for this resource are clearly defined. Second, it is assumed that this resource is traded in a perfectly competitive market setting. Therefore, resource owners are price-takers. Third, it is assumed that the demand for the resource in question will remain constant over time; future resource prices are known with certainty. Fourth, the cost of extraction is assumed to be zero (or negligible compared with the price of the resource). These two assumptions, constant demand and zero extraction cost, are made purely for expository ease. Once the desired model is developed, the robustness of the implications drawn from the use of the simple model can be tested by relaxing these assumptions.

The final assumption concerns the market for time-dated "assets" – that is, the exchange of time-dated commodities. Examples of such assets include houses, major household appliances, shares of a company's assets (stocks) and mineral deposits. A common characteristic of these assets is that their consumption or use could be extended beyond the current period. Therefore, it is up to the owners of these resources to decide how much of these assets to use now and how much to hold for future use.

In the market for assets, interest rate plays an important role because it represents the rate of return from holding the *numeraire* asset. Here another assumption is needed. That is, the real (adjusted for inflation) interest rate is determined by a competitive market force, and long-run real interest rate is constant.

Given the above set of assumptions, in the next two subsections an attempt will be made to determine the conditions under which an optimal price path can be traced for a nonrenewable stock resource.

17.4.1 The time path of nonrenewable resource prices

Let us begin with a simple case where there exists a nonrenewable resource in a known location and in finite quantity. Furthermore, let us say that this resource is owned by an individual and this individual, if she or he wishes, can extract a part or all of this resource for sale at any point in time. The primary objective of the owner of the resource is to be able to sell her or his holding over time in such a way that the *present value* from the sale of the entire stock is maximized. What *decision rule* can an owner of a time-dated asset use to achieve this goal? Ideally, what is needed is a decision rule that can instruct the owner, at any point in time, to either sell or hold a portion of her or his resource stock.

In an effort to construct such a decision rule, let P_t denote the market price at time t for the resource in question. Obviously, at any point in time, given the market price information, the owner of this resource has two options: (a) sell some units of her or his resource stock at the going market price, P_t, and acquire an alternative physical or financial asset; or (b) hold the asset in the ground to be considered for selling at some future time.

Operating within the premise of the above set of conditions, if this individual decides to acquire a unit of the numeraire asset by selling some units of her or his resource stock in time t, that individual's real rate of return during the time interval $(t, t + \Delta t)$ would be r. Alternatively, if the decision is to hold resource stock in the ground at time t and bring it for sale later at time $(t + \Delta t)$ at the prevailing market price $P_{(t+\Delta t)}$, her or his expected return during the time interval $(t, t + \Delta t)$ would be represented by the rate of price appreciation. That is,

$$(\Delta P/\Delta t)/P_t = \dot{P}_t/P_t \tag{17.11}$$

where $\Delta P = (P_{(t+\Delta t)} - P_t)$; $\dot{P}_t$ is the change in price per unit time – that is, $(\Delta P/\Delta t)$; and the subscript t represents time; $t = 0, 1, 2, \ldots, \infty$. The expression $\dot{P}_t/P_t$ tells us the percentage rate at which the price of the resource is changing at a point in time. Since this expression plays a very important role in the analysis that follows, it may be helpful to use a simple example to further clarify this point. Suppose the price for a given natural resource was $40 per pound ten years ago ($P_0 = \$40$). Today, the same resource is traded for $75 per pound ($P_{10} = \$75$) after adjustment is made for inflation. This price information suggests that over the ten-year period, in real terms the price of the resource has increased (changed) by $3.50 per pound *per unit time* (that is, $\dot{P}_t = \Delta P/\Delta t = \$3.50$). If we divide this change in price per unit of time by the value of the original price of the resource, $(\dot{P}_t/P_0)$, the result we obtain would be 0.0875. This figure simply indicates that, on average, the original value of the resource has been appreciating at a rate of 8.75 percent per unit of time. Thus, it is in this sense that $\dot{P}_t/P_t$ indicates the rate of price appreciation per unit time.

Given this, how would an owner of a resource with fixed deposit decide whether or not to sell some units of her or his resource at time t? Ultimately the decision *depends on the relationship between the rate of price appreciation, $\dot{P}_t/P_t$, of the resource during the time interval under consideration, and the rate of return from holding alternative assets, r.* More specifically, if the rate at which the resource price is appreciating is greater than r, then it pays for the resource owner to hold her or his stock in the ground. The opposite will be the case if the rate at which the price of the resource is appreciating is less than r. Therefore, the individual resource owner will be in a state of indifference (or equilibrium) when the rate of resource price appreciation is exactly equal to the rate of return for alternative assets. This equilibrium condition can be expressed as:

$$(\Delta P/\Delta t)/P_t = \dot{P}_t/P_t = r \qquad (17.12)$$

Equation (17.12) is commonly called the arbitrage equation, and in resource economics it is often referred to as the *Hotelling rule* in acknowledgment of Harold Hotelling's (1931) groundbreaking work in this area. This rule suggests that, at each point in time, it is only when the price of the resource rises at rate r that resource owners with fixed deposits will be indifferent between extracting and holding.

One important implication of the condition described by equation (17.12) is this: *provided the rate of return from the numeraire asset, r, is positive, the market price of a nonrenewable resource will not remain constant over time. In particular, the competitive price of a nonrenewable resource will appreciate (rise) over time at the percentage rate of r.* For the sake of clarity, it should be noted that in our discussion so far the market price, P_t, refers to the *net* cash receipt that an owner of a nonrenewable resource would obtain from selling a unit of such resource. This is because the cost of extraction is assumed to be zero. For this reason, for our simple model, P_t represents a *rent* or *royalty* – what an owner of a nonrenewable resource receives net of production costs. Thus, it should be emphasized that, in our simple model, it is the royalty that is appreciating over time at a percentage rate of r.

Furthermore, from our discussion in Section 15.5, we have demonstrated that when something (like a sum of money deposited in a bank) is growing at a constant rate per unit time, the growth is said to be *exponential*. This means, then, that in the long run *the competitive price (royalty) of a nonrenewable resource will tend to appreciate (grow) exponentially*. This is indeed a very significant finding.

Figure 17.6 shows the movement of the competitive price for a nonrenewable resource over time. That is, given the initial price P_0, at each point in time the market price of the resource, P_t, will rise exponentially at the percentage rate of r. It is important to note that, other factors remaining constant, the higher the value of r, the faster will be the rate of price appreciation over time. In Figure 17.6, r_1 is assumed to be greater than r_0. Thus, the curve associated with the higher rate of return, r_1, is steeper than the curve associated with the lower rate of return, r_0.

On the basis of the above observations, the following important inferences can be drawn: given that resources are allocated under a competitive market setting, *the depletion of a nonrenewable resource over time will be accomplished by a steady increase in prices*. In addition, other things being equal, the steady increases in the prices of nonrenewable resources will be accompanied by a fall in the rate of extraction over time. This implies that *an unregulated competitive market system has a built-in mechanism to conserve nonrenewable resources*. This would clearly suggest a prima facie case for leaving resource allocation to the market.

From the discussion so far, we note that the market conserves resources

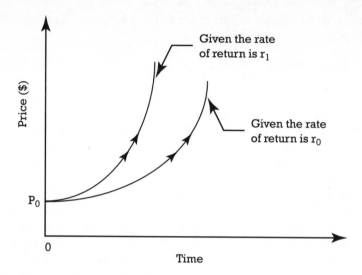

Figure 17.6 **Time path of the price of a nonrenewable resource**

through a steady increase in prices over time. However, nothing is said about the *exact* nature of the price movement over time. This is the subject matter of the next section.

17.4.2 The optimal price path and resource exhaustion

Given the initial price, P_0, and the rate of return from holding long-term assets, r, equation (17.12) suggests that the price path of a nonrenewable resource will behave as depicted in Figure 17.6. That is, the price of the resource will rise exponentially. However, in tracing the price path we have said nothing about how the *initial price*, P_0, is determined. This is a crucial piece of information because, as one would expect, the actual nature of the price path depends on the value assigned for the initial price.

Under a perfectly competitive market setting, as shown in Figure 17.4, the market price that is consistent with the optimal intertemporal allocation of nonrenewable resources is achieved when $P_e = MSB_0 = MEC_0 + MUC$. Thus, if the objective is to trace the optimal price path, the initial price, P_0, must satisfy this condition. The significance of clearly delineating the optimal price path this way is presented using Figure 17.7. Suppose $P_0 = P_e$ – that is, the initial price which is formed under the competitive process that ensures optimal allocation of resources. Using this as a starting point, the price path that follows is shown in Figure 17.7a – which is ascending exponentially at the rate of r. The corresponding extraction path is shown in Figure 17.7b – which is declining monotonically until its eventual depletion at time T_e. This simply suggests that a steady increase in price would be accompanied by a steady decline in the rate of resource utilization. These price and extraction paths are considered "optimal" to the extent that at

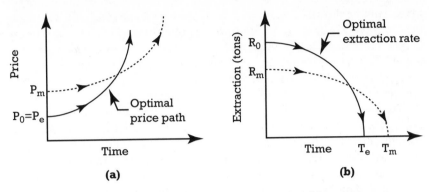

Figure 17.7 **Price and extraction paths for nonrenewable resources**

each point in time the condition for an intertemporal allocation of resources, equation (17.4), is satisfied. They describe the Pareto optimal price and extraction trajectories over time in a perfectly competitive world. To the extent that the real world bears little resemblance to the perfectly competitive conditions that underlie the analysis so far, these "ideal" conditions can be treated as a benchmark.

17.5 RESOURCE PRICES AND EXTRACTION RATES IN THE LESS THAN PERFECT WORLD

The main objective of this section is to show how far reality diverges from the ideal conditions discussed in the preceding analyses. This will be done under the following specific situations: (a) Resource owners are assumed to have significant monopoly power. In other words, resource owners are no longer assumed to be price-takers. (b) The environmental and ecological costs of resource extraction are internalized. (c) The absence of forward markets for natural resources is acknowledged. (d) The divergence between the social and private discount rates is explicitly considered and reconciled. A problem closely associated to this is consideration of intergenerational fairness.

For each of these four situations, an attempt will be made not only to show how far reality diverges from the ideal, but also to offer a clue as to the possible direction of the bias. That is, using the outcomes in a perfectly competitive world as a benchmark, in each of the above cases an attempt will be made to show whether resources are being used too fast or too slowly.

Monopoly Power

Suppose resource owners are monopolists. Basic microeconomic theory confirms that *resource owners with monopoly power will tend to restrict output and charge higher prices than would occur under perfect competition*. This suggests the likelihood of a higher initial price under monopoly. However, although this will not be shown here, under monopoly *it is the marginal revenue, not the price, that will rise at the rate of the interest rate*. Thus, since for a monopoly marginal revenue is less than price, *price will rise at a rate less than the interest rate*. What will be the implication of this for resource allocation over time?

To address this question let us refer back to Figure 17.7a. Let P_m represent the initial price under a monopolistic market structure, which is expected to be higher than the price under a perfectly competitive market setting, P_e. The monopoly price path is shown by the dotted line, and is less steep than the Pareto optimal price path. This deviation is to be expected given that the monopoly price is rising at a rate less than the interest rate. The dotted curve in Figure 17.7b shows the extraction path of the monopoly. This figure clearly suggests that the existence of a monopoly prolongs the depletion period of nonrenewable resources (T_m instead of T_e). Does this mean, as some economists would like to suggest, that "a monopoly is a true friend of conservationists"?

In some respects, this result should not be taken lightly since many resource markets tend to be monopolistic. In addition to the well-known oil cartel OPEC (the Organization of Petroleum Exporting Countries), many mineral-producing companies (such as those involved in the production of copper, bauxite, potash, etc.) operate some form of monopolistic arrangements. *If monopoly is the norm rather than the exception in the extractive resource markets, it suggests that in the real world extractive resources are being used too slowly.*

On the other hand, this bias toward resource conservation may be offset if the following two conditions persist: (a) significant economies of scale occur in the resource extraction sectors – which is not unlikely (see Chapter 7); (b) generous government subsidies are given to industries extracting virgin material resources (see Case Study 17.1). *When these two factors are considered, the remark that a monopoly is "a true friend of the conservationist" may be questionable.*

Environmental externalities

From the above discussion it is clear that the socially optimal price path requires that the initial price, P_0, be set in such a way that the following general condition is met:

$$P_0 = P_e = MSB_0 = MEC_0 + MUC$$

When the allocation of nonrenewable resources is guided through a private market, the *user cost* reflects the forgone future private benefits (profits) to owners of nonrenewable resources when they decide to extract and sell the resource now, instead of holding it for sale at some future date. However, as discussed earlier, when viewed from a societal perspective the user cost may not be limited to the forgone profits of resource owners. It may include external costs, such as the effects of current resource utilization on future extraction costs and the damage to the natural environment. Therefore, a competitive market system which operates solely on the basis of information generated from independent decisions of private individuals may *fail* to fully account for the environmental damage resulting from the extraction of nonrenewable resources for current use. A case in point would be environmental damage arising from the extraction of coal using the strip-mining technique. In such an instance, it is quite likely that the *private* marginal user cost (forgone future benefits to resource owners) will not fully reflect the *social* marginal user cost – which includes the environmental and ecological effects of current extraction methods (see Case Study 17.1). In this case, since what is involved is environmental externality, the social marginal user cost will be less than the private marginal user cost. Consistent with the discussion in Chapter 5, this divergence between marginal social and private user cost clearly indicates market failure.

What this suggests is that the *socially* optimal *initial* price should be set above P_e in Figure 17.7a. This should be the case since market prices do not include external costs. As a result, an unregulated competitive market system would encourage a faster depletion of resources. The upshot is clear. *While the private competitive market system has a built-in mechanism to conserve nonrenewable resources, from society's perspective the level of resource conservation provided by such a system may not be adequate.*

Discount rates

So far, the analysis in this chapter has made no attempt to distinguish between social and private discount rates. In fact, in deriving the Pareto optimal path, the social discount rate has been implicitly assumed. However, when resources are allocated in a private market setting, divergence between private and social discount rates is to be expected. More specifically, as discussed in Section 15.5, the private discount rate tends to be higher than the social discount rate. If the social discount rate is different, then the very claim that resource allocation in a perfectly competitive world will lead to socially optimal intertemporal allocation of resources may not be valid. In other words, when what is considered is an intertemporal allocation of resources, there is a difference between the "Pareto optimal" (of a perfectly competitive world) and the "socially optimal" allocation of resources. The latter insists that future benefits and costs be discounted using the *social* discount rate.

Why would private resource owners tend to discount the future more heavily than society as a whole? It is argued that resource owners will have higher discount rates than socially desirable rates because of uncertainties involved in future resource prices, future taxes and the risk of losing ownership through appropriation by national governments. Furthermore, private resource owners tend to have "myopic" views of the future and, as such, their decisions are based on a shorter time horizon than those of society at large (see Chapter 15 for more on this).

The consequence of the higher rate of discounting in the private resource markets is likely to be a faster rate of resource extraction than is socially desirable. This clearly favors current resource extraction. Thus, if the general bias of the private resource markets is toward a higher level of current extraction, can a resource allocation based on such an institutional setting adequately protect the interests of future generations? Indeed, as discussed in some detail in Chapter 15, the concern for future generations' welfare will remain real and serious provided the divergence between the social and the private discount rate is not corrected.

Absence of forward markets

From the outset, the analysis in this chapter has assumed that resource owners are able accurately to forecast future prices and resource stock (size) conditions. This assumption virtually eliminated consideration of price and stock uncertainties. However, in the real world these uncertainties do exist, and for natural resources in the *long run* there are no forward resource markets – markets that can be used to exchange time-dated commodities in terms of future agreed prices and quantities extending over several decades.

Therefore, in the presence of considerable stock and demand uncertainty, future prices are, at best, *expected* prices. These expectations may be formed on the basis of best available information about future demand and resource size – which is generally acquired at a cost. To some degree they will also be influenced by the individual private decision-makers' risk-taking behavior.

Does uncertainty lead to faster or slower resource extraction? Primarily because of the stochastic nature of the problem, the conclusions to this question on the basis of current theoretical and empirical understandings have been tentative. However, in general, the bias of uncertainty seems to be toward increased rate of resource extraction in the current period. This conclusion is based on the assumption that, in general, resource owners tend to be risk-averse and have myopic views of the future.

17.6 RESOURCE EXHAUSTION, BACKSTOP TECHNOLOGY AND LIMITS TO GROWTH

We have seen in this chapter that depletion of a nonrenewable resource is accompanied by a steady increase in price. Thus, increasing scarcity of a nonrenewable resource is associated with ever-increasing cost; this, in some ways, seems to support the classical doctrine of increasing resource scarcity (see Chapter 7). However, a major difference exists between the notion of resource scarcity discussed in this chapter and the one that is associated with the classical doctrine of resource scarcity. In particular, the discussion in this chapter refers exclusively to a scarcity of a *particular* natural resource over time, whereas the reference of the classical doctrine has been to the *general* scarcity of natural resources. In fact, when the emphasis is on the scarcity of a particular natural resource, as in this chapter, nonrenewable natural resources need not be perceived as a deterrent to economic growth in the long run. The reason is rather straightforward.

First, as noted in this chapter, the depletion of a nonrenewable resource is accompanied by a steady increase in price. However, as the price of a particular nonrenewable resource steadily increases, users of this resource will start to search for substitutes in a variety of ways. This search is expected to be further facilitated by continued *technical progress*. For example, suppose the United States currently generates most of its electricity from the use of fossil fuels, particularly coal. As fossil fuels are depleted, in the long run their price is expected to increase steadily, as shown in Figure 17.8. Of course, this upward price trend will not continue forever. It can be argued that at some price level, the use of an alternative resource such as the production of electricity from solar or fusion energy will become economically feasible. In Figure 17.8, this will occur when the price for fossil fuels reaches P_{max}. In effect, this price indicates a technologically imposed price ceiling on fossil fuels.

The general implication of the simple illustration in Figure 17.8 is that steady price increases of natural resources will ultimately result in a technological breakthrough that will bring the price increase to a virtual halt. This phenomenon is referred to as *backstop technology*. In our example above, the backstop technology is solar or fusion energy, which is expected to become economically feasible at time T_0. Note that at T_0, economic considerations alone will cause fossil fuels to be virtually exhausted (i.e, not in a physical but in an economic sense). However, this should not be a cause for alarm. After all, the depleted resource will gradually be replaced by a virtually inexhaustible resource: solar energy. It is for this reason, as one of the epigraphs to this chapter indicated, that most modern economists share the opinion that "exhaustion of a particular resource is an event, and not a catastrophe." When viewed this way, exhaustion of nonrenewable resources should not be considered a factor that will eventually impede economic growth.

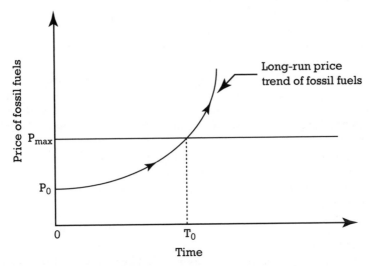

Figure 17.8 **Backstop technology**

However, as discussed in Chapter 7, this view can be supported only if the following three conditions are met. First, there cannot be *general* resource scarcity. Second, there must be no limit to technological progress. Third, resources must be allocated in institutional settings that are highly flexible (adoptive) and efficient.

Furthermore, it should be noted that Figure 17.8 postulates that the price path of a nonrenewable resource steadily appreciates over time. That is, the price path is continuous. This excludes the possibility of discontinuous price changes, which may happen if a sudden and unexpected depletion of a key resource occurs.

17.7 CHAPTER SUMMARY

- In this chapter attempts were made to study the rudiments of the economics of nonrenewable resources.
- For nonrenewable resources the natural rate of stock creation over time is assumed to be *zero*. Thus, in the absence of recycling, with each use the resource is depleted by the rate of extraction. This has the following two implications:

  1 In the limit, continuous use of nonrenewable stock resources will inevitably lead to exhaustion.
  2 The use of a unit of nonrenewable resources suggests a total and permanent loss of future use.

- Consideration of *recycling* does not refute the above two pronouncements. Recycling merely postpones exhaustion.
- Reliable quantitative estimation of total mineral resource deposits depends on a number of economic, geologic and technological factors, and is extremely difficult. Thus, measures of future resource adequacy based on current geologic estimates and current consumption rates are often misleading and inadequate.
- Exhaustion of mineral resources is primarily an economic event, because economic exhaustion precedes geological exhaustion.
- The fundamental economic problem of exhaustible resources is an issue of *intertemporal* allocation of finite geological natural resources. The key issue is, therefore, how much of an exhaustible resource should be extracted for present consumption and how much of it should be left for future use.
- Using a simple model with a two-dimensional graphic approach, it is possible to trace the optimal price path and extraction trajectory of nonrenewable resources over time. The major conclusions arrived from this attempt are as follows:

  1 The optimal extraction rate of a nonrenewable resource is attained when price, or marginal social benefit, is equated with marginal extraction cost *plus* marginal user cost. The inclusion of *marginal user cost* is the distinguishing feature of this optimal condition. As stated

earlier, the use of a unit of nonrenewable resources entails a total and permanent loss to future utilization. The user cost is the opportunity cost of this perceived loss to future generations.

2 Consideration of material recycling lowers, though it does not eliminate, user cost.

3 Resource prices will grow at the same rate as the long-run interest rate – the rates of return on holding other alternative (numeraire) commodities. The fact that this rate of return is stable indicates an *exponential* growth in resource price over time. This has a far-reaching implication, as it suggests that the market has a built-in mechanism to conserve nonrenewable resources – a prima facie case for leaving resource allocation to the market.

- However, conservation of nonrenewable resources through the private market may not be *socially* optimal and, in general, the bias tends to be toward a faster rate of resource exploitation of resources.

- A combination of factors explains this general bias towards over-exploitation. Among them are market imperfection and significant economies of scale in the resource extraction sectors; uncertainty about future prices and resource stock size combined with the absence of forward markets for natural resource commodities; divergence between the social and private discount rates; environmentally and ecologically harmful effects that are not included in resource prices; and the generally myopic views of the future held by private resource owners and planners.

- Policy-makers could use taxes, quotas and other forms of restrictions to correct private-market bias toward overexploitation of nonrenewable resources. The ending of subsidies to exploit virgin material resources should be seriously considered.

- The extent to which nonrenewable resources limit future economic growth was the last issue addressed in this chapter. It was shown that in the presence of *backstop technology*, exhaustion of a particular nonrenewable resource should cause no major economic disruptions. The process of resource exhaustion proceeds gradually until a backstop source of supply takes over.

---

review and discussion questions

1 Briefly identify the following concepts: reserve, resource, resource base, reserve-to-use ratio, crustal abundance, the hypothesis of smooth tonnage grade, intertemporal allocation of resources, user cost, royalty, numeraire asset, monopoly power, forward markets, backstop technology.

2 State *True*, *False* or *Uncertain* and explain why.

    (a) Exhaustion of mineral resources is primarily an economic event.

    (b) User cost is an externality.

    (c) A monopoly is a true friend of the conservationist.

3 In this chapter it is formally demonstrated that in a perfectly competitive market setting, the depletion of a nonrenewable resource over time will be accompanied by a steady increase in prices. The broader implication of this is that an unregulated competitive market system has a built-in mechanism to *conserve* nonrenewable resources. Do you think this observation is simply a theoretical nicety? Why, or why not? Be specific.

4 "Even with recycling capability, nonrenewable resources are eventually exhaustible. Thus, recycling cannot be considered a cure-all remedy." Explain.

5 It is said that "mining's effects on the earth are now on the same scale as those of natural forces." If the very high environmental and ecological costs of mining, as implied by this statement, are real, why do we continue to observe falling price trends for minerals? Discuss.

6 "Reserves are but a small part of the resources of any given commodity. Reserves and resources are part of a dynamic system and they cannot be inventoried like cans of tomatoes on a grocer's shelf. New scientific discoveries, new technology, and new commercial demands or restrictions are constantly affecting amounts of reserves and resources" (Brobst 1979: 115). Discuss.

REFERENCES AND FURTHER READING

Brobst, D. A. (1979) "Fundamental Concepts for the Analysis of Resource Availability," in V. K. Smith (ed.), *Scarcity and Growth Reconsidered*, Baltimore: Johns Hopkins University Press.

Dasgupta, P. and Heal, M. G. (1974) "The Optimal Depletion of Exhaustible Resources," *Review of Economic Studies* Symposium on the Economics of Exhaustible Resources.

Eagan, V. (1987) "The Optimal Depletion of the Theory of Exhaustible Resources," *Journal of Post-Keynesian Economics* 9: 565–71.

Farzin, Y. H. (1992) "The Time Path of Scarcity Rent in the Theory of Exhaustible Resources," *Economic Journal* 102: 813–30.

Gilbert, R. (1979) "Optimal Depletion of Uncertain Stock," *Review of Economic Studies* 46: 47–57.

Heal, G. M. (1978) "Uncertainty and the Optimal Supply Policy for an Exhaustible Resource," in R. Pindyck (ed.) *Advances in the Economics of Energy and Resources*, vol. 2, Greenwich: JAI Press.

Hotelling, H. (1931) "The Economics of Exhaustible Resources," *Journal of Political Economy* 39: 137–75.

Howe, C. W. (1979) *Natural Resource Economics: Issues, Analysis, and Policy*, New York: John Wiley.

Koopmans, T. C. (1974) "Proof of the Case Where Discounting Advances Doomsday," *Review of Economic Studies* Symposium on the Economics of Exhaustible Resources.

Lewis, T. R. (1977) "Attitudes toward Risk and the Optimal Extraction of an Exhaustible Resource," *Journal of Environmental Economics and Management* 4: 111–19.

McInerney, J. (1976) "The Simple Analytics of Natural Resource Economics," *Journal of Agricultural Economics* 27: 31–52.

Nordhaus, W. D. (1973) *The Allocation of Energy Resources*, Brookings Paper in Economic Activity 3, Washington, D.C.: Brookings Institution.

—— (1974) "Resource as a Constraint on Growth," *American Economic Review* 64: 22–6.

Pindyck, R. S. (1980) "Uncertainty and Exhaustible Resource Markets," *Journal of Political Economy* 88: 1203–25.

Polasky, S. (1992) "The Private and Social Value of Information: Exploration for Exhaustible Resources," *Journal of Environmental Economics and Management* 23, 1: 1–21.

Randall, A. (1987) *Resource Economics: An Economic Approach to Natural Resource and Environmental Policy*, 2nd edn., New York: John Wiley.

Solow, R. M. (1974) "The Economics of Resources or the Resources of Economics," *American Economic Review* 64: 1–14.

Solow, R. and Wan, F. (1976) "Extraction Costs in the Theory of Exhaustible Resources," *Bell Journal of Economics*, 359–70.

Stiglitz, J. E. (1976) "Monopoly and the Rate of Extraction of Exhaustible Resources," *American Economic Review* 66: 655–61.

Stiglitz, J. E. and Dasgupta, P. (1982) "Market Structure and Resource Depletion: A Contribution to the Theory of Intertemporal Monopolistic Competition," *Journal of Economic Theory* 28: 128–64.

part eight

RESOURCE SCARCITY, POPULATION, POVERTY AND THE ENVIRONMENT

Part Eight consists of one chapter: Chapter 18, which examines the complex and seemingly paradoxical interrelationship among population, poverty and environmental degradation in the developing countries of the world. The problems of overpopulation, poverty and environmental degradation are addressed with a global perspective. Although the immediate impacts of these problems are confined to developing nations, the developed or industrial nations are viewed as part of both the problems and the solutions to these issues.

Specific issues addressed in this chapter include the following: What exactly is the world population problem? Is the world becoming overpopulated? What can be said about the spatial distribution of the world's population? Should it be a source of concern? What can be said about future global population trends? How significant is the adverse impact of rapid population growth on resource utilization and environmental quality? What can be done to control population growth? What have been the achievements of economic development projects of the past three decades undertaken to ameliorate poverty in the developing countries? Is international trade benefiting or hurting the economic development aspirations and ecological integrity of the developing countries?

Given the seemingly insurmountable political and economic problems the developing countries face, can we realistically expect them to initiate and implement effective population control policies without significant financial and technical support from developed nations? What are the major responsibilities of the developed nations in finding ways to ameliorate the global environmental and resource problems? What exactly is needed to maintain a "proper global balance" of the population–resource–environment interrelationship? Furthermore, if "proper balance" refers to a condition in which the population–resource–environment interrelationship is consistent with the attainment of sustainable development, can we realistically expect to achieve this goal without solid international cooperation? More-over, will the world community be awakened in time to undertake the social rearrangements and moral/ethical transformations that may be essential to make sustainable development a viable option on a global scale?

The above series of questions simply reflects the magnitude of the challenges that humanity will most likely face in its search for viable solutions to many of the contemporary environmental and resource problems.

chapter eighteen

POPULATION, DEVELOPMENT AND ENVIRONMENTAL DEGRADATION IN THE DEVELOPING WORLD

---

learning objectives

After reading this chapter you will be familiar with the following:

- the common elements of the economics, population and environmental problems of developing countries;
- the nature of the population problems of developing nations, both historically and relative to the developed nations;
- the theory of the demographic transition and its implication for population control;
- the microeconomic theory of human fertility and its implications for population control through economic incentives;
- the interrelationships of economic development, population, poverty and environmental degradation in the developing world;
- the vicious cycle of poverty in the developing world;
- why poverty may not be alleviated through the traditional model of development that stresses capital accumulation or engaging in free trade with the industrial countries;
- how economic development projects may actually lead to environmental degradation, which in turn has an adverse effect on productivity and hence income;

- how political instability and tradition-bound and insecure tenure (property rights systems) over many valuable renewable resources, such as forests, fishery and arable lands, continually frustrate public policy efforts to stabilize population, control pollution and conserve resources.
- how trade with the developed nations appears to accelerate the rate of deforestation, mineral resource extraction and the extinction of some animal and plant species in many regions of the developing world.

Economic development and population growth in the poor areas of the earth are essential topics of environmental concern. Much of the so-called Third World suffers extraordinary – and rapidly accelerating – environmental degradation. The patterns of destruction experienced here are markedly distinct from those of the industrialized zone, calling for the development of a separate body of both social–environmental theories and economic–ecological programs.

(Lewis 1992: 191)

Environmentalists have long been concerned with human impact on the environment. Rapid population growth in the developing countries and high levels of resource consumption in developed countries are considered to be important causes of environmental damage, but attempts to study the links between population and environment have demonstrated that the relationship is complex.

(Population Reference Bureau 1997: 4)

18.1 INTRODUCTION

In Chapter 6, the interrelationships among population growth, economic growth and environmental degradation were analyzed within the context of the Malthusian tradition. It was observed that although population growth has not yet threatened us with the immediate Malthusian catastrophe envisioned by many, it remains a serious problem. This is because rapid population growth is considered to be one of the major contributing factors to the vicious cycle of poverty and environmental degradation in many parts of the developing countries. The primary aim of the present chapter is to systematically examine the exact nature of the interrelationships of population, poverty and environmental degradation in the developing world. As will be evident, those interrelationships are not only complex but also, in many respects, paradoxical.

In analyzing this issue, it is important to note that the "developing world" is composed of a heterogeneous group of countries and not all of them are at the same stage of economic development or encounter the same levels of population and environmental problems. As will be shown shortly, some countries in this group have been quite successful both in controlling their population growth and in maintaining a steady growth in their economy as measured by an increase in per capita domestic product or GDP. However, while these countries are making demonstrable progress in their struggle to alleviate poverty, they are plagued by an increasing level of air and water pollution and by an accelerated rate of resource depletion which exhibit themselves through deforestation, soil erosion, overfishing and damage to marine and coastal ecosystems such as coastal wetlands and coral reefs (Trainer 1990). Examples of these countries are South Korea, Taiwan, Mexico, Brazil and Argentina.

On the other hand, many African, Latin American and Southeast Asian countries are confronted with problems of poverty and environmental degradation simultaneously. One of the major reasons for this is the failure of these countries to control the rapid rate of their population growth. In some African and Latin American countries (such as Zambia, Kenya, Nigeria, El Salvador, Honduras and Nicaragua) population has been growing at a rate of 3 to 4 percent annually. In many of the poorest developing countries population has been growing faster than GDP, indicating a negative annual growth in per capita income. In these countries poverty and population growth are exerting dangerous pressure on the carrying capacity of the ecosystem, and producing widespread desertification and deforestation (Lewis 1992; Trainer 1990).

Although these differences exist, the developing world shares certain common characteristics. To a varying extent, population is still a major problem to most of these countries. Urbanization is another problem that these countries seem to share. Most of these countries have unstable government and maldistribution of income and wealth, and they seem to lack the tradition and institutional infrastructure that are necessary for establishing clearly defined ownership over renewable resources, such as forests, fisheries and arable land (Turner *et al.* 1993). As will become evident, these are all factors that tend to intensify both the short- and the long-term economic population and environmental problems of these nations. Until comprehensive solutions to these problems are found, both those countries that seem to be doing well economically and those that are failing to develop will continue to share what appears to be a common experience: a severe form of environmental degradation (Lewis 1992).

In the next section, using published data an attempt is made to examine the growth trends and spatial distribution of world population. This is done to offer a clear picture of the nature of the population problems of developing nations both historically and relative to the developed nations.

18.2 GROWTH TRENDS AND SPATIAL DISTRIBUTION OF GLOBAL POPULATION: A HISTORICAL PERSPECTIVE

Unprecedented steady population growth has been one of the dominant characteristics of the twentieth century. This is a significant change considering that for several millennia, human population was growing at an insignificant rate, with death largely offsetting birth. As shown in Figure

18.1, the world population was growing at a steady but very low rate, reaching the first billion mark in about 1800. In other words, it took millions of years for the world population to reach its first billion. However, as is evident from Figure 18.1, since about the turn of the seventeenth century the world population has been growing at a much faster pace. A look at Table 18.1 makes this point quite clear. While it took millions of years to reach the first billion population, it took merely 130 years to add the next billion. Although the rate of growth seems to have stabilized since the mid-1970s, it now takes merely eleven to twelve years for the world population to grow by a billion. According to Figure 18.1, the world population is projected to reach and perhaps stabilize at about 10 billion by the year 2100.

In addition, the situation becomes even more striking when we focus our attention on the most recent world population trends. At the beginning of the twentieth century there were over one and one-half billion people in the world. For the first half of the century (1900–50), world population grew at a relatively low rate, averaging about 0.8 percent per year (World Resources Institute 1987). By the 1960s there were 3 billion people on Earth, and the annual growth rate was reaching the 2 percent mark (ibid.). In the next decade (1960–70) the world population grew at an accelerated rate until it reached a new plateau – an annual rate of increase of 2.06 percent (ibid.).

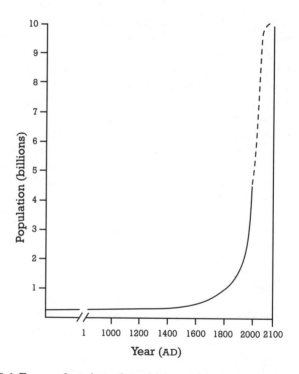

Figure 18.1 Past and projected world population

Source: Reprinted by permission from World Bank, *The World Development Report 1984*, copyright © 1984 (Washington, D.C., 1984), p. 73.

Table 18.1 **Approximate time taken for the world's population to grow by a billion**

Approximate time	Population (in billions)	Time taken to grow (Years)
To 1800	1	(Millions of years)
1800–1930	2	130
1930–60	3	30
1960–75	4	15
1975–87	5	12
1987–99	6	12

Source: Compiled from World Resources Institute (1987).

Rapidly declining death rates, together with continued high birth rates – especially in the developing regions of the world – contributed to this rapid rate of growth.

Yet since the early 1970s, the growth rate of the world population has been showing a slow but steady decline. Specifically, the annual rate of growth has declined from about 2 percent in 1970 to approximately 1.52 percent today (Population Reference Bureau 1996). This drop is attributed mainly to a decrease in birthrates worldwide as a result of intense educational campaigns to promote birth control, along with specific preventive actions undertaken by various government and private agencies. For example, China, the most populous nation in the world, instituted a strict one-child policy during this period.

Despite the progress that has been made to slow down the annual rate of population growth, more people are being added to the Earth's total each year. Several factors explain this, among the most significant of which are the continuing decline in mortality rates, the absolute size of the world population (6 billion was reached in July 1999), and the immense momentum built up from the current age composition of the population (i.e., the fact that a larger percentage of the world population is under 15 years of age, especially in the developing regions of the world). As shown in Table 18.2, the average annual increase in world population has been increasing steadily. During the 1990s, on average, about 84 million people will have been added annually to the human race. This is more than seven times the size of the population of New York City.

So far the focus has been on population trends of the world as a whole. However, these trends, based on aggregate data, do not reveal the wide differences in population growth rates (see Table 18.3) and the distribution of population (see Table 18.4) that persist between the different regions of the world, especially between the developed and the developing nations.

For two centuries, 1750–1950, the population of these two groups of nations grew at low rates – between 0.4 and 0.9 percent, respectively (McNamara 1968). Furthermore, during this period, the rate of growth of the developed nations was slightly higher than that of the developing nations.

Table 18.2 **World population growth by decade 1950-90 with projections to 2000**

Year	Population (billions)	Increase by decade (millions)	Average annual increase (millions)
1950	2.565	—	—
1960	3.050	485	49
1970	3.721	671	67
1980	4.477	756	76
1990	5.320	843	84
2000	6.241	921	92

Source: *Worldwatch* Vol. 2, No. 5, September/October 1989, p. 34. Copyright © 1989. Reprinted by permission of the Worldwatch Institute.

However, as shown in Table 18.3, since 1950 the average annual rates of population growth of the developing nations have started to outpace those in the developed nations by considerable margins. For example, between 1960 and 1965, the average growth rate for the developing nations was roughly twice that of the developed nations (2.3 versus 1.19 percent). Twenty years later, between 1980 to 1985, the population of the developing nations was growing at a rate three times faster than that of the developed nations (2.02 versus 0.64 percent). Stated differently, if these rates persist over a long period, it will take less than 35 years for the population of the developing nations to double, and over a century for that of the developed nations. (It is important to note that, as shown in Table 18.3, the rates of population growth vary among the various groups of the developing nations. Moreover, although very high relative to the developed nations, the rates of population growth are falling everywhere except in Africa.)

Table 18.3 **Annual rates of population growth (as percentages) by regions, 1950-85**

Region	1950-5	1960-5	1970-5	1975-80	1980-5
Africa	2.11	2.44	2.74	3.00	3.01
Latin America	2.72	2.80	2.51	2.37	2.30
East Asia	2.08	1.81	2.36	1.47	1.20
South Asia	2.00	2.51	2.44	2.30	2.20
Developing nations	2.11	2.30	2.46	2.14	2.02
Developed nations	1.28	1.19	0.89	0.74	0.64
Total world	1.80	1.96	2.03	1.77	1.67

Source: R. S. McNamara *Foreign Affairs*, Vol. 62, 1984. Reprinted by permission of the author.

Table 18.4 **Population trends, 1900-2000 (millions)**

Region	1900		1950		1985		2000	
Developing regions	1,070	(66)	1,681	(67)	3,657	(76)	4,837	(79)
Africa	133		224		555		872	
Asia	867		1,292		2,697		3,419	
Latin A.	70		165		405		546	
Developed regions	560	(34)	835	(33)	1,181	(24)	1,284	(21)
Total	1,630		2,516		4,837		6,122	

Source: *World Resources 1988-89*, p. 16. Copyright © 1988 World Resources Institute.
Reprinted by permission.
Note: The numbers in brackets indicate percentage of the world population.

Clearly, then, as seen in Table 18.4, such differences have resulted in a significant shift in the distribution of global population toward developing nations. At the beginning of the twentieth century, a third of the world population lived in the developed nations; this proportion remained constant until about 1950. Since the 1950s, though, the share of the world population living in the developed nations has been declining steadily. By the year 2000, only about one-fifth of the world population is projected to live in the developed nations. That is, approximately four out of every five people in the world currently live in a developing nation.

Moreover, this trend is expected to continue in the foreseeable future. A recent United Nations projection of world population for the year 2050 ranges between 7.7 and 11.2 billion (Population Reference Bureau 1997). However, although the predicted estimate of the world population in 50 years is subject to a wide range of variation, one trend of future global population growth remains indisputable. That is, *the world population will definitely increase in the future, and most of this increase will occur in developing countries*. According to the United Nations estimate, it is expected that in 2050, 88 percent of the people in the world will be living in the developing countries (ibid.).

What the above observations clearly indicate is that the world population problem is predominantly a concern of the developing nations. The question is, then, what can be done to control the population growth in the developing nations? Programs to control population could take several forms. They may range from government-sponsored population programs which are based on subsidized birth control and family planning to a more coercive measure such as the one-child policy of China. Despite the human rights implications, in some situations even coercive measures could be justified.

In this chapter, the discussion of population control is limited to policy measures intended to alter people's behavior in relation to their decisions concerning human reproduction on the basis of economic incentives. While this approach may be conceptually appealing, its practical applications, as will be evident from the discussion to follow, will require fundamental social and political transformations that will be difficult to undertake in most of the developing nations.

18.3 POPULATION CONTROL POLICY: IN THEORY AND PRACTICE

A public policy to control population growth must evaluate and implement specific measures intended to reduce human fertility rates. The *total fertility rate* refers to the average number of children a woman would have in her lifetime on the basis of fertility rates in a given year. Generally, demographic stability is said to be achieved when a nation's total fertility rate drops to about 2, in which case each couple is barely replacing itself without adding to the size of the future population.

Worldwide, total fertility is currently estimated to be about 3. However, as would be expected, a big difference exists in total fertility rates between the developed and developing nations. These rates are 1.7 and 3.4, respectively. In some of the least developed countries, the total fertility rates are in excess of 6 (World Resources Institute 1995).What exactly are the basic determinants of fertility? As will be evident shortly, there is no clear-cut answer to this question. It depends, in addition to the economic and technological factors, on human behavior and value systems with respect to fertility decisions. In this section, two conceptual frameworks of population control are examined. These models are used to gain a clear understanding of the possible determinants of humans' fertility decisions at both macro and micro levels that can be used as a guide to public policy for effective population control through economic incentives.

18.3.1 The theory of the demographic transition

In studying the reproductive decision of humans at the macro level, one view that has been most popular among social scientists is the theory of the demographic transition. This theory derives its appeal from its simplicity and the considerable empirical support for its basic conclusions (Leibenstein 1974). Briefly stated, as shown in Figure 18.2, the theory of the demographic transition is a generalization advanced to explain the transitional stages of fertility and mortality for a nation over time, as it progresses in its modernization process. For our purpose the relevant aspect of the theory is its claim that, as nations develop, they eventually reach a point where the birthrate falls. In other words, in the long run the process of industrialization is accompanied by a sustained reduction in population growth. One important implication of this theory is, of course, that industrialization (which is generally associated with increased GDP) is a possible solution to the population problem (ibid.). Why so?

First, industrialization implies a shift from an economy that is primarily based on agriculture (which is labor-intensive) to one based on industry (which is capital-intensive). This structural change in the economy

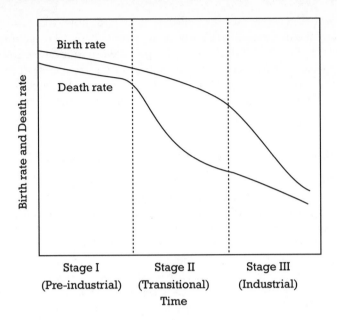

Figure 18.2 **The demographic transition**

increasingly reduces the productivity (hence, the income-generating capacity) of children in the agricultural sector. Furthermore, as often occurs with industrialization and modernization, child labor laws are instituted as a sign of social progress. The combined effect of these two factors reduces parental desire to have more children for the purpose of supplementing the household income.

Second, since industrialization is often associated with an increase in the average per capita income of a nation, the increasing affluence of the average family in the course of industrialization reduces the desire for more children. This is because the need for having children as a hedge for security in old age becomes less and less important as families become increasingly wealthy. In addition, this tendency for smaller family size will be further reinforced by the fact that industrialization is generally associated with declining infant mortality.

Finally, other socioeconomic factors associated with modernization further contribute to a decline in fertility rates. Among them are the rise in the education of women, urbanization and its secularizing influence, increasing participation of females in traditionally male-dominated sectors of the economy, advances in birth control methods, and family planning.

While the association between income and fertility rates sparked interest in this topic within the economics discipline, by and large economists were not satisfied with the above explanations for the decline in birth rates. Economists claimed that the theory of demographic transition simply failed to offer specific and systematic explanations of the very important association between income and fertility. Instead, the theory offers only a broad generalization and does not attempt to deal with the key issue of how parents make decisions about childbearing, and how this choice is influenced by the income of the family (Leibenstein 1974). To economists, this careful examination of decision-making at the micro level is extremely significant because it helps uncover the sources (determinants) of fertility decline – which is essential in designing effective population control policy instruments. As a result, an alternative theory is sought which is the topic of the next subsection.

18.3.2 The microeconomic theory of human fertility

According to this theory, human reproductive behavior is based not just on the passions between the sexes but rather on carefully calculated, rational behavior (Becker 1960). First, it should be recognized that there are *benefits* and *costs* associated with having children. Second, the decision of parents concerning the number of their offspring is based upon careful consideration of these costs and benefits. Basically, there are three basic sources of benefits (utilities) that parents can expect from having a child: (a) consumption or psychic utility – a child is wanted for her- or himself rather than for services or income she or he may provide; (b) work or income utility; and (c) security or old-age benefit.

On the other hand, the costs or disutility of having children are composed of the following two broad categories: (a) the direct costs of providing necessities such as food, housing, clothing and basic education; and (b) the indirect costs of raising children such as opportunities forgone by parents in terms of time and money (Becker 1960; Leibenstein 1974). With this identification of the costs and benefits of having children, and on the general premise that human fertility decisions are made primarily on a purely rational basis, an effort is made in the microeconomics theory of fertility to give an explanation for a seemingly paradoxical negative relationship between household income and family size. In other words, at the micro level, why do rich families tend to have fewer children than poor ones? Or, why is the birthrate lower for families in economically developed countries than in developing ones?

Once the nature of the general problem regarding the childbirth decision is identified in the above context, the economic analysis begins by viewing children as *durable consumption goods* (Becker 1960; Blake 1968). Children are classified as consumption goods because they provide direct psychic utilities to their parents, and durable, since the costs and benefits (utilities) of having children extend over a relatively long period. As with any other consumer durable, then, as shown in Figure 18.3, the demand for children will be downward-sloping. This in turn suggests, other things being equal, that there exists an inverse relationship between the price (cost) of children and the number of children a household (family) would be willing and able to have (Becker 1960). Thus, the more expensive children become, the fewer of them will be demanded. It is important to note that this demand is constructed by treating a number of socioeconomic factors, such as preference and income, as exogenous variables. As usual, changes in any one

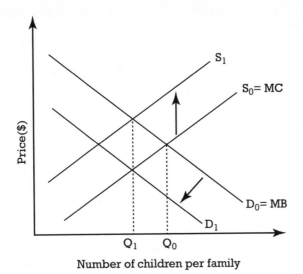

Figure 18.3 **Demand and supply curves for children**

of these exogenous determinants of demand will cause a shift in the entire demand curve. Finally, as discussed in Chapter 2, demand is a measure of marginal benefit.

Similarly, the supply of any good is generally associated with the cost of production (see Chapter 2). In this particular case, the supply for children is assumed to be positively sloped and is related to the cost of raising children. As is the case for the demand function, the supply for children is also affected by exogenous factors such as changes in the economic status of women – which has the effect of increasing the opportunity cost of mothers' time spent for raising children – and any effort to increase the educational level of the general public. As we would expect, a change of this nature will cause a shift in the supply curve. One last point of significance is that, as discussed in Chapter 2, the supply curve represents marginal cost.

According to the microeconomics of reproduction, the initial optimal number of children occurs at the intersection of D_0 and S_0 and, most importantly, at the point where marginal cost equals marginal benefit. As is evident from Figure 18.3, a shift in either the demand or the supply function will not violate this equilibrium condition but will simply cause a change in the optimal number of children. For example, other factors being constant, a leftward shift of a supply curve will reduce the number of optimal children from Q_0 to Q_1. That is, an increase in the marginal cost of raising children will cause a family to desire a smaller number of children.

18.3.3 Population control through economic incentives

The two previous subsections have suggested that there are several economic factors that can be used as a way of influencing parents' decision as to whether to have children – hence, control of their reproductive capacity. According to the microeconomics theory of human reproduction, these factors encompass all the determinants of demand and supply for children. Thus, once the determinants of both demand and supply for children are understood, the economic approach to population control is simply reduced to straightforward applications of traditional demand and supply analysis.

Accordingly, other things being constant, any factor that causes a shift of the demand (marginal benefit) for children to the left will reduce the number of children per family. For example, in Figure 18.3, assuming Q_0 is the initial equilibrium, a shift in the demand from D_0 to D_1 will cause a reduction in the number of children from Q_0 to Q_1. This type of change in demand can be activated by a policy measure that has the effect of raising family income or financial security on a sustained basis. For example, instituting social security programs will have the effect of decreasing the demand for children by reducing the expected benefits or utilities that parents have from security or old-age benefit. In the developing countries this is an important reason for having children.

At a macro level the demand for children can be reduced through a variety of economic policies that have the effect of raising the income or standard of living of the average family. Note that the key policy target is raising the income of the average family. Thus, for most developing countries, where the income distribution profile is highly uneven, a policy of income redistribution could by itself be used as a way of reducing fertility. This is because, under such circumstances, changes to a more even income distribution could have the effect of raising the average family income.

A similar result could also be achieved by implementing a policy specifically intended to affect the supply (cost) curve for children. For example, in Figure 18.3 shift of the supply curve from S_0 to S_1 will cause a reduction in the number of children from Q_0 to Q_1. A policy measure that is designed to materially improve the opportunities available for women to participate gainfully in the labor market will be one way to accomplish this objective. Another way to achieve a similar end is by shifting some of the costs of children's education and health care from the public to the private domain.

The above discussions suggest that a country can use economic incentives to control the rate of its population growth in a variety of ways. Once the determinants of demand and supply for children are known, policy measures can be formulated to trigger desirable change(s) in the demand and/or supply schedules for children.

The discussion of population control through economic incentives is based on the general premise that human fertility decisions are made primarily on a purely rational basis. Furthermore, the underlying motive of the individual family is to promote its self-interest – maximize the *net* benefits from having children (Becker 1960). However, under normal circumstances not all the costs of children are *fully* borne by parents. Education in public-sector schools is almost universally free. In many countries food is subsidized by holding prices below market levels. Even in cases where education and food subsidies are financed through tax revenues, the individual household will not have an incentive to reduce its family size, because the tax is normally not based on the number of children. Clearly, then, since not all costs are borne by parents, the private costs for raising children will be less than the social costs (Blake 1968). What this suggests is the presence of some form of *externalities*. As discussed in Chapter 5, in the presence of externalities, decisions reached by individual actors will not lead to the "best" or optimal outcome for society at large.

Of course, this recognition that real externalities are involved in the parents' decision concerning childbearing underscores the need for adopting a population control policy. Unfortunately, for reasons that will be evident shortly, most countries in the developing world lack the institutional structures, the political systems and the economic resources that are necessary to effectively correct both market and government failures. Until these social infrastructural problems are adequately addressed, the use of economic incentives to control population will continue to be ineffective. However, the situation will be even worse if the alternative is *laissez-faire* policies in reproduction, since these would surely confront society with a ruinous problem of overpopulation (Hardin 1968). This observation should not be taken lightly, given that the right to bear children is a universally held and UN-sanctioned inalienable human right.

18.4 ECONOMIC DEVELOPMENT, POPULATION, POVERTY AND ENVIRONMENTAL DEGRADATION

Population is a concern because it is suspected to be a factor responsible for poverty and environmental degradation in the developing world. As discussed in Chapter 6, some scholars even consider population growth to be the source of all evils (Ehrlich and Holdren 1971). However, the empirical evidence for this claim has not been completely conclusive.

What seems to be increasingly evident is that the economic and environmental problems of the developing countries cannot be attributed to a single factor such as population growth. Instead, population, poverty and environmental degradation are interrelated issues and they need to be addressed in combination (Lewis 1992). With this in mind, in this section an attempt will be made to systematically analyze the interrelationships between population, income and environmental degradation in the developing world.

Casual observation seems to suggest that there exists a negative correlation between the growth of income and the growth of population. Of course, this observation is consistent with the theory of the demographic transition since according to this theory low income is associated with high population growth, or poverty leads to high fertility rates. Another claim that is often made is that there exists a positive correlation between environmental degradation and poverty. This is defended by claiming that the poor nations can least afford to clean up pollution or conserve resources. While these observations may have intuitive appeal, on the whole it is difficult to delineate clearly the population–poverty–environmental interrelationship. This is particularly evident when this interrelationship is examined within the context of the efforts toward economic development of the developing nations over the past four decades.

In the 1960s, when many developing countries were engaged in a desperate struggle to make the difficult transition from colonialism to political independence, a serious push was made to raise the standard of living in these nations (Bandyopadhyay and Shiva 1989). The motivation for this was the depressing level of poverty manifest in many developing nations, especially in the newly independent nations of Africa and Southeast Asia. As a world organization, the United Nations responded to this concern by inaugurating several development programs specifically intended to alleviate poverty in the developing nations.

In all of these efforts, economic "development" was conceived of as the cure for poverty. Economic development was understood as an increase in per capita gross domestic product (GDP), and countries tried to increase their GDP without any attempt to differentiate between economic development and economic growth (Goodland and Daly 1992). Furthermore, it was hypothesized that growth in GDP not only alleviates poverty by creating jobs for the poor, but could also create a surplus with which to clean up the environment and control crime and violence (Homer-Dixon *et al.* 1993). By the same token, in accordance with the theory of demographic transition, achieving a high standard of living is expected to lead to a decline in fertility rates, hence a decline in the rate of population growth. Thus, *economic development is conceived of as a remedy not only for poverty but also for population growth and environmental degradation.*

To further strengthen the above claims, the need for economic development was argued in terms of the "vicious cycle of poverty." The main implication of this is that low-income countries are destined to remain poor indefinitely unless something is done to raise their standard of living on a sustainable basis (Todaro 1989). It was argued that countries with a low standard of living spend a high proportion of their income on current consumption needs. This means low savings and low investments, which leads to low productivity. With no hope of improving productivity, it is argued that these countries will remain stagnantly poor. The question of interest is, then, what can be done to resolve this seemingly persistent problem of poverty?

Using the traditional model of development, *capital accumulation* was sanctioned as the way of alleviating poverty or as a catalyst for economic development (Todaro 1989). This was based on the notion that capital accumulation, by enhancing the productivity of labor and other factors of production, would ultimately lead to an increase in the per capita income of a nation. It was with this in mind that the development projects of the

1960s and 1970s were primarily focused on capital formation to promote growth. These included large capital-intensive projects involving dams, assembly lines and large-scale energy and agricultural projects. These projects were financed largely by international loans agencies, such as the World Bank and the International Monetary Fund (IMF).

In addition, it was argued that the economic condition of developing nations could be further enhanced by engaging in *free trade* with the industrial countries of the West (Bhagwati 1993). The trade relations between these two groups of nations are largely characterized by exports of primary resources (such as plywood, minerals, fruits, spices, etc.) from the developing nations and imports of industrial products from developed countries (such as machines, tractors, transportation vehicles, etc.). The justification for such trade relations is based on the fundamental premise that free trade leads to the attainment of a mutually beneficial outcome for all the parties involved. That is, international trade is not a zero-sum game even when the total benefits are not shared evenly among the trading parties.

By the early 1980s it became increasingly evident that the traditional approaches to economic development, which basically depended on capital formation and free trade, did not live up to expectations. In fact, the evidence seemed to suggest that in many respects these development experiments had failed to improve productivity in many developing countries. Today, there are some who claim that some countries are worse off now than four decades ago when the official United Nations development programs were initiated. More specifically, there are now more people in the developing world who are in desperate poverty than ever before; environmental degradation in this part of the world has reached crisis proportions; and many of the developing countries are politically unstable and are burdened with debilitating international debts. How did this come about? What explanations can be given for such unintended and unfortunate outcomes? Simply put, what did go wrong?

These are indeed difficult questions to address. Any attempt to offer comprehensive answers requires careful scrutiny of the political, social, institutional, economic and environmental dimensions of programs that are specifically intended for poverty alleviation in the developing nations. What follows is an attempt to do this under the following three broadly defined themes: economic growth and the environment; political instability and tradition-bound property rights systems; and international economic relations, development and the environment.

Economic growth and the environment

As stated earlier, the campaign to alleviate poverty in the developing world had as its primary focus the increasing of per capita GDP. Furthermore, this aim was expected to be achieved through increased capital formation. This traditional approach to economic development has two major flaws when consideration is given to the environment.

First, as discussed in Chapter 9, the conventional measure of GDP does not account for the depreciation of natural or environmental capital. Thus, a focus on increasing GDP is likely to have a detrimental effect on the natural environment in the long run.

Second, traditionally, capital formation was conceived of in terms of large-scale capital-intensive projects such as dams, highways, factories, large-scale agriculture, etc.; and these projects were implemented without adequate assessment of their impacts on the natural ecosystem (Goodland and Daly 1992).

The upshot of this has been continued environmental degradation which is manifested in a variety of forms, such as deforestation, soil erosion, increasing levels of urban air and water pollution, and increasing damage to coastal and marine ecosystems leading to diminishing fishery stocks and destruction of coral reefs.

In the developing world, where the economy is primarily agrarian, the environment is an important input of many production activities. Thus, *environmental degradation has an adverse effect on productivity, and the outcome of this will be a reduction in income. The important implication of this result is that poverty-alleviation programs are likely to fail in the long run if they are pursued with a primary focus on increasing GDP or per capita GDP.* Growth ideology of this nature undermines the economic significance of the natural environment. In the developing world the poor depend on the environment, and protecting the environment should be an important element of poverty alleviation (Bandyopadhyay and Shiva 1989).

Political instability and tradition-bound property rights systems

For most developing countries, political instability and insecure tenure over many valuable renewable resources, such as forests, fishery and arable lands, continually negate public policy efforts to stabilize population, control pollution and conserve resources (Turner *et al.* 1993). One of the most unfortunate, but recurring, realities in many developing countries is political instability. It is especially true of countries in Africa, Southeast Asia and Central and South America, which frequently face internal strife that some-times erupts into prolonged tribal conflict and even civil war. Thus, in this kind of political climate it would be, if not impossible, extremely difficult to implement effective population and resource conservation policies based on long-term visions. Instead, public policies are conducted on a piecemeal basis, and generally as a reaction to crisis situations. What this entails is an apparent lack of responsible stewardship in resources that are critically important to the long-term survival of the nation (Homer-Dixon *et al.* 1993).

To make matters worse, in many of these countries properties are publicly or communally owned, and most often ownership is not clearly defined. Consequently, as discussed in Chapter 5, market prices need to be corrected. But this requires that the developing countries have the appropriate regulatory and institutional framework to internalize environmental externalities. In many developing countries, this kind of market failure tends to persist because of their governments' inability to administer and enforce the laws that are intended to correct externalities. One reason for this is that these are countries that can least afford to pay for protecting the environment. As a result, even when the effort to protect the environment or conserve resources is there, regulations are inconsistently applied and regulatory agencies are too poorly staffed and poorly informed to be able to monitor and implement regulations effectively. The ultimate effect of this has been rapid degradation of valuable environmental assets resulting from extensive and random land clearing, imprudent farming practices, and excessive water and air pollution. This situation is likely to continue unless some means are found to strengthen the institutional weaknesses that are at the core of the problems – that is, to define and enforce clear rights of access and use of resources to producers, consumers and government so that societal resources are prudently used. As Case Study 18.1 clearly demonstrates, this does not mean that countries need to adopt private ownership of resources. Effective property rights systems could take several forms; what matters is that governments match property tenure laws with the social context.

In addition to the problems with land tenure systems, in most developing nations the distribution of farmlands is grossly uneven:

> In 1960, the smallest 50% of holdings controlled less than 3% of agricultural land, in 1970, the median of the reported figure is 4%. On the other hand, the largest 10% of holdings controlled 65% of the land in 1960; for 1970, the median for all developing countries figure was 70%.

> (Repetto and Holmes 1983: 610)

The effect of this has been more intensive use of small farmlands, primarily for the purpose of growing crops for domestic needs. This practice is greatly intensified when the internal population pressure increases. Yet owners of large lands allocate most of their holdings for commercial or cash crops, such as coconuts, sugar, fruits, vegetables, cotton and tobacco, primarily for export. Moreover, these crops are grown with extensive application of pesticides. Thus, the unequal distribution of landholdings that exists in most developing countries not only shifts land use from domestic to export needs, but also places these countries at greater environmental risk. This situation can be ameliorated only through land reform (wealth redistribution) designed to more or less equalize landholdings and/or through export restrictions.

The problems of population, poverty and the environment that are facing most developing nations are extremely serious, requiring immediate action. Furthermore, even if action is taken immediately, the fruits of these policy measures will not be seen for quite a while, which implies that the solutions necessitate long-term vision and much short-term sacrifice. This is the dilemma that most developing nations are presently facing. It would be unrealistic to expect these countries to confront their problems effectively

CASE STUDY 18.1   COMMUNAL TENURE IN PAPUA NEW GUINEA

Theodore Panayotou

Unlike most of the developing world, Papua New Guinea has maintained its communal tenure customs while adapting to the requirements of an increasingly market-oriented economy. While the latter requires clear land ownership, Papua New Guinea's experience has shown that converting land from communal to freehold ownership may confuse rather than clarify the rights of ownership. The widespread land degradation encouraged by the insecure tenure, loss of entitlements and open access characteristic of state-owned land elsewhere has been absent from Papua New Guinea.

Most countries have responded to market pressures for clear ownership by imposing a new system of private or state ownership. In contrast, Papua New Guinea's land law builds upon the customs governing its communally held land. The country's Land Ordinance Act calls for local mediators and land courts to base settlements on existing principles of communal ownership. Consequently, 97 percent of the land remains communal, has been neither surveyed nor registered, and is governed by local custom (Cooter 1990).

This communal tenure seems to provide clearer ownership rights, with all their environmental and market implications, than private ownership. Settlements that convert communal land to freehold are often later disputed, and reversion back to customary ownership is a frequent outcome. Yet unlike state-owned land in other developing countries, communal land in Papua New Guinea is neither in effect unowned nor public. Rather, the bundle of rights deemed "ownership" in the West does not reside in one party. For example, individual families hold the right to farm plots of land indefinitely, but the right to trade them resides in the clan (Cooter 1990).

The island's communal systems have long resulted in the sustainable use of its more densely populated highlands. Even with a nine-thousand-year agricultural history, a wet climate and population growth of at least 2.3 percent, the highlands remain fertile. The population, which is primarily agricultural, enjoys a per capita income more than twice that of El Salvador, Western Samoa and Nigeria (Cooter 1990). In marked contrast to much of the developing world, only 6 million of its 46 million hectares of forestland have been converted to other uses (Australian UNESCO Committee 1976).

The lack of deforestation comes as no surprise since those who control the land have an interest in the sustainable, productive use of the forest. Rather than dealing with a distant government in need of quick revenues and foreign exchange, companies seeking logging rights must negotiate directly with those who have secure tenure and who use the land not only to farm, but also to gather fruit, hunt and collect materials for clothing, buildings and weapons (Panayotou and Ashton 1992). Because the communal tenure patterns provide an entitlement to all clan members, individuals have little incentive to sacrifice future value for current use.

Source: *Green Markets: The Economics of Sustainable Development*, San Francisco, Calif.: Institute for Contemporary History, (1993). Case reproduced by permission of the author.

without the presence of a stable domestic government and land tenure systems that preserve prudent use of natural resources.

International economic relations, development and the environment

As discussed earlier, the conventional wisdom has been to view international trade as a vehicle for accelerated economic growth in the developing nations (Bhagwati 1993). However, although somewhat inconclusive, the empirical evidence seems to suggest that commercialization or international trade is an important factor contributing to rapid rates of tropical deforestation and extinction of some valuable animal and plant species worldwide (Repetto and Holmes 1983; Rudel 1989). More specifically, trade with developed nations appears to accelerate deforestation in Latin America and Southeast Asia, and intensify the rate of desertification and the extinction of some animal and plant species in Africa (Rudel 1989). The implication of this is that, contrary to conventional wisdom, free trade has not been consistent with environmentally sustainable trade (Daly 1993). Does this suggest that, from the perspective of natural resource conservation, there is something inherently wrong with the trade between the developed and developing nations? How could this be possible when, at least conceptually, international trade among sovereign nations is based on the premise of attaining "mutually beneficial outcomes"?

From the perspective of natural resource and environmental management, the problem with international trade arises when one examines the way benefits and costs are imputed. Under a free trade regime the value of all international exchanges is assessed on the basis of the *market prices*. As discussed in Chapter 5, a number of factors can lead to distortions in market prices, and the chance for this to happen is even greater when we are dealing with international trade. For our purposes we should note three factors in particular that may lead to price distortions in the natural resources markets of developing countries.

First, as discussed so far, generally the economies of the developing countries tend to be weak and quite unstable. They are often confronted with an urgent need to finance both domestic and international debt. In their desperate attempt to finance such debt, the governments of these countries are likely to offer their natural resources for sale at a discount (Korten 1991). Case Study 2.1 in Chapter 2 also illustrates this point. This case study shows how, because of the pressure to pay its external debts, Brazil in the 1970s and 1980s was aggressively pursuing economic policies that encouraged cattle ranching and in so doing accelerated the rate of deforestation.

The second and probably most important factor contributing to natural resource price distortion is *market failure*. That is, market prices for natural resources in these regions do not take account of externalities (Daly 1993; Ekins 1993). For example, when lumber is exported from a country in Southeast Asia to Japan or France, the importing country will pay the prevailing market price, which is highly unlikely to include the environmental effects of the logging operations and the forgone benefits (these include both the use and the nonuse values) from preserving the resource under consideration for future use. Thus, if no mechanism is used to internalize these externalities, free trade based on market prices will lead to undue exploitation of natural resources upon which a vast number of the poor nations' people depend for their livelihood. Thus, perceived this way, free trade leads to environmentally unsustainable and economically inefficient appropriation of resources on a global scale (Daly 1993; Ekins 1993). The implication of this is even more serious when one considers the magnitude of the per capita consumption of resources in the developed world. This is best illustrated by the following report:

> Taken together, the 24 countries of the Organization for Economic Co-operation and Development (OECD) represent an immense concentration of economic activities. In 1989, these industrialized countries had a combined gross national product (GNP) of $15 trillion and average per capita income of $17,500. The OECD countries also place a huge demand on the natural resources of the planet and contribute a very large share of pollution burden. In 1989, the seven largest OECD economies consumed 43 percent of the world's production of fossil fuels, most of the world's production of metals, and a large share of other industrial materials and forest products. On a per capita basis, the share of consumption of the largest OECD economies is often several times that of the world average. In 1989, the OECD countries released approximately 40 percent of global sulfur oxides emissions and 54 percent of nitrogen oxides emissions – the primary sources of acid precipitation. They generated 68 percent of the world's industrial waste as measured by weight and accounted for 38 percent of the global potential warming impact on the atmosphere from emissions of greenhouse gases. Yet the combined population of the OECD countries, 849 million, represents only 16 percent of the world's population.
>
> (World Resources Institute 1992: 17)

Clearly, this indicates that the developed nations are *directly* responsible for many of the regional and global environmental problems because of their overconsumption of resources on a per capita basis. Moreover, with the increasing globalization of the natural resources market, the developed nations also contribute *indirectly* to environmental stresses and resource depletion in the developing regions of the world.

18.5 CHAPTER SUMMARY

- This chapter dealt with the issues of population, development and environment with specific reference to the developing nations.
- A comprehensive analysis of global demographic trends indicates that the world population problem is predominantly a concern of the developing nations.

- In many developing countries population has been growing at or above 2 percent annually. For some sub-Saharan countries, population is expected to double in about 20 years.
- Just to maintain their existing standard of living these countries have been forced to pursue aggressive economic development policies, often with reckless abandonment of environmental considerations. The result of this has been deepening poverty and mounting environmental degradation.
- Policy-makers can use economic incentives to control the rate of population growth in a variety of ways. Improving the opportunity available for women to gainfully participate in the labor market is one example.
- Population, poverty and environmental degradation in developing countries are highly interrelated. Thus, the economic problems of the developing world cannot be resolved by looking at population, poverty or environmental concerns separately. In order to evaluate the options that are available to raise the standard of living in the developing countries, it is necessary to have a comprehensive understanding of the interrelationships among them.
- The solution to the population, economic and environmental problems of the developing nations requires a mechanism to correct market and government failures.
- However, the political and institutional impediments to achieving economic efficiency are quite daunting. They require, among other changes, the abandoning of traditional land ownership entitlement and cultivation methods, land reform aimed at redistributing wealth, and democratization of the political process. Nevertheless, these are challenges that need to be confronted.
- If *ecological sustainability* is an important consideration, as it should be, the choice of technology is an important factor that needs to be carefully considered (Goodwin 1991; Norgaard and Howarth 1992).
- Public policies should be instituted to encourage the adoption of technological devices that save scarce and costly raw materials and minimize damage to the environment. Furthermore, the adoption of new technologies should always be subjected to comprehensive and carefully designed cost–benefit analyses which search for economically sound, environmentally benign and resource-saving technologies.
- If the developing countries are to succeed in their continued struggle for economic and environmental security, they need significant financial and technical assistance from the developed nations. This assistance, however, needs to be specifically targeted to slowing the pace at which natural resources are inefficiently exploited. Whether or not international assistance contributes to self-sufficiency and resource conservation will depend, in large part, on the discipline with which aid is used by the recipient. When it is not applied appropriately, time and again international aid has proven to be counterproductive (Korten 1991).

- There are two ways in which developed countries could help ameliorate ecological crises in developing countries:

  1 They could eliminate natural-resource price distortions in international markets. This would require the realignment of trade and international relations between the poor and the rich nations.

  2 They could reduce their resource consumption in such a way that an imminent threat of resource depletion and a threat to the health of the global environment are averted. This is important because currently the developing countries supply a disproportionate share of the minerals and ecological resources needed to satisfy the lavish lifestyle of the affluent industrial nations.

- Finally, the main lessons of this chapter are that the population, poverty and environmental problems of developing countries have no simple solutions, and that a comprehensive approach to resolving these problems demands careful assessment of all the political, social, economic, technical, ecological and ethical aspects of these problems. Meaningful resolutions to these problems require international cooperation in the effort to make global resource consumption and international trade environmentally sustainable.

---

review and discussion questions

1 Briefly identify the following concepts: the total fertility rate, the theory of the demographic transition, capital accumulation, commercialism, vicious cycle of poverty, and appropriate technology.

2 State *True*, *False* or *Uncertain* and explain why.

   (a) Long-term population projections are difficult to make because of the unpredictable political and economic environments in developing nations.
   (b) The world population problem is predominantly a concern of developing nations.
   (c) *Laissez-faire* policies toward reproduction will inevitably burden society with the problem of ruinous overpopulation.
   (d) "The vicious cycle of poverty" suggests that, despite the best efforts of the world community to help them, some countries are just condemned to be eternally poor.

3 Using a framework of demand and supply analysis, show how the following events could cause a decline in human fertility rate and hence population growth:

   (a) increase in per capita income due to industrialization;
   (b) a government-sponsored social security program;
   (c) an increase in the mandatory level of education;
   (d) a change in the economic status of women.

4 In what specific ways do political instability and insecure land tenure systems contribute to the environmental degradation of developing countries, especially countries in Africa? Be specific. Also, provide a few suggestions for ameliorating these institutional problems.

5 Free trade could lead to undue exploitation of natural resources upon which a vast number of the poor nations' people depend for their livelihood. Discuss.

6 The root cause of underdevelopment and environmental degradation is the "overdevelopment" of a handful of rich nations. Discuss.

REFERENCES AND FURTHER READING

Australian UNESCO Committee for Man and the Biosphere (1976) *Ecological Effects of Increasing Human Activities on Tropical and Subtropical Forest Ecosystem*, Canberra: Australia Government Publishing Service.

Bandyopadhyay, J. and Shiva, V. (1989) "Development, Poverty and the Growth of the Green Movement in India," *The Ecologist* 19: 111–17.

Becker, G. (1960) "An Economic Analysis of Fertility," in National Bureau of Economic Research, *Demographic and Economic Changes in Developing Countries*, Princeton, N.J.: Princeton University Press.

Bhagwati, J. (1993) "The Case of Free Trade," *Scientific American* 269.

Blake, J. (1968) "Are Babies Consumer Durables? A Critique of the Economic Theory of Reproductive Motivation," *Population Studies* 22, 1: 5–25.

Brown, L. (1989) "Feeding Six Billion," *Worldwatch* 2: 32–44.

Cooter, R. D. (1990) "Inventing Property: Economic Theories of the Origin of Market Property Applied to Papua New Guinea," Memo, Berkeley: University of California.

Daly, H. E. (1993) "The Perils of Free Trade," *Scientific American* 269: 50–7.

Ehrlich, P. R. and Holdren, J. P. (1971) "Impact of Population Growth," *Science* 171: 1212–17.

Ekins, P. (1993) "Trading Off the Future?: Making World Trade Environmentally Sustainable," *The New Economics Foundation* (London): 1–9.

Goodland, R. and Daly, H. E. (1992) "Ten Reasons why Northern Income Growth Is Not the Solution to Southern Poverty," in R. Goodland, H. E. Daly and S. El Serafy (eds.) *Population, Technology and Lifestyle: The Transition to Sustainability*, Washington, D.C.: Island Press.

Goodwin, N. R. (1991) "Introduction – Global Commons: Site of Peril, Source of Hope," *World Development* 19: 1–15.

Hardin, G. (1968) "The Tragedy of the Commons," *Science* 162: 1243–8.

Homer-Dixon, T. F., Boutwell, J. H. and Rathjens, G. W. (1993) "Environmental Change and Violent Conflict," *Scientific American* 268: 38–45.

Korten, D. C. (1991) "International Assistance: A Problem Posing as a Solution," *Development* 3/4: 87–94.

Leibenstein, H. (1974) "An Interpretation of the Economic Theory of Fertility: Promising Path or Blind Alley?" *Journal of Economic Literature* 22: 457–79.

Lewis, M. W. (1992) *Green Delusions: An Environmentalist Critique of Radical Environmentalism*, Durham, N.C.: Duke University Press.

McNamara, R. S. (1984) "Time Bomb or Myth: The Population Problem," *Foreign Affairs* 62: 1107–31.

Norgaard, R. B. and Howarth, R. B. (1992) "Economics, Ethics, and the Environment," in J. M. Hollander (ed.) *The Energy–Environment Connection*, Washington, D.C.: Island Press.

Panayotou, T. and Ashton, P. S. (1992) *Not by Timber Alone: Economic and Ecology for Sustainable Tropical Forests*, Washington, D.C.: Island Press.

Population Reference Bureau (1996) *Population Today* 24, 6–7.

—— (1997) *Population Today* 25, 4: 3.

Repetto, R. and Holmes, T. (1983) "The Role of Population in Resource Depletion in Developing Countries," *Population and Development Review* 9, 4: 609–32.

Rudel, T. K. (1989) "Population, Development, and Tropical Deforestation," *Rural Sociology* 54, 3: 327–38.

Todaro, M. P. (1989) *Economic Development in the Third World*, 4th edn., New York: Longman.

Trainer, F. E. (1990) "Environmental Significance of Development Theory," *Ecological Economics* 2: 277–86.

Turner, K., Pearce, D. and Bateman, I. (1993) *Environmental Economics: An Elementary Introduction*, Baltimore: Johns Hopkins University Press.

World Resources Institute (1987) *World Resources 1988–89*, New York: Basic Books.

—— (1992) *World Resources 1992–93*, New York: Oxford University Press.

—— (1995) *World Resources 1995–96*, New York: Oxford University Press.

Index